King William County Virginia in the Civil War

Along Mangohick Byways

Dorothy Francis Atkinson

HERITAGE BOOKS
2007

HERITAGE BOOKS
AN IMPRINT OF HERITAGE BOOKS, INC.

Books, CDs, and more—Worldwide

For our listing of thousands of titles see our website
at
www.HeritageBooks.com

Published 2007 by
HERITAGE BOOKS, INC.
Publishing Division
65 East Main Street
Westminster, Maryland 21157-5026

International Standard Book Number: 978-1-58549-744-4

DEDICATION

For Ben
and
those who endured

Acknowledgements

Without the assistance and encouragement of my family, friends, and neighbors, this book would have never come into being. Residents of King William and adjoining counties have shared their family memorabilia, John and Jean Leftwich Frawner, Lavalia McGeorge Leftwich, Miriam L. Simmons, Lillian Latane Walters, Betty Latane Walters, Mary Tyler Louthan, Virginia McGeorge Pearson, George D. Pollard, members of the Atkinson family, and many others. My husband, Benjamin Atkinson, and Charlaine Arthur provided me with transportation to wherever the information was.

Staff members of the Pamunkey Regional Library, especially Mae Taylor, the Boatwright Library of the University of Richmond, the Virginia State Library, and the Virginia Historical Society were most cooperative. The Virginia Historical Society has allowed me to quote from the Aylett Family Papers. Willie T. Weathers has approved use of her privately produced information on the Douglas family, which had been supplied to me by James Aldwin Hight, Jr. Betsy Fleet gave her permission for me to quote from *Green Mount*, a Civil War diary of King and Queen County. Bill Gulasky loaned his books on military equipment. Erwin Scott Campbell turned my attention to material on prison life. Dr. Philip B. May, pharmacist, made notes for me on herbs requested by the Pamunkey Indians. Sara Fox Wendenburg loaned maps of King William. Mary Thomas Smith allowed me to use old steamship schedules. Emily Slater Stevens shared a ledger kept for an Ayletts store in 1856. She had collected the church histories in the King William County Historical Society files at the courthouse. Members of the King William School Board made copies of material from their files. Rhoda L. MacCallum supplied the information on the portraits at the courthouse and Thomas T. H. Hill approved its use. Emmett Upshaw, clerk, and Shirley Moore opened the old courtroom so the pictures could be copied.

Teressa Atkinson Pearson, Erwin Scott Campbell, Thomas Mitchell, the Leftwich family, Ron and Alice Steele of "Scotchtown," and staff members of the Virginia State Library and the Library of Congress provided the illustrations. Malcolm Bray Young spent countless hours copying photographs, both private and public.

Rosa Spurlock Brooks and Elizabeth Gwathmey McAllister collected the information on black churches and schools. Virginia Woody Rice supplied the history of Epworth Church.

When the material began to take form, Fran Freimarck, director of the Pamunkey Regional Library, spent her holidays and lunch hours going over the newly written chapters and making suggestions. Later Teressa Pearson and my sisters, Lucie Samuel, Otelia Bodenstein, and Kathleen

Francis helped me ferret out errors on the rewritten pages.

The invaluable expertise of Robert K. Krick, chief historian of the Fredericksburg and Spotsylvania National Military Park, and Harold E. Howard have guided the manuscript into publication.

Dorothy Francis Atkinson

Preface

The last vestige of Mangohick, King William County, Virginia, clings to the sides of Virginia Route 30 between United States Route 301, the north-south highway that connects Richmond to the environs of Washington and Baltimore, and United States Route 360, the eastbound Richmond-Tappahannock Highway. Motorists and truckers use this still-two-lane stretch of road to visit historic Williamsburg and Yorktown or to deliver farm, lumber, and mineral products to barges and ships at West Point and Norfolk. They pass by a few houses, some churches, a few cultivated fields, but mainly through woodland with its lavish growth of pines and hardwood trees under which the mother turkey may be scratching with her spring brood or the white-tailed deer may have secluded her spotted fawn while she does her daily foraging. There is little to indicate that during the nineteenth century the tide of national history touched this inland area and flowed down its dusty byways.

Just shy of or just past the midpoint, depending on the direction of travel, can be seen the sign for Mangohick Post Office, a mere pigeon-holed corner in a green-painted country store. Also to be seen, if one throttles down enough, is the newly erected highway marker pointing to the colonial Mangohick Church. The original building of Flemish bond, now in its restored dignity, stands surrounded by ancient oaks about 200 yards back from the road.

The area's first roads were footpaths over which Indians travelled to hunt, fish, and trade. Route 30 was called the Pamunkey Trail and possibly used by Chief Powhatan to visit his holdings and relations to the west. The route is also known as the Ridge Road, for it passes along the watershed for the Pamunkey and Mattaponi rivers as they flow to their confluence as the York River and hence to Chesapeake Bay. The two rivers form two sides of the narrow triangle that is King William County, which has its apex at West Point, the county's sole incorporated town.

Mangohick was formerly the name of a creek, now shown on United States Geological Survey maps as Millpond Creek, which has its head-waters near the church and post office and then flows westward into the Pamunkey. Soon after the area was opened to English settlement, Colonel William Byrd II, of "Westover," got possession of around 3,000 acres along its banks. At the death of his father-in-law, Governor Daniel Parke of the Leeward Islands, Byrd took over the land in lieu of his wife's unpaid dowry. In an account written in 1732, Colonel Byrd mentioned using a "blind path" near a "new brick church" to reach his "Mangohick Plantation." Much of the county area came to be taken up by large grants of land with their outlets to commerce by way of the two rivers. Other creeks have their beginnings near Mangohick: Dorrell and the Herring creeks flow into the Mattaponi; Hornquarter, Mehixon, Moncuin and lesser creeks flow into the Pamunkey. Interior roads, literally "high-ways" between the streams, were hardly more than foot or bridle paths connecting the holdings, except for those converted to rolling roads for the transport of tobacco and grain to the nearest wharves and warehouses.

Mangohick Church was built as a "chapel of ease" for St. Margaret's Parish of the Anglican Church. When St. David's Parish was formed (1744) the parish church was built on Cattail Swamp, nearer the Richmond-Tappahannock Highway. Through that area ran the Manskin Path. Settlers, like the Indians before them, travelled from their ferry crossings over the Pamunkey from Hanover County at Hanovertown and Newcastle to the King William settlement on the Mattaponi at Aylett's Warehouse, to its ferry and the bridge that came to be built just upstream at Dunkirk in King and Queen County. The parish lines were drawn just below the present highway and ran from the mouth of Moncuin Creek on the Pamunkey to Arnold's Ferry on the Mattaponi. To the southeast of this line the remainder of King William County was in St. John's Parish. To the northwest of St. David's Parish, near Route 301, lay St. Margaret's Parish in Caroline County.

After the American Revolution the land encompassed by the St. David's Parish lines came to be known as Mangohick Judicial or Magisterial District. It is within and from these metes and bounds that I shall attempt to show how the campaigns of the War Between the States carried off the men, along with their fellows from the lower part of the county, and left the home folks of Mangohick to view the passage of hostile troops.

D.F.A.
"Wyoming," 1990.

b

CONTENTS

CHAPTER 1
Between the Pamunkey and the Mattaponi · 1830-1860

King William County, from 1830 to 1860, was similar to the majority of the predominately rural counties of Tidewater Virginia which were to supply their sons to the Confederacy. Along her rivers large farms were flourishing. Yet even with their slave labor these farms were not self-sufficient. They were dependent on artisans, both white and free black, who had settled at the terminals and crossroads of the local byways.

Joseph Martin's *New and Comprehensive Gazetteer of Virginia*, published in 1835, gave the size of this county as 270 square miles, spread out over a mean length of 32 miles with a mean breadth of 8½ miles. The population in 1830 was 9,319 — 3,389 whites and 5,930 blacks (or non-whites, for no separate listing was given for the Indians). Throughout the county there were 1,655 horses, 7 studs, 67 coaches, 14 carryalls and 222 gigs. The land lying in the flats along the two bounding rivers was light sandy loam, quite productive. It was better suited to peas, maize, and cotton than to wheat or tobacco. Corn and wheat were the major crops in the county, although oats and cotton were profitably cultivated. Very little tobacco, as in most other tidewater areas by this time, was being raised. It was predicted that a profitable business might be done by the shipping of timber and wood.[1]

The county at that time seems to have had a natural dividing line running near what is now Route 360 from the area of Ayletts (now Aylett) on the Mattaponi to the flat lands of the Pamunkey where crossings were made to Hanovertown and Newcastle. The area below, or southeast of, this line and through St. John's Parish to West Point was known as the lower part of the county. The area above, or northwest of, this line and through Mangohick to the Caroline County line was known as the upper part of the county. In more recent years Acquinton District, named for the creek that flows near King William Court House, has been interjected between upper King William (Mangohick) and lower King William (the courthouse area to West Point).

The farms in the lower part of the county had their own docks from which they could ship their products. Those in the upper part of the county had to move their produce to the highest point of navigation on the nearest river. At that time the Pamunkey River was said to be "navigable by schooners carrying 1,600 bushels, from Oyster-shell Landing," two miles by land below Dabney's Ferry (Hanovertown). This port was the head of the tidewater and was located 35 miles above West Point and 16 miles north of Richmond. The Mattaponi River was navigable for vessels carrying 2,000 bushels from Ayletts, which was 30 miles above West Point, 28 miles from Richmond and 20 miles from Tappahannock (on the Rappahannock River). Navigation was possible by boats and small schooners with light loads to the Dunkirk Bridge two miles upstream, possibly farther if the river was cleaned out.[2]

Since 1817 Dunkirk had been a ghost town. Most of the houses had been removed to the plantations and only the granary remained. The post road continued to go over the toll bridge there. Dunkirk, or Todd's Bridge as it was formerly called, was a shipping center before the Revolution and continued as such into the nineteenth century. There the Mattaponi was less than 100 feet wide and had high banks. Wagons drawn by four horses could bring up to 40 bushels of wheat, a dozen barrels of flour, or the equivalent to the warehouses from the inland farms on days when the roads were not wet and miry. Additional grain was brought in by canoes (bateaux), lighters, and barges poled or paddled from the farms upstream. Scottish factors and Brittish agents served as the merchants. From the warehouses and wharves the produce would be loaded on sailing vessels 35 to 40 feet in length, which were handled by pilots and buoyed in and out by the tide. The cargo would be transferred to ocean-going vessels downstream at Yorktown or Gloucester Point. In return European goods were brought back.[3]

On the King William side of the river across from Dunkirk (at "Edge Hill," adjoining "Elliott's") a planned settlement to be known as Cochran Town never marterialized.[4] Union forces throughout the war would consider Dunkirk and Ayletts as important locations for passage and supply lines.

―――――――

A working copy of the 1830 King William County tax list, kept by Charles Page, has been found in recent years at "Summer Hill," in Hanover County. It is in a mutilated condition but shows that at least 529 people or estates were assessed for taxes that year. Real estate of more than 300 acres was owned by only 80 individuals. About half of these were in the upper part of the county. There were 189 listings of under 300 acres, 104 of which fell under 100 acres. At least 22 non-whites had been assessed for taxes and about half of them had acreage. Some people were only listed for the "poor rate," apparently a capitation tax for the operation of the county poor farm. Some men were charged a fine for failure to participate in the muster of the county militia; others were given credit for their services in patrolling the county.[5]

The 1850 Census of King William County shows that the free men were predominately farmers, farm managers or labourers (sic). Among the 28 other occupations shown the most popular was carpentry, 36 men.

Some of the carpenters were free non-whites. Non-whites were among the 17 who gave their occupation as sailor, seaman or mariner. They were also among the 15 shoemakers, the 6 bricklayers, and the 2 wheelwrights. The one plasterer was a black man. There were 9 millers and one millwright; 9 coachmakers, 3 saddlers and one tanner; 13 merchants and 11 clerks; 2 dealers in wood; one manufacturer; 2 cabinetmakers and one mason; 8 tailors; one ditcher; and only 2 blacksmiths. There were 14 mechanics, an occupation that may have been so new in such a rural area that the census taker was uncertain of the spelling. He listed them as "machanics." Among the professions there were: 15 physicians (some the more wealthy landowners, others young men still in their 20's with no land of their own); one dentist; 6 lawyers; 10 teachers; and 3 ministers — Baptist, Methodist, and one not designated but known to have preached to those called the Reformers. There were 4 men employed by the county: the clerk of the court, the deputy clerk, the superintendent of the poor farm, and a collector, apparently of revenue. One man listed himself as a "gentleman-at-large" (perhaps a riverboat gambler). No women were listed as employed.[6] The census taker may have been instructed to record only the occupations of the men. For a non-urban county, King William had a diversity of service trades and professions that could well have given her a measure of independence from her neighboring counties with their cities and towns.

There were five post offices in upper King William before the war: Enfield, Ayletts, Greenmount (1832-36), Mangohick, and Sharonville (1848-1854). Rumford Academy had a post office (1832-1860). In the lower part of the county mail came to Acquinton (1849-1866), King William Court House, Lanesville, and West Point.[7]

Enfield Post Office was on the Dabney Ferry Road (Route 604), 3½ miles from the ferry and 300 yards from "Mechanicsville" (a Dabney home at the intersection of Routes 652 and 604 no longer in existence). Nearby were two stores, a blacksmith, a shoemaker, a cabinet maker, a saddler, a harness maker, and a carpenter's shop. A settlement called Brandywine (now Manquin on Route 360) was 7 miles from Ayletts on the road to the Newcastle Ferry and at an intersection with a road from "Mechanicsville" to the courthouse. Here there was an "excellent tavern, a grocery, and a gig maker."[8]

Mangohick (by the roads of that day) was 40 miles from Richmond, 10 miles from Ayletts and 102 miles from Washington. There they had a store, a blacksmith, a gig maker, a shoemaker, and a tailor's shop. (There also stood a colonial church and from it began the often mentioned "road from Mangohick Church to Dabney's Ferry.") Greenmount Post Office was 33 miles from Richmond and 104 miles from Washington, D.C.[9] This may have been in or near the 18th-century house of the same name that still stands near Beulahville and was occupied prior to the war by the Eubanks. Sharonville was probably the location of present-day Central Garage, near the intersection of Routes 30 and 360.

The 1835 Gazetteer characterized the inhabitants of the neighborhood around Aylets as "intelligent, and in easy circumstances." Their homes were "built in a modern and handsome style," adding "importance and beauty to this little village." The village was listed as 27 miles northeast of Richmond and 110 miles from Washington, D.C. It had 15 "dwelling houses," for its 50 white and 60 non-white inhabitants. There were five houses of public worship: one Episcopalian (possibly the colonial church at Cattail Creek), two Methodist, and two Baptist. There were several flour mills, mercantile stores, groceries, and considerable trade involving grain. The gazetteer said that eight miles downstream, below the bar (probably the DeFarges sandbar at Sandy Point), vessels could carry 3,000 to 4,000 bushels with no obstruction in the river.[10]

The community had grown up around the tobacco warehouses owned by the Aylett family in the early days of the settlement of King William. It served as the center for grain shipments to Baltimore and Philadelphia. Standard weights and measures for ports of entry were kept there. The services of house carpenters, blacksmiths, wheelwrights, harness makers and saddlers, tailors, dressmakers, milliners, and confectioners were available. There was a large tavern for the weary traveller. By 1856 there was a large iron foundry and the four groceries listed in 1835 had become "two large stores . . . carrying in stock groceries, fine shirts and laces, silver and jewelry."[11]

Much of the contact with areas outside the county was made through the village of Aylets. Prior to the war the U.S. mail arrived around 11:30 a.m. on Tuesdays and Fridays. With so few post offices in the county, families would pack their lunches and come to Aylets to get the mail and do their shopping. Wheat and other grains were brought from as far away as Caroline County to be loaded on the two-masted vessels, tied up as many as four at a time at the wharf.[12]

Possibly none of the small stores or commissaries throughout the county could compete with the stores in Aylets, with their access by boat to foreign and domestic markets. A ledger for one of the stores, kept by Alexander J. Slater in 1856,[13] shows that life in upper King William just before the War Between the States was far from rustic. The purchases were made mostly by men for their families. The ledger shows how well the people dressed, some of the food they ate, sundry articles they used in housekeeping and farming, and some of the drugs they used for everyday ailments.

At the Aylets store the customers bought material to be sewn (possibly on treadle sewing machines): Irish linen, velvet, silk, alpaca, serge for winter clothes, calico, gingham, silesia (a lightweight linen or cotton twill), and summer cloth for warmer weather. They bought "ozneburg" (osnaburg — course cotton) and domestic material in large quantities. They carried home "bones" to give dresses and bonnets the desired shape, edgings and ruches to give the current style, and even trimming and a pattern for a man's vest. Some bonnets were "ready made." So were an occasional coat, straw hat, cravat, and ladies' and men's shoes, although more often balls of shoe thread were bought for the home manufacture or repair of their shoes. There were suspenders and garters bought, a watch guard, a watch key, and an umbrella. One discriminating gentleman bought the "Best Kid Gloves."

For proper grooming, men bought white soap, Thomas soap, powder, toothbrush and paste, cologne, musk, comb, and even a looking glass to verify the image presented. Also they bought shoe blacking. For housekeeping, they brought: muslin and cambric for sheets, Holland cloth (a sized cotton used for window shades), china cups and saucers, a stone churn, a frying pan, tin pans, and the cooking staples of sugar, coffee, tea, cake chocolate, soda, sarsaparilla, molasses, crackers, rice, eggs, bacon, lamb, fish (salted and by the barrel), tobacco (for those not raising their own), whiskey, and two tons of coal. (The coal must have been for grate fires, a more fashionable way of heating although wood was plentiful.)

For the business of farming (engaged in on just about every homeplace if for no more than supplying the larder) they purchased guano, chickens, bushels of corn, a cow bell, horse collar and traces, weeding hoe, nails, safe lock and lock pad, pistol, fishing hooks, and lines. For home remedies, they bought ipecac, camphor, m. oil (possibly mineral oil) and balsam.

For their children's education they bought: an arithmetic, a geography, an atlas, a spelling book, and an E(nglish) grammar; for their enjoyment, a toy boat, a box of crayons, and some marbles; and for their own enjoyment, a bunch of fiddle strings and a book of undetermined title. From the same store, they purchased a carriage to transport their family over the roads through Mangohick District and beyond.

Through Ayletts rattled the carriages carrying ladies and their trunks, the men following on horseback, as they periodically passed from places like "Fontainebleau" (in King William) to visit "Green Mount," "Smithfield," "Holly Hill," and "The Mount" (all in King and Queen County) and "Cownes" and "Burlington" (in King William).[14] Parties for the young unmarried eligibles lasted over a period of days. At "Montville," one of the homes of the Aylett family, an invitation went out in the 1850's with instructions to bring enough clothes to stay a week. There the young and

5

beautiful Lavalla Lee, from Middlesex, caught the eye of the young King William widower, John F. McGeorge. Later she became his bride and went to live at "Prospect Hill," near Beulahville.[15]

Benny Fleet, a teenage member of the King and Queen County Home Guard, lived with his family at "Green Mount." His father, Dr. Benjamin Fleet, owned the bridge and granaries at Dunkirk and a lighter, *Ben Bolt,* which carried grain and lime on the Mattaponi River. The family appears to have picked up their supplies, mail, and papers at Ayletts, possibly brought in on the stagecoach. Benny wrote that his father took the Richmond *Whig,* The Richmond *Enquirer,* The Richmond *Dispatch,* the Louisville *Journal* and also *Harper's,* both weekly and monthly.[16] Benny's diary and the family letters written during the Civil War, with the family's continuous contact with people and activities in the King William area, are invaluable resources on the way of life in the vicinity of Ayletts during the war years.

Benny seems to have been caught up in the twilight zone between childhood and early manhood. He wrote in 1860 of attending a circus at King William Court House and seeing bears that walked on their hind feet, lions, tigers, a panther, a "white campbell [sic]," parrots, snakes, a baboon, monkeys, a zebra, a horned horse, a show of horsemanship, and a lady who walked on a wire. Benny wrote that the day before there was such a freshet in the river that "the stages" could not cross on the Ayletts Ferry but had to use the Dunkirk Bridge, but by afternoon the skies had cleared and a rainbow appeared.[17] One can almost picture the excitement of the community as the creatures were unloaded from the boat or boats at the wharf, possibly White Oak Landing, Rose Sprout, or Ayletts, and were carted or walked along the narrow roads to the courthouse green. Perhaps the animals were brought in under the brightening skies and the multi-colored arc of the rainbow.

The young man wrote that there were two stages on the route from St. Stephen's (Church) to Richmond — the mail stage and the "Opposition Stage." Either one would take a passenger to any point on the line for $1.00. The rate before the opposition had been $2.50 from Ayletts. On April 24, 1860, he had been to St. Stephen's and had seen eight or nine people waiting for the stages.[18]

———

Post offices were located either on or easily accessible to one or more of the stagecoach routes. The 1835 Gazetteer map shows the state routes as they passed throughout the state. The area of King William is small and almost illegible. The route from Richmond to Tappahannock appears to have passed through the county as follows: it entered King William by crossing the Pamukey River on Dabney's Ferry from Hanovertown; travelled along present Route 604 to the Enfield Post Office; turned

6

to the right on the still-dirt road, Route 649 or 639, to pass "Mt. Columbia" and arrive at the village of Brandywine. From Brandywine it took a less direct route than present Route 360, veering eastward and back again, to pass "Marl Hill," the colonial church at Cattail, "Montville," and from thence into Ayletts. Leaving Ayletts, it headed northwest for a couple of miles on the River Road (Route 600), then crossed the Mattaponi River on the bridge at Dunkirk into King and Queen County.[19]

This lumbering stagecoach carried ten to twelve people. On the back was a "boot" to hold the trunks and on top a railing to hold small packages and the mail bags. The four horses were changed at Old Church (Hanover County), Prince's (Ayletts), and Miller's Tavern (Essex County). The 50-mile-long route between Richmond and Tappahannock was run twice a week.[20]

The Richmond-Alexandria Stage had stops at Hanover Court House and the three-story brick Needwood Tavern in lower Caroline County.[21] Roads from Mangohick Post Office (Routes 601 and 614 to Taylor's Ferry or Norment's Bridge) led to Hanover Court House. The Ridge Road (Route 30) led to Needwood. The River Road (Route 600) led past Greenmount Post Office to Needwood and also connected with the Richmond-Tappahannock Stage just above Ayletts.

Oliver W. Holmes, in his book on stagecoaches up to the time of the war, describes these horse-drawn vehicles. They usually had three seats. Those passengers on the front seat rode with their backs to the horses. The driver sat outside and two lamps dimly lit his way. According to an early advertisement the stagecoaches might be painted thus: body — green, Prussian blue or yellow ochre; carriage wheels — red lead (vermilion); octagon panel on the back — black; octagon blind — green; elbow piece on the rail, front and back — red; and the beads and moulding — patent yellow. The painter would include the lettering "United States Mail Stage" and over those words place a spread eagle of size and color desired.[22]

An American traveller in Boston in 1825 called the stagecoach the "democratic vehicle, something for all people." He said that it was used by "the young, and the old, the rich and the poor" who rode it "for health, for pleasure, or for business."[23]

Yet breakdowns were frequent when one of the leather bands that passed under the body of the vehicle, serving as support and springs, would snap. An English traveller in 1812 wrote that riding on those straps made the coach sway "forward or backward or sideways as the wheels passed over obstructions or dropped into ruts." When a strap broke a nearby fence post or a hickory sapling cut from alongside the road would be shoved under the body of the carriage to support it until the next way station was reached.[24]

No railroad ever passed through upper King William County. The Richmond and York River line crossed the Pamunkey River at the Indian Reservation, many miles downstream, then proceeded on to West Point. The Virginia Central Railroad could be boarded at Hanover Court House (1839) and the R.F. & P. Railroad at Milford in Caroline Couhty (1836).[25]

King William Court House was readily accessible to the upper part of the county by the River Road (Route 600) through Ayletts to meet the Pamunkey Trail (Route 30) which passed by the courthouse; by the Pamunkey Trail from Sharonville; and by the Courthouse Road (Route 618) from Brandywine. The gazetteer stated that the courthouse was 10 miles from Ayletts, 7 miles from Brandywine, 27 miles northeast of Richmond, and 120 miles southwest of Washington, D.C. The court building, clerk's office, and two jails were of brick and all included iron railings (at the windows). At the county seat there were 8 "dwelling houses," several mechanics' shops, and a mercantile store. The population in 1835 was 75, one of whom was an attorney, and there were two "regular" physicians.[26]

An ordinary, or tavern, near the courthouse, had been a favorite stopping place for George Washington as he passed through the county from the crossing at Todd's Bridge (Dunkirk) to the Sweet Hall Ferry, near West Point, into New Kent County and to the home of his brother-in-law, Colonel Burwell Bassett, of "Eltham." The tavern, in the early part of the nineteenth century, was owned by the Gregory family and operated by Mrs. Ann Bickley Gregory. The courthouse building, built of Flemish bond with glazed headers sometime between 1722 and 1735, is thought to have been patterned, with its frontal arches, after the colonial capitol in Williamsburg. The one-story court building, still in use, is in the form of a "T," with the judge's chambers and the jury room flanking the courtroom. The stem of the "T," the courtroom, was lengthened in the early nineteenth century and two exterior doors were cut to give direct access from the court to the jail and clerk's office.[27]

In the 1830's, the County Court was held on the fourth Monday in every month. In the months of March, May, August, and November, the Quarterly Court met. The Circuit Superior Court of Law and Chancery met on the first of April and September under a Judge Semple.[28] Members of the Pollard family served as clerks of King William County over a period of seventy-five years from the first Robert Pollard, who served 1797-1818, to William Dandridge Pollard, who served 1867-1872.[29] The former was one of the early promoters of Rumford Academy and the father of eleven children. As a young man he had come to work in a store at Aylett's Warehouse. He later became a merchant and built his home, "Mt. Zoar," overlooking the village.[30]

The newly renovated (1984) courthouse has among the portraits on its walls many who lived in upper King William during the early and mid-nineteenth century. These officers of the county and others who gave notable service have been described by Thomas T. H. Hill, deputy clerk and clerk of the county, 1933-1977:[31]

(1) Clerks of the County - *Robert Pollard, Jr.,* 1783-1856, of "Mt. Zoar," was both clerk of the County Court and the Circuit Superior Court of Law and Chancery. He loved fox hunting and is shown with a fox horn hung around his neck. Also shown is *James Otway Pollard,* 1820-1873, clerk of the Circuit Court and the County Court, and *William Dandridge Pollard,* circa 1836-1906, clerk of the County Court, who lived at "Octagon," near "Mt. Zoar."

(2) Commonwealth's Attornies - *Thomas Overton Dabney,* 1807-1870, was born at the "Dorrell" (near Beulahville), the son of Major Thomas Dabney and his wife, Lucy Walker. He attended the University of Virginia in 1826 and was a classmate of Edgar Allan Poe. Thomas Dabney succeeded Benjamin F. Dabney (of "Greenville" and Dabney's Ferry) as commonwealth's attorney.

(3) Members of the Virginia Legislature — *General Philip Aylett,* 1791-1848, lived at "Fairfield," near Ayletts, served in both the Virginia House of Delegates and the Virginia Senate, and is thought to have been a brigadier general in the War of 1812 or later. General Aylett's mother was Elizabeth Henry, daughter of Patrick Henry and his wife, Sarah Shelton. *Major Beverley Browne Douglas,* 1833-1878, was educated at the College of William and Mary and Harvard and studied medicine at the University of Edinburg before deciding to return to William and Mary to graduate in law. He built his home "Cownes" near Ayletts, was a member of the Virginia Constitutional Convention of 1850-51, and served in the Virginia Senate, 1852-1865.

(4) Men who served the Confederacy — *Major Douglas* served in the 9th and 5th Virginia Cavalry. *Atwell Tebbs Mooklar,* 1827-1901, served in the armed forces both before and during the war. *Thomas Witt Haynes,* 1827-1877, (of "Brighton") was a captain with Lee's Rangers. *Colonel William Roane Aylett,* 1833-1900, was the son of General Philip Aylett and his wife, Judith Page Waller. He was a lawyer and served with the 53rd Virginia Regiment. William R. Aylett and his wife, Alice Brockenbrough, made their home at "Montville" on (present) Route 360. *Patrick Henry Aylett,* 1826-1870, also son of General Philip Aylett, was a lawyer who served as District Attorney for the Confederacy, on the board of directors of the United States Naval Academy, and as an editorial writer for the Richmond *Enquirer. Colonel Thomas H. Carter,* 1831-1908, was born and lived at "Pampatike" (the Carter family inheritance on the Pamunkey River, on the edge of St. John's Parish as it adjoins St. David's Parish or

9

Mangohick District). Carter graduated from V.M.I. and the schools of medicine of the University of Virginia and the University of Pennsylvania. During the war he was captain of the King William Artillery (Carter's Battery) and served for a while as chief of artillery of the Second Corps. *Dr. William George Pollard*, 1818-1862, was born at "Mt. Zoar" and lived at "Edge Hill," also near Ayletts. He was a practicing physician in the area before enlisting as an officer in the 53rd Virginia Regiment.

There were other notable doctors who practiced either in King William County or who had been born and raised there. Several were members of the Braxton family of the lower part of the county and connected with Carter Braxton, the signer of the Declaration of Independence. Dr. William P. Braxton of King William reported in a Virginia medical journal in 1856 that during the smallpox epidemic of the winter of 1855-56 he had vaccinated twenty-two people. Dr. Corbin Braxton not only practiced medicine in the county but served as a state senator in 1838 and a member of the Constitutional Convention in 1850-51. His son, William Armistead Braxton, born 1824, was a surgeon during the war under Mosby's command and died of wounds on November 16, 1864.[32]

Dr. John Taylor Temple, 1803-1877, was born at "Bear Garden" near Mangohick, graduated from Union College, New York, and studied in Philadelphia and at the University of Maryland. He practiced near Richmond before obtaining a charter for the Homeopathic Medical College of Missouri and becoming its dean. Dr. Benjamin Day Nelson was of the Nelson family of "Bleak Hill," the farm adjoining "Bear Garden." He and his father, Thomas Cary Nelson, moved down the Pamunkey River to "Wyoming" around 1840. Dr. Stephen Sutton of Caroline County had served as a physician's mate in the United States Army during the War of 1812. He married Elizabeth M. Oliver in 1816 and in 1819 bought "Towinque," which lies on the river between "Bleak Hill" and "Wyoming." He died there in 1840. Dr. Sutton was Justice of Peace of King William County in 1833.[33]

The gazetteer said of King William in 1835 that it was a "very religious county, but with little, if any appearance of bigotry, intolerance or fanaticism." The Baptists were the most numerous, of whom the Reformers formed the larger portion. Those meeting at Beulah (at Beulahville on the Mattaponi River Road, Route 600) had an excellent "meeting house" (a frame building 1812-1846) and were "commonly denominated the Old Baptists." There were four brick churches (the colonial churches): Mangohick, Cattail, Acquintance and West Point (St. John's). These were used predominately by the Baptists but were free for the use of all denominations. A few Presbyterians met at Acquintance (in the lower part of the county). The gazetteer stated, "There is a very respectable congregation of Methodists, who have a large and excellent house for public worship, called Powell's chapel." This apparently frame chapel was on the Ridge Road below Mangohick. The Gilmer 1865 map of King William County, prepared for the Confederate army, shows an "Old Chapel" just below the location of the present Epworth United Methodist Church, as its congregation came to be called.[34]

The Virginia Conference of the Methodist Episcopal Church appointed ministers to the King William Circuit. In 1848 the Methodist Episcopal Church divided over slavery and the Virginia Conference became a part of the Methodist Episcopal Church, South. In 1854 Bishop Pierce reported to the Annual Conference that there were 241 white members, 5 colored members, and one local preacher on the King William Circuit.[35] That same year Bethel Methodist Church was organized in the colonial church at Mangohick. The Reverend John B. Laurens was serving on the King William Circuit at the tme. The founders of the church were Robert Sale Peatross, a local preacher who lived just across the Caroline County line and was possibly the one Bishop Pierce referred to in his report, and Thomas Price Jackson, Peatross's near neighbor in King William. Their new church building was completed during the year. Among its members until after the war were many of the black neighbors. Among these were Sam Anderson and his bride, who joined the first Sunday after the church was dedicated.[36] The church stands on the Ridge Road, just across the Caroline County line. This part of the road was sometimes referred to as "the road from Mangohick Church to Needwood" tavern.

Presbyterians also met around 1833 in the colonial church at Mangohick. Perhaps they later joined with others who had been meeting at the Needwood Tavern. The tavern was also used for local weddings,[37] being both spacious and convenient to the stage. No Presbyterian church appears to have ever been built in the area.

The Dover Association of Baptist Churches is known to have met in the colonial church at Mangohick (1814) before any Baptist church was organized in the community. From time to time regular Baptist services were held there also. A prominent Baptist missionary, Luther Rice, passed through the area in December 1819. He received gifts for "the Lot" and spent a night at "Greenville," the home of George Dabney. In 1825 under the leadership of Elder Andrew Broaddus of Caroline County, and aided by Elder Horace White, Mangohick Baptist Church was organized. It operated under that name until 1832, at which time five male and eight or ten female members separated from the Reformers and became constituted as the Union-Mangohick Baptist Church. In 1835 their 174 members were enjoying "the blessings of peace." Temperance reform was favored as well as all "benevolent operations of the day." In conjunction with the Beulah Church a "Female Working Society" was formed which raised $300 for the cause of education. When its new brick church was built one mile down the road in 1854 on land given by Mr. James Leftwich, the name was changed to Hebron Baptist Church. A permanent Sunday School had been established in 1853, after attempts made in 1835 and 1844 were apparently unsuccessful. First the school met only in the summer, but in 1859 under the leadership of James G. White as superintendent it met all during the year and is considered to have been the first "evergreen" Sunday School in rural eastern Virginia. Hebron Church also cooperated in the annual celebration of the Sunday Schools of upper King William.[38]

The Reformers, following the teachings of Alexander and Thomas Campbell, in 1832 organized what came to be known as Corinth Christian Church. Alexander Campbell had held a meeting at Mangohick in June of that year which was attended by members from twelve churches. Following the next Dover Association in November of that year, a group still calling themselves Baptists withdrew from the Mangohick Baptist Church. Those remaining, the Reformers, chose the name Disciples. These Disciples continued to use the colonial church building, alternating with the Baptists, and met in the nearby neighborhood school for worship services when it was not their turn to use the old building. Even after they built their own frame "meeting house" in 1839 (on the Mangohick -Dabney Ferry Road, Route 604), they continued to use the colonial building when larger attendance was expeted. Alexander Campbell wrote in 1855 that he took the early morning "cars" for Mangohick (the train to Hanover Court House), was met at the station by Dr. (Richard) Fox's carriage, had a pleasant 15-mile ride to the doctor's home where he had a "calm repose," and the next day "repaired to the meeting house and found a large and inquisitive audience in attendance." Both Baptists and Disciples assumed responsibility for keeping the ancient building in repair. During the early years the Disciples had no regular pastor yet they met every Sunday for divine worship and observance of the Lord's Supper. Evangelistic services were held whenever a preacher was available. The Reverend Peter Ainslie II was the first pastor and served after the erection of their frame building.[39]

The Beulah Baptist "meeting house" was also a frame building. Its members had come out of the Upper College Baptist Church. They conducted services in that building from 1812 to 1846, at which time the present brick structure was built on the same location. Sometime prior to 1838 the ladies of the church were concerned that the children of the congregation were not being given the proper training. They offered their services to form and teach a class, which they held in the gallery of the church on Sunday mornings. This, their historian wrote, was unusual in the days of "man rule." So successful were they in their undertaking that at the May meeting of the church in 1838 the following resolution was offered by Deacon Richard Gwathmey:

> Resolved: That we consider a well-conducted Sabbath School eminently calculated to promote the best interest of the church, as well as the rising generation, and that we adopt the school kept here as our foster child, and will, by the help of God, sustain it not only by our prayers and contributions, but by our personal labors.[40]

The Reverend Andrew Broaddus of Caroline was the minister at Beulah Baptist Church from 1828 to 1848. He was joined in 1841 by the Reverend John O. Turpin, a young man of 31 years, who served the church until his death in 1884, a man deeply loved by both the whites and the blacks in the congregation. The blacks were in the church for many years prior to the war, some having been made elders and exhorters.[41] The Reverend Turpin made his home near Cattail Creek.

Upper College Baptist Church, having been organized as early as 1775, met in the colonial church on Cattail Creek. The Reverend Dudley Atkinson had been pastor of the church for 19 years when, in 1833, it came under the influence of Alexander Campbell and the congregation was excluded from the Dover Association. The next year, under the leadership of the Reverend Eli Ball, the congregation was reorganized as Rehoboth Baptist Church and was readmitted to the association. In 1843 the membership totaled 445 — 279 blacks and 166 whites. They outgrew the colonial church and, since that building was in such a deteriorated condition, in 1850 they made efforts toward building a new structure. Mr. James Pollard donated land five miles away at the intersection of the Ridge Road (the Pamunkey Trail) and the Tappahannock Highway. The Second Baptist Church in Richmond offered the building they were no longer using on 12th Street to the congregation. The brick building was taken down, loaded onto wagons, brought to King William, and reconstructed on the newly donated land. They changed their name to Sharon Baptist Church. It may have been the first Baptist church in Virginia to have Indian members.[42]

The Reverend John O. Turpin had been pastor at Rehoboth since 1840 and continued as pastor at Sharon (in addition to Beulah). The Sabbath School was organized on the first Sunday in April 1845, with Archie Brown as superintendent and Silas Wyatt as secretary and librarian. Some of the books brought from Rehoboth are still in the library at Sharon. The first school had 68 scholars. Eight of the teachers were men and twelve were women. In 1857 John Henry Pitts, the headmaster at Rumford Academy and an honor graduate of V.M.I., was recorded on the flyleaf of one of the library books as being one of the teachers.[43]

While other churches were prospering in King William, the Episcopal Church continued to be out of favor. A teacher, the Reverend Thomas

Henry Fox, moved to Mangohick in the 1830's from Richmond to get away from the unhealthy climate and cholera there. He opened a boys' school at Mangohick and is said to have enjoyed attending weekly prayer meetings held in the colonial church. It is undetermined which congregation was conducting these services. Mr. Thomas T. H. Hill has said that his great-grandmother, Gabriella Taliaferro, of "Elson Green" in Caroline County, attended Mangohick Episcopal Church in the mid-1830's.[44]

Bishop William Meade of the Episcopal Church wrote in 1857 that the Reverend Dalrymple, of New Kent County, had attempted to revive the old churches in King William. He preached there in 1843 and 1844 and the parishes were accepted into the Convention, but not enough interest was shown for the establishment of a minister. Yet the next year St. David's Episcopal Church, which had met at the colonial Cattail Church, was revived and services were held in the Ayletts tavern while a church was being built in Ayletts. It was consecrated on November 9, 1859. The first rector was the Reverend John T. Poquity, a returned missionary to China.[45]

Attendance at St. David's was apparently from both sides of the Mattaponi River. Benny Fleet wrote in his diary of attending services there and hearing the minister, the Reverend Mr. Kepler, preach. The Sunday School apparently flourished in the mid-1850's, as shown by some of the textbooks and instruction manuals still extant, for instance:

Union Spelling Book for the American Sunday School.
Youth's Friend. 1831.
Small Sins No Trifles. 1853.
Sketches of Character for the Admonition and Improvement of Sunday School Teachers. 1858.

The library must have been large, for many books remain with the Sunday School records.[46]

———

Secular education played a large role in the life of prewar King William. Many young men who would become officers in the Confederate Army, and later civic and public servants, began their education at Rumford Academy, the only public seminary in the county in 1835. It stood halfway between the courthouse and Ayletts. The two-story brick building measured 48 by 26 feet and housed fifty pupils. The academy was considered "an excellent school [where] the usual branches of academic education [are] taught." Originally intended as a preparatory school for the College of William and Mary, it had been started in 1805 on land given by John Roane of "Uppowac." The General Assembly of Virginia passed a law in 1806 permitting a lottery to finance the school.[47] The 1850 Census reported three male teachers living at the academy. Sarah Pitts, the 25-year-old wife of the headmaster, John H. Pitts, must have had her hands full seeing to the physical needs of the 27 boarding students, ages 12 to 18, in addition to caring for her 12-month-old daughter.

An announcement was made in 1827 concerning the opening of a school at "The Dorrell" (on Herring Creek), where females would be taught spelling, reading, writing, arithmetic, history, grammar, geography (with the use of globes), natural and moral philosophy, rhetoric and composition, fine needlework, and Latin if so requested. Board and tuition would be $100 and each pupil would be expected to furnish her own bed (perhaps feather or straw mattress), bedding, towels, and candles. The school was to be taught by Major Thomas Dabney and "Lady," the former Miss Mary E. Tompkins of "Smyrna" (her home on the Mangohick-Dabney's Ferry Road), where she had taught the previous year. By the next year an additional male instructor, Mr. Robert Temple Gwathmey, a graduate of the University of Virginia, had been hired, and the post office was shown as Greenmount. The local King William and Caroline County Baptist minister, the Reverend Andrew Broaddus, and a neighbor, C. W. Taliaferro, attested to the quality of the school.[48]

Dr. Richard Fox conducted the Palestine Female Institute in his home (on Route 604, the Mangohick Road to the River Road). There he educated many young women from King William and the neighboring counties. Dr. John M. Pilcher taught in a school at Beulah during the war years. This may have been a boys' school and the predecessor of the school taught in the Grange Hall, across from Beulah Church, until about 1900.[49]

Thomas P. Jackson had 35-year-old Charles B. Pollard, a teacher, living in his home in 1850. It is not known if he was there solely to be a teacher for the six Jackson boys and three girls, or whether he taught at an "old field school" in the neighborhood. The youngest daughter, Lucetta, later attended the female seminary "Belle Roy" (on the Mangohick Road to Beulahville, Route 609). It was taught by a Mr. Jones and blown up by a Union mine about 1863, pieces of it landing on the neighboring farms.[50]

Many King William families were shown in the census as having young women living with them who were not necessarily related. These were white, black, and perhaps Indian females whom we might say were "employed." The chances are that they were helping out at least for their room and board. Many of them could have been assisting in the education as well as the rearing of the children. Ann Hallowell paid prolonged visits in the home of her sister, Virginia Hallowell Latane, and was referred to as a "professional visitor" while she instructed the children in reading from the *McGuffey Reader*.[51]

15

To learn the role of the women in upper King William County during the period 1830 to 1860, it is necessary to read between the lines of official material, then supplement it with diaries and reminiscences. Although the census for the county does not list any women as employed, certainly all were not the ladies of leisure depicted in romantic novels.

Women must have been involved in the operation of the shops at Ayletts — the millinery, confectionery shops, and the tavern — if no more than assisting their husbands, although no males were listed in the census with the occupations of milliner, confectioner, or tavern keeper. Certainly the wife of the superintendent of the Poor House (on Route 608) had to assist her husband in the care of the twenty-eight women and minor children ranging in age from 95 years to 3 months. Frances and William Pollard, ages 26 and 36, appear to have been running a rooming house in Ayletts. In their home were eight males, ages 16 to 30, with the occupations of tailor, clerks, and coachmakers.[52]

In the 1830 workbook 45 women were assessed for real estate in their own names. Some may have been widows, others unmarried daughters. One was the estate of a mulatto woman. Another estate was noted as being held for daughters.[53]

It can be seen on the 1865 map of the county that many of the households were headed by women. The census reveals that these were in most cases elderly ladies, perhaps widows, with either a son living in the household and having the occupation of farmer, or a young manager living nearby. Yet to the neighbors, according to the map, the homesteads were not known solely by the family name but as Miss Taylor's, Mrs. Dr. Fox's, Mrs. Powell's, and "Wyoming" — Mrs. Nelson's.[54]

In 1840 James Fox died, leaving his 762 acres to his wife, the former Mary (Polly) Burton. Her home was "Retreat," a large two-story brick house on the Mangohick Road (604) to the River Road. Polly Fox became so crippled with rheumatism that she was confined to a wheelchair and could not comfortably use her hands. She needed assistance, in addition to that of her farm manager and her housekeeper, Mrs. Matilda Munday, in carrying on the business of the plantation. An orphan girl, Virginia Thomas Hallowell, a step-daughter of a friend, came out from Richmond to help her with the accounts and correspondence. When Virginia married William Catesby Latane of nearby "Glan Villa" in 1854, the wedding was held in the parlor of "Retreat" and the groom wore a white brocade satin vest.[55]

Although the new mistress of "Glan Villa" could keep books, play the guitar and sing beautifully, do embroidery, read poetry, and was very animated, she was not trained in housekeeping. A very capable black woman was sent along to do the cooking and train the new servants. Mrs.

James Walters (Posie) has described her grandmother's early years as a bride:

> The new home at "Glan Villa" was a time of great loneliness for Virginia. Mr. Latane, as she always called her husband, and his brother, John, often with their good friend, Mr. John Hardy Cocke, who lived at "Edge Hill," were outside a good part of the day and if they came in to be with her all three were together. Being the perfect gentleman they were, if she moved all of them hopped to their feet and said, "Let me help you Virginia," until she felt like an invalid. I don't know how long this lasted but I know Virginia always called her husband, "Mr. Latane."[56]

Mrs. Henrietta Nelson's home "Wyoming," a farm of 1143 acres valued on the census report at $18,000, was actually Henrietta's in her own right. It had been purchased in 1839 by her husband, Dr. Benjamin Day Nelson, and his father, Thomas Cary Nelson, from either her father or brother, Austin Brockenbrough, of Tappahannock. The scorched deed pulled from the ashes of the 1885 King William County clerk's office fire shows that the land was to be held for *her* heirs. The Nelsons had been in King William County since Secretary of the Virginia Colony Thomas Nelson, of Yorktown, Thomas Cary Nelson's grandfather, had moved up from Yorktown during the Revolution. The family had owned "Bleak Hill," "Horn Quarter," "Fork Quarter," "Dorrill Plantation," "Difficult Hill," and "Toler's,"[57] but this is the first time they were owners of "Wyoming."

In 1858 Henrietta Nelson, a widow, applied for a license, in the name of her "infants," to operate a ferry across the Pamunkey River at the former (Thomas Reade) Rootes' Ferry and (John) Hoomes' Ford, or crossing. An 1839 plat of the place shows the house where it continues to stand and just below it, in the bend of the river as it surrounded the farm on three sides, is shown a ford. In 1862 the Union forces found a "new bridge" at Mrs. Nelson's.[58]

Mrs. Nelson's neighbors, W. W. Hutchinson and William D. Downer, had petitioned the county court on July 27, 1857, for a public road and a free bridge from their area in order to have a more ready access to the railroad depot at Hanover Court House. They wanted a bridge built at the former Rootes' ferry or the more recent Hoomes' ford. Mrs. Nelson denied that the road through her land was, or ever had been, a public road, although public use had been allowed for 50 years. The court appointed a commission to view two possible routes to the crossing: William Redd, James L. Latane, James Leftwich, Iverson L. Atkinson, B. J. J. Nicholson, Henry A. Abrahams, and James C. Johnson. Route A was the current road that passed from the main road, near the Hutchinson residence ("Farm Hill") and by the front of Mrs. Nelson's home. Route B would, from near the road to the Hutchinson residence, meet the road to the east used by

17

James Eubank and pass at the bottom of the hill behind the Nelson home. The second route was chosen and Mrs. Nelson was allowed $206.66 for damages to her land.[59] Except for some twentieth century modifications, it is the route used today.

Filed with the court papers on the litigation concerning the bridge at Mrs. Nelson's is a deposition by Samuel Norment concerning his bridge, upstream. He said that the ferriage when he bought the crossing was the same, he supposed, as it has been for 100 years — 6¼ cents per head. He had been given to understand that the bridge at Page's would be discontinued when he had built his. Now he was disconcerted that a free bridge would be built downstream. Henrietta Nelson hired William R. Aylett to represent her interest. She apparently expected to build the bridge and after seven years allow it to revert to public use.[60]

Sam Norment (who apparently lived at "Ferry Farm") had built a bridge at his crossing "on the highway from Sharon to Hanover Court House" in 1850. It had gates that were kept locked and tolls were charged to ride or drive over it. That the majority of the bridges at that time in the area were toll bridges may be inferred by Benny Fleet's diary entry when he went to meet his brother on the train at Hanover Court House and crossed Page's (Littlepage's). He commented that it was a "free bridge."[61]

"Horn Quarter" had passed out of the Nelson family to the Taylors of Caroline. In the 1850's it was owned by George Taylor. He and his wife, the former Catherine Randolph of "Wilton," divided their time between King William and their home in Richmond, "Hanover House." They had five children: Lucy, Ann, John Penn, George, and Eliza. Lucy married Charles Carter Lee, brother of General Robert E. Lee. George had died at the age of six. Catherine Taylor obtained a divorce from her husband in 1856 (and neighborhood tradition says that it took place in the back parlor of "Horn Quarter"). George Taylor then made the county residence his home. On the estate were fountains, gardens, an orangery, an overseer's house, and a school. There was indoor plumbing, with a water closet that froze in the winter of 1859.[62]

It is difficult from official reports to determine the full role of the blacks and Indians in King William prior to the war. A separate census was taken of the slave population. In the census of free inhabitants, each person was listed as either white, black or mulatto. There was no designation of Indian, although two parcels of land in the lower part of the county, 1,500 acres on the Pamunkey River and about 100 acres on the Mattaponi River, had been set aside since the 17th century for the use and occupation of the descendants of the Pamunkey tribe. Apparently by Virginia law a non-black who had at least one negro grandparent was listed as a mulatto and as such the census taker listed all those on the reservations (about

93 people) and those in smaller settlements throughout the county.[63]

A petition of 145 "freeholders and other white inhabitants of the County of King William" (including many in the upper part of the county) was filed on January 30, 1843, with the Virginia General Assembly. These men were concerned that the two reservations had become havens for runaway slaves, free negroes, and mulattoes from all parts of the county and posed a very real danger to their safety and were detrimental to the moral character of the surrounding area. They pointed out that these reservations were "places accessible by a bold and early navigation to every vessel that enters the rivers. They could be readily converted into an instrument of deadly annoyance to the white inhabitants by northern fanaticism." The signers petitioned the legislature to do away with the provisions of the old law and authorize and direct "a division of said lands amongst the same descendants, with power to sell and convey away in fee simple, [which] would in progress of time, lessen or remove the present grievance."[64]

A counter petition was filed by Tazawell H. Langston, one of the chief men of the tribe, pointing out that none of their members had been imprisoned "for stealing or hostility with our white neighbors, or one another, since our tribe has become civilized." He went on to say that they were not lazy. The previous year all but five families had produced all of their own food. In good crop years they were able to produce a surplus. They took care of their own sick and aged without outside assistance. Some among them were descendants of the Catawba tribe who had migrated from North Carolina and had intermarried with them since the American Revolution. He stressed that none of the white petitioners was their immediate neighbor. The initial petition for the sale of the reservation land was rejected on February 27, 1843.[65]

In 1857 some white men, claiming the Indians to be as dangerous as other non-whites who were prohibited by Virginia law from bearing arms, took the Pamunkey men's guns. The Executive Letter Books show the concern of the Indians that they be allowed to keep their guns for hunting. They were assured that there was no law on the Virginia statute books that prohibited Indians from having guns. This latest move was seen by many as an attempt to get the Indians to move from the state. Not all Indians were residing on the reservations. The Upper Mattaponi tribe lived in the vicinity of Sharonville. Members of the Chickahominy tribe had lost their reservation in King William by a land sale in the early years of the county. The Queen of the Pamunkeys had sold her land at "Pampatike," which included two tumuli, or burial mounds, to a settler named Booth in the 17th century.[66] There were probably still a few families scattered from Pampatike Swamp along the Manskin Path, by Muncueing (Moncuin), Mehixon, Cattail, and Machocomico swamps to branches of the Upper,

Middle, and Lower Herring creeks and the Mattaponi River.

William Spotswood Fontaine had married Sarah Shelton Aylett, a granddaughter of Patrick Henry. He built his home, "Fontainebleau," in the southeastern part of Mangohick District, not far from the Newcastle crossing. Fontaine represented King William in the General Assembly in 1840 and in 1852 was made colonel of the King William militia. The following year he was ordained a Baptist minister.[67] He exemplified the combination of civic and religious fervor that would be evident throughout King William, Virginia, and much of the South during the war years.

As has been noted Beverley B. Douglas (age 28) and Corbin Braxton (age 57) were chosen to represent the county at the 1850-51 Convention meeting in Richmond to revise the constitution of the Commonwealth of Virginia. Most of the 135 delegates were young lawyers who had been chosen along the party lines of Whig, Democrat, Radical, or Conservative. Henry A. Wise, later a governor of Virginia and a Confederate general, was prominent at this convention. The "Basis Question," whether the representation from the counties should be determined by "White or Mixed Basis," was the major consideration. The 1830 Convention had already given all white males, not just "freeholders" (landowners), the right to vote. The "White Basis," favored predominately by the western part of the state, was agreed upon and the constitution was ratified.[68]

Harrison B. Tomlin (at age 32) had been elected to represent King William as a delegate in the General Assembly of 1847. He continued to hold office until the last year of the war. After Henry A. Wise was elected governor, Tomlin was made his aide-de-camp and given the rank of "Colonel of the Cavalry." Beverley B. Douglas was elected to the Virginia Senate in 1856, a position he continued to hold until the end of the Confederacy.[69]

Benny Fleet of "Green Mount" wrote in 1860 of attending a "political discussion between the Honorable Joseph Christian and Mr. B. B. Douglas, the former a Bell elector and the latter a Breckinridge elector." John Bell was the presidential candidate running on the Constitutional Union Party ticket and John C. Breckinridge was the candidate of the pro-slavery faction that had bolted from the Democratic National Convention. Virginia at that time had as its governor a Democrat, John ("Honest John") Letcher, from the western part of the state. He had earlier advocated a gradual emancipation of the slaves and after changing his mind was elected by a small majority over the Whig candidate. Benny referred to the governor as "old ball-headed Letcher."[70]

Benny attended a fair at Ayletts on September 21, 1860, for the benefit of St. David's Episcopal Church. This was held at the time of the

20

last general muster at King William Court House. The cavalry from King William, King and Queen, and Essex counties was there and collected $187, supposedly for the outfitting of their units.[71]

Feelings ran high that winter and spring as South Carolina's ordinance of secession was passed in December 1860, and Sumter was fired upon in April 1861. Patrick Henry Aylett became the new co-editor (along with Mr. William Old) of the Richmond *Examiner* and he tried to make it the voice of the Democratic Party in opposition to the Richmond *Enquirer*. He spoke eloquently for moderation and delay at the Peoples' Spontaneous Convention in Richmond on April 16, 1861, (two days after the fall of Sumter) while the citizens waited restlessly for the decision of the elected delegates concerning Virginia's secession from the Union.[72]

Sons and fathers from King William joined the Confederate forces. James G. White, a Mangohick family man of 41 years and superintendent of the Sunday School at Hebron Baptist Church, joined up. He wrote the Misses Susan and Sallie Tuck, of King William (Mangohick) on September 5, 1861, from Allen's Grove, just outside of Richmond, expressing a kindred feeling for them since their father died and having been with them in Sunday School (Hebron). He mentioned seeing 10,000 soldiers around Richmond and wondered when he would see old King William again. White was dreading the prospect of spending the winter in tents, exposed to snow and rain, "while wives were left husbandless and children fatherless, some for life, [yet] he was willing to yield [him]self so that homes not be laid waste or wives and daughters witness scenes too horrible to tell." He asked for their prayers.[73]

War would soon touch the shores of upper King William and its raging torrent flood the Mangohick byways. As the tide rose and fell, local sons, neighbors, strangers, and their horses would trod its paths and their beasts of burden would pull caissons, guns, and supply wagons over its roads until, along the deepening wheel tracks, the waters of the freshet flowed back to the sea, and the union of the states was restored.

CHAPTER 2

Off to Fight for the Confederacy — 1861-62

Stand firmly by your canon,
Let ball and grapeshot fly,
And trust in God and Davis,
But keep your powder dry.

So read the heading on stationery passing through Mangohick Post Office in 1861.[1]

From along the roads of upper King William, her sons travelled to participate with their fellows in nearly all the major battles in Virginia, Maryland, and Pennsylvania. Under the able leadership of their own neighbors, the local boys served in their companies with distinction.

Unlike neighboring counties, perhaps due to its being bounded by two rivers, King William County did not become a battleground. Yet it proved to be a corridor for scouts and foragers of the enemy's cavalry and eventually, in late May of 1864, for Grant's army of around 100,000 as he made his attempt to push into Richmond by its side door. The soldiers' letters to their families and friends show their constant concern for the safety of their neighborhood.

For the families of King William 1861 proved to be mainly a year of mobilization and concern. The minutes of Beulah Baptist Church show that the ladies were instrumental in outfitting Taylor's Grays in May 1861, upon the request of their pastor, the Reverend John O. Turpin. By August it was reported that "a large contribution of clothing and necessaries" were being forwarded to Yorktown for them. Beulah, along with Bruington Baptist Church of King and Queen County, defrayed the expenses of C. H. Ryland to go as a colporteur (deliverer of religious tracts) to the soldiers on the Peninsula.[2]

A letter to Susan Tuck of Mangohick, from one who appears to have been an Essex man stationed at Dunnsville on the Rappahannock River with the 9th Virginia Cavalry, has reference to her making clothes for the soldiers from West Point.[3] The many letters to the Tuck family, although still privately owned, are a valuable source on both life in Mangohick during the war and the experiences of some of the soldiers from the area.

The monument which stands on the King William Court House green has the names of nearly 450 men who served in Confederate military forces. All but 96 of them were members of five predominately King William companies. Unfortunately no listing was made of their local post offices so it is impossible to determine how many were from the upper part of the county. Assuredly they would be, if not residents of Mangohick, at least friends and relatives of residents.

Three early enlistment officers lived in or near the upper part of the county. Major Harrison Ball Tomlin, who lived near the Newcastle crossing, signed up 136 men. Seventy-one men enlisted under Captain Thomas H. Carter. His home, "Pampatike," was near the Piping Tree ferry. Captain James C. Johnson, who enlisted 36 men, made his home after the war at "River Hill," near Beulahville.

Harrison B. Tomlin had inherited a part of the Tomlin farm in King William County, "Eocine," which he came to call "Prestley." He was a member of the state militia and was appointed a major in the Virginia forces (under General Robert E. Lee) by Governor John Letcher on May 3, 1861. Tomlin was a bachelor. In the 1850 census he is shown as living in King William with his sister, July B. Coalter.[4]

Major Tomlin was assigned the command of the village of West Point. The Pamunkey Indians spoke to him of their concern for the safety of the bridge there and he passed the message on to General Lee. He kept a letter book, covering May 3 to October 11, 1861, which is now preserved in the Virginia Historical Society. In it he tells of the muster and training of the garrison of 219 Virginia volunteers. They kept watch over the York River down to Gloucester Point, using the hired assistance of the Pamunkey Indians, who were skilled river boat pilots. Under Tomlin were the Taylor's Grays, led by Captain William R. Aylett, of "Montville;" the Barhamsville Infantry (from New Kent); and the Pamunkey Artillery. A King and Queen infantry (formerly artillery), a New Kent cavalry, and the Virginia Rangers (cavalry later called Lee's Rangers and containing many King William, King and Queen, and New Kent men) were mustered in at West Point but sent elsewhere. As garrison commander Tomlin distributed the limited supply of percussion-cap rifles, to replace the old flintlocks, and called for the election of officers.[5]

The King William men serving at West Point and on the Peninsula in 1861 were members of the 5th Virginia Battalion. Company B had been organized and mustered into service on April 11, 1861. William R. Aylett and 35 others from King William enlisted at West Point on May 13 under Major Tomlin and formed the nucleus of Taylor's Grays. Over the next eight weeks they were joined by ten more from the county.

From May 11 to 21, Captain Aylett was outfitting and equipping Taylor's Grays. They needed blankets, canteens, haversacks, camp kettles, frying pans, axes and handles, hatchets, shoes, and socks. The men signed that they had each received one stand of arms, one flintlock musket, one cartridge box, a bayonet and scabbard, and an accompanying belt with plates. Also the captain requisitioned one bell tent and one wall tent, with the necessary poles and pins.[6]

Company D of the 5th Battalion was made up on July 26, 1861, at West Point. Dr. William G. Pollard of "Edge Hill" was joined by 35 King William men as they enlisted that day for twelve months as members of the Mattaponi Guards under Major Tomlin. Subsequently these Virginia volunteers along with Taylor's Grays were reorganized into regular infantry and in March 1862 went to make up the 53rd Virginia Infantry Regiment under then Colonel Tomlin. Company B, under Captain Aylett, became Company D of the 53rd Regiment. Company D, under Captain Pollard, became Company H of the 53rd. By September 1862, all men of conscript age (18-35 years) had been transferred to the 53rd, and the 5th Battalion was discontinued. Harrison B. Tomlin served as colonel of the regiment until August 1862, when he resigned for reasons of health. He was about 48 years old at the time.

The activities of Taylor's Grays and the Mattaponi Guards may be traced not only through their service records but through the correspondence between William Aylett and his wife, the former Alice Roane Brockenbrough, of the Northern Neck. She was twenty-two at the time of their marriage in 1860 and her husband was twenty-seven. Their letters are filed with the Aylett family papers at the Virginia Historical Society.

———

William Henry Fitzhugh ("Rooney", Lee, second eldest son of General Robert E. Lee) was a resident of the "White House," just across the Pamunkey in New Kent County. Men known as the Virginia Rangers were mustered into service by Major Tomlin. The 28-year-old Lee organized them and became their captain. The unit became known as Lee's Rangers, although officially it was Company H, 9th Virginia Cavalry. Young Lee very soon rose to be colonel of the regiment and eventually became one of his father's major generals. One of his lieutenants has described Rooney thus: "He was of fine stature and commanding and handsome appearance. Though carrying more weight than was suitable to the saddle and the quick movements of the cavalry service, he was, nevertheless, a good horseman and an excellent judge of horses."[7]

Company H's second captain was Beverley Browne Douglas, the lawyer from "Cownes." He rose to the rank of major in the 5th Virginia Cavalry before resigning from service in early 1863. Miss Willie Weathers said of her grandfather, Beverley Douglas, that he was considered to have had a "brilliant and liberal mind and noble character." Although humerous, and a good conversationalist, she said that he also had a love of truth, a tender heart, and a desire to help the underdog. Thomas Witt Haynes, also a lawyer, who had attended the University of Virginia, was the Rangers' sergeant and became their captain when Douglas left the 9th Cavalry. He made his home at "Brighton," near Ayletts.[8]

The activities of Lee's Rangers during 1861 and 1862 may be followed by the extensive accounts written by Captain Douglas and filed with their service records. After he was transferred to the 5th Cavalry, the accounts of the company are sketchy and no letters are yet accessible. One can rely on a few notes made by their sergeant, Fleming Meredith, and references to Company H and Captain Haynes by their colonel, R. L. T. Beale. The memoirs of Colonel (later General) Beale, of Westmoreland County, were found by his son, Lieutenant G. W. Beale, and published posthumously.[9]

Sergeant Meredith recorded that their company was organized at West Point during June 1861. Fifteen King William men travelled to the village to be signed up on June 10 by Major Tomlin. Many of these were to become officers in the company: Douglas; Haynes; Hansford Anderson, corporal; Thomas J. Christian, lieutenant; John Pemberton, corporal; William Todd Robins, sergeant; John L. Slaughter, sergeant; and (from New Kent County) James Pollard, lieutenant.[10]

The company was stationed in Ashland by June 15. Meredith and nine other King William men soon joined the unit. There they were instructed and drilled by Colonels Charles W. Field and Lunsford L. Lomax. During June and July Captain Lee's requisitions revealed that he was busy outfitting his cavalry. For his officers he ordered two wall tents and two sets of tent poles and pins. For his 72 men (four sergeants, four corporals, and 64 privates) he asked for five common tents and five sets of poles and pins, 72 pairs of shoes or boots, 72 jackets and pants, 72 overcoats (cavalry), 72 forage caps, 72 blankets, and 72 horse blankets. Each man in the cavalry was expected to furnish his own horse. When their mounts were killed or disabled, the men were reimbursed the value of their horses.[11]

On June 1, 1861, about 85 men travelled the country roads from their homes in King William to Bond's Store, near the colonial Acquintin Church and a few miles from their county courthouse, to enlist under Dr. Thomas H. Carter in the King William Artillery. What a sight that must have been: boys, young men, and older men. Some were to be released in the ensuing months because they were under 18 years and others because they were over 35 years, some even in their late 40's. It was generally thought in 1861 that the war would be short and apparently little attention was given to the age of those who wished to serve the Confederacy. Tom Carter signed the records as the inspector and mustering officer. They were moved to Richmond and given residence in the "Artillery Barracks — Baptist college" (Richmond College). Other men from King William followed in July to be enrolled under Captain Carter.

Many of Tom Carter's requisitions and a few of his letters are filed with the service records of Carter's Battery. In a thirteen-page letter written by Carter on July 1, 1885, in response to a letter from General D. H. Hill, he told of the battery's activities in some of the major battles. General Hill's two letters to Carter and Carter's response are filed with the Lee papers at the Virginia Historical Society.

Other batteries also were stationed on the college campus. Signed requisitions show that Tom Carter was kept busy over the next several months in the feeding and supplying of the "Baptist College Battalion," which numbered from 119 to 264 men. He ordered flour by the barrel, peas by the bushel, molasses by the gallon, and bacon and beef by the pound. He signed for mess pans and camp kettles, axes, picks, hatchets and spades, blankets, shoes, and wall tents (for the officers). One ordnance order called for 60 rounds of spherical case shot to be used in 12-pound howitzers, 18 rounds of spherical case shot, and 12 rounds of solid shot for the 6-pounders. For the 6-pounder guns, he ordered 15 rounds of shot and 15 rounds of 3-second shells. He included an order for 200 friction primers.

The spherical case shot were to be used against troops at 500 to 1,500 yards distance. Their irregular flight and loss of velocity made them less accurate than shot or shell from the rifled guns. The solid shot was for battering and use against masses of troops, and the shells for use against buildings, earthen works, and troops under cover. Artillerists differed in their opinions of the relative merits of the smoothbore and rifled guns. The rifled ones were for longer range but were hard to place in wooded areas or broken countryside. Also their dense volume of black powder smoke made them difficult to reset but for the marks made by their wheels in the recoil.[12] The powder smoke may have accounted for the artillerists being described later in the POW records as having dark complexions.

Dr. Malcolm Harris tells than Colonel Carter was a man of medium height and slender build, with "clear cut military features." He wore a "grizzled mustache and pointed beard" and a smile would play upon his face. His whole bearing was one of dignity and simplicity. Doctor Harris described Carter's wife, the greatly admired former Sue Roy of Gloucester, as good, true, and kind as well as beautiful. Mrs. Carter followed her husband to camp but before too long she returned to her task of being mistress of "Pampatike."[13]

Under Doctor Carter, the King William Artillery came to be known as "Carter's Battery," first with Tom Carter as its captain. Later, when Tom has been made colonel, his brother, William P. Carter, served as captain of the battery.

———

The third major enlisting officer for King William men, James Christopher Johnson, possibly of "Old Towne" near West Point but later of "River Hill" near Beulahville, like Tom Carter had attended the University of Virginia. He was instrumental in the enlistment on January 31, 1862, of the King William men in the 2nd Artillery, later to become the 22nd Battalion of Virginia Infantry, and was made their captain. He was made lieutenant colonel of the battalion in June 1862, but by November of that year he had resigned for health reasons.[14] This company appears to have been the only one from King William that was not led by local officers throughout the war. The unit apparently remained small. It was one of the few that continued to be designated as a battalion, not as a regiment. In 1864 Andrew Leftwich of the 22nd Battalion, in a letter to his father, spoke of the prospect of his going with General Henry Heth into Richmond to recruit more men.[15]

The records of the 22nd Battalion show that many who enlisted under Captain Johnson were already serving in the 87th Virginia Militia, which was known as the King William Militia. This militia was called out on July 13, 1861, by proclamation of Governor Letcher, for sentry duty at West Point. The proclamation was by requisition of the President of the Confederate States to call into immediate service the militia of counties north of the James River and east of the Blue Ridge. The 87th at that time included at least two local companies, C and D (or F), and was led by Colonel Thomas R. Gresham and Colonel Roger Gregory (of King William) and Major William A. Saunders. Members of the 87th Militia were joined by Companies A and B from the 9th Virginia Militia.

In the summer months of 1861, King William was well represented in four companies: Company B (Taylor's Grays, later to be Company D, 53rd Virginia Infantry Regiment), led by William R. Aylett in the 5th Virginia Battalion; Company D (Mattaponi Guards, later to be Company H, 53rd Virginia), led by Doctor Pollard in the 5th Virginia Battalion; Company H (Lee's Rangers) led by Rooney Lee in the 9th Virginia Cavalry; and the King William Artillery (Carter's Battery) led by Doctor Carter. Those in the 87th Virginia Militia were still only part-time soldiers under the direction of the governor of Virginia. During 1861 enlistment from King William was not confined to these companies. Two men served with the navy. Others joined or later would join the Pamunkey Artillery; the King and Queen Artillery (later to be the 34th Virginia Infantry); the King and Queen Cavalry (a company of the 24th Cavalry); the 4th and 5th Cavalry Regiments; and the 9th, 12th, 13th, and 30th Infantry Regiments. Three Jackson brothers from Mangohick joined the 30th Virginia Infantry between May 13 and July 7, 1861.

Members of Company E, 30th Virginia Regiment, lived along both sides of the King William - Caroline County line. The company had been organized in December 1859, and was called the Caroline Grays. Robert O. Peatross, who lived just on the Caroline side, was elected their captain on March 23, 1861, and remained their leader throughout the war. The road by his house ran from the Ridge Road, just below the Bethel (M. E.) Church, into King William, passed through "Horn Quarter," near Norment's Ferry, and then crossed over the Pamunkey River to Hanover Court House. Serving with Captain Peatross were his three brothers and three of the sons of Thomas Price Jackson, a resident along that same road but in King William. The recruits were drilled in the Bethel churchyard and ladies and girls came out to watch. Young Lucetta Jackson, upon seeing Almar Samuel of Caroline, inquired as to who was that "pretty boy." Perhaps it was due to his size that he could later as a courier slip easily through the lines with messages. In addition to the Peatrosses and Jacksons, others in this company gave their addresses as Mangohick, but may have lived in either King William or Caroline. Their regiment was stationed at Aquia Creek (off the Potomac River above Fredericksburg) at the end of May 1861. The fighting was over and the enemy had fled when they arrived at Manassas on July 21.[16]

None of the King William companies particiated in the first battle at Manassas. Lee's Rangers were on their way to western Virginia. Tom Carter still had his men in or near Richmond. The King William Militia, not yet disbanded to form the volunteer company of the 2nd Artillery and later the 22nd Battalion, still stood sentry duty at West Point. Taylor's Grays were apparently vigilant along the York River and the Mattaponi Guards were not organized until later.

We have no official record of the activities of Taylor's Grays from May 1861 to December 1861, other than that they served in the 5th Battalion with the Army of the Peninsula and were under Major Tomlin and Major E. B. Montague. A postwar register lists their initial engagement as the Battle of Big Bethel (June 10, 1861). However, the service records show only Company A of Major Montague's battalion active in holding the right flank at Big Bethel on June 10 and later busy throwing up breastworks at Yorktown and Williamsburg. There were no King William men in Company A. In a list of opposing forces in the skirmish, a few miles from Fort Monroe, Major E. B. Montague is listed as leading a cavalry battalion.[17]

General Benjamin F. Butler had arrived on May 22 at Fort Monroe, where a regular United States garrison was already stationed. Butler found that the Confederates had abandoned Hampton and burned the bridge. Homes throughout the countryside were also abandoned. The general declared the many slaves who flocked into his camp "contraband of war." Corn and wheat grew in the fields and stock filled the barnyards and his men declared such food also contraband. A Confederate's letter which turned up in the Union camp told of distrust of Colonel Abram Duryea's Zouaves, "red-legged devils around our houses or hen-coops." Their rations were known to include "chicken, roast pig, ham, corn, and other first class food." The Union attack on the entrenched forces, serving under Colonel John Bankhead Magruder, proved to be a fiasco due to mistaken identity among the Union forces.[18]

The organization of the Mattaponi Guards followed a month after Big Bethel. Initial enlistments, as well as that of Andrew Blake on August 16, were at West Point.

From a letter that Captain Aylett wrote to his wife, Alice, at "Montville," it appears that Taylor's Grays remained at West Point at least through September. He wrote that it was quiet down there with no further chance for a fight. He had plans for going into Richmond for blankets and felt that they might be moving to the Peninsula, perhaps to Gloucester. Her response to his letter was that, although the "baby is getting very sweet," she could not come to him now because of the baby, but hoped to see him on Saturday.[19]

The records for Company H, 9th Virginia Cavalry, for late July and August, in which they are called "formerly Capt. W. H. F. Lee's Co. Virginia Rangers," show that they left Ashland on July 18 to join Colonel S. D. Lee's 6th Regiment of North Carolina Volunteers. By the first week in August they were encamped at Moffatt's farm in the Big Springs area (now West Virginia) and serving along the Greenbrier River as a detachment for scouting duty. Captain Douglas reported that they had not seen the enemy and had moved from place to place for health reasons — water and forage. He said that the men were sickly and the horses lean and shoeless.

On September 11, 1861, they joined General W. W. Loring's force two miles from the enemy's entrenched position and took up a position to the rear of the main body of the Confederates, but then had to fall back. Fanning out from their encampment at Big Springs, they watched the enemy's approach to ensure that the Confederate detachments were not outflanked. The Greenbrier River was at their back and there was no bridge at that point. On October 18 they moved east of the river, on the road from Huttonsville (in the Tygart Valley) to Green Bank, and continued to watch out for the approach of the enemy. Captain Douglas reported that their number was much reduced by sickness. Their horses were lean and weak due to scanty forage and exposure to rain and cold by night and day. He said that the company was incapable of very active or efficient service.

In September 1861, Carter's Battery was stationed at Allen's Grove, just outside of Richmond. Tom Carter signed requisitions for the feeding of 50 to 98 horses and one mule. Each horse was to receive 12 lbs. of oats a day and 14 lbs. of hay. At the end of the month the horses were also being fed corn and fodder. The inevitable paper work was closing in on Captain Carter, for he ordered foolscap (paper), blotting paper, pens (points), pen holders and "bottle ink."

By October 1861, the battery had moved from Fairfax Station to Union Mills. Carter continued to sign for fodder, corn, and oats for the horses. From Union Mills the order of December 18 stated the need for four kegs (or 400 lbs.) of horseshoes. One order from Davis Ford for eight tarpaulins shows that they were beginning to feel the wind and weather of the approaching winter. From Manassas Carter signed a requisition for 35 cartridges of powder. Carter and his artillery would return to the defense of Richmond in the spring, but Lee's Rangers remained in western and northern Virginia.

Carter's artillery spent the winter at Davis Ford, seven miles from Manassas. During this time the men checked over their ammunition, emptying all the powder into troughs, mixing thoroughly the fine and coarse powder, and then refilling each canister with an equal amount by weight on the scales. Come spring these shell and case shot would prove to be most effective.[20]

The Mangohick neighborhood must have been much astir in the closing days of 1861 when the 87th (King William) Militia was called out for more active service. The men were assembled at King William Court House on December 16, 1861. Company C was mustered into service by Captain Joseph Boardman Moore. Its other officers were Lieutenant James A. Powell and 2nd Lieutenant Wilson C. Powell. Company D, to be led by Captain J. Beverly Green, was also mustered in that day at the courthouse. By the next day they had marched to West Point, where some men were detailed to do government work, some assigned to the quartermaster and adjutant there, Captain Archer, and others told to report to the president of the Richmond and York River Railroad. By December 22, 1861, this militia had been sent on to near Gloucester Point, where additional King William men were mustered in. Sergeant Ammon Johnson, along with several others, was detailed back to King William to check on those who had not yet seen fit to report to their regiment.

This December muster caused hardships at home. George T. Moren wrote a letter on January 27, 1862, to the Honorable Judah P. Benjamin, then the secretary of war, stating that he had to leave his home on only one day's notice. December 25 was his accustomed day to hire (or rehire) all his laborers for the coming year. Since he was not at home on that day, all had left his employ, leaving no one to assist his family in the feeding of the stock. Should he have to remain in service, he feared that his crops would fail. He requested a discharge, stating that he was a poor man and that his family was dependent solely upon himself. This fact was certified by some who had been called up with him: Silas Mahon, Sterling B. Lipscomb, John T. Floyd, George W. Gravatt, Alexander F. Haynes, Lieutenant Wilson C. Powell, Andrew J. Leftwich, Robert W. Leftwich, Edward F. Eubank, John Cocke, and John W. Marshall.[21] There is no record that his request was honored. A George Moran (sic) is shown as enrolled by Captain James C. Johnson in his company of infantry on March 17, 1862.

Company C remained at Gloucester Point during January 1862, with Lieutenant James A. Powell commanding the company. Lieutenant Powell signed a requisition with Captain Archer, at West Point, for a cord of wood to supply fuel for the captain, two subalterns, and 52 enlisted men. Company D was also stationed at Gloucester that month. Lieutenant Wilson C. Powell on February 3 signed a provisions return for 784 lbs. of fresh beef for the men of the entire 87th and the 9th Militia. By February 8 there was need for an additional 456 lbs. of fresh beef.

At this point both Companies C and D were being broken up. Some men were discharged by the secretary of war due to age or disabilities and others assigned to the new company being made up by Captain James C. Johnson. Together the two companies had reached a total of about 130 men. Major Saunders filed papers stating that Company C, which had been mustered into the service of the Confederate States on December 18, 1861, by order of General John Bankhead Magruder, had remained in service as militia until February 21, 1862, when it was discharged by order of General Magruder. Colonel Powhatan R. Page stated that members of Company D, formerly Captain Harmon Littlepage's company, had been discharged from service on February 21, 1862, and furnished with transportation to Fish Haul (Lester Manor in King William).

Gloucester Point, down the Middle Peninsula and across the York River from Yorktown, was the scene on January 31, 1862, of the enlistment of thirty King William men under Captain Johnson in the 2nd Artillery Regiment. These men were intended to be used in the batteries at Richmond. They were mustered into service by Colonel Page, mustering officer. The men from King William became members of Company G. Twenty-seven men are shown as having been members of the King William Militia.

After February 5, 1862, the 2nd Artillery was no longer near Gloucester Point. Those from King William who wished to enlist had to travel to

Richmond. Captain Johnson, from camp at Howard's Grove, near Richmond, was insisting on his requisition forms, "My men have been mustered into the service of the C.S. [Confederate States] and have not been supplied!" He was ordering shoes, overcoats, jackets, pants, caps, camp kettles, mess pans, skillets and lids, one cooking stove, and 7½ cords of wood. There is no indication that these men were ever used in the Richmond batteries unless there were some at Howard's Grove. They came to be called, for a while, the 2nd Battalion Infantry and Artillery. On March 7, Captain Johnson ordered a drum and fife (perhaps to facilitiate their drilling).

Among those whose names were entered on the muster rolls of the 2nd Battalion that January were three Leftwich brothers from Mangohick. They were Andrew, age 26, a sandy-headed, blue-eyed fellow with a ruddy complexion; William, age 22, of fair complexion, brown hair, and hazel eyes; and Robert, age 20, of similar appearance to William. Their home, "Walnut Hill," a story-and-a-half house now in ruins, stood behind Hebron Church. They were a family of four boys whose mother had died years before. Their youngest brother, Richard, had been raised by an elderly servant and taught by Andrew to read and write. Now, at age 16, he desperately wanted to join his brothers. Finally, after incessant begging for their father's permission, Richard went to serve with "Lee's Rangers" in the final twelve months of the war. Through Andrew's letters home to Mangohick, to his family and to Sallie Tuck, whom he married after the war, we can learn of the activities of his battalion.[22]

Allen C. Redwood, age 27, enlisted in the 55th Virginia Regiment in 1861. Although Redwood was not from King William, his regiment was in the same brigade as the 22nd Battalion and served in many of the same engagements. He was a skilled artist and the scenes he sketched, many done during the war, would be sights witnessed by Andrew Leftwich, the 22nd Battalion, and their friends and neighbors from King William. Redwood sketched the Confederate types: the clean shaven, yet powder-blackened, young artillerymen standing beside his gun with a determined gleam in his eyes as he peered from beneath his forage cap; the cavalryman wearing a jaunty-brimmed hat with a plume as he sat astride his horse; and a beady-eyed sharpshooter standing with his rifle resting on his shoulder, his brimmed hat turned back from his forehead, and a corncob pipe clenched in his teeth. Redwood would sketch the sharpshooters at Fredericksburg in 1862 as they sighted across wooden flour barrels and fired from behind frame houses. He would also show the men as they took off their shoes and rolled up their trousers to ford the rivers and streams on their march to Gettysburg in 1863.[23]

———

The report at the end of December 1861 said that Companies A, F, G, and I of the 5th Virginia Battalion had on December 15 marched from Deep Creek to Yorktown. On that same day Companies B, D, E, and H of the 5th Battalion had marched from Ship Point also to Yorktown. There the companies were united and marched under Colonel Montague to Camp Grafton, York County, where the battalion was subsequently stationed.

William Aylett wrote to his wife soon after arriving at Camp Grafton, three miles from Yorktown. He said that they would be going into winter quarters there. There was a skirmish below Bethel the day before, but there was no "chance of a general engagement." He had been killing some game — snipes and woodcocks — but was almost out of powder. He said that his "comfort is a great comfort" and with it and his blankets and overcoat he slept "as warmly every night as I do at home," although he missed her and their little Sallie.[24]

Captain Aylett signed a requisition at Yorktown on February 20, 1862, for pants and shoes for the men, saying that those they had were worn out and there had been no furloughs during which the men could have reached the government supply depots. Captain Pollard signed a requisition the next week for seven pairs of shoes, saying that his men's shoes were worn out and they were in absolute want of them. During that time several of the men were detailed to work on gunboats at West Point. Others were sent to King William to secure Negroes to work on fortifications on the York River.

In connection with these fortifications, we can catch a glimpse of the role of blacks from King William in the war. The Virginia Legislature approved an act in February 1862 that required all free Negroes age 18-50 to register. These lists were sent to the Adjutant General, and whenever commanders needed laborers they could file a requisition with the local court. A board of three justices would select those who would serve and the sheriff would be sent to notify them. The men were not required to serve longer than 180 days without their consent, but their failure to serve would incur a fine of $50-$100. These laborers were entitled to the same compensation, rations, quarters, and medical services given white laborers. Blacks were used as turfers, carpenters, sawyers, wagon drivers, and ditchers. There were three batteries constructed on the York River for a total of 30 guns. Virginia used the mental and physical capacities of its large black population, both slave and free, in many more phases of the war effort: the employment of male and female nurses in its military hospitals; the use of craftsmen in construction and repair shops at its quartermaster and ordnance depots; and the utilization of skilled, semi-skilled, and common laborers in its mines and munitions factories.[25]

Captain Aylett wrote to his wife on February 26, 1862, from Camp Grafton, telling her that the expedition against Newport News had been abandoned due to the condition of the roads and the fact that the enemy had now been reinforced. He told her that Mr. William B. Pointer of his regiment would be coming to King William to bring back slaves to work on the fortifications. General Magruder was insisting that he must have them. Aylett suggested to his wife the names of those he thought could best adjust to camp life. She was asked to send his "water boots" back by Pointer.[26]

From the Fleet diary and letters we learn that in February 1862 Major Tomlin and Dr. William George Pollard were still recruiting men and officers to make up companies of 80-100 men in the 53rd Regiment.[27] The regiment moved in March 1862 from Camp Grafton to Suffolk; to King's Mill Wharf on the James River; on to Sandy Cross, North Carolina; and then in May back to Suffolk; thence to Zuni and Ivor, on the Norfolk and Petersburg Railroad. Sometimes they marched, sometimes they were transported on boats, and at other times they travelled on "the cars." From their camp at Sandy Cross, Captain Aylett reported that discipline was good; some men were sick and some were on detached duty. At Camp Randolph, near Suffolk, Company H held its election of officers. Dr. Pollard was reelected as captain, John L. Latane elected lieutenant, William H. Burruss elected second lieutenant, and James I. Sale elected third lieutenant. Several more King William men joined the regiment.

Apparently at about this time Lieutenant Latane received the gift of a *Book of Common Prayer.* Later he inscribed in it:

This little book was presented to me by A. Govan Hill [lieutenant of Company D] while camped at Suffolk, Va. and carried during the whole war, even in my confinement while a prisoner and in the many campaigns in which I participated. I value it at a high figure on account of association and other reasons.[28]

Stationed along creeks and riverbanks throughout eastern Virginia and into North Carolina, the men, unaccustomed to camping out, fell victim to pneumonia, typhus, and malaria. Company E of the 30th Virginia was detached for four months during the fall and winter of 1861-62 to build batteries and man them at Evansport on the Potomac. During this time some forty of the company were reported absent and home on leave because of sickness. Nine are recorded as dying from sickness in these early months of the war.[29] At least fifteen of the 53rd Regiment were either hospitalized, died, or were discharged because of disability. Many of the deceased men's families were represented by Richard M. Tuck. He would petition for their back pay and personal possessions. Tuck, more than 35 years of age and a teacher by profession, had served for a while with the 22nd Battalion.

———

From November 1861 through February 1862, Captain Douglas was on leave from the 9th Cavalry to attend the Virginia Legislature. Lieutenant George Washington Bassett, Jr., of Hanover County, commanded Company H during Douglas's absence. Bassett filed the report from Huttonsville for December and January. He wrote that 250 Confederates faced 2,000 to 2,500 Union men on January 3 and were forced to retire, but did so only after a detachment of 75 from three companies, including Company H, withstood the advance for two hours. They withdrew to Monterey and then were ordered to Fredericksburg. The company is shown as being at Camp Mercer in Spotsylvania at the end of February, but no detailed information is given.

Captain Douglas must have come through King William on his way back from the Virginia Legislature. The service records of three men show that they enlisted under him at Ayletts on March 15, 1862. From Stafford Court House in March 1862, Douglas signed for forage for 42 horses and mules — corn, oats, fodder, and hay. On June 13, no location given, he signed for forage for only 25 horses. He wrote the report for the company for March and April from Rouzie's Chapel, Hanover County, and told that they were ordered to reinforce Colonel Lee near Falmouth on the night of April 17 and were in action against the enemy the following morning. That same day they crossed the Rappahannock River and evacuated Fredericksburg, marching as the rear guard of the army. This is the last full report of the company until May 1863. In the 1862 reorganization Beverley B. Douglas was made a major in the 5th Virginia Cavalry and Thomas W. Haynes became captain of Company H, 9th Virginia Cavalry.

Andrew Leftwich wrote his first letter "to ladies," the Misses Susan and Sallie Tuck, in April 1862. His letters that early spring show that they were stationed at Howard's Grove. He wrote that he had been sent in the rain to Richmond to take in some prisoners. These men had first been thought to be Union men but, upon finding them to be loyal, the Governor had sent them on by themselves in "the cars" to join their regiment in the Valley. Andrew returned to camp in the latter part of March to find both his brothers, Robert and William, sick. He inquired about all the folks back home, including Uncle Billy, and wanted to know if they were still playing cards until late at night. The men expected that their unit would be sent to Yorktown with "their heavy artillery (muskets)." Andrew instructed that his mail be addressed in care of Captain J. C. Johnson.[30]

In a later letter that month, still from Howard's Grove, Andrew wrote of the prospect that the company might be in Hanover Junction the next day and he mentioned being under Colonel Tansill. He encouraged Sallie to go to Sunday School to teach the children and cautioned her that the "Yankeys" might be in Richmond the next time she went.[31] McClellan's

Peninsula Campaign was in progress.

The service records show the company was mustered for pay on April 30, 1862, at Camp Anderson, Caroline County, by Colonel Robert Tansill, mustering officer. During the month of May they were listed as near Milford and were mustered for pay by Lieutenant James Ellett. By May 23, 1862, the regimental organization was broken up by the Conscription Act and they had been reorganized as the 22nd Battalion Virginia Infantry. Soon Captain Johnson rose to major and then to lieutenant colonel of the battalion.

In the spring of 1862, Confederate munitions were already in short supply. Their Springfield rifles had to be muzzle-loaded for each shot — the cartridge opened by the soldier's teeth, black powder emptied into the barrel, the bullet pressed down with his thumb, then rammed into place with the ramrod. Even then the rifle would not be ready to be fired until the hammer was half-cocked, a percussion cap placed over the nipple and then the hammer fully cocked. A soldier might emerge from battle unscarred by the enemy yet covered with black soot and cinders from his own gun and those of his fellows.[32] Andrew Leftwich's company became a part of the 22nd Virginia Infantry Battalion in Field's brigade of General A. P. Hill's division.

————

Requisitions reveal the locations of the King William Artillery on the Peninsula during the spring of 1862. Captain Carter signed at Yorktown on April 16 for fodder and corn. The next week he signed for corn and hay or two days' rations for 80 horses. During April the orders for food and staples for the men were signed at Yorktown. These included: bacon, flour, meal, sugar, salt, soap, and whiskey. The order on May 6 for bacon and flour came from Williamsburg, so apparently the battery was moving up the Peninsula with General Joseph E. Johnston. At a camp near Richmond during the remainder of the month their fare was more varied, for they also had peas, apples, hard bread, vinegar, molasses, and a "½ head beef cattle (250 lbs.)."

Fred Fleet, the 19-year-old brother of Benny, was stationed with the 26th Virginia Regiment at Gloucester Point. He wrote home in April that Dr. Thomas H. Carter's men were reported to be on the Peninsula. A month later Benny wrote in his diary of the evacuation of the troops at Gloucester Point during McClellan's Peninsula Campaign. These men were marched up through St. Stephen's Church, King and Queen County, to cross the Mattaponi River into King William at Ayletts and Dunkirk. They thought they were on the way to join General "Stonewall" Jackson in the Shenandoah Valley. As soon as they got to St. Stephen's they were met by provisions for themselves and their horses, which had been sent by the neighboring families. There were about 2,000 to 2,500 infantrymen,

36

two companies of light artillery, and two of cavalry. Fred got to spend that night at home. The next day, May 7, cavalry, artillery, and baggage wagons crossed the bridge at Dunkirk and the infantry crossed the ferry at Ayletts. Fred's company was halted at the Ayletts' wharf to stand guard over the commissary stores, which two vessels had brought up the river. The family visited with Fred at Ayletts during the day. Then the troops headed in the direction of Hanover Court House (possibly along the stagecoach road). The weather was very warm and cotton and corn were being planted. Herrings were being hauled out of the river.[33]

The history of Mangohick Church states that 4,000 Confederate soldiers under a Lieutenant Taliaferro stopped at Mangohick on May 7, 1862, and stayed for two days.[34]

CHAPTER 3

The York and the Pamunkey — 1862

McClellan's Peninsula Campaign during the spring of 1862 brought together assorted "schooners, brigs, sloops, steamers, ferryboats, tugs, canalboats, and barges" which were leased from watermen of the Northeast for the transportation of McClellan's forces to Fort Monroe. More than 100,000 men, their supplies and equipment including pontoons and bridging material, 300 pieces of artillery, and 25,000 horses, mules, and beef cattle with their forage had to be moved.[1]

The Army of the Potomac's supply line stretched toward Richmond along the stem and base of a reversed "L." Between Washington and Richmond lie the many rivers of eastern Virginia: the Potomac, the Rappahannock, the York (made up of the Mattaponi and the Pamukey with their convering streams), and the Chickahominy as it flows through its swamps into the James. McClellan's attempts in the fall and winter of 1861 to push General Joseph E. Johnston's Confederate forces back from their threat on Washington had climaxed only with their withdrawal in March to the Rappahannock.[2] Now McClellan was attempting a flanking movement down the Chesapeake Bay to Union-held Fort Monroe, which stood on the tip of the peninsula between the York and James Rivers as they flow into the bay at Hampton Roads.

The Confederate supply lines in Virginia stretched under the shadows of the Blue Ridge Mountains and along the converging rail lines that fed into Washington and Baltimore. General "Stonewall" Jackson continued to threaten General Irvin McDowell from the flank and President Lincoln had been reluctant all winter to release these men to McClellan.

There was only one east-west railroad that fed into Richmond above the James, the Richmond and York River Railroad. Beverley B. Douglas was one of its founders. It had not been completed until 1860. Matthew Fontaine Maury, as consulting engineer, had suggested that the railroad pass over the Pamunkey on an iron bridge and proceed to its terminal at West Point. From Lester Manor, ten miles above West Point, connections were made with the Northern and Company stage lines to King William Court House, Walkerton, and points beyond. From its terminal the steamer *West Point* plied its way to Old Point Comfort, Norfolk, and Baltimore.[3]

Early in the conflict the strategic position of West Point had been noted with the resulting call up of the militia for sentry duty there, the assignment of Colonel Tomlin to guard the bridge, and the detachment of members of his company to build gunboats. The militia had been sent downstream to guard Gloucester Point, however, then on to the defense of Richmond. The Confederates had destroyed the bridge across the Pamunkey so it could not fall into the enemy hands.

The Confederate ironclad, the *Virginia,* a burnt vessel formerly called the *Merrimack,* had been equipped at the Gosport Navy Yard in Norfolk with plates from Tredegar Iron Works in Richmond, only to have short-lived success in Hampton Roads during March 1862. With the arrival of the more maneuverable Union *Monitor* and General Johnston's withdrawal from Norfolk and Yorktown, it became obvious that the heavy drafted *Virginia* would be of no value in the more shallow inland waters. She was sunk in the Elizabeth River.[4]

The blowing up of the *Virginia* caused quite a stir against the Confederate Navy Department and a Court of Inquiry was called. Thomas DeLeon, in *Four Years in Rebel Capitals,* declared that the ship "drew far too much water to pass the shoal at Harrison's Bar — between her and Richmond." With Norfolk in Union hands and their fleet (in addition to her rival *Monitor)* pressing Confederate shipping, an attempt to remove some of the *Virginia*'s armor only raised the ship two feet in the water. There was no port from which she could draw supplies and unsupplied she could not remain the "grim sentinel to bar all access to the [James] river."[5] Down with her went Confederate hopes of breaking the Union blockade of eastern Virginia by water. King William County became the onlooker as Union forces, supplied from along Virginia's waterways, pushed up the York and Pamunkey Rivers and then westward toward Richmond.

In early April 1862, General Gustavus W. Smith received a lengthy memorandum from Captain B. B. Douglas of Company H, 9th Virginia, concerning a conversation with an Episcopalian minister of Alexandria. The clergyman had recently been taken prisoner while in his pulpit for refusing to offer prayers for the President of the United States. He and a young man, both disguised as sailors, had escaped and landed in King George County, apparently where they had come in contact with Douglas and some of his men. The churchman had told Douglas of the departure of General McClellan and General Joseph Hooker's division for Old Point Comfort (Hampton Roads). The captain also sent information obtained from an informer and an agent that McDowell's division, which had been left to threaten Johnston from the north while McClellan moved up the Peninsula, was "not very strong in number and almost without artillery." All this information was passed on to General Johnston.[6]

. Five U.S. Navy gunboats were propelled up the York River and onto the Pamunkey. The U.S.S. *Corwin* and the U.S.S. *Chocura* were sent up the river from Yorktown on May 5 to determine if the channel was clear to

West Point. The U.S.S. *Currituck* led the army transports up to West Point and later, on May 17, along with the U.S.S. *Sebago*, reconnoitered on the Pamunkey, which resulted in the destruction of Confederate store-vessels. The U.S.S. *Marblehead* remained in those inland waters until June 29.[7]

The Battle of West Point or Eltham's Landing was fought in New Kent County, not in King William. McClellan sent several divisions, including General William B. Franklin's, to the right bank of the Pamunkey near West Point. Franklin's division had been withdrawn from McDowell, near Fredericksburg, and sent to join McClellan at Yorktown. With the Confederate evacuation of Yorktown, plans were made for Franklin to move up the York by water and to land near West Point in order to cover further Union landings and reinforcements. Heavy storms prevented their getting underway immediately. The Confederate rearguard held the advance of the Union land forces at Williamsburg through the night of May 5.[8]

The Union flotilla, made up of civilian boats guarded by Navy warships, set out on the morning of May 6. Clear sky stretched above them and beneath them the river lay smooth and quiet. Colburn Adams, of Franklin's division, described their procession up the river, between beautifully sloping banks beyond which lay green fields and orchards in full bloom. Twenty miles above Yorktown and 1½ miles below West Point they came upon a broad plateau, which Adams called Brick House Point. Their gunboats took position as the infantry and artillery began to embark from the low-drafted steamers and across canalboats and pontoons. A concealed Confederate battery opened on them from a ridge beyond while the gunboats struggled to move closer in the shallow water. A Union man, who was floating in a balloon overhead, thought he saw a mass of Confederate troops north of West Point.[9] The Battle of West Point ensued the next morning on the south bank of the Pamunkey at Brick House. Two Confederate brigades under General W. H. C. Whiting, on their way up from Hampton Roads, pushed Franklin's men back to their gunboats. Union losses totalled 186. The Confederates lost 48.[10]

Prince de Joinville, also with McClellan's forces, described the procession of the army as it moved up the south bank of the York and Pamunkey. He said that they were preceded first by the gunboats, then the next day by the topographers interspersed with cavalry escort. On the third day the army and its wagon trains followed. Transport ships, mostly steamers, moved closely off shore in order to tie up at the improvised wharves to unload supplies and take on the sick. The season was hot and rainy. Joinville wrote, "These lovely meadows of the Pamunkey gave birth to deadly fever."[11]

After passing through the Cumberland (a canal thoroughfare just below West Island), they came to the "White House." Adams described their arrival there on an afternoon of drenching rain. He said that the plantation stretched nearly five miles along the river and extended nearly three miles inland. Mrs. Robert E. Lee was in residence in this her ancestral home and home of her son, Rooney Lee. It was a "small neat cottage . . . with Gothic windows, pointed gables and little balustrades, [which] stood at the upper edge of the ridge overlooking the river." The blacks living in many cabins, also along the ridge, "seemed well provided for and contented." The G. W. P. Custis will (Mrs. Lee's father's) had stipulated that they would be free on July 4 of that year.[12]

George Alfred Townsend, a correspondent for a New York newspaper, travelled up the York and the Pamunkey a few days later on a mail steamer. He wrote that the York River was filled with merchant and naval craft. Apparently near West Point the steamer passed two half-completed Confederate gunboats which had been burned while still standing on their stocks (construction timbers). He said that their charred ribs stuck out "like the remains of some extinct monsters." Just a few days later they would have been armed, manned, and ready to cause "havoc upon the rivers and seas."[13]

Townsend saw the "spit of land" that is West Point with its "few houses built upon the shallow, and some wharves, half demolished." There was only one Confederate water battery for its defense. Now "an array of [Union] shipping scarcely less formidable" than at Yorktown and Gloucester filled the river.[14]

The correspondent considered the winding Pamunkey a beautiful stream, where "densely wooded, and occasional vistas opened up along its borders of wheatfields and meadows." He saw Virginia farm houses, log cabins with mud chimneys, and "manorial" estates and wrote, "Few of the Northern navigable rivers were so picturesque and varied."[15]

Just below Cumberland masts of schooners protruded from the water, sunk in an attempt to blockade the river. The mail steamer found its way by but others had to be towed through the apertures. Upon arriving at the "White House," as darkness began to fall, Townsend saw the twinkling camp fires, heard the lowing of the commissary cattle, and saw some soldiers bathing in the river.[16]

A modern-day writer, Thomas J. Blumer, stood on the banks of the quiet-flowing Pamunkey and talked to those on the Indian Reservation whose family recollections reach back to those days in the spring and summer of 1862. He was told that the landowners along the river who had not already fled into Richmond displayed flags of truce to protect their property. Many of the black people had fled to Fort Monroe. The Indians watched from their log cabins along the river bank. They saw the hasty Confederate evacuation of West Point, saw a locomotive derailment

41

which dumped an undisclosed number of soldiers in the river to drown, and saw the smoke that billowed over the county from the burning railroad bridge, set aflame after the passage of the last troop train and just hours before the arrival of the U.S.S. *Currituck*. Some of the local blacks followed the Federal Army. Although the Indians were determined to remain on their land, some were drafted by the U.S. Navy to serve as river pilots or scouts, for which they were paid $2.00 a day and rations. The Federals confiscated or burned all boats on the river, including row boats, and rebuilt the destroyed railway bridge.[17]

Captain B. B. Douglas was on detached service with men of Company H, 9th Cavalry, in the latter part of May 1862. He had his camp near Ayletts and did reconnaissance along the Mattaponi, the Pamunkey, and a few miles down the York. They saw numerous vessels in the Pamunkey between West Point and the "White House," and watched the disembarkation of troops at the latter, and the unloading of forage and storage supplies. A Federal gunboat had run aground about five miles below Ayletts. It was rumored that a boat of lighter draught would return to capture or destroy the Confederate vessels and stores lying at or near Ayletts. The captain felt that the Federals would not come against General Richard H. Anderson's forces from the direction of King William County but rather would threaten the railroads and communications on Johnston's left. Although Douglas had few cavalrymen in the area and their horses were overworked, he promised to send daily a messenger to Mangohick Church to meet a courier from General L. O'Brien Branch, who was stationed at Hanover Court House.[18]

General McClellan established his base on the Richmond and York River Railroad at the "White House," just across the river from the reservation. He must have deemed it necessary that a way be kept open for possible reinforcements from General McDowell in Fredericksburg and the way closed to an attack on his rear. To this end General Fitz-John Porter was instructed to destroy the bridges over the South Anna and Pamunkey rivers and to clear the peninsula bounded by the Pamunkey and Chickahominy rivers as far north and west as Ashland. On May 27 Porter engaged the Confederates, mostly North Carolinians under General Branch, at Peake's Station on the Virginia Central Railroad, two miles below Hanover Court House. He was joined by Colonel Gouverneur K. Warren, who had come up the Hanover County road along the Pamunkey destroying its bridges and who subsequently was dispatched farther up the river to destroy more bridges and any boats found on the river. The Confederates had already abandoned their camp near Hanover Court House. The next day they were pushed as far as Ashland.[19]

Colonel Richard H. Rush of the 6th Pennsylvania Cavalry "Lancers" reported on May 22 from his camp on the Piping Tree Ferry road in

Hanover of a reconnaissance which he had made to the Newcastle and Hanovertown ferries. He said that he found no town at Hanovertown, only a ferry where the river was not fordable. He found that the country was "very rich, and the farms all stocked — sheep, cattle, &c, rich fields of grain and grass, and the ladies and families at home." Rush heard that some cavalry, believed to have been Captain William B. Newton's, had passed over the Hanovertown — Old Church Road the day before.[20]

On May 24 Rush found a new bridge over the Pamunkey River at Mrs. Henrietta Nelson's (six miles east of Hanover Court House), which he destroyed.[21] Almost exactly two years later some of Grant's armies would be crossing there on pontoons, from the King William side. Warren, by then a general and commanding Grant's V Corps would cross three miles below there, at Hanovertown.

Colonel Rush and the 6th Pennsylvania Cavalry served in the Cavalry Reserve under General Philip St. George Cooke, Confederate General J.E.B. Stuart's father-in-law. The 83rd Pennsylvania Infantry, who wore the colorful Zouave uniform, served under General Daniel Butterfield and were a part of Fitz-John Porter's V Corps. Butterfield was active in the battle at Hanover Court House as was Colonel Hiram Berdan with his sharpshooters.[22] One of the scimitar-like bayonets which the 83rd carried in their belts has been found in the area.

A diary kept by Mrs. Willoughby Newton, who at that time was visiting her daughter-in-law and family at "Summer Hill" and "Westwood" on the Hanover side of the Pamunkey, tells of the arrival of the advance troops, the destruction of the bridge, and the sounds of the fighting at Hanover Court House and throughout the month of June. She began her account on May 18 with the rumor of the enemy's approach from the "White House" through Old Church, and then of the sighting by the servants of a squad of cavalry on the Hanovertown lane. She described the passing by the gate of five or six lancers (light cavalry) with their red streamers and Colonel Rush's visit to the "Summer Hill" house on May 24. On the morning of May 26 Mrs. Newton saw a "regiment of Lancers, one of regulars, one of rifles, and another of zouaves, composed of the most dreadful-looking creatures I ever beheld, with red caps and trowsers; also two guns. They were on their way to the Wyoming bridge, which they destroyed, and then made a reconnaissance of the Court House road."[23]

Were the "Widow Nelson" and her two daughters, Kate and Letitia, in residence at "Wyoming" on the morning of May 26? Did they look out across the river flats to see the flames, hear them crackling along the timbers of the new bridge, and smell the smoke as it billowed into the sky?

About a month before, their brother Cary had gone to Ashland to join

Company G of the 4th Virginia Cavalry, now led by Colonel William C. Wickham, of "Hickory Hill." An 18-man contingent of the 4th Cavalry managed to hold Ashland until May 26. Others of the 4th Cavalry had been sent to Williamsburg, including Cary Nelson's cousin, Captain William B. Newton of "Summer Hill," who headed Company G. Now they were stationed at Hanover Court House and were doing picket duty along the Pamunkey. Captain Newton was not with them. He had mistaken foes for friends at Williamsburg, been taken captive, and would be at Fort Delaware until exchanged in August.[24]

Downstream at "Manskin Lodge" (between Hanovertown and Newcastle), Dr. Carter Warner Wormeley and his family were subjected to even more frightening circumstances on June 2 and 3. Captain August V. Kautz of the 6th United States Cavalry (under General George Stoneman) had been sent to destroy the ferries on the Pamunkey. They were armed with carbines and accompanied by two squadrons of lancers. Captain Kautz said that they found the ferry-boats at Newcastle, Basset's, and Piping Tree already destroyed and they arrived at Wormeley's landing too late to cross over.[25]

That night a runaway slave brought Kautz word at his camp at Newcastle of the location of the Wormeley ferry-boat. The next morning on the doctor's farm in King William they found concealed in a creek the 25-ton sloop *Golden Gate,* from Norfolk; eight wooden boats and one metal boat capable of carrying 20 to 30 men each; and the ferry-boat, which was large enough to carry two teams with their horses. The foliage of newly-felled trees hid the entrance to the creek. The captain said that they burned the sloop and the other boats "were rendered entirely useless."[26]

The river was in flood stage, still rising, and "troops could not be crossed without fixing a line." Kautz sent a lieutenant and six men across in a small canoe to Doctor Wormeley's home and arrested him. Yet the Union officer admitted that he could "collect no satisfactory information that a force was organizing or existed on the north side of the river, as I supposed in my instructions."[27]

Doctor Wormeley, according to a letter which he wrote to his half-brother in New York, was taken to the headquarters of General McClellan and detained there, in the drenching rain and without shelter, for forty-eight hours. Then he was marched through mud eight to ten inches deep in the direction of the "White House," twenty-three miles away. After twelve miles the doctor collapsed and was carried by ambulance the rest of the way. At the "White House" he was put on a steamer for the prison at Fort Delaware.[28]

Confined to the island prison without funds and cut off from contact with his family and friends in King William, Wormeley was nevertheless treated with respect and allowed to return home in mid-December. Back at "Manskin Lodge," Mrs. Wormeley, the former Ellen Bankhead Lightfoot of Port Royal in Caroline County, devoid of a ferry or any type of boat, had to remain with her eight or ten children in King William, away from their summer home, "Forkland" in Hanover.[29]

Life on the Mattaponi River during the spring and summer of 1862 was no less traumatic. After the Confederate troops from the Peninsula moved on westward, Benny Fleet recorded in his diary that a gunboat had come as far as a neighbor's house. His mother was busy purchasing linen and flannel to be made up into shirts for the soldiers and osnaburg for their "drawers." His father carried "12½ doz. herrings, a quarter of lamb, lamb's head pie, loaf bread, biscuit, corn bread, butter & milk, ice, etc. etc. to Lee's Rangers," encamped near Jno. Fauntleroy's gate (perhaps at Dunkirk). Two days later Benny and his father rode by the camp on their way to Sharon Church (King William) to hear the Reverend John O. Turpin preach. The next day he wrote that Captain Beverley B. Douglas had quickly moved his company that evening in the direction of Hanover Court House in order not to be cut off by the enemy said to already be in possession of Guinea and Milford on the R.F.& P. Railroad.[30]

Some of the neighbors' sons were killed in the Battle of Seven Pines but Fred Fleet's regiment was not engaged. On June 17 Benny wrote that he, Daniel, Ned and Wash had been "throwing dirt to corn" all day and had commenced cutting wheat at Dunkirk. Doctor and Mrs. Fleet had gone to a prayer meeting that night when the blacks brought Benny word that 500 Yankees had come up from toward West Point and had burnt the Dunkirk Bridge, the ferryboat, and the granary, including 365 bushels of the neighbors' corn. Later they learned that the black ferryman, William — who received half of the ferriage — had saved the ferry house by telling the soldiers that it was his house. The Fleets continued to attend church, Sunday School, and prayer services, even a "negro Prayer Meeting at Fanny's."[31]

During July the Fleet family was anxious to get food to Fred, whose company was with General Henry A. Wise at Chaffin's Bluff on the James River. Once Benny and his father went in a buggy by way of Mrs. Sutton's ferry ("Towinque," just above "Wyoming"), Hanover Court House, and the Brook Turnpike into Richmond. Returning at night, they came by way of Mechanicsville, Hanover Court House, and Norment's ferry (the next one up from Mrs. Sutton's). They were lost for two miles as they passed over the confusing roads through Mangohick and arrived at Ayletts at 2 a.m. There they learned that the Yankees had again been at Walkerton and that Mrs. Fleet had had the ferryboat removed from the river. In constant fear of coming upon the enemy along those dark roads, they managed to awaken a neighbor at Dunkirk who took word to Mrs. Fleet to send down a boat for them. The weary father and son arrived at home in time for a late breakfast. Mrs. Fleet wrote to Fred that his father went to bed and slept until 11 a.m. and awoke refreshed but that Benny slept all day except when eating or telling a little of the news.[32]

CHAPTER 4

The White Oak Swamp and the Chickahominy — 1862

Neither the 22nd Virginia Battalion nor any other King William company fought at Yorktown or in the rear guard action at Williamsburg.[1] Later, when Major General Gustavus W. Smith wrote of the converging forces in the confrontation east of Richmond, he said that Longstreet's and D. H. Hill's men (which included Carter's Battery) came from Williamsburg; Huger's division (which included Armistead's brigade and the 53rd Virginia Regiment) came from Norfolk; and A. P. Hill's men (which included the 22nd Battalion) came down from the vicinity of Ashland.[2]

Carter's Battery, as it moved toward Richmond, needed bacon, flour, hard bread, peas, sugar, soap, salt, vinegar, and molasses. From their camp near Richmond, the week of May 24-30, 1862, they requisitioned the same staples with the addition of 35 lbs. of apples. By the end of June, during the Seven Days' Battles, they included an order for whiskey.

Captain Aylett brought his men of the 53rd Regiment by rail from Zuni through Petersburg to Richmond between May 23 and May 28. They bivouacked for the night in the Capitol Square. The next morning the regiment marched east out of Richmond for four miles to camp near Oakwood Cemetery.

A. P. Hill's division (including the 22nd Battalion), on its way down from Ashland, was expected in the vicinity of Mechanicsville before midnight on May 28. They received orders to attack McClellan's forces there at dawn on May 29, before the anticipated arrival of General Irvin McDowell from Fredericksburg. Gustavus Smith and David R. Jones, with their divisions, would join them in an attack just beyond Mechanicsville. When General Joseph E. Johnston received word that McDowell had returned to Fredericksburg, the attack was called off and A. P. Hill's men were brought south of the Chickahominy. A map of positions before the Battle of Seven Pines shows the divisions of General A. P. Hill, Smith, and Jones making up Johnston's left flank along the Meadow Bridge Road as it leads northeast from Richmond to the Chickahominy. A listing of forces engaged in the battle shows neither A. P. Hill's division nor the 22nd Battalion.[3] The battalion encamped at Farrar's farm from May 31 well into June. This apparently was located below Nine Mile Road, along Stony Run and just outside of Richmond's defenses.

After an already wet spring, it rained in torrents the night of May 30,

1862. General Joseph E. Johnston had made plans to surprise the entrenched forces of McClellan located between the Richmond and York River Railroad and the White Oak Swamp, near the intersection of the Williamsburg and Charles City roads in an area called Seven Pines. The many branches of rain-swollen Gillies Creek lay between General Benjamin Huger's men and the enemy. The headwaters of White Oak Swamp emerged between D. H. Hill's forces and the enemy's. Off the narrow country roads, the dense woods were a morass of spring growth entanglement. In places, no more than one company could be seen at a time. General Hill had cautioned his men to wear a white strip around their hats to distinguish them in battle.[4]

The Confederates had to contend with mud and water waist deep as they moved across the swampy land. Misunderstood orders concerning troop movements added to the confusion. Although earthen works known as "Casey's Redoubt" were quickly taken by D. H. Hill's men, they then had to face the enemy who had rallied in the woods behind the abatis (a fortification of felled trees).[5]

Just as a Confederate heavy artillery unit was preparing to man the newly captured guns against the enemy and were exposed to attack, Captain Tom Carter and his King William Artillery arrived, apparently from along the old stage road to Williamsburg. They immediately unlimbered and fired upon the Federals until the enemy broke ranks and retreated. Then Carter and his battery moved out 400 yards into the open and fought a duel with a second Federal redoubt. General Hill maintained to the end of his life that he never witnessed anything finer, and Tom Carter remained his ideal artillerist.[6] Dr. Douglas S. Freeman listed among the ten who distinguished themselves at Seven Pines Thomas H. Carter and two other artillerists who gave the infantry support "in the tangle of forest-felled trees and water-covered fields."[7]

In correspondence after the war, General D. H. Hill reminded Carter that at the Battle of Seven Pines, upon the approach of heavy enemy reinforcements, he had directed him to fire upon the infantry and not be concerned about the artillery. Hill also told him that a shell had exploded within twenty feet of one of Carter's guns, knocking down all the men and the horses. When Carter's men ran to their fellows, one man was pulled out alive.[8]

Carter responded to Hill's letter recalling that Seven Pines was the first and bloodiest of his engagements. The ground was so soft from preparation for an oat crop and the heavy rainfall the night before that his guns would mire up to their axles after several firings. At one point sixteen guns played upon his battery, plus what he thought to be sharpshooters. The enemy shells "fell in their midst producing an almost blinding shower of mud and dirt on one's head and shoulders." One shell killed Lieutenant

William B. Newman and another man. John Tebbs was the man pulled from the heap. Also Tom Carter wrote that his brother, William P. Carter, had come to him saying that he was badly wounded and showed him his chest. Tom told him to get on a horse and ride off to find an ambulance.[9]

Carter's Battery was serving under the direction of General Robert E. Rodes, who had been a fellow cadet with Tom at Virginia Military Institute. Carter said that Rodes was a man "blunt of speech" and "given to "blarney." Upon seeing the artilleryman during the fighting at Seven Pines, Rodes said, "Carter, you are late, there's a battery at the edge of the woods on the road that's been giving the Yankees hell!" Carter replied to the general, "Your right humble servant had the honor to command that Battery."[10]

Carter recounted how young Thomas S. Jones, age 18, died at his feet. Soon after the redoubt was taken the boy had gone into an officer's tent nearby and found a bottle of wine and a lemon. Jones offered them to Carter but the captain declined. A few minutes later the lad was taking a cartridge from the ammunition case when a bullet pierced his neck. As Carter reached down to place his thumb on the hemorrhage, the boy's eyes rolled back in death. Carter said that the bullets were rattling on the guns and gun carriages until it sounded like hail.[11]

General Rodes in his report said, "The conduct of the King William Battery has nowhere in the history of the war been equaled for daring, coolness, or efficiency." He had been advised that Lieutenant Newman had behaved with "coolness and gallantry." The general also commended Private Robert B. Johnstone,[12] who had been wounded. This fair-complexioned, blue-eyed farmer from Ireland would be discharged a couple of years later because, at age 50, he was beyond the conscription limits.

The King William Battery had won a name for itself but at a heavy cost. The service records show seventeen casualties from the county: Edward J. Cocke, Jones, and Newman killed or mortally wounded; and at least fourteen others, including William P. Carter, wounded. The next day William Carter received his appointment as captain of the battery. Festus King had sustained a wound through his body. In a letter written the next January, Tom Carter recommended King for a promotion, telling how he had fought gallantly at Seven Pines. George Tebbs was wounded in both feet and had to have one of them amputated. The next year he was recommended for a position in the office of the Secretary of the Treasury C. G. Memminger. King William's representative in the Virginia Legislature, Major Beverley B. Douglas, wrote that Tebbs was "a most excellent and worthy young man, fully capable of performing the duties of [any] position his modesty will permit him to aspire to," and that he had lost a leg and deserved "well of his country."[13]

The elements proved to be too much for the men of the 53rd Virginia Regiment. According to an official report by Colonel Tomlin, the regiment remained at General Longstreet's headquarters on the night of May 31 and did not get to the front the next morning until the other three of Armistead's regiments had been pushed back. They were ordered to join their fellows in the woods, but in the lush growth they mistook friend for enemy. While they were firing at each other, a Federal regiment attacked. The 53rd Regiment withdrew, having suffered one man killed and eighteen wounded.[14]

That afternoon, when there was no further attack on the right, D. H. Hill's men removed 6,700 enemy rifles and muskets, and the captured Federal ordnance, commissary and medical supplies. Ten large guns had been removed the night before. In the early morning hours, the Confederate units withdrew to their former camps. General Huger's men returned to their camp on Gillies Creek to remain for several days.[15]

Company D of the 53rd Virginia spent only a couple of hours at its Oakwood camp before moving on to the Williamsburg Road for two days and nights, then on to the Richmond and York River Railroad, five miles east of Richmond. They had experienced an indecisive two days of fighting with many wounded and killed. W. T. Allen of Company D was wounded in the head. In Company H, Sergeant Thomas Redd was wounded in the face and William H. Tuck mortally wounded. Colonel Tomlin had his horse shot from under him.

Captain Aylett wrote to his wife on June 10 from Richmond that he was returning to his men that day. He said that he had been sick off and on for the last month and that during the last battle a ball had grazed his leg, causing a blister. His weapon during the days of fighting had been his Colt pistol. The regiment had suffered greatly but the "King William Companies" had in a measure been protected by the woods and swamps. He was concerned about the folks at "Wyoming," and wished they were farther from the enemy. Aylett gave Alice instructions for hiding the arms at "Montville" so the enemy could not find them.[16]

During the month of May 1862, the 9th Virginia Cavalry had been stationed along the roads to Fredericksburg. As in the other King William companies, there was much sickness among them that spring. They were sent in the direction of Richmond during the Battle of Seven Pines but did not participate in the action. Prayer meetings, in preparation for the involvements they were sure lay just ahead, were held by the chaplain of the regiment, the Reverend Charles H. Boggs[17] of Enfield. Before the war he had served as pastor of the King William Charge, Methodist Episcopal Church, South.

Rooney Lee and some of his men camped in Richmond at "Rosewood" (near Bryan Park) during May 1862. The Mordecai family has recounted how they "were very glad to have General 'Rooney' Lee as a protector and also as a boarder, and his finely disciplined soldiers gave no trouble." Later generations have been delighted by finding horseshoes and nails at the site of Rooney's blacksmith shop.[18]

General Johnston received a musket shot in his shoulder late in the first day's fighting at Seven Pines. Soon after that a heavy fragment from a shell struck him in the chest, knocking him from his horse and causing him to have to be carried from the field. As a result, President Davis, who had been out and observed the confused movement of the troops, finally gave General R. E. Lee the command of the armies in the field.[19]

———

On June 1, Captain Douglas of Lee's Rangers was at Beaver Dam (on the Virginia Central Railroad). He sent word to R. E. Lee and A. P. Hill: "Some part of McDowell's force has certainly been sent back to Washington or the valley, and if my information can be relied on, he is waiting further intelligence of Jackson's movements to determine his course."[20]

When General J.E.B. Stuart went on his ride to determine the position and extent of McClellan's army along the Chickahominy River (or Chickahominy Swamp as it is known locally), among the 1,200 men he took with him were seven companies of the 9th Virginia Cavalry. Companies A, H, and I were away from the regiment on detached service.[21] Several of Company H were providing courier service for General Jackson during his activities in the Shenandoah Valley.

To the sound of "Boots and Saddles," their fellow cavalrymen set out on the afternoon of June 12, 1862, with three days' rations, sixty rounds of ammunition each, and no idea of their destination. Captain William Latane of Company F of the 9th Virginia was shot while leading a charge against Federal cavalry near Haw's Shop at Studley, Hanover County. Adjutant Robins wrote after the war an account of their experiences as they proceeded under a full moon through New Kent to the Chickahominy and then to the James. He told how each bush looked like a sentinel and every tree hunched over the road resembled a vedette. As they rode along the river road for the last twenty-five miles into Richmond, by the light of the moon they could occasionally see the masts of Federal ships on the James River. Having had no sleep for forty-eight hours, they were constantly falling asleep in the saddle. On the morning of June 17, as the exhausted men and horses passed through the streets of Richmond, beside Lieutenant G. W. Beale of Company C, 9th Virginia, rode a correspondent of the Richmond *Dispatch*, taking notes.[22]

Captain Latane was buried by the neighborhood folk at "Summer Hill," the Hanover farm on Mehixon Neck, which protrudes into King

William as the Pamunkey River winds its way between the two counties. It was the home of Captain William B. Newton of the 4th Virginia Cavalry. After the war William D. Washington, a Confederate soldier and a painter, was inspired by a poem by John R. Thompson describing the event. He visited "Summer Hill" and observed the site. Using models in Richmond who were similar in appearance to the Newton family, Washington depicted the scene in oil under the title "The Burial of Latane." Shown standing around the grave are: the black servant, Aaron, who had made the coffin; Mrs. Willoughby Newton; Captain Newton's wife, Mary Page Newton; and their small daughters, Kate and Lucy; Mrs. Judith White Brockenbrough, of "Westwood;" and two young Dabney ladies, May and Maria, thought to have been from King William.[23]

General William W. Averell, in his account of the cavalry with McClellan on the Peninsula, stated, "Our general's plans were not disturbed by Stuart's raid, and two days after it was over the 3rd Pennsylvania Cavalry crossed the Pamunkey River on our right and rear, ascended to King William Court House and Ellett's [Aylett's] Mills, burned the bridge [Dunkirk] and ferry-boat, and a schooner and other boats, and a storehouse containing 30,000 bushels of grain." Apparently this is the same raid which Benny Fleet recorded in his diary on June 17.[24]

After the war General Porter and Confederate generals D. H. Hill and Longstreet wrote first-hand accounts of the Seven Days' Battles around Richmond following Stuart's ride around McClellan. Hill told of seeing on June 23 a dusty, travel-worn and weary officer leaning over a yard paling. He realized it was General Jackson, whom to that moment he had thought was still facing generals Nathaniel P. Banks and John C. Fremont in the Valley of Virginia. So secret had been Jackson's movements that when he rode ahead the last 52 miles that morning to confer with Lee he wore no insignia of rank and carried a pass from General W. H. C. Whiting, should he be challenged by an outlying sentry.[25]

At a meeting that afternoon between Jackson and General Lee, it was agreed that on June 26 A. P. Hill would cross to the north side of the Chickahominy at the Meadow Bridge; Longstreet would cross farther downstream at the Mechanicsville Bridge; and D. H. Hill would follow Longstreet. Jackson thought he could bring his men from Ashland by way of the Pole Green Road to join them in Mechanicsville. Jackson rejoined his army at Beaver Dam Station, in northwestern Hanover, on the 24th. He had his whole army around Ashland by the night of June 25, but ran into McClellan's pickets the next morning a couple of hours after sunup.[26]

The 9th Virginia Cavalry had been called on to provide screening for Jackson. They met the approaching division on June 25 near Ashland.

Three days later they were sent to seize the Richmond and York River Railroad and arrived at Rooney Lee's home, the "White House," only to find that the Federals had withdrawn. The house was in ashes, the embers still warm. McClellan was changing his base from the Pamunkey to Harrison's Landing on the James. General Stoneman's and Casey's infantry had been loaded on to gunboats and transports and moved down the river. Much of the Federal property had been destroyed at the "White House," but there were sufficient supplies left to replenish Stuart's cavalry. Company H did not rejoin the regiment until they reached Malvern Hill, on the James, about July 1. By this time Captain Douglas had been made a major in the 5th Cavalry. Thomas W. Haynes took his place as captain of Company H.[27]

The other King William companies during the seven days of fighting were still under the same commands and local leaders: Tom Carter's Virginia Battery (King William Artillery) was with D. H. Hill; Colonel Tomlin had Captain W. R. Aylett's assistance with the 53rd Regiment under Generals Huger and Longstreet; and Captain J. C. Johnson directed the 22nd Virginia Battalion. The 26th Regiment, from Wise's command, and the 30th Regiment were assigned temporarily to Longstreet.[28]

The 53rd had picket skirmishes on June 18, while located on the Richmond and York River Railroad. Corporal Andrew C. Blake, Sergeant Harry Timberlake, and John F. Burch were wounded. Robert W. George was taken prisoner. Their activities on June 25 and 27 were listed as picket action, in which one man was killed and two wounded.

The initial day of the Seven Days' fighting was on June 25 on the Williamsburg Road at King's School House. A part of Huger's division was engaged. That night D. H. Hill marched his division to the neighborhood of the Mechanicsville Bridge. Just before reaching the Pole Green Road the next day, Jackson found the bridge over Totopotomoy Creek had been burned. By the time the bridge was repaired and they could cross, night was coming on and they spent the night of June 26 near Pole Green Church,[29] several miles short of Mechanicsville.

By mid-afternoon of the 26th, A. P. Hill felt he could no longer wait for Jackson and proceeded to cross to the north side of the Chickahominy. D. H. Hill's task when he crossed at Mechanicsville was to proceed eastward down the north bank. He has written: ". . . the great want with the Confederates, strange as it may seem, was accurate knowledge of the country in their front. The map furnished me (and I suppose the six other major-generals had no better) was very full in regard to everything within our lines; but a red line on the east side of the Chickahominy and nearly parallel to it, without any points marked on it, was our only guide to the route on which our march was to be made. None of us knew of the formidable character of the works on Beaver Dam." The swampy area was densely covered with tangled undergrowth and young timber. Sharp-shooters were in abundance. Timber had been felled to impede move-ment. The infantry had to advance without artillery to shell wooded areas. It was the next morning before the guns and caissons could find their way through the swamps. On the other hand, the Federal troops had been in the area for several weeks and their engineers had inspected it very carefully. General Porter's forces were well entrenched with his men and artillery well positioned. When the Confederate guns did get through the swamp they proved to be inferior in range and power to Porter's.[30]

When Longstreet's men and D. H. Hill's crossed at the Mechanics-ville Bridge they found A. P. Hill's troops already engaged with the Federals, trying to drive them from behind Beaver Dam Creek. The battle lasted the rest of the day. The Federals did not withdraw until 7 the next morning when they got word of Jackson's approach.[31]

Pender's brigade, with the 22nd Battalion, met rough treatment. The brigade and two of General Roswell S. Ripley's regiments were in on the attack about dark on June 26, at Ellerson's Mill on Beaver Dam Creek. Their movement was across an open field toward an obstructing stream where they were repulsed.[32] John W. Blake was wounded and sent to his home in Ayletts to recover.

Longstreet and A. P. Hill followed the enemy the next day from Mechanicsville to the crest of the hills east of Powhite Creek. There, be-tween New Cold Harbor and Old Cold Harbor, they drew up parallel lines and fought the battle known as Gaines' Mill. D. H. Hill's troops, having been joined by Jackson's, came down from Beaver Dam Creek. Hill took his position on the left and set up his batteries there. A. P. Hill's men, in-cluding those under General Pender and very possibly the 22nd Battalion, took the center and withstood the first severe attack, from 2 to 4 p.m. Jackson, Ewell, and Whiting were also in the center with Longstreet to the right. After darkness fell, the Union forces withdrew. They were ex-hausted, low on ammunition, and had little food.[33]

On June 28, Longstreet and A. P. Hill crossed back to the south side of the Chickahominy at New Bridge. They were to proceed down the Dar-bytown Road to Long Bridge Road and try to intercept what Lee had already correctly surmised would be McClellan's retreat to the James. General Huger and his men moved down the Charles City Road to try to strike the retreat below the familiar White Oak Swamp.[34]

The record of Company D, 53rd Virginia shows that they pursued the enemy down the Charles City Road from the Richmond and York River Railroad on June 29 for six miles. In this skirmish, John B. Fleet was wounded and George W. Brushwood was killed.

Carter's Battery was engaged at Mechanicsville and along the Cold

Harbor Road. On the completion of Grapevine Bridge, they opened up across the Chickahominy. General Rodes said: "Carter's battery had but little to do [on June 27] except receive the fire of the enemy, until late in the afternoon, when for a short time, under my orders, with two of his pieces, and later with his whole battery, under the orders of Major-General Jackson, it engaged the enemy's battery to the left of the Cold Harbor field and silenced it. Fortunately the battery suffered but little loss. Captain [Tom] Carter and his men on this occasion, as on a former one, behaved with distinguished gallantry."[35]

D. H. Hill led Jackson's men in crossing the Chickahominy River. These men arrived at Savage Station just a few hours after General Lafayette McLaws had had a severe fight there. There they found the Union wounded from the battle at Gaines' Mill. At White Oak Swamp, another 500 sick were found. D. H. Hill wrote, "Truly, the Chickahominy swamps were fatal to the Federal forces."[36] Nor were the swamps kind to the Confederates. James Tuck of Carter's Battery sustained wounds at White Oak Swamp on July 1 and by August 1 he was dead from a fever.

June 30 found Longstreet and A. P. Hill (including the 22nd Battalion) engaging the enemy at Frayser's farm (or Glendale) at 3 p.m. The Confederates failed to check the enemy retreat along the Old Quaker Road toward Malvern Hill and the James River. Jackson's troops did not assist them, though Jackson could hear the firing. Huger's division, including the 53rd Regiment, was also nearby on the Charles City Road.[37] On that day Robert H. James of the 22nd Battalion was wounded and sent home to King William to recover. His wounds being more severe, Andrew B. Walker was sent to St. Charles Hospital in Richmond, where he died two weeks later.

On the last day of those seven days, the Federals fought back at Malvern Hill, a few miles farther to the south. D. H. Hill went into battle with 6,500 men and lost 2,000. He had initially crossed the Chickahominy with 10,000 men. General Armistead and the 53rd fought on his right. Below them, on the James, troops under General Theophilius H. Holmes, including Wise's command, were fired at by gunboats on the river.[38] D. H. Hill reported that Armistead was assigned to give the advance signal and a portion of Huger's division drew fire. The enemy retreated during the night. When morning light broke across the trampled wheat fields of "Shirley" plantation they were empty of Union troops.[39] In the fighting the previous day, W. T. Johnson of Company D, 53rd Virginia had been killed and Henry Pollard, also Company D, had been wounded. Pollard, 5'8" in height with a florid complexion, grey eyes and light hair, was over age 35. When reenlistment time came around in August, he chose not to remain in service.

Company D of the 53rd was able to cross a James River bridge on

July 4 Into Chesterfield County. A week later, Company H crossed on pontoons stretched above Drewry's Bluff. They rested on the Richmond-Petersburg Turnpike before moving on to camp with Company D on Falling Creek, near Petersburg.

In May the 26th Infantry had not gone to the Valley, but turned toward Old Church and then headed to the James River to help In the defense of Richmond. They were assigned to General Wise and given picket duty and the job of watching for gunboats on the James River. During this time Fred Fleet was elected 3rd lieutenant. He was able to get letters home to his family and they to him by way of Milford In Caroline County. He wrote, "Dr. Carter's artillery distinguished itself [Seven Pines] & drew a very high compliment from Gen. Hill." He also wrote, "Heard today that poor [Captain] William Latane had been killed, hoped it was a mistake, but borrowed a horse and rode down to see John [Latane]. One look at his face confirmed my worst fears."[40]

56

CHAPTER 5

Across the Potomac — 1862

The same men who faced McClellan at Sharpsburg in September 1862 had fought him from Richmond to the James in May and June and since then had fought General Pope, who was reinforced by some of McClellan's men, from the Rapidan to the Potomac.[1] Both armies must have been battle worn and travel weary.

After the Seven Days' fighting, McClellan was in a strong position at Harrison's Landing, on the James River. D. H. Hill (Carter's Battery's general), R. H. Anderson (with the 53rd), Lafayette McLaws, and J. G. Walker (the 30th Virginia's brigade commander) had their men watching McClellan on the James. They attempted to cut his communications and rested under orders to follow should his main body withdraw.[2]

The 9th Cavalry was at Malvern Hill for a couple of weeks while alternating with other cavalrymen in camp of instruction at Hanover Court House. Their assignment was to picket along the James and support the artillery. While there Company H rejoined them.[3] On July 16, part of Wickham's Cavalry (the 4th Virginia) went with the 9th Virginia into Gloucester to round up deserters. They travelled through King William and King and Queen counties to Gloucester Point where, on July 22, they razed the pier facilities. They had hoped to burn the wharf there; but, having been prevented by Federal gunboats, they returned to Gloucester Court House.[4]

Thomas Blumer wrote that when McClellan's forces moved from the "White House" they again burned the railroad bridge so the Confederates could not make use of it. The blacks who had followed the army to its New Kent base were transported on barges down to Fort Monroe. On July 24 a Confederate marshal conducted an early morning raid on the Indian reservation, charged the men with aiding the enemy, and led seven away in chains. The tribal members recall how Terrell Bradby managed to slip off one of his leather boots and by diverting the guard's attention to the lost boot made his getaway into the bushes. The Indian swam the river to Chamberlayne's Island (New Kent County), then swam back to the reservation and hid in the railway culvert at William's Creek until several weeks later when the Indians were pardoned by the governor of Virginia. Bradby's refuge is still called "Terrell's Culvert" or "Terrell's Hiding Place." Today it stands half submerged in swamp water and on the river bank the charred remains of the old railroad bridge can be seen at low tide.[5]

With McClellan safely at Harrison's Landing, far enough from Richmond so that he could no longer see the church spires, and held down by heavy guns, some using 15-inch shells, there was no longer need for the Confederate armies to stay close by. They withdrew to or near their old positions. A. P. Hill's "Light Division" (including the 22nd Battalion) lay near Longstreet's divisions.[6] The 53rd Regiment camped at Falling Creek.

During July and early August 1862, the troops were kept busy "in front of Richmond" with drill exercises and the training of new men. Food was plentiful and good, with "no variety, but fresh beef or bacon, flour, coffee and sugar were issued in full rations. There was an abundance of whiskey, but comparatively little drunkenness." There were a few books to be passed around. Those volumes sent from home, for instance Victor Hugo's *Les Miserables,* though with rough pages blurred with dirty type and florid designs, were readily "devoured." Gambling flourished and the "greasiest packs of cards were their stand-by." The favorite card game was "Chuck-a-luck." At the same time, one staff officer wrote: "We were rather a devout army. The men came from their homes deeply tinged with religion. Methodists were in large numbers and next to them Baptists and Presbyterians. There were many meetings and addresses conducted by worthy chaplains."[7]

While the companies of the 53rd Regiment rested in camp, a number of the King William men were removed from the rolls. Some had died in Richmond hospitals, including Lieutenant John Newton Brown, Benjamin Butler, and John F. Tuck. Others were declared victims of chronic diseases, such as ulcers of the legs, and phlebitis, and given medical discharges. Some, apparently weakened and demoralized by persistent disease, did not wait for an official release. After being listed as sick in camp, at home or in the hospital, their final record lists desertion. Some men whose enlistment had expired reenlisted and are shown as entitled to the extra payment of $50, certainly a welcome addition to the $11 monthly pay of infantry privates.

Robert and Andrew Leftwich and others of the 22nd Battalion reenlisted and were entitled to bounty. Robert was on sick furlough in King William during July and August 1862. At that time Andrew was also in the county, detailed to enroll conscripts. He is shown as the enrolling officer through November of that year. The location of Company G's camp was not given. Perhaps, during early July, it was still at Farrar's Farm, near Richmond. Lieutenant Colonel J. C. Johnson is listed as the mustering officer.

From Malvern Hill on July 24, 1862, Tom Carter had the painful task of writing to his aunt, Mary Anna Randolph Custis Lee, that Julian (apparently her son), had been killed in a cavalry charge that morning. He told her that her dear one's remains would be taken to "Pampatike" on the morrow.[8]

Carter's Battery was refitting for future action. The captain asked for eleven horses to replace those killed or wounded in recent engagements. The order emphasized that six horses were needed for every piece or caisson. During these summer months Juan Stanley Neale was discharged for being under age 18 and R. H. Lipscomb for being overage. Both men had been wounded at Seven Pines. Patrick Henry Fontaine decided to return to the ministry. His brother, Philip Aylett Fontaine, died with a fever while at home.

President Lincoln called General John Pope from the Western theater to take over the forces of Irvin McDowell, Nathaniel P. Banks, and John C. Fremont as they lay, 50,000 strong, east of the Blue Ridge and between the branches of the Rappahannock. In order to stop the advance of Pope south of the Rapidan, some of Jackson's divisions marched from Mechanicsville in July.[9]

Jackson's "Foot Cavalry," as his men were called, moved under the simple orders: "March to a cross-road; a staff-officer there will inform you which fork to take; and so on to the next fork, where you will find a courier with a sealed direction pointing out the road." They travelled light with three days' cooked rations, tin cans and an occasional frying pan. As July stretched into August, the days were boiling hot. The men marched more than twenty-six miles on some days, twenty on others, and would enjoy a refreshing dip as they forded the rivers and mountain streams.[10]

The 22nd Battalion, along with the 55th Regiment, was now in General Charles W. Field's brigade, under A. P. Hill. According to Allen C. Redwood of the 55th, the brigade was a fairly new one, having first "smelt powder" in the Seven Days' fighting around Richmond. His sketches show: "A Confederate of 1862," bearing a musket with a bayonet; "Our March Against Pope;" "A Straggler on the Line of March;" "Supper after a Hard March," cooking meat on a bayonet held over a log fire; and "Route Step."[11]

On August 9 Jackson challenged Pope's men south of Culpeper, between the Rapidan and the upper Rappahannock, at Cedar Mountain. Field's brigade did not arrive on the field of battle until, according to Redwood, "too late to be more than slightly engaged." Soon thereafter they followed the retreat of the enemy through Brandy Station (Orange and Alexandria Railroad) to the Rappahannock. The illustrator wrote, "While our artillery was dueling with him [Pope] across the stream, I passed the time with my head in the scant shade of a sassafras bush by the roadside, with a chill and fever brought from the Chickahominy lowgrounds."[12]

On July 25, 1862, "Jeb" Stuart had been made major-general, commanding two cavalry brigades. The first brigade was under Wade Hampton and the second brigade, including the 1st, 3rd, 4th, 5th, and 9th Cavalry, under Fitz Lee. At this time Rooney Lee was colonel of the 9th Cavalry. Fitz Lee started from Hanover Court House with his brigade on August 4, 1862.[13]

General McClellan carried out his evacuation plan of Harrison's Landing August 11 to 16 and transported his troops and equipment by way of Norfolk to Aquia Creek, just above Fredericksburg, to be of assistance to Pope. On August 17, Lee sent Stuart word that he wished to confer with him at Orange Court House. There he instructed him to have Fitz Lee move toward the Rapidan to the vicinity of Raccoon Ford. Fitz Lee misunderstood Stuart's instruction that he would meet him at the ford. His men were low on rations so he marched them by the supply depot at Louisa Court House before going on to the ford. When Stuart did not find Fitz Lee at Raccoon Ford, he sent out one of his staff, Major Norman R. Fitzhugh, to look for him, only to have the adjutant captured and General Lee's plan for turning Pope's left flank discovered on him. Stuart's junction with Fitz Lee took place two days later thus giving Pope extra time to move his forces across to the northeast bank of the Rappahannock.[14]

Colonel Beale said that it was near August 15 when the 9th Cavalry left Hanover Court House to march through Caroline to Louisa Court House. There they left the sick, the dismounted, and most of their baggage. Moving rapidly they passed through Louisa and Orange to cross the Rapidan into Culpeper at Somerville Ford, where they left their cooking utensils. Henceforth they would live off of what they could forage for themselves and their horses along the way.[15]

On August 22, Stuart took all of his command except the 7th and 3rd Regiments across the Rapahannock River at Waterloo Bridge, just west of Warrenton. They marched by way of Warrenton to the vicintiy of Catlett's Station on the Orange and Alexandria Railroad. The regiments arrived after dark and in a torrential rain. A captured negro, who had known Stuart in prewar days in Berkeley County, offered to lead him to the wagons belonging to General Pope's headquarters. There the 9th Cavalry captured a large sum of money, some of Pope's staff officers, his dispatch book, and his personal papers, baggage, and other personal belongings.[16]

The weather had grown hot and sulty. The Confederate rations of "unsalted beef, eked out with green corn and unripe apples" were beginning to prove unsuited to men on the march. On August 27 Field's brigade participated along with Fitz Lee's men in the raid that cut Pope's line of communication and captured his supply base. With this coup, food was in abundance and clothing and supplies limited only by what a man could carry, barter, or trade.[17]

The 53rd Regiment, under General Longstreet and R. H. Anderson, remained at Falling Creek until August 16, at which time the regiment moved into Richmond and was transported on the Virginia Central Railroad to Louisa, from whence they proceeded to march to Orange Court House. George S. Bernard of the 12th Virginia Regiment, which was also under Anderson, described the movement from Richmond. He said that his regiment was stationed in Chesterfield County near Drewry's Bluff (in the area of Falling Creek). They marched along the Richmond-Petersburg Turnpike, crossed the James River at Manchester with colors flying and bands playing, and then made their way through the streets of Richmond to the depot of the Central Railroad. There they boarded a freight train for Louisa Court House.[18] This was on a Sunday and the same day the 53rd Regiment boarded the train.

The 12th Virginia arrived at Louisa Court House between dark and midnight. They stacked their arms along the road by the depot and were soon asleep on the ground. On Tuesday, August 19 (like the 53rd), they marched 20 miles to a position just below Orange Court House. When they stopped to rest, they constructed rain shelters of rushes and oil cloths and sat around blazing fires until the "long roll" sounded again.[19]

Just before passing through the Bull Run Mountains, Bernard noted: "The country through which our line of march lay was beautiful, the many hills over which we passed furnishing the most magnificent views of the mountainous country which surrounded us. At dark we were passing through Thoroughfare Gap."[20] G. Moxley Sorrel of Longstreet's staff reported that the mountainous gorge was long but narrow and precipitous. "Its echoes were wonderful — a gun fired in its depths gave forth roars fit to bring down the skies. ...Pushing through we saw the dust of Jackson's masses miles away and heard his guns. Forward we pressed almost at a run, and in time. The attack on Stonewall ceased as soon as Longstreet came on the scene."[21]

Bernard wrote that Anderson's division by 8 or 9 a.m. on August 30 was in line of battle on a commanding hill, with their forces stretching perpendicular across a turnpike. Their artillery was 400 yards to their left and their skirmishers were one half mile in their front. General Lee's headquarters was in the woods 500 yards in their rear. The men, tired and hungry after their marching, were soon removed to the rear for their rations, but before they could be fed they were moved back into the field of wheat stubble and briers, where shells continued to pass over their heads.[22]

Company H, 53rd Virginia, marched night and day with hardly time to rest. They came within sight of the enemy at Fauquier Mountain Springs on the Rappahannock (near Warrenton). There was an unexpected picket fight on August 26 in which Robert G. Taylor was killed, Absalom A. Atkins was mortally wounded, and John Hill was wounded slightly in the hand. Then the unit pushed on through the counties of Rappahannock, Fauquier, and Prince William to arrive on the field of battle at Manassas after the fighting had begun.

All day on August 30, the 53rd was exposed to the shells of the enemy and part of the time to sharpshooters. Company H reported having no casualties, "Thanks to Almighty God." The 22nd Battalion was not as fortunate. Their brigadier general, Charles W. Field, was severely wounded and during subsequent days Colonel J. M. Brockenbrough commanded the brigade.[23] On August 28, Robert H. Prince was killed in action and George W. Gravatt mortally wounded. The next day Lieutenant James E. Johnson was wounded.

The fighting continued on August 30 until 10 p.m. when Pope managed to move away under cover of darkness. It rained during the night, giving him reprieve from pursuit. Jackson challenged him at Ox Hill on September 1. On the following day, Fitz Lee's brigade occupied Fairfax Court House.[24]

For two days, from Waterloo Bridge to Centreville (north of Manassas and just west of Fairfax Court House), the 9th Cavalry operated "over fences, across ravines, and through swamps," with little or no food for themselves or their horses. The men received a few crackers while they sat astride their horses at Manassas. At Centreville they found the advance guard of Pope's army. Led by Rooney Lee, they charged into the village and pushed the guard back onto the infantry. Captain Haynes and several privates chased the fleeing horsemen through the woods. By this time, according to Colonel Beale, the regiment's horses were nearly exhausted. Late at night they found hay for their mounts. The next day they remained in camp northeast of Manassas Junction, received their rations, and watched the fighting going on during the Battle of Second Manassas. For the next couple of days the 9th Cavalry was assigned picket duty in the area. They observed as an ambulance bearing the body of slain U.S. General Philip Kearny moved back into Federal lines.[25]

Lee's Rangers marched to Fairfax Court House and took the road (past the present Dulles Airport) to Dranesville, where they met their baggage train and had a day's rest. The colonel wrote that they knew that the next day they would be crossing into Maryland. "These facts brought paper, pens, and pencils into demand, and many letters were prepared for loved ones at home." The cavalry forded the Potomac at Edward's Ferry, just east of Leesburg. Major Douglas, in the lead with the 5th Cavalry, led a charge into Poolesville. The 9th Cavalry was in the rear. By the time they arrived the village was quiet and Confederate Treasury notes were accepted for shoes.[26]

A detachment of men remained at Barnesville while others of the 9th Virginia Cavalry went farther north toward New Market, Maryland. Upon their return they found that McClellan had instructed General Pleasonton and the 6th U.S. Cavalry to take Sugar Loaf Mountain, where General Lee had a signal station which overlooked much of the surrounding countryside. The attacking Federals outnumbered the Confederates three to one. Colonel Beale had only one squadron armed with carbines, and those were of "inferior quality." Under Colonel Rooney Lee the regiment helped hold the base of the mountain until darkness fell. During the night they withdrew through New Market and crossed the mountain near Frederick to receive and cook rations, the first received in two days.[27] Among the few Confederate casualties at Sugar Loaf Mountain was John B. Lacy, of King William and Company H, who was mortally wounded. He died on September 19.

The 30th Virginia coming with General Walker from the defense of Richmond arrived on the Manassas Battlefield only to find the fighting over but the dead still on the field. With the withdrawal of McClellan, Walker left one brigade behind and marched northward with the other two hoping to assist in the fight against Pope. He found that Lee's men were marching toward the upper fords of the Potomac River. On September 7, Walker crossed his men by Creek's Ford, at the mouth of the Monocacy where Jackson had crossed earlier. He conferred with Lee at Frederick and was instructed to return to their crossing and destroy the aqueduct of the Chesapeake and Ohio Canal. Lee spoke of his plan to rest his men for a few days at Hagerstown; to get shoes for the barefooted and clothing for the most needy; to destroy the Baltimore and Ohio road; and then to march on to Harrisburg and the railroad bridge over the Susquehanna River before turning his attention to Philadelphia, Baltimore, or Washington.[28]

The day after the battle at Manassas, George Bernard had expected he would be able to provide himself with shoes from a slain Federal soldier only to find that all shoes had been removed from the Federal dead during the night and early morning hours. A friend was able to furnish him with a pair of boots that were so hard that on the march to Maryland he wore them dangling around his neck except when fording a rocky stream. Upon their arrival at Frederick, Bernard was given the last pair of shoes purchased by their quartermaster that day in the city.[29]

Allen Redwood sketched Jackson's men as they removed their shoes and trousers and waded across the Potomac at White's Ford. Some were already barefooted. Another of the 55th Regiment wrote that as they passed through Leesburg "an old lady with upraised hands, and with tears in her eyes exclaimed: 'The Lord bless your dirty ragged souls!' " He added, "Don't think we were any dirtier than the rest, but it was our luck to get the blessing."[30]

The canal aqueduct proved to be too sturdy to be blown up. On September 10, General Walker received his copy of the now famous "Special Orders no. 191" telling him to join Jackson and McLaws in the capture of Harper's Ferry and detailing the Confederate position over the next five or six days. D. H. Hill's copy, which he claims he never saw, was found by one of McClellan's men as they passed through Frederick. Walker found that the Federals were already at Creek's Ford so he crossed his men at Point of Rocks and had them on the Virginia side by daylight of September 11. On September 13, the 30th Virginia was stationed on Loudoun Heights overlooking Harper's Ferry. They were positioned with five long-range Parrot guns and some men from the signal corps to communicate their readiness to Jackson. McLaws with his infantry artillery was on the Maryland Heights. A. P. Hill with his "Light Division", of which the 22nd Battalion was a part, was on the lower slopes of Loudoun Heights.[31]

On September 14 they could hear the sound of artillery in the direction of South Mountain, a few miles away in Maryland. Later they learned that McClellan was confronting D. H. Hill at Turner's Gap. The Confederates fired down upon Harper's Ferry that afternoon and resumed again the next morning although a dense fog clung to the side of the mountain. Firing from the Federals ceased at 8 a.m. and the garrison surrendered unconditionally. In the early morning hours of September 16, Walker's men joined with Jackson's, crossed back over the Potomac just below Shepherdstown, and headed toward Antietam Creek and Sharpsburg.[32]

William Aylett had gotten home on furlough in the late summer of 1862. A letter from Gordonsville, written on September 11, shows that he reached there the morning before and would go on the next morning to Rapidan Station and from thence to join his regiment in Maryland. He advised Alice not to sell the old carriage. Although she could get $400 for it, a replacement with any kind of vehicle would not be found at any price.[33]

Company D of the 53rd Virginia marched from Manassas to Frederick, Maryland, arrived there on September 6, and remained until September 8, when they were ordered to Harper's Ferry. Company H was mustered for pay on the Manassas Battlefield, then marched to Fairfax Court House and crossed the Potomac at Leesburg. Upon arrival at

Frederick, they too were sent to Harper's Ferry, where they "played a small part in the capture." Afterward they again crossed the Potomac, this time on pontoon bridges, and moved toward Shepherdstown, where they recrossed to Sharpsburg.

———

D. H. Hill had been assigned the rear-guard action as Lee and Longstreet moved from Frederick toward Hagerstown by way of Boonsboro. He was to protect Lee's wagons and artillery and to watch all roads from the east until Jackson finished at Harper's Ferry. To the south of Boonsboro stretched South Mountain of the Blue Ridge chain. To the southeast and across a narrow valley lay the Catoctin Mountains, where Stuart was to watch any approach from Washington through the mountain passes. On September 13, Stuart sent Hill word of the advance of two brigades of Federal infantry and asked for a brigade to check them at South Mountain.[34]

The road from Frederick to Boonsboro crossed South Mountain at Turner's Gap. There D. H. Hill held on September 14 until 4 p.m., when Longstreet came to his assistance. Darkness put an end to the conflict. During the night Longstreet and Hill withdrew toward Sharpsburg.[35] Colonel Carter wrote after the war that his artillery was not engaged at South Mountain. They had taken the road to the left but had been ordered back to prevent their being cut off.[36]

The movement to Sharpsburg was covered by Fitz Lee, who took position east of Boonsboro where the road descended from South Mountain. Then as the Confederate forces moved westward, he called upon the 9th Virginia Cavalry under Colonel Rooney Lee to make a continued stand at his rear as troops passed through the town of Boonsboro. The streets were so narrow that this could be done only in squadrons of fours. Henry McClellan, Stuart's adjutant general, recounted, "As one squadron retired from the charge, to form again in rear of the regiment, the one next in front took up the battle. By a rapid series of well executed attacks, the 9th regiment thus covered the retreat of the remainder of the brigade and gave it time to take position west of Boonsboro."[37]

They were not just facing the enemy in the streets but were subjected to shots from the windows of houses, and were pushed steadily through the town. At a bridge Colonel Lee fell from his horse. Captain Haynes of Company H reclaimed the bridge and raised the fallen horse, but Rooney Lee was too sore and bruised to remount before Haynes was forced back across the bridge. Dazed and unnoticed by the enemy, Colonel Lee managed to crawl to a body of woods. There he was met by two Confederates who helped him to a farmhouse and secured a horse for him. When Fitz Lee was no longer pursued by the enemy, he moved his command to Sharpsburg and positioned it to the left of the Confederate line in order to guard the upper fords of Antietam Creek.[38]

Robert Krick calls September 15 one of the hardest days of the war for the 9th Virginia Cavalry. Eighteen of the regiment's men were killed or mortally wounded, ten captured, and Lieutenant Colonel R. L. T. Beale had his horse killed.[39] Yet injury sustained by King William's men was negligible: Richard Gwathmey had his horse killed.

A member of the 9th New York Volunteers wrote of meeting the Confederates in the cornfields along the slopes of the mountains. As they emerged from the woods, he heard for the first time the "rebel yell." He described it as "a high shrill yelp, uttered without concert, and kept up continually when the fighting was approaching a climax." In his memory of one of these battles, there lingered long afterward the smell of "pennyroyal, bruised by the tramping of a hundred feet."[40]

When Jackson joined Lee on September 16 at Sharpsburg, a few miles from Shepherdstown, McClellan's army had already reached the east bank of Antietam, just a few miles away. Lee positioned his forces on the "irregular range of high ground" west of the creek.[41] During twelve fateful hours on September 17, all the organized infantry of Lee's army was put into action.[42] D. H. Hill assigned Captain Tom Carter and the King William Artillery to a ridge ¾ of a mile northwest of Sharpsburg and they were brought closer into action when needed.[43]

The activities of Carter's Battery are described in a letter which Tom Carter wrote on March 17, 1864, to further promote his recommendation for a commission for Sergeant Festus King. More than a year before, General W. N. Pendleton, Lee's chief of artillery, had authorized Sergeant King to act as junior first lieutenant subject to the action of President Davis. Carter's letter, filed with the service records, states:

At the Battle of Sharpsburg in the afternoon when Burnside's forces crossed the Antietam Creek & attacked our right, S. D. Lee, then Colonel of Artillery, requested me to take position with my battery a short distance in front of the town & on the right of the turnpike to aid in repelling the attack made by this force.

As the battery was unlimbered to engage the guns on its front, a heavy & enfilading fire of Artillery was opened from our left which swept through the battery from left to right and Colonel Lee who accompanied me at once remarked that the position was untenable.

Several of the guns were drawn off, but the fire becoming more accurible & more concentrated & the cannoneers being fatigued and reduced in numbers by the heavy engagement earlier in the day it was impossible to get them to the last gun.

66

On this occasion Sergeant King remained by his gun alone & with the assistance of Lieutenant [Wm. P.] Carter limbered it up & brought it off. Earlier in the day the accuracy of the fire from his gun was such as to cause Lieut. Carter repeatedly to call my attention to it during the engagement.[44]

Lieutenant Alexander T. Dabney was mortally wounded during the action.

The 53rd Regiment, serving under General "Dick" Anderson, arrived to support D. H. Hill around the Piper house, just north of town and in the midst of the heaviest fighting. They initially sustained heavy casualties but after their general was wounded and, as the afternoon progressed, they could give only occasional fire.[45] Company H of the 53rd arrived on the field at 2 p.m. While Company D was moving to take a position on the left, a shell exploded in their midst, mortally wounding their captain, Dr. William G. Pollard. Family tradition states that Pollard, with a furlough in his pocket, had remained to command both Companies D and H because his friend, William Aylett, was sick.[46]

On September 5, Doctor Pollard had resigned his commission in order to return to medical practice in King William. His request, signed by Generals Armistead, R. H. Anderson, and R. E. Lee, had been sent on to the Secretary of War on September 12 for approval. Pollard died at a hospital on David Smith's farm. He was almost 45 years old. James T. Neale was also shown on the company roll as wounded on September 17. There is no further record on him.

General J. G. Walker commanded in the center of the line in the fierce fight around Dunker Church, north of Sharpsburg. His men helped Jackson and Hood in clearing the woods.[47] Captain Robert O. Peatross's company of the 30th Virginia suffered seventeen killed or wounded, including his brother Walter who was wounded and Edwin Jackson who was killed. Lewis Tunstall (who gave his address as Mangohick, but who probably lived in Caroline County) was taken prisoner.[48]

A. P. Hill and his men had been left behind at Harper's Ferry to deal with the prisoners and captured supplies. When they did arrive at Sharpsburg on September 17, they moved onto the field swiftly and drove the enemy off, thereby saving the day for the Confederates although there had been tremendous lost. The men of the 22nd Battalion were under fire,[49] but apparently did not take a large part in the action.

The 9th Cavalry bivouacked the night of September 17 on the Sharpsburg turnpike. The next morning they had the task of rounding up Confederate stragglers in the cornfields. They found them out of ammunition and exhausted from fighting and hunger. As night fell the cavalrymen replaced the infantry outposts on the left. In the fields the "dead in many places covered the ground," and nearby Federal surgeons worked over the wounded who had been laid on straw. During the night Lee's Rangers could hear bugle calls and movement of wagons, but the enemy did not attack. At sunrise on the 19th a signal gun was fired and they slipped quietly across the Potomac at Shepherdstown, leaving as Colonel Beale observed, many Confederate wounded "to the care of the foe, and many of our dead lay on the field unknelled."[50]

The 9th Cavalry camped along Opequon Creek between Martinsburg and Harper's Ferry. There was nothing but green food from the cornfields for the horses. R. L. T. Beale said that the animals soon became sick and a more remote camp had to be established to treat them. Pickets were maintained along the Potomac. Fitz Lee was absent and Colonel Rooney Lee, although temporarily disabled by a kick from a horse, was in charge of the brigade. On October 18 young Lee was elevated to the command of a third cavalry brigade made up of the 5th, 9th, 10th, and 15th Virginia Cavalry Regiments and the 2nd North Carolina. R. L. T. Beale became colonel of the 9th Regiment.[51]

Pleasonton's Union cavalrymen crossed the Potomac at dawn one morning and encountered some of the 9th Cavalry on picket duty. As Pleasonton moved toward Martinsburg, Stuart strove to entrap him between that town and Shepherdstown. The 9th Cavalry reached Shepherdstown after dark, just as the Union cavalry crossed back across the Potomac.[52]

Lee's Rangers broke camp on October 28 to march by Berryville and bivouac near the Shenandoah River. Many of their horses were suffering from a foot disease. They moved eastward through the Blue Ridge at Snickersville to make camp on the road to Bloomsfield. Captain Haynes remained with Companies G and H on picket duty near Bloomsfield (northeast of Upperville) while the regiment operated in the area from Mountsville to Aldie (at the Bull Run Mountains).[53] Harmon H. Littlepage was taken prisoner at Bloomsfield on November 9.

During the latter part of October McClellan moved both infantry and cavalry southward. Stuart was assigned the task of operating between the Union forces and Lee's men in the Valley and along the Blue Ridge. Major Beverley Douglas and the 5th Cavalry patrolled along the Manassas Gap Railroad while the 3rd and 9th Cavalry kept Ashby's Gap open for Jackson and Longstreet to pass to the east. D. H. Hill took his men back through Ashby's Gap and then through the Valley to Front Royal.[54]

Companies D and H of the 53rd Regiment had remained on the field at Sharpsburg until September 18, when they were ordered back to Martinsburg. In the early morning hours of September 19 they crossed the Potomac back into Virginia. The regiment remained in the vicinity of Martinsburg a few days and then encamped six miles north of Winchester.

William Aylett wrote Alice from a camp near Winchester on October 20 that Colonel Tomlin's furlough had been extended because of illness. John Grammer, the lieutenant colonel, continued absent, so Aylett was still in charge of the regiment. He said that the enemy had seen a fire from a burning house and, thinking that they were retreating, had advanced almost to Charlestown. In her response, Alice expressed the hope that his regiment would winter again in North Carolina. Her sister Etta had offered to keep the girls so she could be with him.[55]

Along the Shenandoah River on October 31 the companies of the 53rd Regiment were mustered for pay by Major Aylett. The record of Company H shows that they left Winchester on November 1. After four days of hard marching (68 miles, but without incident) they arrived at Culpeper Court House.

Aylett's next letter, written on November 15, was from near Culpeper Court House. It gave a foretaste of the winter to come. Already there had been two snows. During the second one the regiment was out on picket duty, but he had a "fine quilt in a low place where the enemy couldn't see it & slept comfortably all night." She must send him some new flannel drawers for those he had came only to his knees. He reminded her to pay the taxes and to buy some salt.[56]

CHAPTER 6

Fords of the Rappahannock — 1862-63

By foot, by horseback, by rail, and on caissons, men from King William, both black and white, were on the move to entrench, supply, and support Lee's Army of Northern Virginia.

Andrew Leftwich was home on furlough at Thanksgiving and rejoined the 22nd Battalion in Staunton after travelling by "the cars" and the stage. No sooner did he join them than they set out to march the 180 miles back to their camp in Caroline County, near Guinea Station. Although they were often travelling without food, his dominate recollection would be of the beauty of the Blue Ridge and their "sport" in catching rabbits and squirrels. He showed concern in his letter written home that the Yankees might be in King William by Christmas.[1]

The battalion's lieutenant colonel, J. C. Johnson, had received his medical discharge on November 5 and had been replaced by Lieutenant Colonel Edward P. Tayloe, a native of King George County and a graduate of Virginia Military Institute. Serving in A. P. Hill's "Light Division," their brigade continued to be commanded by Colonel John M. Brockenbrough.[2]

President Lincoln removed General McClellan from the command of the Army of the Potomac early in November 1862, and put General Ambrose E. Burnside in his place. The Federal army, with its three grand divisions under generals Edwin V. Sumner, William B. Franklin, and Joseph Hooker lay around Warrenton. Across the Rappahannock from them stretched Lee's army from his and Longstreet's headquarters at Culpeper to across the Blue Ridge and into the Valley to Jackson's headquarters at Winchester.[3] Rooney Lee's brigade was assigned to guard along the lower Rappahannock while Fitz Lee's and Hampton's brigades watched along the river higher upstream.[4]

According to Jed Hotchkiss, Jackson's cartographer, they were in the Valley to protect "that great Confederate granary, and as a menace to McClellan's right." Jackson was busy breaking up the Baltimore and Ohio Railroad and "keeping the Federal authorities uneasy about his whereabouts," for he posed a threat to the Federal capital. Longstreet was sixty miles from Jackson and faced McClellan across the Rappahannock. Ambrose Burnside, the new Federal commander, planned to execute an "on to Richmond" move by way of Fredericksburg.[5]

Lee summoned both Longstreet and Jackson to Fredericksburg. The latter took the westerly route — by the Valley to New Market and across Massanutten Mountain and then the Blue Ridge at Fisher's Gap (probably the scenic route which Leftwich wrote about). Jackson took two days to reach Orange Court House by way of Madison Court House. He arrived in the vicinity of Fredericksburg by the beginning of December and went into camp above Guinea Station.[6]

Captain Thomas H. Carter and his artillerymen were still under D. H. Hill and Jackson. The records for Carter's Battery do not show their location in the fall of 1862 until November and December, when they were near Milford. Armistead's brigade and the 53rd Regiment had been placed under George Pickett in Longstreet's corps. The records for Companies D and H of the 53rd Regiment show that from November 21 to 23 they marched the sixty miles to Fredericksburg.[7]

Moxley Sorrel of Longstreet's staff described the plight of Longstreet's men as they made their way to Fredericksburg. It was bad weather, he said, and the roads were almost bottomless. Longstreet advised them to rake "the coals and ashes from your cooking fires and sleep on the ground; it will be dry and warm." As many of the men were barefoot, he also advised them, "Take the rawhides of the beef cattle, killed for food; cut roughly for a moccasin-like covering for the feet, and there are you are with something to walk in." But this did not prove practicable. The make-shift shoes had no outer soles for stiffening "and in the mud and icy slush of the Virginia roads the moist, fresh skins slipped about as if on ice." The wearers, after many falls, kicked off the useless "shoes" and either marched barefooted or with their feet wrapped in rags and straw. Sorrel stated that Richmond did its best to supply shoes even to purchasing some from England. He tried a pair of those and they fell apart after the first day's wearing.[8]

General Longstreet knew that by November 18 or 19 that General Edwin V. Sumner was moving toward Fredericksburg. A few days later Sumner's provost-marshal crossed the Rappahannock under a flag of truce with a letter to the Mayor and Common Council of Fredericksburg stating that the town would be shelled in 16 hours because it was providing provisions and transportation facilities for a rebelling army. This threw the townspeople into a panic. Some were able to board a train while others, the sick and infirm men, women, and children, fled their homes to "seek shelter in the wood and brave the icy November nights." Longstreet arrived on the heights overlooking the town. When he sent word to the Federals that he would not be using it as his military base, shelling was postponed until mid-December.[9]

Winter arrived early in Virginia that year. It was extremely cold as they stood watch over Fredericksburg. William Aylett felt that they were in a strong defensive position. Should the enemy consider crossing, Jackson,

A. P. Hill, and D. H. Hill were there to discourage them. On December 7 it was snowing and William's hand stiffened as he sat writing by an outside fire. He urged his wife not to let Mr. Pitts (the overseer) neglect getting in the ice.[10]

At Fredericksburg the river was winding, wide, and difficult to cross. Major Wesley Brainerd, of the 15th New York Engineers, and Major Ira Spaulding, of the 50th New York, reported that on November 27 they had in place on the Rappahannock two full trains of material for two 420-foot-long pontoon bridges capable of spanning the river. However, these were not utilized until December 11 and 12, when General Sumner's men crossed at Fredericksburg and General William Franklin's men crossed farther downstream.[11]

There was still a light snow on the ground when they crossed the river. A dense fog enveloped the area on the morning of December 13 until the sun broke through and a light breeze wafted the fog away. Lee's men could be seen dominating the heights overlooking the flats along the Rappahannock. His forces stretched from northwest of Fredericksburg and across from Falmouth, through Marye's Hill and Telegraph Hill (Lee's and Longstreet's headquarters) to the lower elevation above Hamilton's Crossing, where Jackson had his men. Pickett was with Longstreet on Telegraph Hill and would be called on to assist on Marye's Hill and along the Sunken Road. The 53rd Regiment was placed near the center of the line. Brockenbrough's men, including the 22nd Battalion, stood in Jackson's second line of defense. D. H. Hill, with Carter's Battery, was near the crossing. Stuart's stance was at the end of the line, near Massaponax Creek and three miles below Fredericksburg. The usually disheveled Jackson appeared in a new uniform said to have been supplied him by Stuart.[12]

Dr. D. S. Freeman has credited Tom Carter with always being alert and diligent. On the mid-winter afternoon of December 13, after the repulse of the Federal onslaught, he already had his artillery where it was needed. Also, when calls were made for volunteers to "dash out of the woods and open up on the weary Federals" in preparation for the infantry advance planned by General Jackson, the King William boys offered their services. The advance was to include A. P. Hill's "Light Division" (and the 22nd Battalion), but there was not sufficient daylight left to carry out the plans. No additional attack was made during the next couple of days. On the night of the 15th, during a fierce storm of wind and rain that muffled their movement, Burnside withdrew his men back across the Rappahannock.[13]

The 9th Cavalry had been called from its activities farther down the Rappahannock at Leedstown (King George County). Colonel Beale said that they received orders on December 12 "to march with dispatch to

Fredericksburg," forty miles away. At sunrise on December 13 they were crossing the Massaponax. When the fog lifted they could see enemy guns posted in their front. They retreated back across the run and were fired upon by guns beyond the river at intervals during the day. The cavalrymen could see smoke rising from the firing near Fredericksburg and observe nearer by the fighting between Jackson and the Federals at Hamilton's Crossing. The colonel said of his command, "No damage, save a few slight wounds and the loss of six horses."[14]

As darkness fell there was the smell of "sulphurous smoke and the lurid glare from the explosion of shell" as Confederate artillery fired at the enemy near the river and the Union batteries replied. Beale said that they bivouacked that night on the edge of the woods. The next morning was cold and rainy and rations were scarce. On the 15th they moved to a camp site overlooking Port Royal and served on picket duty up the river to Moss Neck (Caroline County).[15]

Those Union men who recrossed the river under a flag of truce to bury the Federal dead, after a period when the thermometer dropped below freezing, found the earth frozen nearly a foot deep and many of the bodies frozen to the ground.[16]

The men from King William were more fortunate. None were reported killed or seriously wounded. Relief came on December 18 for the weary and weakened Albion Jackson in the form of a substitute, Henry Kelly. Albion returned to the household of his wife, children, younger sister, and parents. During the year his brother, Edwin, had been killed at Sharpsburg and his 14-year-old brother, William, had died of diphtheria. Before the war was over, Albion would die of pneumonia.[17]

Along the Rappahannock, after the fighting was over, the pickets resumed their posts and became "friendly; more given to trading than shooting at each other at less than one hundred yards," although trading was discouraged by the authorities. When a Federal band came down to the river, Confederates called out for some of their songs. The Federals played "Dixie," "My Maryland," and the "Bonnie Blue Flag," and ended with "Home, Sweet Home." Cheers went up from both banks and "many wet eyes could be found among those hardy warriors under the flags."[18]

Captain William J. Turner, Company D, 53rd Regiment, recorded that they left Fredericksburg on December 29 to camp near Guinea. The regiment was in good health and well clothed.

Immediately after Christmas Day, the 9th Virginia Cavalry assisted in what has come to be called the "Dumfries Raid," Stuart's harassment of Federal communications along the Potomac. On the afternoon of December 26, the cavalry command of Hampton, Fitz Lee, and Rooney Lee crossed the Rappahannock at Kelly's Ford and encamped for the night at Morrisville. When morning came they headed toward the Potomac with Rooney Lee's assigned designation being Dumfries. There his men captured the Union pickets and caused their forces to withdraw north of Quantico. That night a squadron of the 9th Virginia was sent back to the Rappahannock with the prisoners and wagons taken by Hampton's men.[19]

Tom Carter's men, under Jackson with General Robert E. Rodes, were near Grace Church in Caroline County. Nearby was A. P. Hill with his "Light Division," Field's Brigade, and the 22nd Battalion.[20]

The Leftwich letters and the letters and records of the 53rd Regiment show that the units had their winter quarters in Caroline County around Guinea Station (where in a few months Jackson would lie dying). Andrew wrote to Sallie on January 2 to tell her about the battle at Fredericksburg and to ask her about the parties she had attended at Christmas. Apparently he received a furlough in January. His January 25 letter from a camp near Fredericksburg told that he had been in command of the company since his return. The "Yankeys," he said, had been badly "whipped" there previously. He had taken a working party out through six to eight inches of mud.[21]

General Burnside had been "whipped" by the elements during January. His attempt at a recrossing of the Rappahannock above Fredericksburg, known as the "Mud March," thoroughly demoralized the Union forces for several months. Lincoln lost confidence in Burnside and replaced him with "Fighting Joe" Hooker.[22]

Major Aylett, of the 53rd Regiment, from his camp near Guinea Station, wrote to his wife on December 30 of his concern at not hearing from her. A month later he became discouraged about getting a furlough. He had heard from home that Alice had a new baby (another girl, Pattie). The major had a new horse, which he said was "getting quite accustomed to drums, glittering arms & flaunting banners. Camp is a great place for gentling horses." Bob, his orderly, had been making soap and candles. Aylett did not believe the enemy would attempt another crossing due to the continued cold.[23] Douglas Brown Benson joined the 53rd Regiment as assistant surgeon on January 1, 1863. He had to furnish his own horse and was allotted $110 for its forage.

General Lee remained in his headquarters southwest of Fredericksburg. He had an army depot and artillery winter quarters at Guinea Station, twelve miles below the town of Fredericksburg. Farther south, toward Richmond, Lee had another supply base at Hanover Junction, where the Virginia Central crossed the R.F.&P. to head west to Gordonsville and the Orange and Alexandria Railroad. Just north of Hanover Junction flows a protective barrier, the North Anna River. Lee had a line of defense along the Rappahannock from just above Fredericksburg to Port

Royal and Port Tobacco and made it more heavily entrenched as the winter wore on.[24] With the railways and many roads and turnpikes, he could readily move his troops to any point the Union forces might choose to threaten.

Around Richmond and Petersburg, the Engineer Bureau of the Confederacy, under the command of Colonel Jeremy F. Gilmer, had been busy since the fall of 1861 with entrenchments and earthen works. The bureau hired blacks, both slave and free, to construct these defenses.

In November 1862, King William furnished its entire quota of 100 men for work on the Richmond defenses. Other counties were lax in meeting their quotas due to the need for men in harvesting crops, the smallpox epidemic, and the ineptness of sheriffs in delivering the laborers. In anticipation of the spring campaigns, on March 19 King William County was requisitioned for 20 free blacks.[25]

There was smallpox at Ayletts. William Aylett wrote to Alice to instruct Mr. Pitts not to allow the servants to go to Ayletts because of it. Doctor Fleet was busy vaccinating. He wrote to Fred, "I would be obliged to you for two or three good scabs at the earliest possible moment as mine are giving out rapidly, there being so many and frequent calls for vaccination." Two weeks later Doctor Fleet wrote to his son that he had heard that Mr. Pitts, Aylett's manager, had been beaten so badly with a large wagon pin that he had died two days later.[26] Did the curtailment of visiting privileges have anything to do with it?

After the activities in Fredericksburg during December 1862, Longstreet, with Pickett's and Hood's divisions, was sent south to replenish Lee's commissary supplies. The Tuck family later received a letter from one of "two sojourners" in King William County at this time to obtain food and forage. They were Georgians of General Henry L. Benning's brigade in Hood's division.[27]

While their fellows collected supplies and worked on local defense, the men of the 53rd Regiment were used to hold the line against the Federals elsewhere. On January 27 both companies from King William were sent north of Fredericksburg to work on the fortifications on the Plank Road at Salem Church. There they found the snow 15 inches deep so they returned to their camp until February 6 when they could complete the fortifications.

Lee was concerned because Federal troops (the IX Corps) were being transported to Hampton Roads. Pickett's and Hood's divisions had already been dispatched to the Chickahominy when on February 18 Lee instructed Longstreet to place them where they could guard both Richmond and Petersburg. On March 27 he left it to Longstreet's discretion whether to attack Union-held Suffolk. Lee was also concerned about whether his men were getting sufficient food from the area. Each regiment was "directed to send a daily detail to gather sassafras buds, wild onions, lamb's quarter, & poke sprouts" to supplement the meager vegetable supply and thereby ward off scurvy.[28]

Starting on February 19, Company H of the 53rd Regiment marched southward to Richmond in double-quick time, crossed the Mayo Bridge, and encamped for a night near Manchester before moving on to Chester. The Company D report for that spring was signed by Captain William J. Turner. He reported that his company left Fredericksburg on February 15, marched the 60 miles to Richmond, and then went on south of the James to encamp at Chester.

William Aylett's furlough may have come through for the latter part of February, after his regiment had moved to Chester. By March 2 he had returned to camp by way of Piping Tree ferry, because, as he stated, he could not cross at Newcastle. (Perhaps the river was in flood stage). A few days later he was made full colonel following Colonel Grammer's resignation. William wrote to Alice that he had retained his brother as his adjutant-general and Dr. Thomas P. Temple as the surgeon, but still had need for an assistant adjutant-general and a chaplain. He had been in Richmond, occupied his brother's office while there, and had purchased a "pair of ready made pantaloons" for $35.[29] There is no record that Patrick Aylett ever served as an adjutant in the 53rd Regiment.

During March the men of the 53rd Regiment worked on the fortifications at Fort Powhatan and during April they stood picket duty outside Suffolk. On one occasion they drove the Union forces back into their fortifications. Thomas D. Quarles was wounded at Suffolk on April 12 and sent to the hospital in Petersburg. On April 26 they took position on the White Marsh Road and on May 3 they fell back to the Blackwater River near Franklin.

———

Others from King William remained nearer Fredericksburg with Lee. The 22nd Battalion's brigadier was now Henry Heth, a 37-year-old native of Chesterfield County and a graduate of West Point who had served in Mexico and the West before the war. He was brought from his services in West Virginia, Kentucky, and Ohio to assume command of Field's brigade in February 1863.[30]

We can almost trace Andrew Leftwich's steps, and perhaps those of his fellows, home to Mangohick, and then back to camp on the road (Route 600) by Vernon Church and Reedy Mill, to the R. F. & P. Railroad at Penola. There Andrew would catch a ride back to camp on the passenger train or the freight. Once, when neither would stop, he walked to Guinea, covering the distance between sunset and midnight and apparently following the railroad track. When he set out from Guinea across the heavily wooded countryside of Caroline County, he was lost fifty times before he arrived at camp an hour before daybreak. He suffered from rheumatism for the next couple of days. On Sunday he went from camp to services at Liberty Baptist Church. There he heard the Reverend George W. Trice preach and found it very much like his home church, Hebron.[31]

This same route may have been the one over which Andrew's letters passed to Mangohick — by rail along the R.F.&.P. and then by carrier along the winding roads to the River Road (Route 600). On an undated scrap of paper Leftwich wrote that he was sending his letter by private conveyance for the cars were not running while a bridge was washed out. The majority of his extant letters were addressed to the Ayletts Post Office, only a few to the Mangohick Post Office. Once he instructed Sallie Tuck to inquire at the Ayletts Post Office for letters because he had heard that the mail was not running to or through King William.[32]

Leftwich's letters after January 2 were addressed from Camp Gregg. He wrote in March of being back in camp after returning on the cars. He was writing to Sallie while sitting in his "cloth house" after having seen her 48 hours before. In early April he wrote of being back in camp after having passed through Bowling Green at church time. He said that the men were allowed to carry only one change of clothing in their knapsack and the officers were allowed to carry only what one knapsack would hold. On April 26 he wrote that he had been helping build a large guardhouse and that the "Yankeys" had crossed 200 men at Port Royal the week before.[33] This was apparently Hooker's feint to lure Lee downstream before the Union crossing above Fredericksburg.

The Fleet letters contain several from a neighborhood boy who, as a substitute in the 5th Virginia Cavalry, wrote of travelling through King William in March 1863. Upon arriving at Mangohick Church one rainy day, he dried himself, got a good night's sleep in the church, and then went on to join his unit at Chesterfield Station (on the railroad below Penola).[34]

The Reverend James Power Smith, an aide to Jackson, wrote: "Fresh from the long winter's waiting, and confident from the preparation of the spring, the troops were in fine condition and high spirits. The boys were all back from home and sick leaves."[35]

Changes had been made in the assignment of the artillery in early 1863. Theretofore batteries had been assigned to individual brigades. Lee set up battalions of four batteries each, making a total of sixteen or more guns, to be directed by two field officers. By an order dated April 16, 1863, Dr. Tom Carter was made one of these officers. Dr. Douglas S. Freeman called Carter one of those who "added most to the luster of the 'Long Arm'."[36]

Over the next two years the young men of the King William Battery would travel many miles throughout Virginia and into Pennsylvania. On the march from one engagement to another, each gun was hooked behind a limber (a two-wheeled vehicle) carrying an ammunition chest and water and grease buckets, and drawn by six horses. Following would be a caisson carrying additional ammunition boxes (usually three) and a spare wheel, and pulled by 4 to 6 horses. A driver rode on the left of each pair, designated in the case of six horses as lead pair, swing pair, and wheel pair. Following would be a battery wagon with additional supplies and forage and possibly a forge wagon. The cannoneers sometimes rode on the ammunition chests. Although they were covered with tarpaulins and had handles one could hold on to, at the normal trotting pace of 5 miles per hour the chests proved to be a spine-rattling perch which could be an explosive "powder keg" should they unexpectedly come into enemy fire. The officers, sergants, buglers, and guidon bearers rode alongside on horseback. Once the command "Action Front" was given a battery could unlimber and fire a round in twenty-five seconds.[37]

During February 1863, General Hooker consolidated the cavalry of the Army of the Potomac under General George Stoneman. Stoneman had been a classmate of Jackson. According to Edward Stackpole, Stoneman was "entirely too cautious and conservative for the new role that he was now being called upon to fulfill," and no match for "Jeb Stuart and his cocky troopers."[38]

Hooker made plans to cross the Rappahannock by its upper fords and attack Lee's forces at Fredericksburg and below from behind. To Stoneman he gave the assignment to cut Lee's supply line and communications with Richmond by way of the Virginia Central and the R.F.& P. railroads. He instructed Stoneman to cross the Rappahannock west of the Orange and Alexandria Railroad, to disperse the Confederate cavalry at Culpeper, to destroy all bridges over the North and South Anna rivers, and to inflict as much damage as possible on the Pamunkey all the way to West Point.[39]

Stoneman received his orders on April 12. By the next night he had his troops at Morrisville. That same night Rooney Lee's scouts informed him of the Union presence and he promptly reinforced his picket at Kelly's Ford. To oppose the crossing Lee had only the 9th and 13th Virginia Cavalry and the 2nd North Carolina Cavalry, 143 dismounted men whose horses had been killed or disabled, and two batteries of horse artillery. At daybreak they confronted General Buford's men at Kelly's Ford and General Gregg's men at the nearby railroad bridge. At the latter some Union forces were allowed to cross; but upon the arrival of the 9th Cavalry, they were pushed back to the north side of the river. The 9th Cavalry also assisted at Beverly's Ford where Colonel Chambliss's men (the 13th) captured twenty-four men of the 3rd Indiana Cavalry as they attempted to recross the river. Twelve hours of heavy rainfall had swollen the tributary streams. Some Union men were drowned in the rapidly rising Rappahannock. Henry McClellan reported: "Thus ended this expedition. The bold action of two small regiments [9th and 13th], aided by a swollen stream, thwarted the plans of the Federal commander and delayed . . .the advance of the Grand Army of the Potomac."[40]

During March and April 1863, Company H of the 9th Cavalry had been stationed at Rapidan Station, on the Orange and Alexandria Railroad between Culpeper and Orange Court House. They were engaged in the rifle pits on the Rapidan River on May 1 against General Averell and his Union cavalry. Lee's Rangers were able to hold the railroad bridge there for two nights and a day before burning it and withdrawing to Gordonsville, and then going on in pursuit of the enemy cavalry to Trevilian's on the Virginia Central Railroad. There they met another squadron of cavalry, charged them on foot, drove them back and then pursued them to Columbia on the James River. From Columbia they returned to Culpeper and to their camp, two and a half miles below the courthouse. The official report credits Rooney Lee's small command with containing the enemy's damage to the railroads so that they could be readily repaired and with saving the James River-Kanawha Canal from damage. On one occasion they had to cover 80 miles in 24 hours.[41]

Meanwhile, an intense engagement raged at Chancellorsville, about twenty miles from Rapidan Station. There had been a misunderstanding between Averell and General Hooker. The cavalry had been expected only to block immediate opposition and then to return to the assistance of the main army — not to remain for two nights and a day facing Rooney Lee's small forces.[42]

At the end of April, General Richard H. Anderson's division guarded Lee's extreme left above Fredericksburg and General Lafayette McLaw's division stood nearer to town. Late in the afternoon of April 29, cavalry pickets brought word to General Mahone of the movement of an enemy column along the plank road from the Germanna Ford, of an approach toward Ely's Ford, and of a demonstration at U.S. Mine Ford on the Rappahannock. Within an hour Mahone's men had abandoned their winter camp and were in position north of the Chancellor house with two guns covering each road along which the Federals were approaching. But Hooker halted before making contact and Anderson's men went into bivouac that night in line of battle.[43]

In the early morning hours of May 1, McLaw's men were drawn up beside the turnpike so A. P. Hill's "Light Division," including the 22nd Battalion, could pass. A witness wrote:

They were in light marching order, and I thought I had never seen anything equal to the swinging, silent stride with which they fairly devoured the ground. The men were magnified in the morning mist which overhung the low flat-lands they were traversing, and at the same time imparted a ghostly indistinctness of outline, which added to the impressiveness of the scene.[44]

A shout went up as Lee and his staff rode by shortly thereafter. A Southern artillerist wrote that he could not recall a moment of higher enthusiasm:

I cannot say that it was his [Lee's] habit, but I distinctly remember that on this occasion he lifted his hat, taking it by the crown with his right hand and holding it suspended above his majestic head as far as we could see him. I remember, too, that the men greeted him, shouting, "What a head, what a head! See that glorious head, God bless it!"[45]

Jackson arrived near Tabernacle Church early on May 1. He at once took charge and ordered the entrenching to cease. At 3 p.m. Jackson's musketry could be heard and by nightfall Jackson had established his line on the Plank Road within sight of Chancellorsville.[46]

The next morning, May 2, the sun was barely up when Jackson, with Lee's approval, took his men on a circuitous route which had been sketched for him by his cartographer, Jed Hotchkiss. The first division in the line of march was Rodes's division (with which Carter's Battery was serving). The second division in line was Raleigh Colston's. Last came A. P. Hill with General Henry Heth (and the 22nd Battalion). This road took them by Catherine Furnace and brought them in position to charge Hooker on his right flank and rear at about 5:15 p.m.[47]

Colonel Tom Carter had under his command during the battles at Chancellorsville the King William Battery under the direction of his brother, Captain William P. Carter; two other Virginia batteries, Fry's Orange Artillery and Page's Morris Artillery; and Reese's Alabama Battery. He reported that they followed Jackson on May 2 and took position in an open field 1½ miles west of Melzi Chancellor's house while the infantry formed in the dense woods. A Parrot gun of Carter's Battery was among the three unlimbered guns. Others could not be brought to bear during that day's attack due to the heavy forest on both sides of the turnpike.[48]

General Rodes's forces routed the Federals of General Oliver O. Howard's XI Corps. In less than an hour, the Confederates had the high ground near Talley's in their possession. At 6:30 p.m., General Hooker, seated, peaceably on the front porch of the Chancellor house, saw men, horses, cattle, and vehicles in their flight eastward toward the turnpike. The Wilderness had muffled the sound of musketry and the use of artillery fire had been slight. Immediately Hooker began shifting his forces and guns to stop Jackson's advance. Pleasonton had already positioned his cavalry and whatever guns he could get his hands on. Rodes's division was stopped near Hazel Grove as darkness fell. Colonel Carter reported: "The fire from our three guns was promptly responded to from the enemy's whole line. At this juncture, General Hill ordered the firing to cease. We remained in this position until the front line (Rodes's division) was relieved by Hill's division, which, it was understood, would resume the attack."[49]

Jackson ordered A. P. Hill, his third line, to cut the Federals off from the U.S. Mine Ford. A bright moon had risen, giving an eerie light to unfamiliar surroundings. Jackson and several of his men rode ahead to locate the road to the ford and the position of the enemy. On returning at 9 p.m., they were mistaken for Union cavalry and Jackson was shot by his own men. While Jackson was being carried from the field, Heth's brigade was arriving on the left. They advanced to the entrenchments under heavy fire of enemy artillery. Soon A. P. Hill was also wounded. Neither Heth nor Rodes were major generals. Rodes called off the night advance at 10 p.m. and Jeb Stuart took over the command at midnight.[50]

When Jackson was fired upon by his own men, Carter said that it drew fire from the enemy's artillery upon them causing "considerable damage done to my battalion, still on column of pieces on the turnpike, behind (with exception of the three pieces in position)." When further action was called off for the night, he withdrew the battalion "to the entrenchments near M. Chancellor's house, where the guns were placed in position and broken poles replaced and preparation made for the battle of next day." With Lee's approval the next morning Carter collected guns from other battalions and moved them with his guns to the crest of a Hazel Grove hilltop that had been abandoned by the enemy. Colonel Carter sent Major Carter M. Braxton with Carter's and Fry's companies along with Colonel Hilary P. Jones down the turnpike to engage the enemy while he opened from the crest of the hill. This made an effective line of fire. Hill's division remained in the front of the attack while Rodes's men assailed the earthworks on the left of the Plank Road.[51]

Stuart, with the forces of the fallen Jackson, resumed the attack on the right center of the enemy line early on May 3. Three times Hooker's entrenchments were taken and three times, under heavy fire of musketry and artillery, had to be abandoned. The fourth attempt, "aided by an enfilading fire from thirty pieces of artillery under Cols. Thos. H. Carter and Hilary P. Jones, proved irresistible, and the enemy gave way in confusion."[52]

Lee praised the artillery in his report, mentioning Colonel Carter among those deserving special commendation. Carter himself reported that Major Braxton praised Captain William P. Carter's company, and he himself pointed out the admirable conduct of the detachment under Lieutenant L. D. Robinson of Carter's Battery.[53]

Both men and horses suffered from the consequences of long marches followed by extensive fighting. As May 3 wore on, Major Robert A. Hardaway was told to follow General Anderson to the vicinity of Banks' Ford, on the River Road northwest of Fredericksburg. He took with him four guns from Carter's battalion, two of which were from the King William Battery. Hardaway was instructed to shell the supply wagons which Hooker had left on the north side of the Rappahannock, near Scott's Ford. Hardaway's engineer at 3 a.m. pointed out three positions. He selected one of them and had fifteen rounds fired into the camp fires. Then they "limbered up" the guns to return in the mud toward Chancellorsville.[54]

The next day General Lee ordered Hardaway to take charge of all the guns the Smith house, above Banks' Ford. On the north bank of the river the enemy had a battery that could enfilade any at advance of Anderson's men toward Fredericksburg. Hardaway was assured that he would find rifle pits ready for use. He did find positions for four of his guns, but for the others to bear his men had to advance beyond the abatis to cut the tree stumps closer to the ground. The major reported that the evening was sultry and oppressive and some of his men and horses had not had rations for 24 hours. Carter's guns halted on a 40-foot high bluff near the rifle pits. When the Confederate infantry started its movement to the right, the guns commenced firing and continued until after dark. Even with defective fuses they were able to disable six of the enemy's guns and drive two others from the field.[55]

That night Carter's Battery moved into the rifle pits. Major Hardaway was awakened about 1 a.m. by the sound of heavy musketry fire in the direction of the ford. He ordered his guns to fire at intervals of twenty minutes to each gun, changing direction so as to cover all approaches to the ford. This sequence put a shell into the air every minute until one half hour after sunrise, May 5. A gun of Huger's Battery got the range on a wagon park, three miles away where the roads to Aquia Creek and the U.S. Mine Ford branched. Hardaway wrote: "We plied them with solid bolts as long as . . . it would pay." All the while his men acted with commendable spirit. With daylight supply wagons could be seen hurrying off in all directions. At 10 a.m. the batteries of the special rifle battalion were told to report back to their regular commanders.[56]

Just to the south of Banks' Ford, on May 4, had been fought the Battle of Salem Church. General John Sedgwick, following Hooker's instructions, had driven Jubal Early's Confederates from the heights overlooking Fredericksburg and then attempted to join his commanding general at Chancellorsville. But Lee had not chosen to wait there until Hooker was reinforced. Sedgwick found Anderson and McLaws in his front at Salem Church. Early moved south only long enough for Segwick's forces to pass then he returned to the heights. Between 2 and 3 a.m. on May 5, Sedgwick's entire corps, his trains and 55 guns, crossed on two pontoon bridges back to the north side of the Rappahannock.[57] This was near where the Confederate rifle battalion had fired its rounds across the river 24 hours before.

Throughout Monday night and Tuesday morning, May 5, Hooker's men cut roads from their positions to the U.S. Mine Ford. An afternoon storm turned the new roads into muddy streams and the rising river threatened to wash their pontoons downstream. But the Rappahannock soon crested and then receded. Sometime during the day Hooker himself recrossed the river and during the hours of darkness all his corps followed.[58]

Lee's greatest battle had been a time of anguish for Andrew Leftwich and the 22nd Battalion as they moved with A. P. Hill and his "Light Division." Andrew wrote home that they marched up the river near Fredericksburg, formed a line of battle in Hooker's rear and fought the hardest battle that he had been in. He was delivered without a bruise, although badly shocked, and had been sent to the hospital. When he wrote the letter on May 9 from Hamilton's Crossing, he was nearly starved because no food had been rationed in the last few days. There was no prospect of food anytime soon.[59] The official report shows that six from the 22nd Battalion had been killed and twenty-three wounded.

Soon after the battle, Lee called for Longstreet to join him at Chancellorsville. As soon as the general could collect his wagons from along the coast he headed for Petersburg and Richmond. Some of the troops covered 34 miles in a single night, never knowing when they might come upon General George Stoneman and his men who were known to be raiding north and west of Richmond. There was a brief layover in Richmond when word was received of Lee's success at Chancellorsville and of the mortal wounding of General Jackson. Longstreet's men, including the 53rd Regiment, then joined a grieving Lee in Fredericksburg.[60]

CHAPTER 7

Ayletts, Brandy Station, and the South Anna — 1863

As Lee and Longstreet made plans to take the armies into Maryland and Pennsylvania, the days when the valor of King William men would be tested and their county invaded by the enemy lay just ahead. There were four "invasions" of the county that spring and early summer. The first came in May with the quartering of soldiers in West Point by General George H. Gordon. The second "invasion" was a raid on Ayletts in June, led by General Erasmus D. Keyes and under the direction of General John A. Dix from the headquarters of the Department of Virginia at Fort Monroe. During the latter part of June and early July, Dix also directed the third and fourth "invasions," which were expeditions across the county. It appears that only during the second "invasion" would any of the local men be put in a position for their county's defense. During the expeditions King William soldiers were engaged, or on the way to be engaged, elsewhere: in Fredericksburg and Culpeper prior to the battle at Brandy Station in early June, and on the way to and at Gettysburg during the latter part of June and early July.

Upon the death of Jackson, Lee divided the Army of Northern Virginia into three corps. (For clarity they will be designated as the *First, Second,* and *Third* Corps as against their counterparts in the Union forces to be referred to by Roman numerals, e.g., I, II, III Corps.) Longstreet continued to command the First Corps. Jackson's command was divided between General Richard S. Ewell, for the Second Corps, and General A. P. Hill, for the Third Corps. Men from King William would be serving in all three corps. The 53rd, under Brigadier General Lewis A. Armistead, was in General George E. Pickett's division of the First Corps. Carter's Battery was in an artillery battalion led by Colonel Carter in General Robert E. Rodes's division of the Second Corps. The 22nd Battalion was in a brigade led by Colonel J. M. Brockenbrough in General Henry Heth's division of the Third Corps. Both Fitz Lee and Rooney Lee were now brigadier generals under Stuart. Those men in the 4th and 5th Cavalry would be serving under Fitz Lee and those in the 9th Cavalry would be under Rooney Lee, with Colonel R. L. T. Beale as their leader.[1]

On the Union side, Colonel Judson Kilpatrick and Colonel Percy Wyndham of Averell's command were helping to carry out Stoneman's instructions to operate between Lee, on the Rappahannock, and his base in Richmond. Their assignment was to destroy the bridges and telegraph lines over the Chickahominy and then either to return to the Rappahannock or push on to Yorktown or Gloucester Point.[2]

Benny Fleet told his diary that the 12th Illinois Cavalry (under Wyndham) passed through King and Queen on May 5 and destroyed the boats at Dunkirk and the ferry at Ayletts. Kilpatrick and Wyndham were in the area for the next week, taking horses, mules, corn, and fodder. Melville Walker, Benny's friend, was making his way back to camp at Orange Court House when, on arriving at Mangohick Church, he heard that the "Yankees" were at Chesterfield Station. He stayed at Mangohick long enough to feed his horses and then took the road to Bowling Green.[3]

West Point was occupied by a Federal brigade during a portion of May and early June. Quartered in the town were: the 22nd Connecticut; the 127th, 141st, 142nd, and 143rd New York; and the 40th Massachusetts Infantry; two or more batteries from Wisconsin; and some cavalry — all under the direction of General Gordon. President Lincoln's Emancipation Proclamation took effect on January 1, 1863. During the following months, blacks from the farms surrounding West Point flocked to the Union lines. The men found employment under quartermasters and the women did the needed washing and cooking for the troops.[4]

General Gordon had his headquarters in West Point at the "Grove House," near the Richmond and York River Railroad. Troops were set to building earthworks and rifle pits along the railroad. Cannon emplacements, using or converting the Confederate works, were put along the road (perhaps Route 30) to the courthouse and at the "point." Soldiers proceeded to "liberate" the stock from nearby farms, although General Gordon tried to discourage the taking of cows and pigs and sent back some of the horses. The elderly and infirm citizens pleaded with him for the return of their servants, but he remained adamant in his role of liberator. There were a few skirmishes with the Confederates. Union gunboats were sent out to destroy a battery that had "fired on the Union's Yorktown-to-West Point mail steamer." But the artillerists fled with their guns, so the soldiers burned some of the houses in the area. By the end of May, Gordon had been replaced by General Edward O. C. Ord, and soon the men were shipped back to Fort Monroe and Yorktown.[5] Thus ended the first "Invasion."

After Hooker's withdrawal across the Rappahannock, Pickett had not taken his men all the way to Chancellorsville, but established his headquarters at Hanover Junction. By June 3 Lee commenced withdrawing his forces from around Fredericksburg. He left A. P. Hill's corps, including the 22nd Battalion, in a position to meet any crossing there, and he had plans to call up Pickett if Hill needed any assistance. Andrew Leftwich's letter written on June 12 from the battlefield near Fredericksburg, stated that they had been in a line of battle there for the last seven days.[6]

William Aylett had his men encamped at Salem Church, near Fredericksburg. They broke camp on the morning of May 27, 1863, and marched twelve miles until they were within five miles of Fredericksburg and six miles of Falmouth. There they threw up fortifications. Their assignment was to reinforce Pickett's line and to keep the enemy from fording the Rappahannock.

The records of Companies D and H of the 53rd Regiment show that they were moved instead into a position to defend their home county. On June 3 they made a drive into Caroline County as far as Newtown. Then on June 5 they were sent to Reedy Mills and from there made a 10-mile march into King William before being recalled to Hanover Junction. This appears to have been at a time when Union forces were at Ayletts, or the second "invasion." A letter written by Colonel Aylett to his wife on June 23 told that his brother had received the letter which he had sent to him as they passed through Mangohick.[7]

Hooker was aware on June 6 that Lee had already drawn two of his brigades out of Fredericksburg by rail from Hamilton's Crossing and that Pickett could very likely have 10,000 men between the "White House" and Newtown (in Caroline County). He put a bridge across the Rappahannock, crossed a portion of his troops, and expected that this action would draw some of Lee's forces back to that front.[8]

While Hooker held A. P. Hill at bay at Fredericksburg, he received word from General John A. Dix that he had fewer than 5,000 men and some cavalry at West Point, which was not enough force to take and hold the "White House." But a combined army-navy expedition under General Eramus D. Keyes had been sent up the Mattaponi to Walkerton, twenty-three miles from Richmond, and had destroyed "a large amount of property and stores."[9]

This is recorded in the *Official Records* as: "June 4-5, 1863 — Expedition from Yorktown to Walkerton and Aylett's, Va." It gives both versions, the Federal as told by General Erasmus Keyes and his subordinates and the Confederate defense as told by General Henry A. Wise. The fifty-six-year-old former governor of Virginia was now in control of the district between the Mattaponi and the James. With his brigade, made up of the 26th, 34th (also known as the 4th Heavy Artillery), and 46th Infantry, were a battalion of artillery and a squadron of cavalry.[10]

According to Colonel C. Carroll Tevis, commanding the Union infantry, the expedition used 100 men each from the 4th Delaware Infantry, the 168th New York Volunteers, and the 169th and 179th Pennsylvania Drafted Militia. The navy furnished the transport (ferryboat) *Winnisimet* and the gunboats *Commodore Morris* and *Commodore Jones.* The army supplied the U.S.S. *Smith Briggs* from Yorktown. They started up the York at 7 p.m., June 4, disembarked at Walkerton at 3 a.m. and by 4:30 a.m. had commenced their march up the King William side of the Mattaponi to Ayletts, ten miles distant. One detachment of men was left at the intersection of the King William Court House road and the road leading to Dunkirk (perhaps Route 30 to 600). Two other detachments were positioned at crossroads leading to that main road.[11]

On their arrival at Ayletts at 7 a.m., June 5, the Federals occupied all the approaches to the town and put out pickets. Then they proceeded to destroy "a large iron foundry [Cardwell's], where were molds for cannon and projectiles, and a number of shell and solid shot lying on the ground." While there they also destroyed a large machine shop, a lumber yard, a storage house containing agricultural implements, tobacco, cotton, turpentine, and other articles, and what they called "five Government houses, containing several thousand bushels of corn."[12]

General Wise reported from the "White House" in New Kent to General Arnold Elzey, commanding the Department of Richmond, at 10:30 a.m. on June 5 that three Union transports and one gunboat had landed men at Walkerton and that the enemy had crossed into King William and were near Piping Tree. Wise had sent Major John R. Bagby with about 100 infantry, one section of artillery, and two companies of cavalry over the Pamunkey River to below the enemy in King William. He was calling up four more companies of infantry from New Kent Court House and had a small guard of infantry with him. Colonel W. P. Shingler was at Tunstall's on the Richmond and York River Railroad in New Kent with a small guard of cavalry. Wise asked that extra forces be sent to Piping Tree Ferry on the New Kent side since it was reported that houses were being burned there.[13]

Bagby, with his infantry, artillery, and cavalrymen, went by way of Lanesville to Frazer's Ferry, below Walkerton and King William Court House. There, posted on the bluffs overlooking the Mattaponi, they would be in a position to attack the enemy as they moved back down the river toward the York River and Fort Monroe.[14]

The wires of communication between the Confederate forces were buzzing. General Elzey telegraphed to General J. Johnston Pettigrew at Hanover Junction to go to Wise's assistance and to communicate with Pickett, said to be near Tappahannock, to attack on the far side of the Mattaponi. President Davis wished that the enemy either be captured or destroyed and felt, with Wise's help from the "White House," that this could be done.[15]

Unfortunately the former governor received instruction from General Elzey that he should keep his men on the New Kent side of the Pamunkey. The general had no choice but to withdraw his troops from King William. Those under Major Bagby got back to the "White House" about the time that Colonel J. T. Goode and the 4th Heavy Artillery arrived from New Kent Court House. By this time General Wise had received a dispatch giving him permission to have troops across the Pamunkey in King William.[16]

It was 8 p.m. before Goode had his infantry and guns back at Frazer's Ferry. The main body of Union forces had already passed back down the river at 7 p.m. The Confederate cavalry, which had remained in the vicinity of King William Court House, rode into the Union pickets and the rear guard of 150 infantry. A gunboat began to shell the cavalrymen as the Union forces returned to their transports. The woods were very dense in the area and the Confederates were not able to operate effectively. Only one Confederate was wounded while, according to Wise's report, they killed three of the Union men and took two prisoners.[17]

The damage inflicted by the Federals had been extensive. On their way back to their boats at Walkerton, according to the Union report filed later by Colonel Tevis, they burned the grist-mill of Colonel Aylett "of the rebel army," together with eight "run of stone," 2,500 barrels of flour, and 2,000 bushels of wheat. Also, they destroyed twenty barns and ten wheat stacks containing about 20,000 bushels of grain, stores of bacon, tobacco, cotton goods, and 80 gallons of whiskey. They drove the horses, mules, and "horned cattle" which they captured to the wharf at Walkerton.[18]

General Wise said in his report that the Union forces burned, in addition to Aylett's Mill, the barns and outhouses on the farms of Dr. D. H. Gregg, Dr. A. H. Perkins, James Roane, Warner Edwards, and Hill King. They destroyed grain, fodder, machinery, implements, and bacon. A. T. Mooklar, "an intelligent and respectable citizen" (apparently not in service at this time) made out a paper showing damage inflicted being at least $300,000 to $500,000.[19] Local tradition holds that all houses at Ayletts, except the old post-office tavern and the "Berkeley" house, where black families resided, were burned, either at this time or during subsequent raids.

Judith McGuire, living at Ashland at that time, wrote in her diary that raiding parties had gone up the Pamunkey and Mattaponi rivers recently. A large party rode to the home of Mr. Roane on the Mattaponi ("Uppowac," off of Route 600 below Ayletts). Their commander accosted him on the lawn with the statement, "Mr. R., I understand [that] you have the finest horses in King William County?"

"Perhaps, I have," replied Mr. R.

"Well, sir," said the officer, "I want those horses immediately."

"They are not yours," replied Mr. R, "and you can't get them."

The cursing officer threatened to burn all the buildings on the place if the horses were not turned over to him. Handing a box of matches to a subordinate, he said, "Burn!" Within thirty minutes Mr. Roane saw four-teen of his houses, including his dwelling, aflame. But the horses had been taken off into the woods by a loyal servant for safe keeping.[20]

Commander James H. Gillis of the *Commodore Morris* reported that the expedition did not get back to Walkerton until 5:30 p.m. Word had been received that the Confederates were planning to obstruct the river downstream at "Mantapike" (King and Queen County). The U.S.S. *Smith Briggs* had been sent down at 2 p.m. to keep the river open. By leaving most of the animals behind, all the men were soon boarded and they were on their way downstream by 6 p.m. About 60 or 70 "rebels" had collected on the bluff at Indian Town (Frazer's Ferry). Captain John C. Lee of the *Smith Briggs* said that his shells dispersed them. As they proceeded downstream, the Union gunboats shelled both sides of the river and the Confederate sharpshooters were kept from firing upon them at all but one point. The navy sustained only one casualty. The Federal infantry report was that they sustained one man killed, one wounded, and one reported missing. They had taken two prisoners and picked up two deserters. Gillis said that the whole countryside had been aroused and the banks were lined with those who would have delighted in taking the lives of the "in-vaders of their soil" (his quotation marks).[21]

The Federals considered it a fact that Longstreet (actually Pickett) was at or near Newtown, 10 miles from Ayletts, and Pickett (actually Wise) was at or near the "White House," 12 miles from where they had landed. Gillis could only conclude "that the enemy was under the impression our small force was but the advance of a large body of troops." The expedi-tion arrived back at Yorktown at 2 a.m., with "all hands pretty well tired and worn out with their two days and nights of constant work and watch-ing."[22]

On June 6 Pickett had his men back in camp at Hanover Junction. He told Pettigrew that the Federal gunboats had left Walkerton at 6 p.m. the day before and he did not know what had become of them. A day or two later Companies D and H of the 53rd Regiment commenced their three-day march to Culpeper. General Wise, in his report to General Elzey on June 9, was disgruntled because neither Pickett nor Pettigrew had as yet cooperated in the defense of King William, although some forces of the former had been within five miles of Walkerton and turned back. Wise suggested that such a raid could be perpetrated again unless General Pettigrew could be ordered to picket and hold the upper ferries of the Mat-taponi, and unless he (Wise) be allowed at discretion to cross the Pamunkey as emergency might require. He stressed that this had been a daring and destructive raid.[23]

The Federal expedition and subsequent cavalry raids caused reverberations throughout King William County, into King and Queen

County, and consternation around the camp fires of local companies. Benny Fleet recorded in his diary that sixteen to eighteen houses, as well as the foundry, warehouse, and mill, had been burned at Ayletts. On June 12 he attended a large citizens' meeting at Ayletts that had assembled to organize for local defense. He recorded in his diary that they elected Major B. B. Douglas as their captain and Colonel J. C. Johnson as their first lieutenant. (Major Douglas had apparently left active service in order to tend better his responsibilities in the legislature. Colonel Johnson had resigned because of a long-standing health condition.) There were many reported sightings of the enemy during the ensuing months, many of which proved to be false alarms.[24]

General Pleasanton had received orders on June 5 from General Hooker to take three divisions and four batteries of horse artillery across the Rappahannock River to determine the position and intentions of Lee's army. Jed Hotchkiss had drafted maps of Maryland and Pennsylvania for the Confederate commanding general who was already positioning infantry and cavalry beyond the Blue Ridge for movement into those states. Longstreet and Ewell's corps had arrived at Culpeper. A. P. Hill was on the way with his men from Fredericksburg. Stuart was assembling his cavalrymen to be reviewed by General Lee.[25]

On June 6 the 9th Cavalry moved from its camp near Culpeper on up the Orange and Alexandria Railroad to camp on a fork of the Hazel River as it flows to the Rappahannock River near Beverly's Ford and Brandy Station. Two days later they returned to their old camp to be a part of the cavalry review.

This review was not as pretentious as the one held just before Lee's arrival. Lee allowed no galloping of horses or firing of artillery in order to save men, powder, and horses for what lay ahead of them.[26] He wrote to his wife:

I reviewed the cavalry in this section yesterday. It was a splendid sight. The men & horses looked well. They had recuperated since last fall. Stuart was in all his glory. Your sons & nephews well & flourishing. Fitz Lee was on the ground not in the saddle tell Sis Nannie, but sitting by some pretty girls in a carriage. He says he is afflicted by an attack of rheumatism in his knee. I fear it is so, but he is getting over it & expects to be on duty in a few days. Fitzhugh [Rooney] was on his black charger tell Charlotte [his wife] & Rob [the youngest brother] by his side ....The country here looks very green & pretty notwithstanding the ravages of war. What a beautiful world God in His loving kindness to His creatures has given us. What a shame that man endowed with reason & a knowledge of right should mar His gifts. May He soon change the hearts of men, shew them their sins & enable them to repent & be forgiven![27]

Back in their camp on the Botts Farm at Brandy Station, the 9th Virginia was in just the right place for the large cavalry engagement on June 9. Fairfax Downey, in his book on the Battle of Brandy Station, described the calm of the early morning hours of June 9. He said that a "bright moon set about two o'clock." A haze settled over the Rappahannock, "blinding sentries and dulling sound."[28]

Upon hearing firing at Beverly's Ford, Robert E. Lee's son Rooney advanced his men to the assistance of General William E. ("Grumble") Jones's cavalry brigade. General John Buford and his First Division of Union cavalry had slipped across the ford. Rooney Lee soon positioned his men on the Cunningham farm and put dismounted men behind a stone fence there.[29] Company H of the 9th Cavalry engaged as sharpshooters from 8 a.m. to 5 p.m. that day.

Colonel Beale of the 9th Cavalry described the regiment's resistance during the afternoon, when "the enemy's cavalry, which seemed not less than three regiments, were seen moving towards our left flank, and apparently seeking the ravines and woods to conceal their line of march . . . .The regiment, which was resting in column of fours, was ordered to charge up the hill to save the dismounted men." General W. H. F. Lee arrived while the enemy was in retreat, but was wounded in the leg. After several charges by the regiment up the hill, only to be pushed back to the foot of the hill in hand-to-hand fighting, the colonel of the 9th received the following message from General Stuart: "The General sends his thanks to Colonel Beale and the men of the Ninth for gallantry in holding the hill, and if you will hold five minutes longer he will send reinforcements." When reinforcements were sighted, the Union cavalrymen were already, according to Beale, in "full and rapid retreat." With Rooney Lee now incapacitated, Colonel John R. Chambliss of the 13th Virginia Cavalry took charge of the brigade.[30] Three men from King William had been wounded: Walker Hawes; Hansford Anderson, who sustained a wound in the hip; and James R. Burgess, who received a mortal wound.

General Ewell's men, with those of General Rodes in the advance, were marching to the assistance of the cavalry by way of Culpeper and the Botts Farm to Brandy Station. They did not arrive in the area until Pleasanton and Buford were in the act of retiring back across the Rappahannock.[31]

Rooney Lee was sent the next day to "Hickory Hill," the home of W. F. Wickham (his wife's relative), near Hanover Court House. His younger brother, Rob, went along to care for him. Rooney was put in the office in the yard and his wife, sisters, and mother came from Richmond to be with him. Federal cavalry came a few weeks later and took Rooney prisoner.

"Hickory Hill" is at Wickham's Station on the Chesapeake & Ohio Railroad then the Virginia Central, just northwest of Hanover Court House. A few miles beyond, the Gum Tree Road (Route 738) leads to the South Anna just upstream from its confluence with the North Anna and the Little River to form the Pamunkey. The railroad bridge there was a vital link in Lee's supply line.

Upon hearing that Union cavalrymen were at the gate, Rooney told his brother to flee with the horses across the Pamunkey to "North Wales," but Rob was watching from the limbs of a fir tree when the soldiers took him away. That night they camped at Mrs. Nelson's and she gave Rooney supper and "her best room for his quarters." The young general was held hostage at Fort Monroe for the next nine months for the safety of several Union officers who had been captured by the Confederates.[32]

General R. E. Lee wrote to his wife from Williamsport as he struggled to return his army from the disaster at Gettysburg: "I have heard with great grief that Fitzhugh has been captured by the enemy. Had not expected that he would be taken from his bed and carried off, be we must bear this additional affliction with fortitude and resignation, and not repine at the will of God."[33]

The cavalry which appeared at "Hickory Hill" was part of a raid called in the *Official Records,* "June 23-28, 1863 — Expedition from Yorktown to the South Anna Bridge, Va., and skirmish." General Dix reported from Yorktown to Major General Henry W. Halleck that he was moving his cavalry under Colonel Samuel P. Spear and General George W. Getty's artillery by transports from Yorktown. General Keyes was moving his infantry by land from Cumberland, five miles below the "White House." When the cavalry landed at the "White House," they surprised two companies of Confederate cavalry and a small force of infantry, who soon burnt their own store house and left. General Keyes's men did not arrive there until June 27. There had been a long drought followed by three days of continual rain, making the roads very difficult to travel. When the transports returned to Yorktown, General Dix sent General Isaac J. Wistar with a part of his brigade and a battery of artillery to West Point. They landed during the night, after pulling down two small buildings and building a wharf.[34]

In the meantime Colonel Spear with his 1,500 cavalrymen — eleven companies of the 11th Pennsylvania and a detachment of Illinois and Massachusetts cavalry — had gone up the south side of the Pamunkey to Hanover Court House. There the raiders found a Confederate quartermaster depot. They burned the office, the wheelwright's and blacksmith's shops, the stables, 300 complete sets of harness, and thirty-five wagons. Apparently they sent the "100 good mules," the horses, and other stock to Mrs. Nelson's Bridge. They also found a large Confederate safe which they were unable to open. Then they went on to the South Anna River, burned the Virginia Central Railroad bridge, and captured some men of the 44th North Carolina Infantry. By the time the cavalrymen reached the R.F.& P. bridge, farther upstream, they were too exhausted and their ammunition too low to allow them to take and destroy it. They paroled the badly wounded prisoners and started back to rejoin General Keyes and the infantry at the "White House."[35]

A Confederate scout, led by Sergeant W. T. Thorn, had followed the Union cavalry up the south side of the Pamunkey River to ascertain their destination. At Mrs. Nelson's Bridge, now reconstructed, they ran into the Union picket, captured one prisoner, and released Lieutenant W. P. McKnight of the 17th Virginia Regiment and six of his men, who had been taken prisoners. The Union picket also had a large number of horses and mules which they ran across the river and Sergeant Thorn's men were unable to retrieve them. From the freed prisoners the scout was able to learn that possibly as many as 1,500 Union cavalry were headed toward the Central Railroad Bridge over the South Anna River. A dispatch to this effect was sent on June 26 to Colonel William P. Shingler, with the Holcombe Legion at Bottom's Bridge.[36]

At "Wyoming" the Nelsons may have heard the braying and nickering of the mules and horses and the lowing of the cattle as they moved restlessly in make-shift pens on the Hanover side. They could have witnessed the utter pandemonium when the animals, forced to swim the river, came crashing through the underbrush and trees to streak in all directions across whatever crop, perhaps wheat or corn, stood in the river flats.

At Hanover Junction on June 25, General Montgomery D. Corse, serving under General Pickett, had turned over the defense of seventeen bridges and fords from Milford Station to the South Anna River to the 44th North Carolina Infantry, under the direction of Colonel Thomas C. Singletary. Colonel David J. Godwin, commanding the cavalry there, received word at 10 a.m. on June 26 of the approach of the enemy. Just an hour later they were attacked by what he reported as three cavalry regiments, one battalion, and two pieces of artillery. Inspite of the loss of Company G and the severe fight sustained by Company A, both of the 44th North Carolina Infantry, a few companies were able, Colonel Godwin reported, to keep intact all the stores and buildings at the junction and retain all but one of the bridges, that of the Virginia Central. The cavalry pursued the Union forces along the north side of the Pamunkey River until they came within the cover of the Union gunboats at the "White House."[37]

Upon the Union countermarch to Hanovertown, Colonel Spear reported, they learned that should they attempt to return along the south bank of the Pamunkey River they would be intercepted by General Wise.

So they crossed over the Hanovertown Bridge, taking up the planks behind them, and returned via "New Castle" and King William Court House to the crossing to the "White House." They had been assured that there would be a small force at West Point and gunboats in the river to protect them. En route they captured a Confederate agent who was carrying $15,000 in bonds to make payment for "purchased stores."[38]

On June 27 Benny Fleet and seven others had been sent on an advance guard to Hebron Church (Mangohick). Upon arrival there they heard that the Yankees, coming from Hanover, were at Mrs. Nelson's Bridge. Soon their pickets were run in. Their entire guard, consisting of Captain R. H. Bagby's Company, tried to cut the enemy off by another road. Benny was left on picket duty and got separated from the main force until evening, but returned home safely. He wrote in his diary, "The Yankees were on a raid with about 2 or 3000 Cav: & 3 pieces of Art: — We couldn't do anything with them, we had about 100 or 130 men."[39] This Union passage through Mangohick District probably took them through Dr. Carter Warner Wormeley's "New Castle Estate" ("Manskin Lodge" and "Wormeley Grove"[40]) to strike the Richmond-Tappahannock stage road, and from it to bear right at Brandywine (Manquin), to pass "Fontainebleau" and Acquinton Church, to King William Court House (perhaps Routes 618 and 629).

When the Union cavalry arrived back at the "White House" on the evening of June 27, besides their North Carolina prisoners they had about 500 mules and 200 horses as well as wagons, carts and harness. A large number of slaves — men, women, and children — had followed them. The men were set to work there and the women and children were sent on to Fort Monroe. The Federals' greatest prize was Rooney Lee, taken from his recuperation near Hanover Court House. The next day General Dix wrote to his commander, General H. W. Halleck, that the Confederate general had been brought in "an easy carriage," had been examined by the medical officer to determine that the flesh wound in his thigh would not be injured by further movement, and then had been sent on to the Chesapeake Hospital.[41] Certainly it was with sadness that Rooney passed as a prisoner through his ancestral estate and viewed, although probably not for the first time, the ruins of his own home.

General Dix continued to be a threat to Richmond and the surrounding areas. Word came to the Confederate War Department on June 28 that there were 25,000 Federals at Williamsburg and an additional 5,000 at the "White House." Four days later they were reported to be eighteen miles from Richmond, in New Kent County. The capital's volunteer troops were sent out the Darbytown Road to assist D. H. Hill's regulars in repulsing three Union regiments in their attempt to cross the Chickahominy at Bottom's Bridge.[42]

This was a diversionary move by General Dix while he made another

94

attempt at more completely cutting Lee's supply line at the South Anna. On a second expedition, July 1 - 7, Dix sent out 10,000 men under General George W. Getty, including his own division, General Robert S. Foster's brigade, a provisional brigade (of Wistar's men), the 99th New York Volunteers, and Colonel Spear with his cavalry. During the evening and early morning hours of June 30 - July 1, they crossed their artillery and wagons over the Richmond and York River Railroad Bridge, on which planks had been laid, into King William County. General Dix instructed them that there should be no pillaging and no private property taken except what could be used for military purposes. To emphasize this order, Articles of War numbers 52 and 54 must be read at the "evening parade" of each regiment. The soldiers were instructed to take five days' rations, two of which were to be cooked rations.[43]

Moving in advance of the column and on its left flank was Colonel Spear, this time with 1,200 cavalry made up of the 11th Pennsylvania and five companies of the 2nd Massachusetts. They found a small Confederate picket at King William Court House and captured two men, their horses, and a quantity of small arms. The prisoners were sent to the rear and the arms destroyed. Proceeding on to Brandywine, they captured two detectives of the Richmond Police Force. By the time they bivouacked at Taylorsville (Taylor's farm), they had taken prisoner a lieutenant, a commissary officer, and seven privates, and had destroyed six ferryboats, including the one there, and had burnt to the water's edge the 70-yard-long, well-built bridge at the Widow Nelson's.[44]

Colonel Edward D. Hall of the 46th North Carolina Infantry, serving under General John R. Cooke, was stationed near Hanover Court House and appears to have been in charge of the Confederate troops eastward into King William County. He and his men had joined Colonel Singletary at the South Anna on June 27, but then retired to the courthouse. Hall received a telegram on July 2 from Milford telling him that a large enemy force and fifteen pieces of artillery had been at Rumford the night before. He sent the information on to General Elzey and said, "I have a strong scout at Mangohick Church, which has not yet reported. Will advise you as soon as their course is determined. Two deserters came in yesterday, and report a large force under General Dix." Apparently later in the day Colonel Hall reported to Secretary Seddon that the enemy had burned Nelson's Bridge over the Pamunkey and captured a company of cavalry at Mangohick.[45]

The heat and dust on the march had been oppressive, and many Union men suffered from sunstroke and exhaustion. They left one brigade, two batteries, and some cavalry, with the sick, exhausted, and foot-sore, to guard Taylorsville and all their wagons and baggage. The expedition on July 4 moved on to Littlepage's Bridge by a narrow road that passed over high hills and proved to be difficult for the movement of artillery and troops. After crossing into Hanover, General Getty set up his headquarters at Hanover Court House. General Foster was given charge of those who continued on to the South Anna.[46]

The route that General Getty and his men used has not been definitely determined. We can be fairly certain that they used the main road (Route 633) from the "White House" crossing to their first night's bivouac near Lanesville and to their second night's encampment across the road from King William Court House. The second day they could have taken Route 629 and Route 618 to Brandywine. Colonel Spear and his men had traversed this road only a few days earlier. Recollections of the Fontaine family tell of the encampment by Getty on their place in 1863, when the soldiers, "laid waste the crops, burned the outhouses and fences, carried off and slaughtered or mutilated the horses, mules, cattle, sheep and hogs, leaving not a chick on the place." Also they broke up the furniture in the house and were about to set a fire at the doorway when they were stopped by an officer with a drawn pistol. The Reverend Fontaine was away at the time and his sons were with the army. Mrs. Fontaine and their daughters retreated to the third floor. That night two of the Negro servants took them to "Pampatike."[47]

From Brandywine, near the old Drewry home "Bellevue," it is uncertain whether the raiders would have taken Route 605 by "Chestnut Grove" and "Pleasant Green" or the old Richmond-Tappahannock stage road (Route 649, a still unpaved road by "Mt. Columbia") to "Mechanicsville," on Route 604 from Hanovertown. Either route would have taken them to Enfield and past the present Pollard home, "The Point." From there they could have travelled along Route 604, passed "Plain Dealing" and "Smyrna" before branching off on Route 614 at Corinth Fork. Route 614 would have taken them through Hickman's Gatepost (now Etna Mills) and over McDowell's Mill (now Gravatt's Mill site) to "Bleak Hill" and "Horn Quarter," both owned by George Taylor.[48]

Route 615, now slightly altered as it passes through the "Wyoming" farm, is the only presently public road the cavalry could have travelled past "Widow Nelson's" to destroy the bridge. However, there were many roads from the adjoining farms (e.g., "Farm Hill," "Difficult Hill," and "Towinque") which met at an intersection called Seven Roads, which now lies abandoned in the woodland of "Wyoming." From this crossroads Colonel Spear and his cavalry would have passed through Mrs. Nelson's yard and over Sturgeon Creek on their way to the wooden bridge, thought to have been about two hundred yards upstream from the present bridge.[49]

Their apparent route from Taylor's farm to Littlepage's Bridge (on Route 301) lay along what, except for the last few miles, are no longer public roads. My husband, Benjamin Overton Atkinson, travelled on horseback in his youth along a sandy road and through seven gates from "Horn Quarter" to Thomas Price Jackson's farm (now Camp Discovery). He said that the road was hilly and narrow, as their reports describe, and from it he could overlook the Quarters around Hanover Court House. A 1918 map shows the road as it passed Jackson's home and then entered Caroline County. The Federals could have taken a now-abandoned road that crossed Mill Creek and entered the Richmond-Alexandria stage road (Route 651) between "Mt. Gideon" and "The Grove" and from thence have gone on to cross the Pamunkey into Hanover County at Littlepage's Bridge.[50]

From Hanover Court House they would have again followed Route 646 across the railroad at Wickham's Station, passed by "Hickory Hill," near the previously destroyed Virginia Central Railroad Bridge, and then along the south bank on Route 646 to below Taylorsville, just east of U.S. Route 1. The Confederate engineer's map shows heavy fortifications extending from the north bank of the South Anna to Little River.[51]

Lieutenant Colonel Richard Nixon of the 99th New York Infantry reported that his regiment encamped at 3 p.m. on a very warm July 2 at Brandywine. Starting out at 7 a.m. the next morning, they marched all day before encamping in a cornfield on Taylor's farm at 10 p.m. On the morning of July 4 they were in the advance with the 11th Pennsylvania Cavalry and 7th Massachusetts Battery, leaving at 6 a.m., and did not arrive in the vicinity of the R.F.& P. Bridge over the South Anna until 7 p.m. On their arrival the Confederates "opened a vigorous fire of shot and shell" and continued to fire during the night. General Foster, not wanting to give away their position, did not reply but sent out two companies of the 118th New York and one of the 99th New York as skirmishers.[52]

At 10:30 p.m. another company of the 118th New York was called upon to support the earlier skirmishers. It was a moonlit night and as they moved forward their whole line was visible along the railroad. Captain Edward Riggs of that company said that the enemy retired behind its breastworks from whence the musketry fire became more vigorous and frequent. In their front, canister and shrapnel fell in showers. Cross fire of shot and shell struck around them and also passed over their heads. They were almost out of ammunition and their guns were heating up due to rapid fire. Although it was night, they were anxious to charge the breastworks. But at 2:30 a.m. the order came to fall back, firing all the while. By 1 p.m. on July 5, Captain David W. Wardrop of the 99th New York Volunteers said, they were back in bivouac on Taylor's Farm. Now that they were across the Pamunkey, Littlepage's Bridge was destroyed.[53]

General Cooke, commanding the Confederate forces at the South Anna Bridge, on July 5 reported to Richmond that three brigades of infantry, 1,500 cavalry, and three batteries of artillery had attacked at about dark on the evening before and had continued at intervals into the night along a 2½ mile line south of the South Anna. Companies of Colonels E. D. Hall's and William McRae's regiments had "repulsed them repeatedly in handsome style." Cooke reported that two pieces of artillery, one Blakely and one Napoleon, were almost out of ammunition. He requested also some Parrot cannon and some Enfield rifle ammunition. He ended his communication with the comment, "I would much prefer my two regiments to the convalescents now here, though they may do very well, if called on."[54]

Since the railroad bridge had not been destroyed at the South Anna, Major Franklin A. Stratton took two companies of the 11th Pennsylvania Cavalry in the early morning hours of July 5 to Ashland to hamper rail access from Richmond. They tore up the tracks above and below the town and burned the station and a trestle a mile below town. They destroyed railroad buildings, a warehouse, switches, platforms, three freight cars, several carloads of bridge timber, and 100 bags of salt. They carried off the telegraph equipment and cut the wire in small pieces for about 400 yards. One "dwelling house" near the depot was in danger of also going up in flames. Major Stratton reported that he impressed a "party of citizens" to protect it.[55]

The Union troops returned to the "White House" by way of the King William "Ridge Road" through Ayletts instead of Brandywine. They found this road "dryer, more level, somewhat shorter [twenty-three miles from Taylor's farm to King William Court House], and altogether a much better road than the other." The 99th New York arrived at 4 p.m., July 6, at the courthouse, after marching through hard rain that afternoon. Colonel Spear and his men, as they had led in the advance, now brought up the rear.[56]

For their return through King William along the Ridge Road to Ayletts, they would have passed through Mangohick either from Route 601 at Bleak Hill Fork to Calno and then down Route 30, or along a less desirable and now no-longer-public road from Route 601 by "Bear Garden" and across the headwaters of Mangohick Creek to Route 30 at Hebron Church. A few miles past the old Methodist chapel, they would have diverged from the more rambling route now replaced by Route 30 by either bearing left at Pollard's Corner, near the Alms House and "Cherry Hill," on Route 608 to pass "Brighton" and "Warsaw" before entering Ayletts; or they could have turned left at Turpin's Corner (Route 611) to pass the colonial Cattail Church before reaching the Richmond-Tappahannock Highway (Route 360) and travelling north to Ayletts. This may have been the time that a Union visit was made to "Cherry Hill." The hams and family valuables had been hidden under the chimney closet floor in the girls' bedroom. An appeal to the raiders' honor not to enter the ladies' room proved to be successful.[57]

A surviving undated scrap of a letter from Andrew Leftwich to Sallie Tuck was probably written about this time. He sent his regards to her sister and Lou and asked, "Oh, what has become of Old Dick? I suppose that he is frighten[ed] almost to death on account of the Yankeys — has he hid[den] his meat, corn &c tell him I would be glad to hear from him by letter."[58]

When Benny Fleet rode down to Dunkirk on July 6, he found that ten Yankees had been there the night before to check the crossing and finding no boat there they had returned to Ayletts. Benny could hear the Union drumbeat as he rode down the river on the King and Queen County side. He soon came within 50 yards of 100 men either on the shore or swimming in the river. Captain R. H. Bagby and his company were also watching them from the King and Queen side. Benny wished to shoot into their midst but Captain Bagby feared that it would cause them to do more damage in King William. The Union forces began leaving Ayletts at 9 a.m. and "were passing out until 3 in the evening going down to the White House." Aferward Benny "rode over to Ayletts & found that the Yankees had taken all the horses, mules, bacon, flour, and fowls that the people had."[59]

From their last bivouac at King William Court House, some of the Union men started out at 6:30 a.m. on July 7 and were back at the White House Landing by 1 p.m. General Getty reported that his expedition arrived back at the "White House" after having received "no annoyance from the enemy" on their way.[60]

The simultaneous expeditions to the South Anna and Bottoms Bridge had both been unsuccessful. General Dix had expressed the hope that he could control the whole countryside from the "White House" to the Rappahannock River from a base at West Point. He planned to destroy the railroad bridge there and do away with the long circuitous navigation of the Pamunkey to the "White House" by having a closer access to Richmond over a pontoon bridge at Newcastle or Hanovertown.[61] Fortunately for King William in 1863, the general's dream did not materialize.

Fred Fleet wrote from camp to his mother expressing uneasiness about affairs at home, his gratitude that the Home Guard had kept the enemy out of their county, and his anger: "What a brutal set of wretches that destroyed everything at Fontainbleau."[62] Andrew Leftwich wrote Sallie Tuck on July 31 that he had not heard from her since the "Yankey" raid through the county. He wondered whether she "caught the Yankey officer," although he felt in no mood for jesting due to their recent reverses.[63]

CHAPTER 8

The Susquehanna and Falling Waters — 1863

To follow the sons of Mangohick to and from the disastrous days at Gettysburg, one must monitor the movement of all three of the corps that made up Lee's Army of Northern Virginia. They moved to the protection of the Blue Ridge Mountains, then on to the northeast into Maryland by way of the fords of the Potomac River between Williamsport and Shepherdstown, and thence into Pennsylvania. The experiences of Colonel Aylett and the 53rd Regiment paralleled those of Pickett in the First Corps, Colonel Carter and his battalion those of Rodes in the Second Corps. Andrew Leftwich and the 22nd Battalion reflected the activities of Heth in the Third Corps. The 9th Cavalry was under General Chambliss while Rooney Lee was in prison.[1]

General Hooker's headquarters were at Fairfax. His army stretched eastward from Thoroughfare Gap in the Bull Mountains to the Potomac River at Leesburg. Starting on June 13, Hooker began to move his army northward to interpose it continuously between Lee and Washington, D.C. On June 28 his command would be turned over to General George G. Meade, who would meet Lee at Gettysburg.[2]

Aylett's men took the more westerly route through the Valley of Virginia. They would be the last of the King Wiliam men to reach Gettysburg. Carter's artillerymen preceded them and, having pressed on eastward to the Susquehanna River, which empties into the upper reaches of the Chesapeake, they had to return to Gettysburg from the northeast. Colonel Beale's cavalrymen, who had come from the environs of Washington, also approached Gettysburg from near the Susquehanna. Lieutenant Leftwich and the 22nd Battalion, having been among the last to leave the area of Fredericksburg, would be among the first to be engaged at Gettysburg.

The First Corps was at Fredericksburg on June 3; at Culpeper on June 6-9; at Brandy Station on June 12; at the Blue Ridge on June 17; at Hagerstown, Maryland, beyond Williamsport, on June 24; and at Chambersburg, Pennsylvania, west of Gettysburg, on June 28-30.[3]

On June 15 Longstreet began to move his men of the First Corps from Culpeper to pass through Ashby's and Snicker's gaps (two passes in the Blue Ridge south of Harper's Ferry). Stuart assigned the brigades of Fitz Lee, Rooney Lee (Chambliss), and Beverly H. Robertson to move in the advance and on the right of Longstreet's column. Rooney's brigade was sent to reconnoiter Thoroughfare Gap to Longstreet's right.⁴ As the 9th Cavalry moved east and then to the north, they were often in pursuit of the enemy cavalry or operating on the flank of the Federal army.

Longstreet continued along the slopes of the Blue Ridge and expected Stuart to continue on his right. Stuart told him that his instructions from Lee were to use only some of his men to cover the gaps and for the remainder to follow the movements of the Federal army. Longstreet made junction with A. P. Hill in Maryland and moved on to Chambersburg. With the absence of any news from Stuart, their only information of the enemy's movements was that brought by individual scouts and spies.⁵

Companies D and H of the 53rd Regiment started on June 15, moving with General Longstreet from Culpeper along the eastern side of the Blue Ridge in the direction of Pine Gap, then on to Snicker's Gap, where they crossed to the west of the mountains and forded the Shenandoah River.

The 53rd Regiment camped near Berryville on June 23. According to Colonel Aylett, they were there for 36 hours in a beautiful valley, awaiting the enemy. He said that he had supplied himself with a saddle taken from a Yankee. At 10 p.m. that night he added a postscript to his letter saying that they had orders to march at 3 a.m., carrying three days of cooked rations in their haversacks and "don't reckon that we will stop short of Pennsylvania. Ewell is already there." He had just received two letters from Alice and replied that she need not fear another enemy raid "for Lee will be keeping them busy near their homes." General Lee had given instructions that personal property should be respected, but the colonel said that he had "ordered several boxes of matches and expects to make the path of his regiment a smoking ruin."⁶ Considering what had been done in the Ayletts neighborhood and to his private property, the colonel's feelings are understandable. Yet there is no indication in the record that he disobeyed his commanding general.

Averaging fifteen miles a day, the 53rd crossed the Potomac River at Williamsport on June 25 and encamped near Chambersburg, Pennsylvania, on June 27. There Company D kept busy destroying the railroad bridge and serving picket duty. Its officers mustered the men for pay on June 30. They marched from there to near Gettysburg on July 2, and the additional six miles to the battlefield on the next day. Company D's records show that they arrived there a few minutes before 5 o'clock.

———

The Second Corps was at Fredericksburg on June 3; on the Rapidan on June 6; near Brandy Station on June 9; in the Valley, at Front Royal, on June 12; at Winchester and Martinsburg on June 13; at Winchester and Shepherdstown on June 17; and had crossed to Chambersburg and Greenwood, Pennsylvania, on June 24. They were at Carlisle, York, and

Wrightsville, near the Susquehanna River northeast of Gettysburg, on June 28-29; and at Heidlersberg, just north of Gettysburg, on June 30.[7]

Carter's Battery was among those of Ewell's Second Corps who had been nearby during the Battle of Brandy Station. They had left their camp at Grace Church in Caroline County on the morning of June 4. Travelling with three days' rations in their haversacks, three days' rations in their brigade train, and three more in the division commissary train, they arrived at Culpeper on June 7 and on June 10 they were at Gourd Vine Church on the Hazel River.[8]

In their march on to Pennsylvania, Carter took his battalion through the Blue Ridge at Front Royal by way of Chester Gap. Some of Ewell's men participated in the simultaneous attack on the Union forces at Winchester and Berryville. But General Rodes left this business to the other divisions and took Carter's battalion with him on north to Martinsburg. There Carter was told to find the best position for his artillery to silence an opposing battery, which he soon did. The enemy burned some of their provisions and then, in their flight to the Potomac, abandoned grain, other commissary stores, and some ammunition. The Confederates found soldiers hidden in the homes of Union sympathizers in the town. These they took as prisoners. After crossing at Williamsport, possibly on pontoons four or five miles below the town, the division bivouacked on June 22 at Greencastle, Pennsylvania, in the Cumberland Valley west of Gettysburg. According to General Rodes's report, three of his brigades were encamped on the campus of Dickinson College at Carlisle on June 27.[9]

Stuart's men were at Fredericksburg, Culpeper, and Brandy Station on June 3-13; in Middleburg and Salem, near the Bull Run Mountains, June 17-24; at Rockville, Maryland, across the Potomac above Washington, on June 28; at Westminster, Maryland, below the Pennsylvania line, on June 29; and at Hanover, Pennsylvania, below Gettysburg, on June 30.[10]

The record of Company H, 9th Virginia Cavalry, describes fully their movement toward and into Pennsylvania. On June 16 they crossed the Hazel River. On the following day they marched to Thoroughfare Gap, where for two days they were engaged as sharpshooters against the 1st Rhode Island Cavalry. Their squadron, consisting of 50 men, killed seven Union men, wounded 30, and took 147 as prisoners. Also they took three stands of colors, a regimental flag staff, valuable medicine, surgical instruments, and arms. Company H was put in charge of the prisoners at Upperville and from there a detail (including John Hill and Robert Semple Ryland, formerly of the King William Artillery) was sent with the prisoners to Winchester. Those who remained with the company moved on the next day, June 19, toward Middleburg.

Outside of Middleburg, Colonel R. L. T. Beale of their regiment was shot in the arm on June 20. He returned to lead the action on June 21. That day Captain Thomas W. Haynes of Company H was painfully wounded and had to be furloughed. Lieutenant James Pollard assumed command of the company.[11] They engaged the enemy from 10 a.m. to 5 p.m. That night they camped at Ashby's Gap and the following day they succeeded in driving the Union forces back to Middleburg. Company H remained on picket duty at Middleburg until it was ordered to join the regiment on the Warrenton Pike and to proceed eastward through Thoroughfare Gap. Then, moving by way of Buckland and Fairfax Court House, they arrived at the Potomac River three miles below Dranesville at 10 p.m. on June 27.

The cavalry had been taking by-paths since sunset and now, under the stars, the majestic river stretched before them. They were at a ford where no highway touched either side. The far bank appeared to be a quarter-mile away. As they crossed, the water came at least to their saddle skirts and at times covered their seats. By the gray light of drawn all four brigades had reached the Maryland hills overlooking the river and the Chesapeake and Ohio Canal. A couple of miles from the river they halted for food. Then they moved out at a trot through Rockville, fifteen miles west of Washington, D.C., and on down the turnpike toward Georgetown. It was a Sunday morning and the villagers appeared ready for church. Some of the ladies in their scarves and bonnets waved from the doorways.[12] Company H, soon after leaving the river, met a squadron of Federal cavalry from which one was killed, one wounded, and sixteen taken captive. Now between Rockville and Washington the company assisted in the capture of the wagons and mules of a supply train.

Colonel Beale later wrote that as they overtook the wagons they sent them back under guard to Rockville. The Virginians were almost to the District of Columbia line, and they would soon be able to see the dome of the Capitol, when they captured the quartermaster of the train. Then the forty or so men from the regiment who were still in the pursuit turned back to Rockville. The Union caravan had consisted of 175 new wagons pulled by 900 mules. Some were loaded with corn and oats, while others had "bakers' bread, crackers, whiskey in bottles of great variety, sugar, hams . . . tin and woodenware, knives and forks." They soon regretted the capture of the train. Their being in "enemy country" made it difficult to guard. Between Rockville and Westminster they were aware that they had crossed the enemy's line of march and were satisfied that the Federals were between them and Lee's infantry.[13] All night long the rangers marched, through Mechanicsville, Brookville, and Cooksville, to arrive at the Westview Station on the Western Maryland Railroad. There they encamped until daybreak of June 30. By noon of that day they were engaged in a battle at Hanover, Pennsylvania, that lasted on into the afternoon. Harmon Littlepage, from King William, was killed in action.

After the fighting was over at Hanover, the regiment continued to ride night and day, stopping only for an hour's rest in the evening. This was now nostalgic country for Colonel Beale. He had attended Dickinson College and hunted along Yellow Breeches Creek. He expected to find the Confederates at Carlisle, but they had left for Gettysburg and the town was held by Union forces.[14]

The Third Corps was at Fredericksburg on June 3-12; on the Rapidan on June 13; near Brandy Station on June 17; had crossed over to Boonsboro, Maryland, near Turner's Gap in the South Mountain, on June 24; at Fayetteville, Pennsylvania, east of Chambersburg, on June 28; at Fayetteville and Fairfield, to the south, on June 29; and at Cashtown and Greenwood, just west of Gettysburg, on June 30.[15]

A. P. Hill's instructions had been on June 16 to follow Longstreet as closely as possible and to keep his divisions in supporting distance, that his artillery and trains might "take the Sperryville Road as far as Woodville, and there turn off for Chester's Gap to Front Royal and so down the Valley." Longstreet crossed the Potomac at Williamsport while Hill was instructed to cross at Shepherdstown,[16] about ten miles downstream.

General Heth reached Cashtown on June 29 with his division of Hill's men. Cashtown lies at the base of South Mounain, on the Chambersburg Road and nine miles west of Gettysburg. While three brigades, including Colonel Brockenbrough's, remained in bivouac the next day, General J. Johnston Pettigrew took his brigade on a mission to Gettysburg to obtain much needed supplies, especially shoes for the barefooted men. On finding some Union forces, both cavalry and infantry, already there, the Confederates did not enter town, but returned to Cashtown. That evening General Hill arrived and ordered the entire division and Pegram's artillery into Gettysburg, starting at 5 a.m. the next morning, July 1.[17]

Both Lee and Hooker had crossed the Potomac on June 25, but Lee was unaware of Hooker's position until word came through the scout Harrison that Hooker was threatening Lee's line of communication through Hagerstown, Maryland. The Federal general had seven corps at his command (I, II, III, V, VI, XI and XII) — four at Frederick, Maryland, and three at Middletown, Maryland. Pleasonton and his cavalry — the divisions of John Buford, David McM. Gregg, and Judson Kilpatrick — also reported to Hooker. The general's plan to use the garrison stationed at Harper's Ferry and the XII Corps to cut Lee's supply line and to follow in the Confederate rear was rejected by Lincoln. Thereupon Hooker requested that he be relieved. His command of the armies was given to Meade.[18]

According to Jed Hotchkiss, Lee was "where the topographical conditions were all favorable for a defensive battle." He had the fertile Cumberland Valley to his back. Ewell was in the Susquehanna Valley, across from Harrisburg, where he posed a threat to Philadelphia, Baltimore, and Washington. His move down to York, Pennsylvania, directed Meade's attention to those strategic cities and his own line of communication. Lee ordered Ewell to move back in the direction of Gettysburg, by way of Heidlersburg.[19]

By the time he reached the second crest of hills west of Gettysburg on July 1, Heth could see that there was a much larger force around the town than he had expected. Besides infantry and cavalry there was also artillery. A mile from town he put two brigades in line of battle along the turnpike. Pettigrew's and Brockenbrough's men remained in reserve. When General James J. Archer and a number of his men fell into enemy hands, Heth reorganized his battle line to the right of the road with Brockenbrough's men on the left of his line. This brigade continued to push the Union forces before them, capturing two stands of colors and a number of prisoners. After breaking through the Union's first line, Heth's division was relieved by General William Dorsey Pender's, which continued the pursuit on beyond Gettysburg.[20]

Allen C. Redwood of the 55th Regiment sketched a picture of his recollection of that day's fighting and called it "Assault of Brockenbrough's Confederate Brigade (Heth's division) upon the Stone Barn of the McPherson Farm." He showed a big barn with smoke drifting from the slits as the Federals fired their rifles.[21]

With the arrival of General Ewell and the Second Corps that afternoon, the sound of the artillery under Tom Carter was added to the din of the battle. Colonel Carter reported that he placed Captain William P. Carter's Battery (the King William Artillery) and Captain Charles W. Fry's Battery on a high point north of Cashtown Turnpike to enfilade the Union lines and batteries along a small crest to the railroad cut. He said, "The batteries fired with very decided effect, compelling the [Union] infantry to take shelter in the railroad cut, and causing them to change front on their right. The enemy's guns replied slowly. Owing to the exposed position of Captain Carter's battery, which was unavoidable, it suffered much at this point, having 4 men killed outright and 7 more or less severely wounded."[22] Of these only Mordecai Kelly, who died in a Winchester hospital sixteen days later, appears to have been from King William.

Later, upon receiving word that a large force was massing on General Rodes's left front, Captain Carter's and two other batteries were moved to the foot of a high ridge to the rear of General George Doles's men to prevent the enemy from turning their left. Colonel Carter reported, "Captain Carter's battery was particularly effective in its fire at this position." As the batteries under General Jubal A. Early, Doles, and Rodes advanced, his battalion followed, with "a few pieces unlimbering from time to time to break up the formations of the enemy as they endeavored to rally under cover of the small crests near the town."[23] By the end of the day the town of Gettysburg was in the hands of the Confederates.

The 9th Cavalry arrived in Gettysburg on July 2, weary from riding and fighting. General Stuart sent word that they should remain in the saddle all night and added "that the promise was fair that Pennsylvania would on the morrow be open to our army." Colonel Beale sent word back that the request would be honored but the men and their horses needed rest and rations. They were allowed to dismount, graze their horses, feast on some captured sheep, and soon "the grassy sod supplied a couch softer to the wearied limbs than any downy bed in days of moping peace."[24]

Men from King William do not seem to have been involved in any action on July 2. The artillery under Colonel Carter remained idle in its position on the north edge of town. Heth's division remained to the west, across Willoughby Run, with Lee's reserve artillery and the ammunition trains. July 3 was a different story. Brockenbrough's men, though still nursing their wounds from the action on July 1, were committed to the attack. Colonel Brockenbrough continued in command of the brigade, but he assigned control of one-half of it to Colonel Robert M. Mayo of the 47th Virginia Regiment.[25] Two King William men of the 22nd Battalion were wounded, John Slaughter and Joseph Slaughter (not brothers).

General Heth had been incapacitated by a slight head wound on July 1. General Pettigrew, theretofore only in charge of his now much-battered North Carolinians, was put over the entire division. Another of Hill's division commanders, W. Dorsey Pender, had also been wounded and General Isaac R. Trimble was elevated to his command. These two divisions were assigned under General Longstreet to reinforce Pickett's division (consisting of the brigades of General Richard B. Garnett, James L. Kemper, and Lewis A. Armistead), who had come up from Chambersburg where they had been guarding the supply trains. The three divisions would be making a renewed attempt on July 3 to take Cemetery Hill south of Gettysburg. Colonel Aylett and his men of the 53rd Regiment would be fighting under General Armistead, a veteran of twenty-five years who had served under General Lee at Fort Riley, Kansas, in 1855.[26]

On July 3 the 9th Virginia Cavalry participated under Stuart in the midst of a cavalry battle east of Gettysburg, said to have been fiercer than the one they had experienced at Brandy Station. They entered into the fighting around Rummel's barn near Cress Ridge. Henry McClellan said: "All the Confederate regiments had been greatly reduced in numbers by the arduous services of the previous month. Some idea of this depletion may be gained from the following statement of Lieutenant G. W. Beale, of the 9th Virginia Cavalry: 'My own company [C] could muster for duty that morning only fifteen men . . . .The 9th Regiment was not more than one hundred strong, and the brigade could hardly have exceeded three hundred.' "[27]

The 3rd Pennsylvania Cavalry, one of the units against which they were contending, was also showing the strain of the campaign. One of their captains wrote: "By this time we had become a sorry-looking body of men, having been in the saddle day and night almost continuously for over three weeks, without a change of clothing or an opportunity for a general wash; moreover we were much reduced by short rations and exhaustion, and mounted on horses whose bones were plainly visible to the naked eye." Much of the fighting was by saber and pistol. One grand charge left 30 dead horses on Rummel's field. By the end of the day the Union troops had "established a skirmish line along Little's Run, by Rummel's spring-house, and along his lane toward the cross-road." The Confederates held "their line along the edge of the woods on the summit of "Cress Ridge."[28]

As Pickett's men waited to go into battle on Seminary Ridge, the chaplains came out and knelt among the boys in the front of Armistead's and Garnett's brigades. Armistead was heard to say, ". . .the issue is with the Almighty, and we must leave it in His hands." the enemy artillery was trying to reach them as they stood there. Colonel Aylett was hit by a fragment of a bursting shell.[29]

Colonel Rawley W. Martin, also of the 53rd Regiment, heard General Armistead ask of their color bearer, "Sergeant, are you going to put those colors on the enemy's works today?"

"I will try, sir, and if mortal man can do it, it shall be done."

Kemper called to Armistead to hurry, and he wanted his support to take the heights. Armistead replied, "I can do it! Look at my line: it never looked better on dress parade." And to his men he said, "Attention, Second battalion, the battalion of direction! Forward, guide center! March!" As he moved forward, he held his hat high on his sword and his white head was an easy target for bullets. Nineteen battle flags fluttered in the bright sunshine of that mid-summer afternoon.[30]

Dr. Douglas S. Freeman wrote concerning July 3, 1863: "The powerful artillery of the Third Corps was not used heavily at a time it would have been most useful. To the extent that the artillery cf the Second Corps was employed on the day of the charge, Col. Tom Carter's was the one battalion that was effective." Colonel Carter reported that he stationed ten rifled guns on the ridge overlooking the railroad cut. They were directed upon the Union batteries on Cemetery Hill to divert their fire as Pickett's and Hill's men crossed the valley.[31]

Tom Carter wrote after the war that he witnessed the charge but had too few long-range guns to be of much assistance. Over a range of about a mile he could see the line as it passed over ascending and open land, "up, up, up," until it disappeared "in the cloud of smoke left by the now silenced & captured cannon." Then he heard the Confederate cheer on the heights of Gettysburg. He considered it "an unparalleled feat of arms . . . .But alas, they were not supported."[32]

Carter's Battery sustained five casualties during the fighting on July 3: James C. Beadles was killed; John C. Longest was taken prisoner and by the end of July was dead from his wounds received at Gettysburg; Benjamin Cary Nelson received a shell wound in his knee which caused him to be assigned to the invalid corps; Corporal Thomas Catesby Jones sustained a wound in his left arm and had to have it amputated a few weeks later; and Sergeant William H. Robins was also wounded.

According to Jed Hotchkiss, it was Trimble and Pettigrew (with the 22nd Battalion) and Pickett's first line (Kemper and Garnett) that took possession of the wall and silenced the batteries. Then it was Pickett's second line, the Virginia brigade under Armistead, that followed their general up over the wall as he led them with hat still held high on his sword. But the general fell mortally wounded and his men "retired behind the stone wall, anxiously awaiting reinforcements." Someone called out "Retreat!" and many of those approaching turned to do so. Soon the Federals were upon them from all sides and "captured the 4,000 Confederates that, unsupported, were still holding the stone fences."[33]

Lieutenant James Irving Sale of Company H, 53rd Virginia, was among those taken prisoner. He wrote to his mother from Johnson's Island: "We took their Battery, broke their line of battle but didn't have the reinforcements & therefore cd [sic] not hold it."[34]

Sale told his mother that Lieutenant William H. Burruss of Company H had been wounded and died at Gettysburg on July 9 (August 15 on his official record). William Pointer and Robert Pollard, both of Company D, and Colonel Aylett also had been wounded. Lieutenants E. D. Robinson and Robert Campbell of Company D, Captain John L. Latane, and seven other officers from the 53rd Regiment were with Sale on Johnson's Island.[35] Latane was captain of Company H. Sale had received his promotion to first lieutenant on the day of the battle.

It was indeed a disastrous day for the officers and men in the three brigades that Pickett had taken into Pennsylvania. Not only had Armistead and Garnett been killed, but the wounded Kemper had been taken captive. Of the colonels who were commanding the regiments six had been killed; six wounded, as well as one major who was in charge of a regiment; leaving only one full colonel who was not incapacitated. In addition some of the lieutenant colonels had also been killed.[36]

There are several letters filed with Colonel Aylett's service records that attest to his courage and valor at Gettysburg and later at Williamsport. The surgeon who helped him from the field as he hemorrhaged from his lungs considered the colonel to be seriously if not mortally wounded and instructed him to be on his way to Williamsport with the least exertion and as quietly as possible.[37]

The 53rd Regiment sustained the loss of twenty-eight from King William. In addition to those mentioned by Lieutenant Sale, they were:

In Company B, 53rd Regiment: William Harvey Bray, whose promotion to captaincy would have been effective on July 27, was killed in action on July 3. A ball lodged in Daniel Robins' back and he was dead before the month was out.

From Company D: Captain William J. Turner was wounded so he could not return to duty until after October. During much of this time while Robinson and Campbell remained in prison, Second Lieutenant James B. Hill commanded the company. Sergeant W. A. George died in a Gettysburg hospital and John H. Siegle and James F. Wilson died in prison. James W. Sullens and Charles Bray were wounded and taken as prisoners and there is no further record of them. Sergeant John R. Lewis and Lorimer B. Robinson, both wounded, along with Lewis Littlepage, were prisoners and would later be exchanged. Henry Carneal was killed in action. Sergeant Thomas A. Lipscomb, Corporal Anderson Tuck, Corporal John F. Burch, and Selim Slaughter were among the wounded Lee must now try to get back to Virginia.

Company H sustained the following losses: Captain Latane and Lieutenant Sale remained in prison. Sergeant Marius Campbell (brother of Robert) was made a prisoner and died just two days before his scheduled release in September. Corporals W. T. Gary and George P. Tuck were made prisoners and later exchanged. Nineteen-year-old Americus Floyd was wounded and furloughed until he was again fit for duty. After his return to the regiment, his brother, William Columbus Floyd (although married and the father of three children)[38] would come from Mangohick to join the depleted ranks of the regiment. It appears that no member of Lee's Rangers from King William was a casualty at Gettysburg.

General Lee's instructions on July 4 were that the Army of Northern Virginia was to vacate its position that evening. A. P. Hill was to commence the movement, by the Fairfield Road to the pass in the mountains, after darkness had fallen. Longstreet would follow with the prisoners and Ewell would bring up the rear. General Stuart was to designate forces to precede and follow the army in its line of march. Stuart directed one or two brigades to Cashtown that afternoon, to hold it and to occupy the gorges until the army had passed and to guard the right and rear of the army in its march to Hagerstown and Williamsport. The remainder of his cavalrymen were ordered to take the route to Emmitsburg, Cavetown, and Boonsboro in order to guard the army's left and rear. Lee in the early morning hours had already assigned to General John D. Imboden, with his independent brigade of cavalry of fresh men and horses and a six-gun battery of horse artillery, the duty of taking home the wounded whom it was thought could survive the journey. Another seventeen guns were assigned to the defense of the train.[39]

Allen Redwood's sketches entitled "Goodbye," "Retreat from Gettysburg," and "Carry Me Back to Ole Virginny" depict the dismal journey home. General Imboden wrote of the difficult passage through and out of enemy territory. As they assembled the wagons and ambulances, he reported: "Shortly after noon of the 4th the very windows of heaven seemed to have opened. The rain fell in blinding sheets; the meadows were soon overflowed, and fences gave way before the raging streams." The wounded soldiers, in most cases lying on the bare boards of the wagon-bodies, were drenched. As the thousands of wagons moved into positions along the road from Gettysburg to Cashtown, the fury of the wind and water maddened and blinded the horses and mules, making them almost unmanageable. The seventeen-mile-long train moved out with orders from General Lee to push through Greencastle and then take the direct road to cross the Potomac at Williamsport. Colonel George W. Imboden (the general's brother) with the 18th Virginia Cavalry, led the advance. At the head of the train were ambulances carrying wounded generals Dorsey Pender and Alfred M. Scales, of Pender's division.[40]

The storm continued throughout the night, protecting the train from the enemy, who, in the rain, fog, mist and darkness, could not distinguish friend from foe. At dawn the next morning they were at Greencastle, 12 to 15 miles from the flooded Potomac crossing at Williamsport. The wounded were exposed now to occasional cavalry raiders and to the enmity of the local people, who chopped the spokes out of the wagon wheels. Upon their arrival at the river, they took the town of Williamsport and buried their dead. The wounded were tended by doctors brought along and the people of the town were ordered to either cook food for the wounded or have their kitchens taken over for that purpose. But the wagons could not cross the rain-swollen river, risen ten feet above fording stage. Only the walking wounded could be ferried across on the two small ferry-boats or "flats" available there.[41]

Early on the morning of the 6th, word was received of the approach of twenty-three regiments of cavalry, a force of 7,000 men and 18 guns.

General Imboden had only 2,100 men, including cavalry and mounted artillery with their batteries. By noon he had assembled 700 drivers of the wagons, armed them with the weapons of the wounded, and put them under the direction of commissaries, quartermasters, and wounded officers, including Colonel Aylett. The cavalry, artillery, and this meager force were able to hold out until Stuart's men arrived that night. Imboden later wrote: "My three regiments, with Captain John H. McNeill's Partisan Rangers and Aylett's wagoners, had to sustain a very severe contest ....The 62nd [Virginia Mounted Infantry] and Aylett, supported by the 18th Cavalry, and McNeill, charged the enemy who fell back sullenly to their horses."[42]

A letter written by General Imboden tells that Aylett, although badly wounded and suffering great pain, upon his arrival at Williamsport and finding the forces there threatened by the enemy, asked to be assigned to duty wherever he was needed. Imboden placed the colonel in what proved to be the most important position, the right flank next to the river. It was an extended line, far from the center, and Aylett had to rely on his own judgment. William Aylett must have left his sword in Pennsylvania for it turned up years later in an antique shop in that state. Now bearing a carbine (although, according to a letter written by his brother Patrick Henry Aylett, the colonel had a mutilated hand), he led his command of convalescents, wounded men, and wagoners in a critical movement that helped "defeat the efforts of Gen'l Buford and Kilpatrick with 13 regiments of Cavalry & 16 pieces of Artillery to capture and destroy vast trains of Gen'l Lee's whole army." When his own division arrived the next day, Colonel Aylett, seeing the scarcity of field officers, again reported for duty.[43]

As darkness fell on July 3, Longstreet withdrew his men to the Fairfield road. On the night of July 4 they followed Hill. Their movement was impeded by the heavy rains and bad roads, yet they reached the "top of the mountain" by early in the night of July 5. On the 6th his command passed to the front, marched on to Hagerstown, and arrived there at 5 p.m. Then they moved down the Sharpsburg road to encamp two miles from Hagerstown. They had now arrived in the vicinity of Williamsport and in time to relieve the pressure on the trains there.[44]

The records of Companies D and H of the 53rd Regiment show that they took charge of 4,900 prisoners. As they covered the 25 miles to Williamsport, they would march nine or ten miles, rest a few hours and then move on, passing through the Fairfield Gap of South Mountain, Waynesboro, and Hagerstown.

Rodes's division fell back toward Hagerstown on July 4. At Waterloo Bridge, Maryland, on July 5 five of Carter's Battery were taken prisoner:

111

Robert S. Beadles, James Hillard, W. A. Prince, Benjamin H. Beadles, and Richard T. Redford. On July 6 members of Rodes's division became the rear guard for Lee's army and were attacked as they moved along the Emmitsburg Road.[45]

Andrew Leftwich, with Heth's division of the Third Corps in it's retreat from Gettysburg, wrote a letter from Hagerstown on July 8 stating that they had been in trenches or fighting for the last 32 days with only two days rest, from Fredericksburg and Berryville to Maryland and Pennsylvania. In his next letter, dated July 31 at Culpeper Court House, he was still writing that they had been in skirmishes most of the time. He said that he had been in the battle on July 1 and 3 at Gettysburg. One man was shot in his front, shielding him from the shot. He declared that 100 balls had been shot at him alone and not one had touched him.[46]

The 9th Virginia Cavalry during these days of withdrawal helped shield Lee's army on its left. Whenever the services of Company H are noted they were being used dismounted. As the regiment passed along a narrow road from Emmitsburg and through the Catoctin Mountains, Lee's Rangers, under the direction of Lieutenant Pollard, served as the advance guard. At Hagerstown, the company used its carbines in "the enclosed space about the market-house" against the charging of Kilpatrick's cavalry until mounted cavalry could drive the Union men into an open field. By the time the skirmishers reached the edge of town, the main street was secure and Chambliss's cavalry moved down the macadamized pike in the direction of Williamsport, six miles away. After the regiment retraced its steps back through Hagerstown and Funkstown, it engaged Buford's and Kilpatrick's men for two days on the road from Boonsboro. Again Companies G and H, this time under the direction of Lieutenant Nick Davis of Lunenburg County, "were acting as foot skirmishers."[47] Braxton Seldon and Pulaski Sutton were taken captive. Seldon had been wounded, and in a few weeks he would die in prison.

Meade sent the I Corps (whose general, John F. Reynolds, had been killed in the first day's fighting) and the VI Corps, under General John Sedgwick, to press Lee to the mountains. Martin McMahon, chief of staff of the VI Corps, said, "Every house and barn along our route of march was filled with wounded Confederates." The main body of the Army of the Potomac assembled around Emmitsburg and passed through the Catoctin Mountains at Hamburg. By the 10th they came upon some of the Confederates along Beaver Creek, which flows into the Antietam. Both armies were on familiar territory, having fought in this area the previous year. It appeared that Lee might be preparing to make a stand. His position was a strong one. On July 13 his forces stretched from the Conococheague Creek to the Potomac at Downsville. Stuart was on the left, then Ewell, Hill in the center, with Longstreet and more of Stuart's cavalry on the right. Meade's forces faced them along Antietam Creek, except for Buford's cavalry which was near South Mountain.[46]

The building of pontoon bridges were going too slowly for the Confederates, so joist beams were pulled from warehouses along the canal, boats built and then floated on the flood current down the river for a bridge at Falling Waters. The rain continued to fall. General Lee, while conferring with General Imboden at Hagerstown about all the likely fords across the upper Potomac, asked the general, "You know this country well enough to tell me whether it ever quits raining about here? If so I should like to see a clear day soon."[49]

Longstreet's men had begun to entrench on July 12 when word was received that the pontoon bridge was ready. His command led in the crossing as soon as it was dark. Fires had been lit to mark the road and signal torches to delineate the bridge. Another heavy rainstorm had flooded the roadway. One wagon with wounded men ran off the bridge and a few of the men were rescued from the water. For the next two hours the engineers were busy repairing the bridge. By 9 a.m. the rear of Longstreet's command had crossed and was back in Virginia at Hanesville.[50]

Company H, 53rd Virginia, first remained at Williamsport then marched to two miles east of Martinsburg and crossed the Potomac back into Virginia. Preston Crow of Company H was taken prisoner at Falling Waters.

Heth had recovered enough from his wound of July 1 to not only bring his own men out but to serve as a rearguard as other divisions crossed the river. During the skirmish at Falling Waters, General Pettigrew, who had led Heth's men in the charge on July 3 and had been one of the last to leave the field, received a stomach wound which would prove to be fatal.[51]

General Heth reported that on July 13, after receiving word that the pontoons had been constructed at Falling Waters, they withdrew at dark from the entrenchments near Hagerstown. The night was totally dark and they marched ankle deep in mud, sometimes halting to allow the wagons and artillery in their front to pass on. It took twelve hours for them to cover seven miles. Then with only a mile and a half to go to Falling Waters, General Hill placed them in line of battle and they were soon charged by a few of Kilpatrick's cavalry. Brockenbrough's men were stationed on the right of the road, where they were attacked by dismounted cavalry. First they were able to push the attackers into the woods, but when they were forced to fall back Brockenbrough deployed them as skirmishers. When more of the enemy appeared on Heth's left and front, General Hill ordered them to withdraw as speedily as possible across the river.[52]

When they were engaged at "fallen waters," Andrew Leftwich wrote home, their captain and lieutenant were taken prisoner and he was put in charge of the company. He commented, "Life is but a bubble that is liable to disappear at any time." He prayed, "May the Lord deliver me from Yankey cavalry in the future, especially when I have marched all night in the snow [sic] and rain."[53] The company record shows that at Falling Waters Lieutenant James E. Johnson and John H. Beadles were declared missing, but later appeared on the roll of the Old Capitol Prison, Washington, D.C.; Ira Huckstep and John H. Atkins were taken captive and would both die and be buried at the prison; and Reuben Gardner would be paroled from a Baltimore hospital in September.

Colonel Carter reported, "My whole battalion took position at Falling Waters, to cover the crossing on the pontoon bridge. A few rounds were fired at the enemy's line of sharpshooters as they attempted to press our skirmishers approaching the bridge. The pursuit was checked without further difficulty."[54]

Those of the Second Corps who remained at Williamsport waded across the river after dark. There was just enough light on either shore to mark their entrance into and exit from the murky water. It was still raining and the banks were steep. Many men lost their shoes as they slid down the banks. The water was still up to the armpits of average-sized men, so the taller ones carried the shorter ones across. Each man had his cartridge box swung around his neck. Yet all remained in good spirits and crossed with cheers and laughter. Not a man was lost, but as much as 30,000 rounds of ammunition slipped into the swirling water.[55]

The waters of the Potomac had receded somewhat when the jaded men of the 9th Virginia forded the river at Williamsport, but it still came up to the horses' backs. It was raining that day, like it had been for the past two weeks, in hard and almost constant showers. This did not overly concern them, their colonel said, for they "had not been dryly clad for fourteen days."[56] If not as footsore as their neighbors in the infantry, they were no less battle weary, a weariness extending back several months to their stands against Stoneman between Gordonsville and Richmond in May.

The plight of the Federal prisoners has been described by John L. Collins, a member of the 8th Pennsylvania Cavalry of Gregg's division. While taking part in an attack on the Confederate train in Pennsylvania, near Monterey, his horse was injured. Separated from his regiment, Collins was captured while he was washing and examining his horse's shoulder. He was put under the guard of a young cavalryman from King and Queen County, a fellow about his own age. Later in the day, as the prisoner watched his own regiment being fired upon by sharpshooters from across a cornfield, he recalled that "a quiet, pleasant-faced man, as

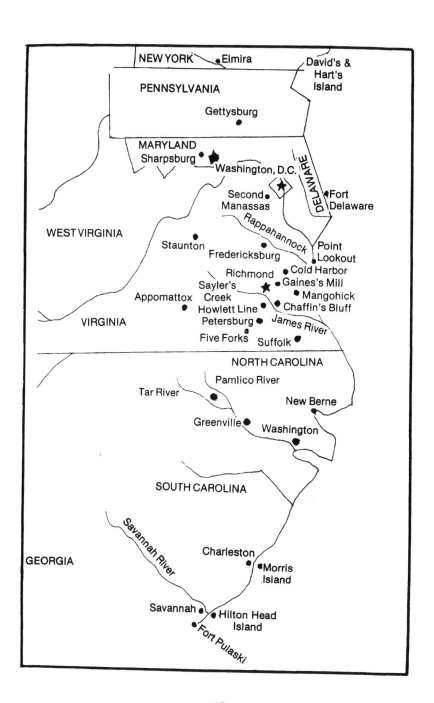

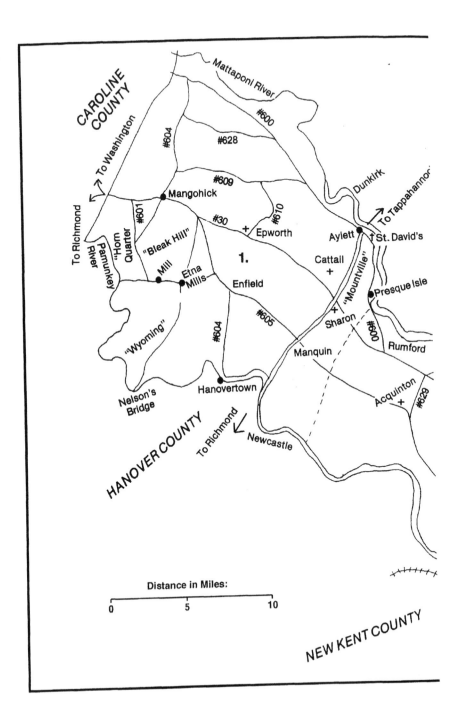

Map of
King William County, Va.

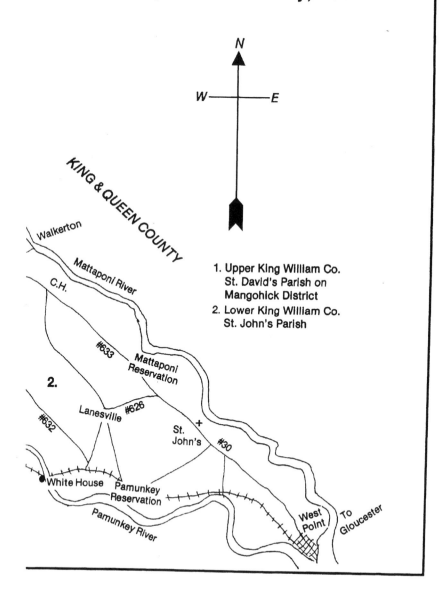

N

W —— E

KING & QUEEN COUNTY

Walkerton

Mattaponi River

C.H.

#633

Mattaponi Reservation

2.

Lanesville #626

#632

St. John's

#30

White House

Pamunkey Reservation

Pamunkey River

West Point

To Gloucester

1. Upper King William Co.
   St. David's Parish on
   Mangohick District
2. Lower King William Co.
   St. John's Parish

Sallie Tuck Leftwich

Captain William G. Pollard

Atwell T. Mooklar

Richard T. Leftwich

Colonel William R. Aylett, a painting

Lieutenant Andrew J. Leftwich

Captain Thomas W. Haynes

Reverend Patrick Henry Fontaine

Patrick Henry Aylett

Colonel Thomas H. Carter

Colonel Harrison B. Tomlin

Major Beverley B. Douglas

Archibald, Almar, and William Samuel, a painting by Teressa A. Pearson

Alice Brockerburgh Aylett

Bethel M. E. Church

Pontoon Boats and Wagons

Mangohick Church, 1864, a drawing by Teressa A. Pearson

123

Courtesy: Library of Congress

Gunboat on the Pamunkey

Courtesy: Library of Congress

Pontoon bridge on the Pamunkey River at Mrs. Nelson's

"Horn Quarter", 1932

"Montville", 1932

125

Courtesy: Virginia State Library and Archives

"Bleak Hill", 1932

Courtesy: Virginia State Library and Archives

"Fontainebleau," ca. 1865-1933

King William County Courthouse, 1990

Hebron Baptist Church, 1990

127

were many of the others, noticed my dejected look, came to me, and, swinging himself from his saddle to a fence-rail, took a Testament from his pocket, and asked me if I objected to his reading a chapter aloud. I thankfully asked him to do so, as I had not had heart enough to read my own that day."[57]

Collins was among the prisoners who were turned over to Pickett's men and escorted to Williamsport, where they were sent across the swollen river by a "rope ferry" and on "flat-boats." From there Imboden and his men conducted them to Staunton and arranged for them to be carried by "box, or gravel cars" to Richmond. The young Pennsylvanian's boots had given out early in their trek. With sore feet and a diet consisting of "about a pint of flour every other day," which the men mixed with water and drank as a paste saying "It stuck to their ribs longer that way," and "now and then a piece of rusty flitch [side bacon]," Collins' strength gave out. He became temporarily blind and despaired for his life.[58] The news got to King William by July 21 that the remnant of Pickett's men would be returning with the prisoners.[59]

CHAPTER 9

The Rapidan, Neuse, Stono, and Mattaponi — 1863-64

In the fall and winter of 1863 and the early months of 1864, men from King William would be scattered from camps along the Rapidan and near Charlottesville to the Neuse River in North Carolina and the Stono River in South Carolina. Others would be in Tennessee or on picket duty along the Mattaponi and the James.

Lee began taking his army back to its supply lines in Virginia and away from the rain-swollen Potomac basin, where high water had closed down the mills along tributary streams, making flour in short supply. They stopped for rest at Bunker Hill and Darkesville, West Virginia. The main body of Meade's forces had not followed, except for some of his cavalry who crossed the Potomac at Harper's Ferry on July 16 and proceeded toward Martinsburg.[1]

Upon learning of the cavalry advance, Stuart sent Fitz Lee's men and Lee's Rangers along the Martinsburg road to meet the enemy. They drove the Union men to within a mile of Shepherdstown. There the terrain was not suitable for cavalry operations and they fought dismounted. The Federals, having placed themselves behind stone fences and barricades, withdrew when darkness fell.[2]

Colonel Beale wrote that he was "sick and broken down" and the major had to take over his command. They were involved in the heavy skirmishing near Shepherdstown. The 9th Cavalry was able to find a "blind ford" across the Shenandoah River and a path through the Blue Ridge Mountains to the left of the enemy who were beginning to range along the slopes. The cavalrymen passed through Rappahannock County to first take up picket duty at Gourd Vine Church and then to move back to their old camp on John Minor Botts's farm, near Brandy Station. Now the exhausted colonel could take his ten-day leave of absence.[3]

Stuart received word on the evening of September 12 that the enemy cavalry would be crossing Kelly's Ford and other fords of the Rappahannock. His cavalry regiments were strung from Brandy Station to Culpeper Court House. There was just time enough to remove the disabled horses and supply wagons. The large force of Union cavalry caused Stuart's men to retire toward Rapidan Station. By daybreak of September 14 the Union advance was at the Rapidan River.[4]

In the action a bullet lodged in Colonel Beale's leg. He was taken to

Orange Court House, where the bullet was removed, and then he was sent to the care of his sister in Charlottesville and eventually to his home. The injury was painful and complications arose. It was Christmas before the colonel resumed his command. In the meantime, according to Beale, "...the movements of the regiment were carefully noted and recorded for him by another hand."[5]

Lee had chosen to bring his men back into the heart of Virginia by way of the Valley, then across the Shenandoah and through the mountain passes to their old camps in Madison, Culpeper, and Orange counties and their patrol stations along the Rapidan.

Longstreet brought the First Corps (including the now much dimished ranks of Pickett's men and the 53rd Regiment) by way of Front Royal, across the Shenandoah, through Chester Gap in the Blue Ridge, to camps in Culpeper. A. P. Hill followed with the Third Corps (and the less battered 22nd Battalion). Ewell, with the Second Corps (and Carter's artillerymen), arrived in Orange a week later. They had come by way of Thornton Gap, near Luray. All three corps joined for a line along the Rapidan. General Meade faced them across the Rappahannock with his headquarters near Warrenton.[6]

The report of Company D, 53rd Regiment, signed by James B. Hill, second lieutenant, and the unsigned report of Company H show that from Falling Waters they moved up the Valley through Bunker Hill and Millwood to Front Royal and through the mountains there. Some of the men of the 53rd must have been left to guard the Manassas Pass through the Blue Ridge for Patrick Tuck was captured there on July 31. Company D returned to its camp on the Stearns farm, four miles from the Rapidan, while Company H camped at Rapidan Station. During August they were at Somerville Ford in Orange County and it was there they were mustered for pay at the end of the month. Colonel Aylett may have remained a few weeks at Williamsport to rest from his injuries. He filed a requisition for stationery from there at the end of July.

There remains only an undated page four of a letter written by William Aylett during the summer following Gettysburg. He told Alice that he had gotten over his dysentery, "but have been attacked with Rheumatism in my back produced by exposure & exhausting effects of my previous complaint. I can walk about & have a pretty good appetite, but my back is pretty painful." He reminded her, "You had two brothers & a husband in those fights [at Gettysburg] & have lost but one loved one. How many there are who have lost all!"[7]

During at least part of this time Alice Aylett did not know where her husband was. She wondered if he had rejoined his regiment in Culpeper

130

and why he had not been sent home. She wrote that Cousin Henrietta (Mrs. Nelson) had offered to keep the children should she go to be with him. The "Montville" horses had been taken, leaving only four mules and a young bay horse with a sore back, which had been found on the place apparently after being "turned out to die." The enemy was no longer in the area on July 21.[8]

Neighbors were leaving the Ayletts neighborhood for safer localities. Alice would have liked to go too, but felt if she did what little they had left would be destroyed. She had had no success in getting anyone to stay with her. The Negro farm workers left voluntarily before they "saw the Yankees." John, a house servant, had gone to New Kent to visit his family but found that his "wife had gone to the Yankees, taking [their] children & all his property." Alice wrote that John took it very well and was already on the "grapevine" (courting). She was distressed at what had happened at "Fontainebleau" and said that Pat Fontaine expected to join the 53rd as chaplain, although the family opposed it because of his health."[9]

Colonel Aylett's wife wrote that her meat was still safe in their garret and that she had been making blackberry wine. "Brother Henry" (Patrick Henry Aylett) had gotten a large furniture wagon to bring supplies from Richmond to "Montville." Earlier she wrote that the stage was not running but a wagon was passing by. At that time her sister, Etta, was waiting for a conveyance so she could go to the "springs." Alice wrote that William must not send her the horses because it would not be safe. She closed her letter with the comment that it was sad for him to have children and not to know them. A few days later she wrote about her fear that he was not gaining his strength back due to the shock and loss of blood and that he was "not strong at best." He must not worry about his law books. They were safe in the cellar at "Wyoming," having been packed up and moved before the enemy's last visit there.[10]

On August 11 General Pickett wrote to William Aylett that he was recommending that, now that General Armistead was dead, Aylett should be given command of the brigade. A note signed by R. E. Lee and filed with the colonel's records, however, shows that, from August 12 to September 8, Lee did not give credence to the report that the general had died. By Aylett's account he did command the brigade for "three months after Gettysburg [through] New Bern [North Carolina] and various other places."[11]

Lieutenant James Hill of Company D, 53rd Regiment, ordered pants, shoes, drawers, a cap, jackets, and socks during July and August. Before moving south in September, he ordered a fly tent, camp kettles, and one skillet and lid. Apparently for his own paper work he requested four quires of letter paper, four pens, fifteen envelopes, and one "Blk bk" (blank book). The 53rd Regiment was not a among those Lee kept along the

Rapidan. Both Companies D and H broke camp in Orange for their march to Richmond. Company D left on September 8, but Company H had already started promptly at 7 a.m. on September 7. At Richmond on September 15 they took "the cars" for Petersburg and encamped about a mile from town.

The removal of Longstreet's and Pickett's men from the Rapidan was the result of several conferences between Lee and President Davis in Richmond. Knoxville had fallen and Longstreet was to be of temporary assistance to General Braxton Bragg and his Army of Tennessee. Lee wrote to the President from Orange Court House that Longstreet's troops were on the march to Richmond. Lee said, "Pickett's division wants many officers, owing to the numbers wounded and captured, which cannot now be replaced." According to the quartermaster general, they would be the last to be moved. Longstreet suggested that Pickett's men be kept around Richmond, but Lee would leave that to the President's discretion.[12]

General Henry Harrison Walker, an 1853 graduate of West Point, was given charge of Field's brigade in July 1863. While lieutenant-colonel of the 40th Regiment, he had been twice wounded at Gaines' Mill. Now he was brought from command of a convalescent camp to be head of his old brigade.[13]

The 22nd Battalion remained on familiar territory, on the Rapidan and along the Orange and Alexandria Railroad, near Orange Court House. Andrew Leftwich's July 31 letter was from Culpeper. He instructed Sallie Tuck to direct her letters to Walker's brigade, Heth's Division. She wrote that she was going to "singing school" and Andrew answered that he hoped she would teach him some "new Sunday School hymns" if he ever got home. In September he wrote to her from a camp near Rapidan Station, where they were watching the enemy cavalry across the river. He had heard that Sallie was taking dancing lessons and had been to a watermelon feast at his father's place.[14]

Other letters which Leftwich wrote during August and September tell of the religious "meetings" being held in all the corps and that three preachers could be heard at one time. Twenty-nine men had "professed religion." He commented on the fact that the Dover Baptist Association would be meeting at Beulah Church and a "protracted meeting" was being planned for the 3rd Sunday in October at Hebron. Sallie had mailed her letter to him at Hanover Court House. In order to get mail through to her he sometimes addressed his letters to Mangohick, other times to Ayletts or Enfield post offices. He assured her that he was destroying all letters from her before going into battle.[15]

Carter's Battery was at Liberty Mills in Madison County at the end of August. From there Colonel Carter ordered 12-pound shot, shells, caps, and friction primers.

The artillery had greatly improved its efficiency since its reorganization in May 1863. About September 1863, Colonel Armistead L. Long, of Lee's staff, was made a brigadier general in the Second Corps and given the responsibility for its artillery. His book, *Memoirs of Robert E. Lee,* assembled after Lee's death, is a valuable resource on the role of the artillery from this point.[16]

The roster of Carter's Battery shows that its men were engaged at Somerville Ford on the Rapidan River in Orange County on September 14. There five King William men were wounded: James W. Allen, William H. Butler, Obediah R. Ellett, Benjamin F. Davis, and James Nelson Eubank. Davis would die from his wounds; Allen would have his leg amputated; and Eubank would be sent on to a Richmond hospital.

As the leaves began to turn on the rolling hills of Orange County, Colonel Carter was making every effort to clothe, shelter, and supply his battalion. His requisitions show their needs: for shelter — wall, fly, and hospital tents; a Confederate flag; for clothing — jackets, pants, woolen shirts, drawers, and socks; for cover — blankets; for supplies — skillets, camp kettles, and water buckets; and for transport — artillery horses. Carter also requested poles, primers, halters, forges, curry combs, harness oil, bridles, linch pins, axle grease, priming wires, knapsacks, collars, harness, lamp black, lard for greasing handles, pick axes and handles, sheepskin, and a spare wheel. Captain William P. Carter's men had need for "five artillery arms" and one bridle to replace those which had been "commandeered."

General Meade and his Federals were encamped north of Culpeper Court House. General Lee's plans in October 1863 were to use the Second Corps under General Ewell (and possibly Carter's Battery), the Third Corps under General A. P. Hill with General Heth and Walker (directing the 22nd Battalion), and Stuart's and Fitz Lee's cavalry to push Meade toward his Manassas base and the Washington defenses and possibly to intercept his retreat. General Hill took his troops by a circuitous route from Culpeper Court House to Warrenton. Upon arriving at Bristoe Station he thought he could successfully attack and would soon be relieved by the Second Corps. But there were additional Federals hidden behind a railroad cut. The divisions lost 1,300 men in a few minutes. By the time the Second Corps arrived, the battle was over and it was growing dark. Walker's men, who formed Hill's rear guard, had moved to the left flank and crossed Broad Run before they realized their fellows were in trouble. They recrossed the run and made an unsuccessful attempt to recover the lost artillery of General John R. Cooke's brigade. Walker's losses were less than the other brigades.[17]

Fitz Lee's division (including Rooney Lee's men) and two brigades of Infantry remained at Raccoon Ford on the Rapidan to hold Lee's former line. The day after Lee left, as reported by Fitz Lee, General Buford with his cavalry from the Stevensburg area crossed the river to his right. Fitz Lee attacked with his cavalry and drove them back across the Rapidan to Stevensburg. He expected that they would do battle at Brandy Station, but upon pausing there he found that Buford had moved on to the Rappahannock.[18]

During this drive Captain William B. Newton of "Summer Hill," near Hanover Court House, and the 4th Virginia Cavalry, was leading his regiment and was killed by a wound to his head. Fitz Lee eulogized him as "an officer of extraordinary merit and promise" and Lieutenant G. W. Beale of the 9th Virginia said that that night, in their camp at Brandy Station, the men wept openly over Newton's death.[19]

After the fight at Bristoe Station, General Warren massed his corps of Federals in the vicinity of Centreville and awaited further attack. Lee's main army went no farther, but Stuart continued the pursuit and made contact on Bull Run at Manassas, Groveton, and Frying Pan Church.[20] Captain Haynes, of Lee's Rangers, commanded a line of skirmishers on October 15 at Manassas. The lines were too long for him to command on foot. According to Colonel Beale: ". . .as he [Haynes] rode on horseback from point to point encouraging his men and directing their fire, he became a target for hundreds of rifles. He presently fell, pierced by a bullet which, passing near the spine, paralyzed his lower limbs." It was thought that the captain was mortally wounded. His men took Haynes to rest in the brick house which Beauregard had used for his headquarters during the first Battle of Manassas. Beloved by all in the regiment, Haynes was visited that night by many with tears in their eyes.[21]

The captain did not die but was disabled for life. Robert Semple Ryland of Mangohick was put on detached duty for the next twelve months to serve as Haynes's nurse. In March 1865, after spending many months in the hospitals, Captain Haynes was assigned to the Invalid Corps. Philip Lipscomb of Company F was also wounded near Manassas.

Lee's Rangers continued on the move that fall and winter. Their records and the requisitions of James Pollard, their lieutenant from New Kent (who was called "Cousin Jim" by his King William relatives), show that the cavalrymen during October and November 1863 were at Peyton Ford, Martin's Ford, and Barnett's Ford. Rooney Lee remained in prison. He would not be exchanged so he could join Stuart in Orange until nearly springtime.

Andrew Leftwich's letter of October 20 was addressed from Rappahannock Station. He wrote that the army had begun to move out but his brigade had been left to guard the "Yankeys" and to tear up and burn the rails to Bristoe Station. He was commanding the company since his fellow officers had been taken prisoner.[22] From July 1863 through April 1864, Leftwich filed the reports and requisitions for the battalion. Except for August, when he listed two subalterns (commissioned officers in the company), he showed one subaltern and from eighteen to twenty-four noncommissioned men and privates. They had need for pants, jackets, one overcoat, caps, shirts, canvas shoes and leather shoes, blankets, four axes, one tent, and a skillet with a lid. Andrew needed for his reports and correspondence note paper, foolscap, letter quality paper, and one blank book.

During that winter and early spring, Andrew Leftwich's letters to Sallie Tuck began to sound notes of sadness and despondency. His mood was not brightened with a visit to their camp by Edward Eubank, a Mangohick neighbor, who brought news of Sallie having a good time dancing. He wrote Sallie to have her "likeness taken" in Richmond because the one he had had been defaced with use and was not a good likeness. He also wrote her that no officers were getting furloughs at that time, but he hoped to get one soon.[23]

After Christmas Lieutenant Leftwich's letters were addressed either from Mt. Jackson, Shenandoah County, or from a camp near Harrisonburg. He was expecting to be moved down the Valley and considered himself no longer with "Lee's Army," his unit having been sent to assist General Early. He wrote to Sallie while sitting on the ground and writing on his knee. He said that he was in fine health, weighed 156 pounds, and sent his regards to "Sue, Lou, Charles, and Belle." By February Leftwich's unit had made a "flying trip" down the Valley to Mt. Jackson to guard the pike and the gap in the mountains. He had attended Baptist, Episcopal, Dunkard, and Lutheran churches since he last saw her. He still had hopes of a furlough.[24]

The confrontations along the Rapidan River and near Culpeper had resulted in no particular advantage gained by either side. Kilpatrick's cavalry and Stuart's cavalry proceeded to heckle each other. After the alignment on Mine Run (General Warren, William H. French, and Sedgwick facing Ewell and A. P. Hill in late November), the season ended with Meade's withdrawal across the Rapidan. Although the Second Corps artillery settled for the winter at Frederick's Hall (in Louisa County on the Virginia Central Railroad above Beaver Dam Station), its infantry remained on or near the Rapidan, above Mine Run.[25]

From their winter quarters at Frederick's Hall, Carter's Battery requested leather, shoe thread, additional shoes, jackets, and drawers. William E. Hart signed as commanding officer and inspecting officer of the battery.

A First Corps artillerist described the winter camps. He told how each group of four tentmates built a ten-foot-square enclosure. They dug into the earth for three or four feet and built up three sides another three feet with logs chinked with mud. The fourth side was made up of a mud-lined log chimney and a blanket covered the doorway. A tent fly, held up by a pole and fastened to the log sides, served as the roof. They slept on cedar-bough bunks. A ditch dug around the outside of the walls kept the rain from draining into this sunken enclosure. Similar but larger buildings were constructed as stables for the horses. On those one side was left open to the sun and the roof was made of large slabs held down by heavier logs.[26]

In December each regiment in Rooney Lee's brigade was issued a distinguishing emblem. That of the 9th Virginia was in shape of a star and bore the inscription (in cursive writing) "Co. __ 9th Va. Cavalry." Most of the men wore the emblem attached to the front of their hats or caps.[27] Some of the cavalrymen were allowed to go home for fresh horses. After Christmas Chambliss took Rooney Lee's men from their camp above Charlottesville into West Virginia on a search for Averell's Union cavalry. It was cold and there was already snow on the ground when the rain began to fall heavily, swelling the streams and turning the roads into sheets of ice. On the way back many of the men had to dismount and lead their weary and poorly shod horses down the mountain slopes and along the slippery roads. Colonel Beale, now back from his convalescence, watched as the men, "ragged, frost-bitten, and worn out, returned limping into camp in squads."[28]

At year's end they were at Ivy Depot on the Virginia Central Railroad near Charlottesville. There were forty-five men and two officers with the company. In a later report, after more limped into camp, there were sixty-four men and three officers present.

On January 25, 1864, the 9th Cavalry was dispatched to Centre Cross, Middlesex County, and from there Lieutenant Pollard and Company H were detached for picket duty from West Point to Urbanna.[29] By the end of February Pollard, from the detachment in King William, had ordered pants, shirts, drawers, overcoats, caps, shoes, blankets, cords of wood, and an axe for the men; and saddles, bridles, stirrups and straps, and grain sacks for their horses.

———

Some men from King William were sent south with General Wise to assist Beauregard in the defense of Charleston, S.C. Two Gresham brothers, John, age 22, and Richard, age 18, and James H. Eubank and James R. Reid, both age 19, were members of the 4th Virginia Regiment Heavy Artillery (later the 34th Infantry) under Major John R. Bagby. With them also went Fred Fleet and members of the 26th Infantry. Fred wrote that from engaging gunboats, even one ironclad, on the James in August 1863, they were sent to guard "Charleston in the rear." Both regiments were located at Camp Wappoo, four miles from Charleston. (Wappoo Creek runs into the Stono River to the southeast of the city.) The brigade was used to defend the islands, James and John, which lay between the city and Federal installations on Morris and Folly islands, in the Atlantic Ocean. During December Benny Fleet visited them after delivering his wheat to Richmond.[30]

General Longstreet, after being sent to assist Bragg at Chattanooga, was dispatched by Bragg to try to capture Burnside at Union-held Knoxville. Those of Pickett's division who had not been with him at Gettysburg (Corse's brigade with the 30th Regiment) were sent into Tennessee, although they are not listed among the opposing forces of the unsuccessful Knoxville Campaign that winter.[31] Almar Samuel, of upper Caroline County and later of Mangohick, served as a courier in Tennessee. A diarist from Mangohick wrote, "It looks like they don't know exactly what to do out here since Bragg's defeat. We keep marching backwards and forwards."[32]

While in Tennessee the troops often encamped for less than one week at any one place and then only under the shelter of their small fly tents. The weather was terribly cold and their food so scarce that they were often on half rations. There was "a little fight this side [east] of Knoxville" in early December. With the beginning of February, they were again on the rails to join their fellows in the Kinston — New Berne area. There they remained, often shelled by gunboats on the river, until taken back to Virginia to assist General Pierre G. T. Beauregard in the defense of Drewry's Bluff.[33]

On October 6 Companies D and H of the 53rd Regiment were sent by rail 130 miles from Richmond to Kinston, North Carolina, arriving at night. They marched three miles to an encampment on Dunn's farm, where they were mustered for pay at the end of the month. James B. Hill, 2nd lieutenant, was still in command of Company D.

In November Alice Aylett had gone to Tappahannock or the Northern Neck to visit some of her relatives and stay at "The Cottage." She was enjoying the oysters and fish and busy making shoes out of black cloth. There was the promise of a new felt hat for her husband at a cost of $40 to $45. In recent days she had received two letters from him, one from Petersburg and one from Garysburg, North Carolina. She wrote that Tina (probably a cousin) said that he must come for a visit since they had a big swamp he could hide in. Colonel Aylett's letter to his wife from Petersburg on December 11, 1863, told that they would be leaving there within the hour for Kinston, North Carolina. As soon as they arrived he would put in an application for a furlough.[34]

During November and December the 53rd Regiment was often on the move, being shuttled between Kinston, North Carolina, and Hanover Junction, Virginia, and passing through Petersburg and Richmond. At the end of December they were "comfortably quartered" in Kinston, according to the Company D record.

Kinston is about twenty miles from New Berne, at that time a fortified town at the junction of the Neuse and Trent rivers, thirty miles off of Pamlico Sound. New Berne had been captured by General Burnside in March 1862.[35] By January 1864, Lee was writing to President Davis, "The time is at hand when if an attempt can be made to capture the enemy's forces at New Berne it should be done." Lee could spare men from his forces at that time better than in the spring. Already, or so he had been informed, General Seth Maxwell Barton's brigade (formerly Armistead's) was in the area in sufficient number should a secret attack be made.[36]

Barton, the new brigadier over the 53rd Regiment, was a native of Fredericksburg and an 1849 graduate of West Point. He had taken part in the siege of Vicksburg and was taken prisoner on July 4, 1863, but soon thereafter exchanged.[37]

Colonel Aylett wrote to his wife on February 5, 1864, that they were back in Kinston from the New Berne exposition. On February 12 he wrote that they would leave the next day for Richmond, but might stop in Petersburg. The colonel's letter of February 17, after a "worrying trip from Kinston," shows that they were encamped on the Nine Mile Road, near the Richmond and York River Railroad and three miles from Richmond. It was intensely cold and already he had built a chimney to his tent. There was a possibility that he might be able to get a room for her in the home of a Dr. Friend, who had married a Miss Johnson from King William. Alice would have to leave the children with someone. Bob (Aylett's orderly) left camp on February 26 to bring Alice back to stay at Dr. Friend's house.[38]

There is a scrap of a letter that begins to tell about the controversy concerning General Barton's decisions at New Berne. In succeeding letters Aylett expressed his feeling that Barton was right in not attacking because of the enemy's superior strength. William wrote that he had "climbed a tree on the very advanced skirmish line & made reconnaisance."[39]

Alice had started back home when William wrote on March 14 that everything was quiet at present. He said that Lee, Longstreet, and "other notables" were in Richmond concerning something "hatching to be executed *somewhere*." A few days later Aylett wrote that he had heard she had gotten home all right through William Edwards, at whose home Bob's wife lived. The colonel said that he had finished deposing in General Barton's case.[40]

The regimental roster shows that they were being supplied with new men. John T. Floyd, Eugene V. Clements, Otway Pollard, and William H. Wright passed through Camp Lee (located on the present site of the Virginia Science Museum) in Richmond to join the ranks of the 53rd. George Hargrove had joined the first of the year in Kinston and Sterling S. Thornton, who had previously served with the regiment in 1861-62. reenlisted in King William on the last day of April.

Andrew C. Blake was commissioned 2nd lieutenant of Company H in April and given the responsibility for the new members of that company. From Chester he filed a requisition for jackets, pants, shoes, shirts, drawers, caps, and blankets. Captain William J. Turner, now apparently sufficiently recovered from his wounds at Gettysburg, was commanding Company D. In an undated requisition he ordered jackets, pants, shoes, shirts, drawers, caps, and blankets. Now in the spring he requested one wall tent and fourteen "shelter tents." His report shows one captain, one subaltern (Lieutenant James B. Hill), and forty-two noncommissioned men.

From a camp near Richmond on April 1, 1864, Eli B. Tucker, a teamster with the 53rd Regiment's supply train, wrote a letter to Secretary of War Seddon requesting leave so that he could be married. He said that he had volunteered at the beginning of the war, but had had only one furlough and that two years ago. Tucker said that he had applied "during the winter to no effect" and that he had always been at his post doing his duty to the best of his knowledge. His request was signed by Lieutenant Hill and approved for fifteen days by General Barton.[41]

———

Andrew Leftwich was fortunate to receive a furlough of twenty days to visit his family in King William. It was dated February 15, 1864, and signed by Brigadier General H. H. Walker and Major General J. A. Early. Even so, his letters continued to sound notes of sadness and despondency. After his furlough he returned to join his unit in the valley, travelling on the platform of the train as far as Gordonsville with W. W. Hutchinson, of Mangohick, on the way to visit his daughter in Charlottesville. Andrew saw that the "Yankeys" (Kilpatrick) had burned everything around Beaver Dam, even the fencing. He left his baggage at the Madison Post Office and walked, apparently through steady rain, to join his company. He wrote Sallie that his coat got so wet that it weighed 100 pounds and it was "still sad — shedding tears."[42]

With the approach of spring Meade had renewed his activity with a cavalry expedition. General Judson Kilpatrick and young Colonel Ulric Dahlgren staged a cavalry raid around Lee's left in an attempt to reach

Richmond and free the prisoners there. Dahlgren had not long before lost a leg and was wearing an artificial one. They started out on February 28. However, Kilpatrick kept just out of the reach of Colonel Beale and the 9th Cavalry. Later the Federal general said, "When he knew the 9th Virginia was in front he always put three regiments to fight it, that they were the best cavalry in the Confederate service."[43]

Dahlgren started from Culpeper with intructions to first destroy the artillery at Frederick's Hall before joining General Kilpatrick at Richmond. The general destroyed the buildings and rails of Beaver Dam Station (on the Virginia Central) while Dahlgren, having separated from him, struck the railroad just east of Frederick's Hall but stayed clear of the Confederate artillery bivouacked there.[44]

General Long, suspecting such an attack, requested two regiments of infantry. Lee felt that he could not spare any of his men from along the Rapidan. Long did receive 125 muskets to arm the artillerymen and organize sharpshooters in each of his four battalions (two of which were under Colonel Carter, two under Colonel J. Thompson Brown).[45]

Long had just enough advance notice of Dahlgren's approach to enable him to send Carter M. Braxton with one battery and sharpshooters along the road to meet him. Brown's batteries were placed in command of the approaches below the station. Cutshaw's and Carter's batteries were placed in their rear for support. When he glimpsed the bayonets of the sharpshooters, Dahlgren halted with surprise. Upon questioning a newly captured black servant as to whether the artillery was supported by infantry, he received the reply "plenty of it." On further questioning to ascertain why the man was sure it was infantry, he got the reply, "Because infantry has stickers on the end of their guns." Dahlgren then made a maneuver to the left out of the range of the muskets and did not attempt to destroy the artillery.[46]

Dahlgren was unsuccessful in an attempt to cross the James River from Goochland to come into Richmond from the south. Later his troops became divided as he tried to meet Kilpatrick at Atlee Station, on the Virginia Central just north of Richmond. One portion, along with the young colonel, crossed the Pamunkey at Hanovertown.[47]

They were apparently proceeding toward Ayletts on March 2 when the advance guard came upon young Benny Fleet as he scouted for the Home Guard. The Confederate Congress had just passed a law calling out all men 17 to 18 and 45 to 50 years of age. Benny, aged 17½ years, having decided to go with Colonel John Mosby within a few days, had his uniform made and was wearing it that day.[48]

The Richmond *Whig* for March 12, 1864, had an article stating that B. Fleet, Jr., and Willie Taliaferro, from King and Queen, and Mr. Gus Sizer, from King William, had been on a reconnaissance concerning "the late raid." About a mile from Ayletts they saw three men in Confederate uniforms. They continued to ride to within thirty yards and then called out, "Are you friends or enemies?" The reply was, "Friends." But, "perceiving the Yankee column in the rear," they turned and tried to escape. The paper stated that Tallaferro was dangerously wounded and Fleet was found dead the next morning.[49]

Benny, shot in his left arm, had been able to escape into the woods but died during the night from loss of blood. His horse was grazing on the lawn of "Green Mount" the following morning. Members of the Fleet family started out to search for Benny and met his dog which led them to find the body near Mr. Anderson Scott's home in King William County at Turpin.[50]

Colonel Beale had taken 175 men from Centre Cross to Hanover Junction, Hanover Court House, and Old Church in the wake of the raid. When word was received that Dahlgren was headed toward Gloucester Point in an attempt to join General Butler at Williamsburg, Lee's Rangers joined with several other cavalry units and the Home Guard to stop him. After the war Lieutenant James Pollard of Company H, 9th Virginia Cavalry, wrote an account of the raid for the Philadelphia *Times* (September 17, 1887). He said that the regiment had been sent "to protect the transportation of supplies from the Northern Neck of Virginia, which was very much interrupted at that time by the enemy's gunboats on the Rappahannock, Mattaponi, and Pamunkey rivers. Besides, they would frequently land parties from the boats and make incursions into the country to plunder."[51]

Lieutenant Pollard was ordered to stretch a picket line from the Mattaponi to the Pamunkey. He said:

I moved over into King William county, quartered my men in the court-house, being a convenient point to both rivers, and established a picket post at West Point. . . .The distance by water to my camp was three times as great as by land, which would enable my pickets to bring me word of the entrance of a boat into the mouth of either river, and give me time to meet her with my sharpshooters on some of the bluffs.[52]

The lieutenant made several trips into Richmond to try to obtain ammunition for some captured Spencer rifles, but eventually he had to be satisfied with exchanging them for Sharp's carbines. It was during one of these trips that he heard of the approach of Kilpatrick and Dahlgren. He immediately returned to camp, stationed pickets at the lower Pamunkey ferries, and placed a "courier on the road about half way to the upper ferries." On the next morning, March 2, he received word that Dahlgren had crossed at Hanovertown. Pollard then had his baggage wagon put across the Mattaponi at Mantua ferry (off Route 637 near King William Court House), had all boats on the river put out of sight, and sent for the boat at Dunkirk to be brought to him as he awaited the raiders on the King and Queen side.[63]

The raid was now in three parts. Two of these, consisting of Kilpatrick's column, were being pursued by Colonel Bradley T. Johnson and his men. The third, consisting of Dahlgren's small command, having despaired of making connection with the others south of the Pamunkey, had made its way across King William to Ayletts. There they found a flat boat for the transport of the men while they swam the horses across. The Confederates came upon their rear near Bruington, causing enough delay that Lieutenant Pollard, Company H, and some of the Home Guard were able to get below them.[64]

At Mantapike (a few miles down the river from Mantua), near where the enemy had gone into camp, Pollard said that he put his men in line of battle after dark on the edge of a body of woods. He instructed them to hold their fire until they heard a signal from Sergeant Fleming Meredith, whom he had stationed on his left. At 11 or 11:30 p.m., Dahlgren, having sighted some of the Confederates, called out for their surrender. The Union colonel's pistol snapped as he tried to fire upon them, whereupon the Confederates fired on him. His horse wheeled and Dahlgren fell dead, killed instantly by "five balls" (buckshot). Captain E. Campbell Fox of the 5th Virginia Cavalry now took command of the Southerners. Both sides fell back until daybreak.[65]

The next morning Pollard rounded up prisoners from the surrounding woods and fields, some 100 Union men and officers. A thirteen-year-old boy, William Littlepage, who had followed his teacher from school, brought to Pollard some papers which he had found on the young colonel's body. The papers told of a plan for the release of the prisoners, the destruction of Richmond, and the capture of Davis and his cabinet. The lieutenant made copies of the papers before sending them to Colonel Beale, who sent them on into Richmond. Orders came the next day for Dahlgren's body to be brought into the capital city for identification. Pollard said that he had the body taken up and a coffin made. He accompanied the corpse into the city and turned it over to General Elzey on Sunday evening, March 6. Later he heard "from an authentic source" that the provost marshal had the officer buried in Oakwood Cemetery. Union sympathizers took up the body, held a funeral at the home of Miss Elizabeth Van Lew, and reburied it in Hanover County, from whence it was "returned to his friends" after the war.[66]

Although the veracity of some of the papers was denied by General Kilpatrick and General Meade, General Stuart commended Pollard for his gallantry. Lee forwarded the report to Secretary of War Seddon, who also praised the lieutenant for his "gallant exploit." Ironically Lieutenant Pollard, like young Dahlgren, was to lose his leg a year later after the Battle of Nance's Shop. He was discharged from service and wore a peg leg the rest of his life.[57]

Kilpatrick made his way to Gloucester Point. Colonel Beale said that they were assigned to watch for Kilpatrick's movement up the Rappahannock or the Mattaponi. Company H was sent to hold, for a short while, the picket line between the Mattaponi and Dragon Swamp (between King and Queen and Middlesex counties). Then, with Fitz Lee's permission, Lieutenant Pollard took his men back to King William, leaving the picket line to be serviced by the Home Guard.[58]

While they were in the area nine new men from King William came to join Lee's Rangers: M. R. Beadles, John L. Cardwell, D. C. Clements, W. L. Garrett, Miles C. King, Richard T. Leftwich (brother of Andrew), Cornelius Luckhard, and William B. Martin. W. R. McGeorge joined Company F at Centre Cross and Spencer Roane Waring was transferred to that company from Carter's Battery.

Fred Fleet had been home on leave when his brother was killed. After his return to General Wise and his men in South Carolina, Fred met the general on the street in Charleston and explained why he had overstayed his leave. He wrote that Wise seemed "much affected & disturbed" at the news of the event. Fred said the he was reminded hourly of his brother's death and wondered how young Willie was doing.[59]

With Benny Fleet's death ended the almost daily account of the effects of the war on the environs of Ayletts and Dunkirk. However, Fred's letters continued. Often he referred to what he heard from home and provided information on the 34th Regiment (the former 4th Regiment Heavy Artillery), a sister regiment of his own. He continued to wear a black arm band in mourning for his brother.[60]

CHAPTER 10

The Ni, the Po, and the James — 1864

On March 12 the United States War Department announced that General Ulysses S. Grant had been placed in command of all the Union armies. He set up his headquarters at Culpeper Court House, near those of Meade, who was still in charge of the Army of the Potomac. The Federals at that time held almost all of Tennessee and West Virginia. They controlled in northern Virginia the area east of the Blue Ridge Mountains and north of the Rapidan. Grant's men also held some coastal areas from Virginia to Florida, including in Virginia, Fort Monroe and Norfolk; in the Carolinas, New Berne, Morris Island, and Hilton Head; and in Georgia, Fort Pulaski. General William T. Sherman assumed Grant's old command in the Mississippi region.[1]

That spring Grant decided to make simultaneous moves against all the Confederate lines: the Army of the Potomac would go against Lee across the Rapidan; Sherman would move against General Joseph E. Johnston's army and Atlanta; Butler would move up the James River toward Petersburg and Richmond; and Franz Sigel would drive up the Valley in order to cut Lee's supply line and prevent another invasion from that region.[2]

Lee's headquarters were at Verdiersville, about 10 miles from Orange Court House. Both the Third Corps under A. P. Hill, including Heth's division, and the Second Corps under Ewell, including Cutshaw's and Page's battalions directed by Colonel Carter, were nearby.[3]

That winter Tom Carter's artillery battalion had become quite settled at Frederick's Hall. They had their own chaplain and quartermaster. Carter's wife, Sue, and their baby come to stay with him. Tom was concerned that his request for a commission for Festus King, dating back to January 1863, had not been acted upon. Concerning this he wrote to Secretary of War Seddon in April saying that "the time for active operations [is] rapidly approaching" and "we are making arrangements to move to the front as soon as the roads will permit."[4]

As the spring campaign began the artillery of the Second Corps consisted of the two groups. One led by Colonel Brown, consisted of three battalions: Hardaway's, Nelson's, and Braxton's, with a total of 45 guns; the other, directed by Colonel Carter, consisted of two battalions, Cutshaw's and Page's, with a total of 28 guns. Captain William P. Carter's battery of King William men and their four guns was in Page's battalion.[5]

The 9th Virginia Cavalry had moved back to near Hamilton's Crossing in the latter part of March. Toward the end of April they moved through Orange Court House and pitched camp in the fork made by the Rapidan and Robinson's River, just beyond Madison Court House.[6] From there Lieutenant T. J. Christian of Company H requisitioned ten jackets, twenty-four pairs of pants, seventeen pairs of shoes, forty-four drawers, twenty-eight cotton shirts, and twenty pairs of socks.

Andrew Leftwich's letters from March 12 through April 21 were written from Orange Court House. His company had been sent back to General Heth as soon as he rejoined them in the Valley of Virginia. Leftwich wrote to his father that they had been kept busy since his return in preparation for the big battle between Meade and Lee. He said that he might be going with General Heth to Richmond to recruit more men. He wished that John be sent up by Mr. John Fox, also his shirt which Richard Thoms was going to have made for him if his brother Will did not bring it. He reported that Robert (his brother) was better.[7]

Andrew wrote to Sallie that his battalion might be sent to Richmond, probably to join Pickett's division, but he would prefer to be in a smaller army. He told her that he and Benjamin Cocke messed together. Their "bill of fare" was three tablespoons of rice, two small pieces of bacon, and so far plenty of bread. He did not like rice for breakfast so had been eating dry cornmeal. In a later letter he said they were receiving: "½ lb. bacon, 1¼ lb. meal, ½ oz. salt, teaspoon of sugar, 13 grains coffee, and ½ oz. rice per day." He and Ben Cocke sometimes alternated meals eating meat. They had had a grand dinner a few days before when it had snowed and they caught fifteen snowbirds. He wanted to know, "How does Miss Belle get on with her shoe making? Has Mr. Prince finished any of her shoes?"[8]

By April 1864, Andrew Leftwich had become concerned because Sallie was not receiving his letters. He thought perhaps someone was recognizing his handwriting and removing his letters from the Mangohick Post Office "for sport." Apparently he dictated this letter, for it appears to be in a handwriting other than his. Both it and the succeeding letter told of deserters being shot. In the letter, he wrote that the enemy had come the night before to find out something about their position. They had been having "a meeting in camp with the following preaching: Dr. Burrous of Richmond, Mr. Granberry of M. E. Church, and Mr. Brown of Baptist [Church]."[9]

The Army of the Potomac began its movement at midnight on May 3, with two divisions of Sheridan's cavalry leading the way. The II Corps, under General Winfield S. Hancock, the V Corps, under General Warren, and the VI Corps, under General Sedgwick, used canvas and wooden pon-

145

toon bridges to cross the Rapidan at Germanna, Ely's, and Culpeper Mine fords, where the river was about 200 feet wide. They took up the canvas pontoons behind them but left the wooden ones for their trains and the IX Corps, under Burnside, which would follow. General Ewell had met with Lee at the signal station on Clark's Mountain on May 2 and told him that he was of the opinion that the enemy would cross at these fords below them.[10]

Ewell took his Second Corps along the Orange Turnpike on the morning of May 4. Hill, with General Cadmus M. Wilcox's and Heth's divisions, set out along the Orange Plank Road about midday. Longstreet left the vicinity of Gordonsville during the afternoon. Heth's division led Hill's advance. When they came upon George W. Getty's men of the VI Corps near the Brock Road, they took their position across the Plank Road. Walker's brigade was on the right. The affluents of the NI River were on their front, right, and left and Wilderness Run on their left and to the north.[11]

General Long received orders from Ewell on May 4 to move his artillery from its grazing camps near Liberty Mills, Orange County, to the front. Colonel Carter was already at Raccoon Ford on the Rapidan with Page's battalion. By the next day the Second Corps artillery was concentrated at Locust Grove, on the old Orange Turnpike to Fredericksburg. Colonel Brown's guns were on the right and Colonel Carter's on the left. There were few opportunities, due to the denseness of the wilderness, for use of the artillery. Colonel Brown was killed by sharpshooters the next day.[12]

Unfortunately Andrew Leftwich's letters do not cover his activities during the first three weeks of May. Perhaps they were kept too busy for him to write. The big battle or battles he had expected between Lee and Meade had come. The 22nd Battalion, along with the other regiments of Walker's brigade, was engaged in General Heth's actions with Hill's Third Corps. The 53rd Regiment, although members of Longstreet's corps, remained on the James.

The Brock Road was narrow. There was dense woodland on either side and thick undergrowth. The countryside was a tangled mass of scrub-oak, stunted pine, sweet gum, and cedar. Through this morass on May 5 at 4:15 p.m. General Getty attempted to advance against Heth's division, part of which was lying behind the crest of a small hill. General Hancock's report says that the fighting became very fierce. The battle lines were close and the musketry deadly along the entire line. Officers could not see their whole command. The approach of the enemy could only be determined by the crunching sound of the underbrush and the flash of their guns. The lines became so entangled that in the darkness that night men on the prowl for water would stumble into the enemy's lines and be taken captive.[13]

In the late afternoon Lee sent word to Ewell that General Heth had been able to withstand the enemy at the intersection of the Brock and Plank roads. General Richard H. Anderson of the Third Corps and Longstreet should be there to assist Heth in the morning. He wished Ewell to make preparation either to drive the enemy from the Wilderness Tavern ridge or, if that was too great a sacrifice, to reinforce the Confederate right.[14]

The Federals attacked again at daybreak. Wilcox's and Heth's men held for about thirty minutes but had begun to retreat when the First Corps arrived to save the day. Hill's two divisions had sustained their position against the six divisions led by Hancock on the preceding day. Now they were allowed to pass through Longstreet's lines to regroup in the rear. Later in the day they joined with brigades from Florida and Alabama to push back men of Burnside's IX Corps. The confusion of the Wilderness fighting had taken its toll. Longstreet had been shot in the neck by some of his own men. By the next day both sides were so heavily entrenched that only skirmishing was done. That afternoon Stuart brought Lee word that the Federal trains were moving southward.[15]

Colonel Beale said that after Grant recrossed the Rapidan the 9th Cavalry moved down the river to bivouac near Morton's Ford. The colonel wrote that they were not used in the Wilderness fighting, but he was allowed to ride out to watch the enemy's charge on the second day.[16] We can trace the activities of Lee's Rangers from February 1864 through June 1864, from the obituary for Richard Leftwich which appeared in a Staunton newspaper on June 20, 1920. It shows that Richard was with the regiment during the Dahlgren incident, in the fighting along the Rapidan, and at Spotsylvania Court House.[17]

On May 7 Ewell ordered the artillery to be in readiness to move. The enemy appeared to be shifting toward Spotsylvania Court House and Lee's armies would be moved in that direction. Braxton's and Page's battalions would remain with the infantry while the others encamped at Verdiersville. General Long took Carter's Battery on a reconnaissance along the Germanna Road. They met up with some Federal cavalry near the Beale house and drove them back toward the river.[18]

The march of the 9th Virginia Cavalry on May 9 took them through Stevensburg, past Grant's deserted camps, and along the Plank Road near the old Wilderness Tavern. They passed two Federal field hospitals which held both Federal and Confederate wounded and removed as many of their fellows as their ambulances could carry. According to their colonel, there were "cast-off arms in piles" nearby. Still stretched on tables were men who had died while their limbs were being cut off. As the cavalrymen rode along they saw many of the dead still lying in the burning sun where they had fallen, their faces already "quite black from incipient decay."[19]

For the next several days the men from King William would be engaged along the waterways that make up the Mattaponi River — the Mat, the Ta, the Po, and the Ni rivers. Spotsylvania Court House is situated on a ridge between the Ni and the Po rivers. The Mat and the Ta rivers lie more to the south and west in the direction of the North Anna River. These rivers, though not very wide, have abrupt banks, making them difficult to cross except where bridged.[20]

The Confederates won the race to Spotsylvania, Stuart's cavalry having covered the advance along the Brock Road. Longstreet's line, now under General R. H. Anderson, was placed eastward from the Po River; Ewell was in the center north of the courthouse; and Hill's Corps, now under General Early because Hill had fallen ill, was placed crossing the Fredericksburg Road on the right. They were to hold these positions over the next several days with only some occasional shifting back and forth of divisions.[21]

Early in the morning of May 10 it was found that Hancock had crossed the Po River and was threatening the Confederate rear. General Early shifted Heth's and Wilcox's divisions to push the enemy back through burning woods until they recrossed the river. General H. H. Walker (commanding the brigade containing the 22nd Battalion) was so badly wounded that his foot had to be amputated. Other attacks were sustained by the First Corps on the left and the Second Corps on the right.[22]

Lee's new chief of engineers, General Martin L. Smith, had designed a line of defense that would make the best advantage of the lay of the land. Lee would use the steep banks of the Po River to anchor his left flank. The center of the line formed a narrow salient that came to be known as "The Mule Shoe," being little more than one half mile wide and one mile deep. The artillery was placed at the apex of the angle. On the afternoon of May 10 Lee had his headquarters about 150 yards from the center line when it was broken into by the Federals. A portion of one brigade of the Confederates was taken captive before the enemy forces could be pushed out and back into their own lines. That night the Confederate band played "Nearer My God to Thee" while the Federals played the death march from "Saul." Lee wrote to Ewell to be sure that every man was supplied with ammunition, because Grant might attack at night as he had done in Vicksburg.[23]

During the heavy fighting around the courthouse on May 10, the 9th Cavalry watched the enemy's left flank, to the south. The next morning they emerged dismounted from some woods and came upon a body of well-posted infantry about the Gayle house. Colonel Beale wrote that they charged across the open field and "drove the enemy from the garden palings and fences into and behind the dwelling." The cavalry was then ordered to retire quickly to the woods. Just before reaching cover they were fired upon by additional infantry and two privates were killed instantly. One of these was R. C. Pemberton of Company H (and King William). Colonel Beale said that Pemberton fell by his side. Others were mortally wounded. Later in the day a detail was sent for the bodies of Pemberton and his fellow, which lay where they had fallen that morning.[24] The company records do not tell of Pemberton's death. He had joined the company that February and may have been in his mid-thirties. Corporal John Pemberton (perhaps the brother of R. C.) had joined Lee's Rangers in 1861 and is shown as mortally wounded in the right arm on May 12. He died a week later in a Richmond hospital.

Toward the end of May 11 a conference was held by General Lee and the sick General Hill in Heth's headquarters at Spotsylvania Court House. Reports had been coming in for the last two days from Rooney Lee in the enemy's rear that there were signs of movement. Ewell was told to withdraw his artillery along the narrow, woody, winding roads. All but eight of Colonel Carter's twenty-eight pieces were removed from the salient to about one and one half mile in the rear, near the courthouse. A section of Page's battalion was sent with an infantry guard and the wagon train to the depot at Guinea.[25]

Apparently the "long season in May," a cold, rainy spell experienced periodically in Virginia, had set in. A Union band struck up at 11 p.m., playing on into the night and adding its din to the muffling effect of the atmosphere. Major General Edward Johnson, still within the salient, sensed the movement of troops and the eminent threat to his front and requested the return of the artillery. Colonel Carter was also apprehensive because they had been moved. Johnson was assured that they would be back by 2 a.m.[26]

The attack came in the early hours of the morning on the apex of the salient. Page's guns were moving in and the drivers were ordered to lash their horses. One of Captain William P. Carter's guns was the first unlimbered. He leaped forward to help load it. Only one round had been discharged when he heard a shout. The captain turned and "looked into a score of rifles held by determined men in blue. The enemy was in the salient and was in the rear of guns and infantry." Twenty cannon, twelve of Page's and eight of Cutshaw's, were permanently taken. Others were taken and then recaptured as Cutshaw and Garber slipped away and regrouped to return and fight on.[27]

Taken captive that morning from King William were: Captain Carter; the lieutenants, William E. Hart and Festus King; Sergeant Beverly A. Littlepage; and Privates William B. Blake, William Brown, William H. Butler,

149

Andrew M. Dunstan, Obediah R. Ellett, William M. Ellett, Gustavus A. Lipscomb, Charles J. Madison, James R. Madison, Andrew J. Moore, William A. Nicholson, John W. Pemberton, William H. Penny, L. B. Slaughter, Harvey Terry, and T. N. Verlander. Sergeant John Waller Burke, John W. Griffith, and James D. Nicholson (brother of William) were either killed or would die on the way to prison. Corporal Augustine W. Atkins and Private Silas D. Tignor were wounded but not captured. James Madison would die in prison of smallpox. Ten would be exchanged, seven in September or October and three in the early part of 1865, but nine would remain in prison until the war's end.

General Long reported that the morning was so dark and foggy that it was hard to distinguish friend from foe. Colonel Carter commanded the guns posted on the hill, but as they day wore on he joined Long on the front and "rendered valuable assistance; his coolness and judgment everywhere had their effect." Major Page was put in charge of the remnants of his and Cutshaw's battalions. Portions of the artillery assisted Rooney Lee on the right of the line and other portions went with Stuart and Fitz Lee to try to stop Sheridan's raid against Richmond.[28]

The hand-to-hand fighting was so fierce that "The Mule Shoe" came to be called "The Bloody Angle." A Union man of the 95th Pennsylvania Volunteers wrote that as the rain fell in torrents they stood in mud half way to their knees. They would fire in what they guessed was the direction of the enemy. The Confederates would crawl under cover of the smoke until, leaping up with the characteristic yell, they appeared in the very muzzle of the Federal pieces. The Union men fought until their fallen comrades were almost buried in the mud at their feet. The head logs of the works became frazzled until they resembled "hickory brooms" and large oaks toppled on the Confederates. The fighting went on until midnight, sixteen hours of neither rest nor food until a new line was completed at the gorge of the salient and Lee gave orders for the units to fall back. During the past nine days five Confederate generals had been killed or mortally wounded. Nine more generals had been injured and two, including General Edward Johnson, taken prisoner.[29]

General Long concluded his report on the fighting in the Wilderness and Spotsylvania with an expression of thanks to "Colonel Carter, who commanded a division of artillery, and also rendered valuable assistance in selecting positions and the general supervision of the lines."[30]

———

In the opposition against Grant south of Richmond, General Pierre G. T. Beauregard was determined to take New Berne. He felt that Burnside, when he left Tennessee, would either move against the Petersburg and Weldon Railroad or against Richmond by way of Petersburg. Instead, Burnside went to the assistance of the Army of the Potomac and Butler began to threaten Petersburg and Richmond. President Davis sent orders on May 4 that the New Berne expedition should be abandoned. A few days later Beauregard was ordered from North Carolina with all his available forces to assist General Robert Ransom in the defense of Richmond. General Pickett was in command of Petersburg but was reported to be ill. General W. H. C. Whiting was called from Wilmington to replace Pickett, and he would eventually bring Wise's command (with the 26th and 34th Regiments) by way of Port Walthall junction to come up on Butler's rear.[31] Later in the year some King William men, held as prisoners of war off the coast of Georgia and South Carolina, would witness the culmination of Sherman's movement from Atlanta to the coastline of the Atlantic.

Lincoln had visited General Butler at Fort Monroe on April 1. They made plans for Butler to land on a "bottle of land" made by the James and Appomattox rivers, called Bermuda Hundred. From the location of the Confederate fortifications at Drewry's Bluff, on its south side, and Chaffin's Bluff, on its north side, the James River meanders around Farrar's Island, past Varina, around Jones's Neck at Deep Bottom, around Curls (Curles') Neck, past Malvern Hill, and around Turkey Bend before reaching the Bermuda Hundred landing and the river's confluence with the Appomattox, just above City Point.[32]

Drewry's Bluff, or Fort Darling as it was sometimes called, rises 200 feet above the James River. It had been hastily fortified during the Peninsula Campaign. During the siege at Yorktown the Confederate ironclad *Virginia* (or *Merrimac*) had played a vital defensive role. But with the fall of Norfolk and the scuttling of the ironclad the Federal gunboats could proceed up the James River toward the uncompleted batteries at Drewry's Bluff. The Confederates then took some of their ships from Norfolk up the James and sank them below the bluff. Piles were driven across the river and gunners from the *Virginia* were sent to reinforce the garrison.[33]

On May 15, 1862, the U.S.S. *Galena* (an ironclad) and other sister ships shelled the bluffs. The batteries and the C.S.S. *Patrick Henry*, stationed above the barrier, answered the fire for three hours and twenty minutes, until the *Galena* ran out of ammunition and limped out, having been perforated in eighteen places. The fort could not be taken except with the cooperation of land forces, which McClellan at that time did not choose to employ.[34]

Two years later General Grant was not as reluctant. General Butler came up from Fort Monroe on May 5, 1864, with an assortment of "coasters and river steamers, ferry-boats and tugs, screw and side-wheel steamers, sloops, schooners, barges, and canal boats" under the direction of the Union admiral, Samuel P. Lee. On landing, Butler's men stretched their entrenchments across the neck of the "bottle," a distance of three and one half miles, from Walthall's Landing on the Appomattox to

151

the James River just south of Farrar's Island. They were just four miles from Drewry's Bluff and nine miles from Petersburg. Petersburg was twenty-one miles by turnpike from Richmond. Between them and Petersburg flowed the narrow but steep-banked Swift Creek, the equally unfordable Appomattox River, and the Richmond-Petersburg Railroad. Confederate forces guarded all the railroad and turnpike bridges.[35]

General Butler sent out two cavalry expeditions, one of 1,800 men to move through West Point and be available to make junction with him wherever he might make foothold and another 3,000 men, under General August V. Kautz, to go through Suffolk and to operate south of Petersburg and Richmond. Kautz cut the Richmond-Petersburg Railroad, leaving some of Beauregard's men below the railroad. Butler wrote to Secretary Stanton on May 9 that Grant would (or so he thought) no longer be troubled by reinforcements to Lee's army from Beauregard.[36]

The 53rd Regiment, having left the New Berne area in February to be under the command of General Seth Barton and General Robert Ransom, was now participating in the defense of the James. There had been some scheme afloat which Colonel Aylett referred to as a "fishing expedition." He wrote to Alice that they were having difficulty getting the "boat & seine." The former was "being built by the Engineer Corps in Richmond." In the same letter he mentioned that cotton would be brought down from the Rappahannock, near Fredericksburg. On April 22 the colonel wrote that they would "start fishing that morning." He had heard from home that "Uncle Spot" (William S. Fontaine) was advertising "Fontainebleau" for sale.[37]

The latter part of April found the 53rd Regiment at Tunstall's Station on the Richmond and York River Railroad in New Kent. Their colonel wrote home that their encampment was considered a better place to fight than their former location three quarters of a mile away. Union cavalry and infantry were in the area and two Federal gunboats had been at West Point the day before (April 29). With May came rumors of Yankee raids in King William. William Aylett was concerned about reported smallpox cases in his home county. The time was near for Alice to give birth and it was rumored that Doctor Fleet had smallpox. William told Alice that he had written to the doctor. He told him, ". . .if he would not be able to serve to get an old & reliable Dr. to fill his place."[38]

The 53rd broke camp on the Brantley Farm, New Kent County, on May 3, 1864. Then they covered the thirty-two miles to Hanover Junction in two days, but stayed there only two days before being sent back by rail to Richmond. From the capital city they were ordered to go the thirty-five miles down the James River to the entrenchments at Drewry's Bluff.

Colonel Aylett wrote that his sister had sent them a most welcome box of edibles as they passed through Richmond, and he had gotten a chance to see "Brother Henry." From Richmond they went by steamship down the James to the fortifications at Drewry's Bluff. There they found General Barton in charge.[39]

The companies of the 53rd Regiment left the entrenchments at Drewry's Bluff on May 10 to go with Barton's brigade to near Chester Station. Members of the 53rd Regiment served as skirmishers in a second line of advance across an open field and then over a ridge of tangled undergrowth of hickory, young oak, and fallen timber. The woods were soon fired and the blinding smoke added to the difficulties of the terrain. The denseness of the morass prevented the regiments from connecting closely. When Colonel Aylett found that his advance had left some of the enemy between them and the 14th Virginia Regiment, he had to retire his men. This was done in order and secretly so as not to draw enemy fire. The general commended his officers saying, "The skill and gallantry of Colonels Aylett, [William] White [14th Virginia], and [James J.] Phillips (9th Virginia) were conspicuous."[40]

Colonel Aylett wrote to Alice that his regiment was in a "very severe fight yesterday [May 10] on the turnpike leading from Richmond to Petersburg." Having gone out "to see what the enemy was about & ascertain their force" they found the Federals in a large number. The 53rd and the 9th Infantry drove the Union men to within a mile of their fortifications. They captured a Union battery but could not bring it off the field because all the horses had been killed. William Aylett said that he had escaped injury but forty had been killed. Lieutenant James B. Hill of Company D had been shot through the hand. The report of J. D. Darden, assistant adjutant for Barton's brigade, shows thirty-six killed, three of them from the 53rd Regiment. Thirty men and three officers from the regiment had been wounded.[41] Sergeant Thomas Edwards of Company H sustained a gunshot wound in his abdomen and died in a Richmond hospital the next day.

Four days later William Aylett wrote to his wife that he was "relieved of much anxiety" to learn that King William had not been visited by the Yankees. Aylett did not write at this time that General Barton was again in trouble. The general had been removed from his command on May 11 and Colonel B. D. Fry given charge of the brigade. Aylett had nothing but praise for Colonel Fry and would defend Barton's actions and decisions. In a letter written later to General Cooper, Colonel Aylett said that his "regiment had fought most gallantly [that day] against overwhelming numbers until ordered away." Realizing that further action was eminent, he waited until later to file a complaint concerning the reassignment of command. Aylett took it as a personal affront that he, Colonel Fry's senior, had been passed over.[42]

Aylett and the other officers commanding regiments in the brigade sent a letter to General Cooper stating that their withdrawal on May 10, when against heavy odds, should cast no aspersions upon their commanding general. They asked that Barton be returned to their brigade. General Lee later wrote to the Secretary of War stating that he knew of no obloquy or censure cast upon the men and officers of Barton's brigade.[43] While Captain Latane and First Lieutenant Irving Sale remained in prison, Andrew Blake was in charge of Company H. Blake's apparent inexperience led to questions about his deportment on the battlefield in May 1864.[44]

Grant sent General Sheridan from Spotsylvania to cut Lee's supply line. He came from Todd's Tavern on May 9 and passed through Chilesburg and Beaver Dam. General Stuart and Fitz Lee followed the Union cavalrymen. They met at Yellow Tavern on May 11 and Stuart was mortally wounded. Sheridan then moved on to Haxall's Landing on the James River on May 14.[45]

Beauregard arrived at the Drewry Mansion on the morning of May 14. He brought with him grandiose plans of how he could defeat General Butler should he be sent more reinforcements from Lee's army at Spotsylvania. But, upon making this request to President Davis, he was promised only 10,000 men from the Richmond defenses. Half of these were General Robert Ransom's 5,000 men, who joined him on the evening of May 15. Already the enemy was erecting rifle pits about Drewry's Bluff. On May 16, using those three divisions now at his command, Beauregard began his attack at daybreak by sending General Ransom against the Federal right flank. Of the four brigades under Ransom, one was led by Colonel Fry (with the 53rd Regiment). The fog was so thick that morning that a horseman could not be seen fifteen yards away. The Federals had surrounded themselves by telegraph wires which they had pulled down from along the turnpike and strung from tree stump to tree stump. Yet by 6 a.m. Ransom's men had carried the breastworks, captured 500 men, and halted to regroup themselves in the still dense fog and to send for ammunition and reinforcements.[46]

Companies of the 53rd Regiment had been pulled out of the Confederate entrenchments on May 12 to meet the raid under Sheridan and they "marched and countermarched on the line of breastworks from Mechanicsville to [the] Williamsburg Turnpike" for three days before returning to Drewry's Bluff. On May 16 they assisted in driving the enemy back to Howlett's farm on the James, just above Farrar's Island. That day Colonel Aylett and Lieutenant Andrew Blake were wounded.

Corse's brigade was used in the fighting but Whiting did not arrive from Petersburg until the next day around noon. By that time General Ransom had been ordered back to the defense of Richmond. Butler had been defeated and "bottled up" but Beauregard felt that the Confederates should have captured his entire army.[47]

The King William and Caroline men of the 30th Virginia Regiment, under Corse, had fought in the center of action. Coming from North Carolina, they had been put under temporary assignment to General Robert F. Hoke. They moved from Petersburg to Mattoax, on the Appomattox River at the Richmond and Danville Railroad crossing, on May 12. From there they were called to rejoin General Corse, already in the trenches at Drewry's Bluff, on May 16, and were assigned to the movement across an open field on the Confederate left. They were able to rout the Federals in their front. Major Peatross was wounded slightly in the side and Lieutenant Philip Samuel was wounded severely in the arm. Two other officers were wounded, one mortally. Of the four men wounded, two would die from their wounds. Thomas Price Jackson, Jr., received a slight wound in his leg.[48]

The fourth simultaneous movement that spring was taking place along the Shenandoah. Under Grant's orders General Franz Sigel tried to push up the Valley from Winchester through the small town of New Market. He was faced by General Imboden and General John C. Breckinridge with mounted infantry, cavalry from Virginia and Maryland, and a six-gun battery of horse artillery. The generals decided to call out the reserves of Augusta and Rockbridge counties (boys under 18 and men over 45, armed mostly with rifles and shotguns) and the cadets from Virginia Military Institute. Colonel Francis H. Smith, commandant of the institute, had reduced the admission age to 16 and filled the school with boys below conscription age. From "Marl Hill" in King William County, on the stage road from Richmond to Tappahannock, young Henry Jenner Jones, age 17, had left home in the fall of 1863 to attend V.M.I.[49]

Colonel Scott Ship, a professor, reported to General Imboden with 225 cadets and on May 15 they were engaged in a charge across a muddy field to take an enemy battery. The boys were agile and surged ahead. The charge was successful. But eight of the cadets were among those killed and 46 of the wounded were from the institute. Henry Jenner Jones, of King William, was the second cadet to fall, killed by a canister ball.[50]

In Spotsylvania, after the extensive fighting on May 12, General Long reported that all remained relatively quiet along their lines until May 18. That morning at 9 a.m. a force of 10,000 to 12,000 infantry came against them. Using 29 pieces of artillery, the Confederates drove them back in thirty minutes. On the 21st the Federal forces appeared to be shifting eastward. With no enemy now in their front, the Second Corps, with its artillery, passed through the other corps to the Telegraph Road, south of the Po River, and on to Hanover Junction. Hill's men took a road to the west of the Telegraph Road and the First Corps (under Anderson) took the

Telegraph Road and roads to the west. By the 22nd they had all reached the south bank of the North Anna near Hanover Junction, with the Second Corps extending down the river, and the Third Corps upstream. The next day the Third Corps, including Heth's division and the 22nd Battalion, went to make a demonstration at Jericho Ford. That night a new line for the armies was selected a little farther from the river, with the Second Corps guns posted from the center eastward.[51]

A letter written on May 22 (no year) from Milford Depot may well have been Andrew Leftwich's last letter written while he was still with the 22nd Battalion. He told of a midnight drill and that he was writing during wind and rain. The tent fell on him, but he hurried to finish writing so he could send it on by a Mrs. Harrison.[52]

The fighting over at Drewry's Bluff, the companies of the 53rd Regiment left on May 19 to be of assistance to Lee in Spotsylvania. They travelled twenty miles to Richmond, twenty-four miles to Milford Station, and finally thirty-five miles to the vicinity of Spotsylvania Court House, arriving on May 21. Immediately they were sent back to Hanover Junction. Apparently Colonel Aylett remained behind in Richmond to recover from his wounds.

The 30th Regiment rejoined the First Corps on the North Anna on May 22 after having served in a blocking action the day before on the road below Milford, in Caroline County.[53]

After the fighting stopped at Spotsylvania, the 9th Cavalry was assigned to picket duty on the roads near the Ni River. Colonel Beale was surprised that General Lee knew every by-road and path in the area. Their brigade moved to the Po River and engaged in two cavalry skirmishes. By daylight on May 21 Beale's regiment was on the hills overlooking Guinea Station and could see some of Grant's army moving down the road to Bowling Green.[54] The next two nights they were engaged in ambuscades and on May 22 they moved at the rear of Lee's column to encamp that night south of the North Anna and near the Virginia Central Railroad.[55] Sometime during this period Sergeant William Todd Robins, of King William, received a thigh wound.

On his return from the James River, through "Saint Mary's Church" (Samaria Church in Charles City County) Sheridan found the railroad bridge at the "White House" only partially burned. He sent mounted parties throughout the countryside to gather planks and the bridge was readied for their use in one day. After crossing on May 22, they passed through Lanesville and King William Court House to encamp at Ayletts, on the Mattaponi River. There they learned that Grant was on the North Anna River near Chesterfield Station. Their next encampment was at Reedy Mills (apparently after travelling on Routes 600 and 601 into

Caroline County). General Wilson went on reconnaissance south of the North Anna as far as Little River. The other two divisions bivouacked May 24-26 near Pole Cat Station (Penola).[56]

According to the reminiscences of the family of Major Beverley B. Douglas, Sheridan spent three days in the latter part of May 1864 encamped at their home, "Cownes" (two miles north of Ayletts on the River Road, Route 600). He bivouacked in their yard and established his headquarters in one of two summer houses which stood on the circling front driveway. During the evenings his officers danced with the major's daughter and her cousin and their spurs left picked places on the parlor rug. All was not conviviality, for they searched the house and grounds for valuables and food, knocked down fences, and flattened the almost ripe field of wheat.[57]

Butler, like McClellan, had failed to push up the James River into Richmond. Sigel had not been able to break Lee's supply line through the Valley. Meade, like Hooker, had met disaster at every turn in Spotsylvania. But Grant was undaunted and his thrust would still be toward Richmond. Lee had lost his "eyes and ears" in the death of Stuart. But Grant still had Sheridan at his beck and call. King William and Mangohick would soon become an area of passage for Grant's armies.

CHAPTER 11

Through Mangohick — 1864

The quiet countryside of Mangohick and King William, with its narrow roads and lonely households, would be subject to the passage of 125,000 men, their equipment, and their 56,000 or so horses and mules. In addition to those horses ridden by the officers and cavalry, draft animals were used to move the artillery pieces, caissons and limbers, the supply wagons and ambulances, and the bridging equipment.[1] King William residents were accustomed to the distant sounds of battle and the passage of raiding parties of cavalry and small expeditions that included some infantry and artillery, but not to an invasion of this magnitude.

General Hancock and his forces of the II Corps were sent by Grant and Meade to determine how far they could proceed down the railroad toward Richmond. If the Southern commander would take the bait and come to meet them, the other three corps were ready to follow before the Confederates would have time to entrench. They moved after dark on May 20, by way of Guinea Station and Bowling Green, and reached Milford with little opposition. General A. T. A. Torbert and his cavalry found some of Pickett's division entrenched there. They drove them out of their works across the Mattaponi River (the south side) and secured both the wagon-road bridge and the railroad bridge.[2] This position was just below where the Ni and Po rivers which, having come together with the Ta a few miles upstream, are joined by the Mat, or South River, to form the Mattaponi.

Early on the morning of May 21 Lee sent a telegram to Secretary Seddon stating that Grant was putting the Mattaponi between them and would probably be secure from attack until he crossed the Pamunkey.[3] Hancock's circuitous movement had served no purpose. Lee moved his troops nearer to his supply depot at Hanover Junction. The North Anna River, yet to be joined by the South Anna and Little River, still lay between them.

Lee found General Pickett with his 9,000 men (including companies of the 53rd Regiment) awaiting him at Hanover Junction. There he could hold his supply lines from Richmond by both railroads, the R.F.& P. and the Virginia Central, and from Staunton by the latter. Ewell, with the Second Corps and Carter's men and guns, had crossed over the North Anna at the Telegraph Road bridge with General Lee on the morning of May 22.[4]

Colonel Beale, Rooney Lee, and Chambliss fought together on the North Anna. The 9th Cavalry joined the brigade on the Telegraph Road on

May 22. They camped on the railroad that night and then moved camp to Newfound Creek to serve picket duty along the North Anna for two days. During that time a "colored servant" arrived in camp driving a two-horse wagon. He had travelled from Westmoreland County by way of Spotsylvania, eluding the enemy all the way. Mrs. Beale had sent the man with birthday gifts of "pastries, cakes, bacon, eggs, etc." for her husband and sons. On his return, the colonel said, the Negro man "flanked the Federal army, going almost to Fredericksburg, and reached home without an accident."[5]

Grant and Meade instructed the II Corps (Hancock) to move to the Chesterfield ford (Ruther Glen) of the North Anna, near the railroad. The IX Corps (Burnside) was to move to the Jericho bridge and the V Corps (Warren) to move to a point on the river west of there. The VI Corps (Wright) would be following from Mt. Carmel Church.[6]

Hancock's corps took possession of the bridges on May 23, but the Southerners burned the far end of the railroad bridge during that night. In the morning it was discovered that the Confederate main line of defense extended about three miles "along a chord of a bend in the river." These were Ewell's and Longstreet's men. Burnside was ordered to take Ox Ford, just above the Chesterfield Bridge, on the morning of May 24. He crossed at Quarles' Mill, one and a half miles above the ford. Upon marching toward the ford he found the enemy so heavily posted that, after a brief encounter, he withdrew.[7]

Warren's corps found the banks of the North Anna high and rocky. On their arrival on May 23 no enemy was in sight. They immediately began building a pontoon bridge and crossed their infantry over by 4:30 p.m. and formed lines one half mile from the river. Hill attacked their center and right at 6 p.m. There was some loss on both sides. That night the V Corps entrenched and the VI Corps waited on the far side of the river to join them in the morning. By morning the Confederates had withdrawn their line along the river. Hill's corps and Pickett's men had a well entrenched line extending one and a half miles from Ox Ford to Anderson's mill on Little River.[8]

Official records show that Andrew J. Leftwich was captured at the North Anna on May 24, 1864. Because of the scarcity of Confederate records it is hard to fit Andrew's capture exactly into accounts of Lee and Grant at the North Anna. It was General Wilcox's division of Hill's corps who faced Warren's V Corps when they crossed at Jericho Mills. Heth's division was brought up to join then on the afternoon of May 23.[9]

Colonel Charles S. Venable of Lee's staff wrote that between May 23 and 26 Lee lay ill in his tent and had his reports brought to him from the field. In his impatience Lee would say, "We must strike them! We must never let them pass again."[10]

159

General Breckinridge, having succeeded against Sigel, was sent word on May 17 to move his two brigades of infantry by railroad to Hanover Junction. He boarded his troops at Staunton and arrived at the junction on May 20. Then three days later Lee moved him to Hanover Court House, where as Lee wrote President Davis, with the assistance of Colonel Bradley T. Johnson and his Maryland cavalry, he was in a position "to check any movement in that direction if made."[11]

As we have seen, the Confederate cavalry, including the 9th Virginia, had served as "eyes and ears," escort and rear guard as Lee's army pushed into Maryland and Pennsylvania, fought and then moved back onto familiar territory. As the war progressed the Union cavalry too had become skillful. They could move swiftly with an element of surprise, ford streams, swim their horses or improvise a bridge. But the infantry with their supply wagons and artillery with its caissons could soon become mired in the many rivers and streams that flowed eastward through Virginia.

Grant's army as he withdrew them across the North Anna can be likened to Arabs who quietly folded their tents and slipped away. But it was not over soft sand but through alluvial forest where, as one officer stated, there was a "carpet of pine boughs [needles] that hushed the usual noise of moving columns and the heavy step of feet."[12]

There were no maps of Virginia at the beginning of the war that could be depended upon. A nine-sheet map which had been devised by Herman Boye in 1826 and revised by Ludwig von Bucholtz in 1859 proved to be of little or no value for military use. One authority on maps noted, "All too often the common road (as marked on the Bucholtz maps) turned out to be a quagmire in which long columns of infantrymen floundered knee-deep and baggage wagons sank up to their hubs."[13]

"Stonewall" Jackson had come to rely on Jedediah Hotchkiss, a native New Yorker, teacher, and self-educated civil engineer who, with his notebook on his knee and a compass in his bridle hand, could sketch for his maps without dismounting. The one among the Federals who came closest to being his counterpart was Peter S. Michie, a West Point graduate who was assigned to the Federal Corps of Topographical Engineers. His immediate superior was Major Nathaniel Michler, who accompanied Major J. C. Duane to Mangohick and filed the official report of the movement through King William.[14]

During the winter months of 1863-64 the Federal engineers had been working on their maps, anticipating all directions the army might move after coming out of winter quarters near the Rappahannock River and the Orange and Alexandria Railroad. Major Michler reported in October 1864 "that however well the only accessible maps might have served the purposes of general knowledge, still they furnish but little of that detailed information so necessary in selecting and ordering the different routes of marching columns, and were too decidedly deficient in accuracy and detail to enable a general to maneuver with certainty his troops in the face of a brave and ever-watchful enemy."[15]

Although they were able to capture a few of the maps recently made by surveying parties of Confederates, the Federal engineers found that they had to remain near their marching armies, though scouting somewhat ahead, to revise their maps and serve as guides. One of the engineers had ridden with Kilpatrick and his cavalrymen to the James in March 1864, mapping the way for any future army advance. Another engineer had ridden with Sheridan from Chancellorsville to Haxall's Landing and back through King William that May.[16]

It was over the old "highways" through Caroline and King William counties, used by the Indians for centuries before white men came to fight over the land, that Grant was to make his flanking movement toward Richmond from the northeast. Along the old trails between rivers and creeks the corps marched to convenient places of portage where the white man's wheeled vehicles could pass over on canoe-like pontoons.

On the route chosen there would be only one or two rivers to cross — the Pamunkey, for the main body of Grant's army corps, and the Mattaponi, for the supply trains, ambulances, and hospital equipment that would come down from Port Royal on the Rappahannock River. Sheridan's cavalry and the 50th New York Engineers, led by Lieutenant Colonel Ira Spaulding, conducted the corps along these roads and arranged their crossings over or through its rivers and streams.[17]

With the movement of the entire Army of the Potomac (the II, V, and VI Corps) and the IX Corps under Burnside, time was of the essence. The supply train and ambulances would follow, but the corps must bring their bridging equipment with them. This consisted of pontoons, either wooden ones already made up and each carried on its own wagon with its oars, ropes and anchors, or canvas pontoons to be assembled on dismantled wooden frames. The canvas would be wrapped around the frame and the resulting pontoon then lashed and soaked to make it wateright. Following would be wagons carrying the 27-foot-long, 5x5-foot balks and side rails and the 13-foot-long, 12x1½-inch chesses or decking. The pontoons would be placed parallel to the river banks, spaced 20 feet apart, and each anchored upstream with every other one also anchored downstream. The balks would be placed across the gunwales; then the chesses placed at right angles to the balks. The side rails would be lashed into place and the bridge floor covered with straw or earth to muffle the sounds of passage.[18]

From their bivouac near Ayletts, Sheridan and his men had marched back toward the sound of artillery. When they joined their fellows at Chesterfield Station, they had been on the move for sixteen days, averaging 18 miles but not exceeding 30 miles a day. When 250-300 horses had given out, they were shot by the rear guard so as not to be of use to the Confederates. Sheridan had found little forage or sustenance between the Pamunkey and Mattaponi rivers.[19]

The next day, May 26, after Wilson's cavalry division was sent from Pole Cat Station on a diversionary reconnaissance as far as Little River, Torbert's and Gregg's divisions were sent back into King William. Gregg was told to proceed to Littlepage's crossing of the Pamunkey River (between Caroline and Hanover County), and Torbert's division was instructed to proceed downstream to Taylor's Ford (between King William and Hanover County). Each was to demonstrate as if the general army crossing would be at that point, but after dark to leave only a guard there to continue the demonstration. They were then to proceed with the pontoons to effect the real crossing at Hanovertown (from King William to Hanover County).[20]

In these demonstrations there was an element of truth. Grant would be crossing the Pamunkey, not its tributaries. By the time the streams reach the Littlepage crossing, used by the Richmond-Alexandria stage, the North and South Anna rivers have formed the Pamunkey. Upstream the Newfound and Little River flow into the North Anna. The Littlepage family had been granted land on both sides of the river in Hanover, Caroline, and King William counties. They called their acreage in Hanover "South Wales" and in Caroline "North Wales." At Calno, in King William County and on the Ridge Road just above Mangohick, the Littlepage home was called "Wales." Early land grants referred to that portion of the Ridge Road as a "Path to North Wales." Troops that would not be demonstrating at Littlepage's need not have travelled all the way to the stage crossing but could have branched off to the Ridge Road. At Mangohick Church they could have taken the old road (Route 604) by Dabney's Mill to arrive at Hanovertown. This road follows the high ground between Mehixon Creek and its headwaters and Moncuin Creek and its tributaries. It too is a very old road which if not part of at least made connection with the old "Manskin Path" from the Mattaponi River. Over it would be coming the supply trains and reinforcements.[21]

The VI Corps withdrew across the North Anna at 9 p.m. on May 26 and proceeded to Chesterfield Station. Because of the "heavy rains, the roads were wretched and the march slow and fatiguing." They arrived at 4 a.m. at the station, met the supply train from Fredericksburg, and then resumed the march at 7 a.m., proceeding southeast until they turned west from the main road at Niagara Church. Their bivouac that night was a mile from Taylor's Ford. One account from the corps says that they camped for the night on the "Taylor plantation, in King William Valley."[22] The identity of Niagara Church and the road west is uncertain. It might have been Route 650 below Bethel M. E. Church, or the no-longer-current road over which the 1863 "Expedition to the South Anna" had passed from and to Taylor's farm.

The accounts of the artillery, which was moving with the VI Corps, are very graphic concerning travelling conditions. They say that their journey gave them a fair sample of Virginia mud. For several miles during the night march the mud was knee deep. The next day was exceedingly hot and proved to be the severest test of stamina one of the regiments ever experienced. The 12th New York Independent Battery reported that they came by way of Bethel Church and camped near Taylor's Ferry. The 1st Rhode Island Light Artillery took the road nearest the Pamunkey River and went into camp at sunset at the Taylor house, three miles from the river.[23]

The last pontoon was taken up from the North Anna at 5 a.m. The wooden bridge was burnt and they started marching at 10 a.m. toward Hanovertown, proceeding until they encamped at 10 p.m. three miles from the Pamunkey River. Confederate Colonel Bradley T. Johnson, in his report of May 29, 1864, to Fitz Lee, said that the V and VI Corps had encamped at "Bleak Hill," a farm of Mr. George Taylor. He also reported that Burnside was said to be in about the same locality.[24] Warren's V Corps and Burnside's IX Corps were apparently a number of miles away; Johnson should have reported that it was the II and VI Corps.

As the Pamunkey River circles around "Horn Quarter" farm, "Ferry Farm," and "Bleak Hill" farm it leaves low grounds or flats which are subject to flooding and may have been part of the river bed in ancient times. Hornquarter Creek, an insignificant stream, flows through these flats and into the river below Norman's (Norment's) Bridge, the crossing of Route 614 to Hanover Court House. Taylor's Ferry is shown on the 1865 Gilmer map as a private crossing a short distance upstream. The Taylor home, "Horn Quarter," is a brick mansion built in 1810. The McDowell home at "Bleak Hill" and the Norment home at "Ferry Farm" are no longer standing. To this "King William Valley" marched the major portions of the II and VI Corps and their artillery to encamp the night of May 27. The massing of troops in these lowgrounds near "Taylor's" could well have given credence to Grant's feint that he intended to cross at this point. An encampment three miles from the river would have put the II Corps beyond Bleak Hill Fork.

Members of the V Corps had recrossed the North Anna at Quarles' Ford at 8 p.m. on May 26. While waiting from 11 p.m. to 3 a.m. for the VI Corps to pass, they spent their time issuing rations. They marched for ten miles and stopped for coffee at St. Paul's M.E. Church at 6:40 a.m. Then they continued until they crossed Dorrill's Creek and stopped for the night at 5:30 p.m., the main column being two miles from Mangohick Church and the trains strung out along the road for many miles. They had covered 23 miles in 21½ hours. One of their colonels said, "Toward the last part many men gave out. The morning showery, middle part hot, last part cloudy and cool."[25] Apparently Warren took one of the old trail roads, just south of Pole Cat Creek and the R.F.& P., that would take them by St. Paul's and to the River Road (Routes 601 and 600) along the Mattaponi. After crossing Dorrill Creek, a right turn on Route 604 would have taken them by "Catalpa Grove," Sallie Tuck's home, and on to Mangohick Church.

Charles A. Dana, the Assistant Secretary of War, reported to Secretary Edwin M. Stanton at 5 p.m. on May 27 from the command headquarters which had been set up at Mangohick Church. He said that the whole army had been drawn north of the North Anna during the night without loss or disturbance. At 9 a.m. that morning General Sheridan, with the 1st and 2nd Divisions of his cavalry, had taken the Hanover Ferry and Hanovertown. The 1st Division of the VI Corps, under General David A. Russell, had arrived at 10 a.m. and was holding the crossing. The 2nd, 3rd, and 4th Divisions of that corps were already near Mangohick and were being followed by Hancock's II Corps. The V Corps (Warren) had not stopped at Mangohick. They and the IX (Burnside) had taken the road by Moncure's plantation. The army supply base would be at the "White House" or at Newcastle, according to the preference of General Ingalls (the quartermaster). Dana went on to say: "The men are much jaded with hard work and night marching . . . .Weather fine, and roads perfect." By 7 a.m. the next morning he was reporting: "Everything goes finely. Weather splendid, clear, and cool. Troops coming up very rapidly, and in great numbers. The whole army will be beyond the Pamunkey by noon." He also reported that Wickham's and Lomax's brigades of Confederate cavalry as well as Breckinridge's force of 3,000 to 10,000 men were at Hanover Court House.[26]

Colonel Ira Spaulding had under his command eleven companies of engineers numbering 1,500 men and 40 officers. They were divided among four battalions with the following assignments:

First — Major Wesley Brainerd with 14 French (wooden) pontoon boats and with the entrenching tools of and assigned to the II Corps.

Second — Major E. O. Beers with 13 French pontoon boats and with the entrenching tools of and assigned to the VI Corps.

Third — Major George W. Ford and Captain J. H. McDonald with 13 French pontoon boats and with the entrenching tools of and assigned to the V Corps.

Reserve — Captain W. W. Folwell's no. 4 train with canvas pontoons and Captain Martin Van Brocklin's no. 5 train with canvas pontoons, under their own immediate command. These were sent ahead with the cavalry.[27]

Captain Walker V. Personius with his bridging train remained at the North Anna until the cavalry under General Wilson had finished their assignment there. Lieutenant C. W. Howell, who had travelled with Sheridan to the James and back, was given the assignment to lead the IX Corps.[28]

The Reserve Battalion and its two trains of canvas pontoons reached the Hanovertown crossing about daylight on May 27. About a mile from the river Van Brocklin assembled two canvas pontoons, which were carried on the men's shoulders to the river. The Confederate vedettes were driven away and two squadrons of dismounted cavalry were ferried across to hold the far bank of the river while two pontoon bridges were being constructed. The first, 180 feet long, was completed within an hour. By 7 a.m. a second bridge of 164-foot length was finished a few yards upstream. The brigades of Torbert's division — General George A. Custer's, General Wesley Merritt's, and Colonel Thomas C. Devin's — crossed the bridges.[29]

During the afternoon Major Michler went from the Union headquarters at Mangohick Church to examine the road from "Rider's" (at Caino on the Ridge Road) to Taylor's ford, Norman's ferry, and the Widow Nelson's ferry, and to determine if a crossing could be made at the latter. Some of Torbert's men, the 19th Pennsylvania Cavalry, had possibly passed down the same road. While others pressed on to Hanovertown, they had been detached to make a demonstration at Jones's ferry.[30]

Jones's ferry was another name for either Taylor's or Norman's ferry. This too was Littlepage land, but had been sold to two Jones brothers. During the lifetime of Colonel William Byrd II the Jones land, "Horn Quarter," had adjoined his holdings along Mangohick Creek in King William County, which he called his "Mangohick Plantation." Byrd told of visiting his land on a return from Germanna in 1732. He used a "blind path" near a new brick church (Mangohick) that took him down between his land, which included "Towinque," and that of Colonel Thomas Jones.[31]

The "blind path" may have been a road that is no longer for public use which passed through or by "Bear Garden" to "Bleak Hill." The road the soldiers took appears to have been the one which connected the Littlepage land on the "North Wales Path" with the "Ferry Farm" at Norman's ferry or bridge. Route 601 follows the elevation between the headwaters of Hornquarter Creek and those of Mangohick Creek. At Bleak Hill Fork it joins Route 614, which has come from the Mangohick-Hanovertown road (604) by way of Etna Mills (then Hickman's Gatepost) and Gravatt's Mill (then McDowell's), to pass over Hornquarter Creek and the Pamunkey to go on to Hanover Court House.

Some land off of Route 601 and along Mangohick Creek is referred to on local plats as the "Campgrounds." It is uncertain whether this name originated from use by Fitz Lee as his headquarters (at an unknown date) or from the use by Federal troops at this time.[32] The road from Bleak Hill Fork over the millrace to Hickman's Gatepost, and then a right turn on present Route 615, would have been the widest route to Mrs. Nelson's crossing, although private paths through "Bleak Hill" and the Sutton farm "Towinque" would have been shorter. There is no mention of any consideration of possible crossing of the armies at the Sutton ferry.

General Frank Wheaton's brigade of the VI Corps, from its bivouac a mile from Taylor's Ford, started out at 4 a.m. on May 28. They continued their march southeast, crossed Hornquarter Creek and halted at the Pamunkey three miles north of Hanovertown. They soon crossed over and formed an entrenched north-south line. The 1st New York Independent Battery (serving with the VI Corps) went via McDowell's Mill to cross the Pamunkey. The 14th New Jersey Infantry, after crossing at "Widow Nelson's house" at 11:30 a.m. on May 28, formed a line and threw up breastworks near the Pollard house ("Williamsville").[33] This would have taken those units over Mangohick Creek and possibly through Etna Mills.

About dark on May 27, Captain Folwell of the engineers had been sent from Hanovertown to Mrs. Nelson's to select a bridge site. It was too dark for him to gain much information but, upon his return to Hanovertown about midnight, he was told to take all the surplus material of trains number 4 and 5 and, if possible, to have a bridge at Mrs. Nelson's by daylight. Captain Folwell and his men reached Mrs. Nelson's by 6 a.m. and by 7 a.m. had completed a canvas bridge 146 feet in length. Due to the scarcity of materials it was built in spans of 21 feet (instead of the usual 20 feet) and the 27-foot balks had to rest on alternate gunwales. Over that frail bridge passed two divisions of the VI Corps and their artillery without incident.[34]

At the North Anna, Major Beers and Major Ford dismantled the bridge at Jericho Mills after the V Corps had crossed. They were on their way with their trains and were joined by Captain McDonald during the march. Major Brainerd took up the bridge at the railroad after the II Corps had completed its crossing. Accompanying the II Corps, he was that morning only five miles away from Mrs. Nelson's. He and his battalion spent the major portion of that day working on the roads and approaches to the bridges. Ford's and Beers' men had done a great deal of work on roads and bridges all the way from the North Anna. At 3 p.m. they arrived at Mrs. Nelson's and immediately threw across a wooden pontoon bridge of 140 feet below the canvas one and facilitated the passage of the II Corps and its artillery. A photographer took a picture of a "Pontoon Bridge over Pamunkey River at Mrs. Nelson's."[35]

General Meade reported that the II and VI Corps crossed at Hundley's (the name for the Hanover side of the Nelson crossing) and the V and IX Corps crossed at Hanovertown. But that was not true for each unit of the various corps. The morning of May 28 found the major portion of the II Corps three miles from the Pamunkey. (This could have been anywhere between Bleak Hill Fork and Calno or Mangohick, even the "Campgrounds.") Breaking camp at 5:30 a.m., they marched in the direction of the river to cross at 12:30 p.m., following the VI Corps. They formed a line on the south side of the river, connecting with the VI Corps near the Pollard house ("Williamsville") or the Jones home ("Hilly Farm"). During that afternoon they were able to communicate with the V Corps, which had crossed at Hanovertown, but could not make a junction. At this time the cavalry was engaged (at the battle of Haw's Shop, between Studley and Enon Church) on their front. The report of a number of units, both infantry and artillery, show them crossing at "Wyoming," although they called it by various names: "Nelson's ford," "Nelson's ferry," "Nelson's farm," "Holmes ford," and "Hundley's ford."[36]

The 28th Massachusetts Infantry, of General Francis Barlow's division of the II Corps, remained behind to bivouac in the mud on the North Anna, and were deployed on the railroad "warping rails and turning crossties." Starting at 10 a.m. on May 28, they marched through alternate rain and intense heat until 4 p.m., when they stopped for one half hour in Bowling Green. Their march then took them through Guinea and Milford to arrive at the Pamunkey at 1 a.m. and to cross near Newcastle. Their captain said, "The soldiers, notwithstanding their fatigue, were cheerful and spirited; many straggled and fell out on this march. Water being scarce the men suffered greatly."[37]

As noted the V Corps had come by way of Mt. Carmel Church, St. Paul's Church, and Dorrill Creek to bivouac two miles from Mangohick. They continued their line of march (probably along Route 604) at 5:30 a.m. on May 28 to Dabney's ferry (Hanovertown), crossed on pontoons and hurried to form "two lines a mile from the river and erect barricades." Some encamped near the Brockenbrough house ("Westwood"). The 18th Massachusetts Volunteers served as the picket guard behind the ammunition train, marching all day on May 27 until they bivouacked at mid-

167

night. After a long day's march they crossed the Pamunkey and joined their brigade. The artillery reports of the V Army Corps show that they passed through King William near Mangohick and Brandywine.[38]

Captain Personius of the engineers had remained at the North Anna until General Wilson and his cavalry arrived from Beaver Dam and Little River and crossed the log bridge. Then he was ordered to proceed with the supply trains down the east side of the Mattaponi River. Personius overtook the rear of the trains at Milford Station and moved with them to Newtown. His men and teams were "very much worn and exhausted with excessive heat and long marches." Yet they were able to pass all the line the next day, May 28, to arrive at Dunkirk and, in one and a half hours, build a 180-foot pontoon bridge in time for the supply trains to start across. During the afternoon and evening they also built a bridge of ferryboats for the crossing of the infantry and cavalry reinforcements coming from Port Royal and also for the light ambulance trains.[39]

Some of the IX Corps had held the line while the last of the troops crossed the log bridge across the North Anna. Then as they marched away they watched the sky turn crimson from the burning bridge. They travelled for 31 of the next 36 hours, through Newtown and Dunkirk until they arrived at "Hanover City" and were covered by the Federal artillery as they crossed on the pontoons there. This may have been the same route over which the supply trains, ambulances, and hospital trains travelled. A few ambulances had followed each division over other roads. The remaining ambulances were soon filled due to such rapid marching on a sultry day over dusty roads. Some men had to be unavoidably left behind. The putrefaction of the slain horses of Sheridan's cavalry along the road added to the unpleasantness of the journey. A regiment was left at Dunkirk to guard the pontoon bridge over the Mattaponi while others moved on to Hanovertown on May 29. They crossed the Pamunkey on May 30 and June 1.[40]

At 9 p.m. on May 28, Captain McDonald was sent with his bridge train across the river at Mrs. Nelson's and on to Hanovertown to throw a wooden pontoon bridge in place of Captain Van Brocklin's canvas one. This was done during the night and Van Brocklin's bridge was dismantled and parked with its train on the south bank to be ready when needed elsewhere. About midnight on the 29th he was sent with eight boats and part of his train to Dunkirk to help bridge the Mattaponi for the passage of the reinforcements.[41]

By 6:45 a.m. on May 27 Lee had word that Union forces had crossed at Hanovertown, although some could still be seen on the far bank of the North Anna. Lee wrote to Secretary Seddon that he would move to

Ashland. The next day, from his headquarters near Hughes' Shop, Lee wrote to President Davis that he would position his men on the "ridge between the Totopotomoi and Beaver Dam creeks, so as to intercept his [the enemy's] march to Richmond." He had been told that the enemy cavalry was moving from Hanovertown by Haw's Shop toward the Mechanicsville Road, and their infantry had been seen passing down the River Road which he understood to be the road from Hanover Court House to Hanovertown.[42]

Grant had shifted his corps to threaten Richmond from another angle but found Lee still holding in his front. Lee had moved south along a shorter route. The Second Corps (including Carter's men) came down the Virginia Central Railroad past Merry Oaks (a tavern on the stage road below Hanover Court House and west of Peake's Station). They went by Atlee Station and Shady Grove Church to the crest overlooking Totopotomoy Creek.[43]

A. P. Hill and his men (including the 22nd Battalion) had followed in the rearguard from Little River, moved along the Telegraph Road, and stopped for the night of May 28 near Atlee Station. Lee was sick. By the next day Ewell, suffering from an intestinal complaint, had turned over his command to Early. They took position near Pole Green Church. General Long was also unwell and Colonel Carter assumed command of his artillery.[44]

Willie Dame, a private in the 1st Company, Richmond Howitzers, with the First Corps, described the march from the Rapidan to Richmond. In his account Dame noted that Grant had crossed the North Anna River on both sides of them but soon found that his army was cut in two and gave it up "as a bad job." Dame's company moved back and forth for several days and was subject one day to sharp infantry fire on the Doswell farm. They then made an all-night march through the "Slashes of Hanover." It had been raining heavily and long sections of the road were under water. That night they were often wading through water from an inch to a foot deep. The gun wheels would mire up to the hub and have to be pried up and nearly lifted out. At dawn the troops rested for an hour or two before moving on to take a position on the far edge of a flat, open field. Two hundred yards away, on the edge of a body of woods, was Pole Green Church. Dame was told that the Pamunkey River (actually Totopotomoy Creek, which empties into the river just below Hanovertown) was only a mile away.[45]

Pickett's division had not started from the South Anna with Hill's troops but joined them during the night of May 27. They had moved by Ashland to encamp between Hughes' Crossroads and "Half Sink" (on the Chickahimony in Henrico County). They went on the next day by way of Atlee to bivouac that night between Hundley's Corners and Walnut Grove

Church.[46]

Fitz Lee's cavalry continued to report the enemy's position. With the newly arrived South Carolina cavalry they threw up meager breastworks near Haw's Shop, where they fought dismounted. The fight lasted for seven hours until the Confederates withdrew to their horses and left. Wickham's brigade of Virginia men had been heavily involved and the green Carolinians had proved their mettle. The 9th Virginia Cavalry arrived during the afternoon. They dismounted but were never pressed. Lieutenant G. W. Beale of the 9th Cavalry wrote that as they rode off at twilight the rifles were still flashing and a trooper was heard to remark, "Lor's, they beat the lightning bugs." General Sheridan felt certain that he had faced 4,000 men armed with long-range rifles. General George A. Custer thought that they had engaged "mounted infantrymen." He included in his report the probability that the private who had given "Jeb" Stuart his mortal wound had himself died from a wound at Haw's Shop.[47]

The Federal cavalry ambulances coming by way of Dunkirk had not caught up with the horsemen by the time of their engagement at Haw's Shop. A small building at the shop was used for operating and dressing wounds. Several shells struck the building. One even fell under a table while an operation was in process, but fortunately it did not explode. The wounded were sent to the large house and outbuildings belonging to Mrs. Newton ("Summer Hill"), a couple of miles from the scene of action. A hospital was set up on her shady lawn and the men laid on beds made from corn husks found nearby. By May 30 the cavalry hospital train had arrived at Hanovertown and supplies were ample. On the same day the "depot hospital boats and barges" arrived at the "White House." Ambulances and wagons were organized to carry the sick and wounded to the "White House." Some were sent across the Pamunkey at Hanovertown and down the north bank (through King William) to arrive on June 2. Others went by "the direct road" (through Hanover and New Kent) and reached the "White House" on June 1.[48]

After protecting the flank at Haw's Shop, Colonel Beale took his men to bivouac at Atlee Station. The regiment was used to watch Grant's infantry around Hanover Court House. They were told by some prisoners that Warren's headquarters was at Cash's Corner (Route 637). The cavalrymen moved one day in Warren's rear to near the courthouse, where minie balls and shells screamed and whistled harmlessly over their heads during a "spirited fight." Beale's men snatched a couple of hours of sleep that night before moving to General Wickham's farm ("Hickory Hill"), to form a line of battle. However, no fighting occurred there and they moved on to Ashland, where a mounted squadron under Lieutenant Christian (of Company H), was "warmly engaged."[49] Richard Leftwich's 1920 obituary shows that he was "in engagement near Hanover C.H., at Hanover C.H.,

Ashland, Va., Gains Mill, [and at] Mare Shop."[50]

Certainly the "Widow Nelson," her daughters, and the remaining servants must have remembered for the rest of their lives the sound of marching troops, the clatter of horses' hooves, the rattle of passing caisson wheels, and the crackle of rifle fire from across the river. Major Brainerd, the head engineer with the II Corps, and Major Beers, the head engineer with the VI Corps, had parked their wagons under the old mulberry and locust trees at "Wyoming." Confederate Colonel Bradley T. Johnson reported to Fitz Lee on May 29 that the II and IV (sic) Corps had crossed on pontoon boats at Mrs. Nelson's and a portion of their train was encamped at her house. He had left her yard at 2:30 a.m. that morning but could not speak to anyone in the house because there was a Union "safety guard established at her door."[51]

Captain Folwell took up his canvas pontoon bridge from the river at "Wyoming" on May 29 and moved his train to Hanovertown, where there was still one canvas bridge in use. When on May 30 Major Brainerd and Major Beers moved their battalion elsewhere, Beers left Captain Palmer and Company H in charge of the bridge at the Nelson crossing. Folwell took up the canvas bridge at Hanovertown and the Reserve Battalion moved its trains from Hanovertown to encamp at the widow's place.[52]

Over the next several days the Confederates harassed Captain Van Brocklin on the Mattaponi at Dunkirk so that his men had to remain armed and throw up temporary defenses. After dismantling the bridge there and moving back to Hanovertown, they were called upon to erect a 160-foot bridge at Newcastle for the crossing of one regiment of cavalry and a battery of artillery on June 3. Then they took up that bridge and reported to Cold Harbor.[53]

William Aylett did not know how Alice was faring at "Montville." While still recuperating in Richmond, he wrote to her, "If the Yankees have been near you, God grant you may have been able to stand all you were called upon to endure." Nor did Alice Aylett have the details concerning her husband's injury on May 16. His "13 to 14 pages (foolscap)," telling of his "sufferings, griefs, and sympathies," had apparently been lost in transit.[54]

CHAPTER 12

Cold Harbor and the James · 1864

For the last ten or eleven months of the war it is hard to determine where the various King William companies were located. Searching out their whereabouts becomes more difficult as leaders were lost or wounded, units shifted, and official records filed less often. For the 22nd Battalion, now that Andrew Leftwich was languishing in prison, we have to rely on accounts concerning Heth's division or General Henry H. Walker's brigade.

Walker, having lost his foot as a result of injuries at Spotsylvania, relinquished his command for a while to Colonel B. D. Fry, who led the brigade at Cold Harbor.[1] Fry had been wounded and captured while leading Archer's brigade during Pickett's charge at Gettysburg. Upon his release from prison he had been given charge of Barton's brigade at Drewry's Bluff in May when that general was temporarily relieved from duty.[2]

The records of Company H, 53rd Virginia Regiment, show that the unit went from line of battle at Hanover Junction on May 25 to Cold Harbor. There they were in process of throwing up breastworks on May 27.

The swampy banks of the Chickahominy River and the farm lands of eastern Hanover County are not a likely locale for a "cold harbor." General Humphreys surmised that an early settler had named his new homestead for a farm, or for one of a cluster of houses on the Thames River near London, called Great Cold Harbor, Little Cold Harbor, or just Cold Harbor. While the Union forces occupied themselves "with securing the roads from the Pamunkey to Richmond upon which to advance against Lee, Lee was endeavoring to cover those roads."[3]

"Cold Harbor was important to us," General Humphreys said, "as it was on the line of our extension to the left, and roads concentrated there from Bethesda Church, from Old Church, from White House direct, from New Bridge, and, directly or indirectly, from all the bridges across the Chickahominy above and below New Bridge."[4]

The river road along the south side of the Pamunkey led from Hanover Junction through Hanover Court House, past Mrs. Nelson's crossing to Hanovertown and Newcastle, and to the head of navigation at the "White House." The network of roads which these roads intersected was:

1. The old stage road to Richmond by Littlepage's Bridge and Han-

over Court House.

2. The road from Hanovertown through Haw's Shop (Studley), by Pole Green Church on through Hundley's Corner (Rural Point), by Shady Grove Church and across the Meadow Bridges to Richmond.

3. The road from the "White House" by way of Old Church to Hundley's Corner.

4. The road from Newcastle Ferry through Old Church, past Bethesda Church and on to Mechanicsville.

5. The road from Old Church by way of Cold Harbor and New Bridge over the Chickahominy.[5]

Lee was well aware of the lay of the land. Not only had he fought there before, but there was a new map of the area which had been drawn by Captain Albert H. Campbell on April 26, 1864.[6]

The Jed Hotchkiss map for May 27 to June 12 shows the Army of Northern Virginia's line extending from Totopotomoy Creek, east of Atlee Station and Shady Grove Church, southeastward across the Old Church Road to Mechanicsville (360 and 156), and through the Gaines farm to the Chickahominy at Grapevine Bridge.[7]

The Second Corps artillery continued to be under the command of Colonel Carter because General Long was "unwell." They were engaged with Rodes's division on the Old Church road on the evening of May 30 and were able to drive the Union force from Johnson's farm to Bethesda Church. The guns of Cutshaw's battalion were held in reserve. On June 1 General Long resumed his command. The next day the Second Corps, with Heth's division (and the 22nd Battalion) fighting with them, "advanced against the right flank of the enemy, making a wheel, the pivot of which was the Johnson house." Cutshaw's battalion (and probably the men from Carter's Battery) took position in front of the Confederate works but were relieved that night.[8]

At dawn on June 3 the Federals made a heavy attack on the Confederate left. Cutshaw's battalion, from a distance on the left, "delivered a telling enfilade fire on the enemy's line in front of Rodes's division." The enemy that day was "bloodily repulsed along the entire line," and the Third Corps, except for Heth's division and the guns supporting him, was able to move to or near the Gaines farm and rest its right flank on the Chickahominy River. Pendleton, on June 3 and 4, was able to check the fords down to the railroad bridge and post batteries to guard them.[9]

It was portions of General Warren's and Burnside's troops who, on June 3, attacked Rodes's and Heth's divisions under Early on the Shady Grove Road with great loss to the V Corps. General Early reported that the threats by the cavalry on Heth's left were "kept off by Walker's brigade under Colonel Fry."[10]

Perhaps the pressure by Burnside's cavalry continued into the early hours of June 4. Rufus W. Waters, of the 22nd Battalion, is shown as having been taken prisoner at Cold Harbor on that day. He appears to have been the only one captured from among the King William men during those disastrous days for the Union army at Cold Harbor, nor were there any serious injuries reported.

Remaining with the artillery, after the calamity for Carter's Battery in Spotsylvania, were very few men from King William. Lieutenant Lucian D. Robinson had charge of the company. Four men from the company joined during the year. A. E. Brooke, J. R. Douglas, and William T. Slaughter joined in March, and Walker Jones joined at an undetermined time during 1864. Corporal John M. Davis and W. T. Douglas, veterans of three years of fighting, were still with the battery. Silas D. Tignor, who had been wounded at Spotsylvania, returned at some time to be with his fellows. Robert B. Johnston, age 50, James Martin, age 45, and Ezekiel Woody, age 45 — all veterans of three years of service — were discharged on June 1, 1864, due to their age. Several were on detached duty: John Hay, as a harness maker; William A. Davis, as an ordnance officer for Cutshaw's battalion; and Egbert E. Lipscomb, as a guard at Chimborazo Hospital. Sergeant Spencer R. Waring had been transferred to the 9th Virginia Cavalry. Sergeant James N. Eubank was still suffering from a wound sustained at Somerville Ford. He was sent to the hospital for a resection of his shoulder in January 1864, and would spend July through October on medical furlough at his home in Enfield. James W. Allen, who had lost a leg as the result of an injury at Somerville, received an artificial leg and a discharge from service in July.

As the Confederates followed Grant to the James on June 15, Heth and his men (including Walker's brigade) were given the responsiblity of holding the White Oak Swamp Bridge while the rest of Hill's corps opposed the enemy at Riddell's Shop, at the intersection of the Long Bridge and Charles City roads.[11]

The 9th Cavalry was assisting in local defense and scouting Meadow Station Bridge on the Chickahominy when Grant was crossing the Chickahominy at Long Bridge. With Grant's shift toward the James, Colonel Beale said that they "moved close up to the blood-stained trenches at Cold Harbor, and went into camp on the now classic and famous Gaines' farm."[12]

The record of Colonel Aylett's men tells only that they remained at Cold Harbor until they were moved to Malvern Hill on June 13. Pickett's line was on the extreme right, toward the Chickahominy, until that date, where the "fighting was incessant at very short range, the opposing lines being at some points not a stone's throw apart." At Beauregard's call for assistance, Pickett's division was the first to be sent across the James.[13]

Grant's army had moved out of Cold Harbor on the night of June 12-13, and arrived on the north bank of the James at Wilcox's Landing below Bermuda Hundred. Using ferries from Fort Monroe the Federal engineers built a pontoon bridge across the James where the river was 700 yards wide and had four-foot tides. Hancock crossed his men on the night of June 14-15. General William F. Smith brought his XVIII Corps by transport from the "White House" to return to the assistance of Butler's army. He crossed his men over the Appomattox River on pontoons and assaulted the Petersburg fortifications on June 15. Hancock arrived at Petersburg that afternoon. Beauregard's indirect call through Richmond to Lee for assistance was slow in being processed. That night he abandoned his line across Bermuda Hundred and moved to Petersburg, leaving the rail lines between Richmond and Petersburg exposed.[14]

On June 15 it fell to General Henry A. Wise and his 2,200 men to hold the Petersburg line against Smith's corps until reinforcements from Bermuda Hundred could arrive. General Wise had with him the 26th and 34th Virginia Regiments. James Robert Reid, a Beulahville man of the 34th Regiment, was possibly with Wise at this time. Fred Fleet, of the 26th, had been wounded on May 22 while doing courier duty for General Wise and was recuperating at a cousin's home in Petersburg. Beauregard wrote, "No event of our war was more remarkable than the almost incredible resistance of the men who served under me at Petersburg, on the 15th, 16th, 17th, and 18th of June, before the arrival of Lee."[15]

Lee had his headquarters at Drewry's Bluff by June 16 and then at Clay's House (on the south end of the Howlett Line) on June 17. He wrote to President Davis that the line there had been reestablished and that he had ordered the railroad line at Port Walthall, which the enemy had destroyed the day before, repaired and reopened. Lee watched as the Federals sank five of their own vessels in Trent's Reach (a wide, shallow part of the James), supposedly to prevent his gunboats from descending the river to Petersburg. Ten of the Federal steamers remained in the Reach and the ironclad monitors lay downstream. The commanding general wrote to the president that he had left General G. W. C. Lee (his son) with the Richmond forces guarding the outer defenses of Richmond. Assisting Custis Lee, General Lee assured the president, would be "two battalions of artillery under Colonel [Thomas H.] Carter," who would guard against any enemy landings and embarrass navigation on the James. The commander said that he had ordered General W. H. F. (Rooney) Lee and some North Carolina infantry to Petersburg, a move necessitated by the crossing of Wilson's Federal cavalry to the south side of the James. On the 18th A. P. Hill and his men were approaching Petersburg and Pickett's division was left holding Bermuda Hundred.[16]

The 53rd Virginia crossed the James on June 16 (probably by the pontoon bridge between Chaffin's and Drewry's Bluff) to go to Chester, in Chesterfield County, just above Petersburg. On the Richmond-Petersburg Turnpike, near Port Walthall, they met, engaged, and pursued the enemy and recaptured some of the Confederate works which Beauregard had abandoned by going to Petersburg. The following day they assisted Pickett in a charge at the Howlett House and regained all of the Confederates' works. They remained there on the Howlett Line across the neck of Bermuda Hundred the "balance of June." It is the last official record of Companies D and H, 53rd Regiment, however inspection reports show them on Bermuda Hundred at the end of August.

Colonel Aylett wrote two letters to Alice in June. In the first he told her that his wound was completely healed and he was returning to camp. In the second he answered her letter of June 21 in which she told him how she and Etta had fared in the "last and *worst* visitation of Yankee thieves and barbarians." William urged her to "go *anywhere* you will feel better off." He told her that she must keep his servant, Bob, to help her and also to try to get a white servant woman. As for the other Negroes who had been at "Montville," Aylett said, "They have their freedom & can leave the land."[17]

Patrick Henry Aylett wrote a plea to President Davis that his brother be given the temporary rank of brigadier general. He pointed out that the colonel's family resided in that part of the county (Ayletts) through which the enemy had passed, at various times, 70,000 going through his brother's plantation, "destroying everything — even the clothing of his wife and children," and laying waste the land. He told the president that William Aylett's pay as an officer remained the only means of support for his family. He had entered service at the beginning of the war in spite of having a "mutilated hand [which would have] exempted him from conscription." Copies of Pickett's and Imboden's letters attesting to the colonel's exemplary service were enclosed. General Cooper replied to the colonel's brother that, since Aylett remained the senior officer in the brigade and by virtue of this the commander of the brigade, it was not necessary that he be given the temporary rank "at least until the case of Gen'l Barton shall have been finally diposed of." The adjutant general went on to say that neither General Lee nor General Longstreet recommended the promotion.[18]

Sheridan had left Cold Harbor with Captain Personius and a pontoon train for a raid on Trevilian's Station (on the Virginia Central Railroad) in Louisa County. They left the Newcastle Ferry on June 7, marched through King William to Ayletts, and encamped on Herring Creek before moving on to Pole Cat Station. Did they take the old winding stage route near

"Hollyfield," "East Bassettaire," "Mt. Pleasant," "Mulberry Hill," and to the east side of "Montville"? This was possibly the old Manskin Path mentioned in the early land grants, which has now been replaced by the more direct Route 360.[19]

Among Rooney Lee's men, at least the 9th Virginia stayed on the north side of the river while Fitz Lee and Hampton took other regiments to cut off Sheridan from the Valley. Then the 9th was engaged in the battle at Nance's Shop (also called Samaria Church by the Confederates and St. Mary's Church by the Federals) in Charles City County. Sheridan by this time had returned from Louisa, but not along the same route due to the complete lack of forage between the two King William rivers. He had moved south of the Mattaponi to Walkerton, had crossed out of the county at West Point and had arrived at the "White House" in time to escort the wagon trains on June 24 in the Federal movement to the James. He reported that in the process they engaged the Confederate cavalry at St. Mary's Church, Charles City County, in a "stubborn fight that lasted until dark."[20]

Sheridan found Hampton's men, whom he had fought in Louisa less than two weeks before, now covering the road to the James at Samaria Church, 2½ miles from the Chickahominy. Wickham's men were held in reserve on June 24 until noon. At 2 p.m. the Confederates charged a Union line of log breastworks. Fitz Lee commanded the charge and they fought dismounted. A lieutenant of the 9th Virginia said that the heat was "overpowering" and that they suffered from "unappeased thirst." The 12th Virginia Cavalry pushed the Federals to within 2½ miles of Charles City Court House, where darkness enveloped them. Some fighting went on until 10 p.m. The wounded were taken the next day from the makeshift hospital at Samaria Church into Richmond. Young Cary Nelson, who had been wounded in the thorax, died either in the ambulance or upon arrival at a Richmond hospital. Lieutenant James Pollard of Company H, 9th Virginia Cavalry, had to have his wounded foot removed.[21]

Certainly there was extreme sadness at "Wyoming" when word came to Mrs. Nelson and her daughters that Cary was dead. Was he brought home to be buried in an unmarked grave in the Nelson cemetery at "Fork Quarter," near Mangohick, or was his body interred in nearby Oakwood Cemetery? Had he stopped off at home just a few days before on his way back from Louisa?

The cavalry engagement in Louisa and then in Charles City County gives some idea of the mobility achieved by both the Federal and the Confederate cavalry. Stuart and his men in 1862 on his way south from Chambersburg had travelled 80 miles in 27 hours. Up to 35 miles in an eight-hour day was not considered undue strain. Cavalry travel need not be, and often was not, in the day. Moving in columns of four, they could

177

sleep in their saddles with the capes of their overcoats thrown over their heads and chins resting on their chests. The columns were spaced only a yard apart. Yet it has been said that Sheridan's movement through Yellow Tavern in May 1864 of three divisions, totalling 10,000 men and six batteries, stretched out for thirteen miles.[22]

The Confederate cavalry seldom fought on horseback except on scouting expeditions. According to General John H. Morgan, they were often held in reserve on the flanks of the action to press a victory or cover a retreat and were more apt to be utilized as mounted riflemen. When the need arose they fought dismounted, with a skirmish line in the forefront and their main body following. In this type of action some companies would remain mounted on the flanks and the horse holders in "as sheltered position as possible" but near enough to be readily available should the tide of battle turn against them.[23]

In July the 9th Cavalry took up the pursuit on the south side of the James as Wilson's cavalrymen tried to destroy the Weldon Railroad to the south of Petersburg. Their regiment (including Company H) and the 10th Cavalry gave support to other regiments under Rooney Lee already engaging the enemy near Stony Creek. It was past twilight one evening when they dismounted in the yard of Sappony Church and occupied the road. Colonel Beale wrote, "Seizing upon rails, boards, the stalks of green corn, any and everything we could get hold of, the best barricade we could make was hastily thrown up." The enemy was only two hundred fifty yards away, but they also stopped to form a barricade and bring up their artillery. Then in the darkness the enemy shot and shell passed harmlessly overhead and into the church walls. Twice the 9th and 10th Cavalry opened with volleys on the enemy advance, causing them to retreat. Then the Holcome Legion (South Carolina) arrived and took over the center of the line to relieve them. The enemy's firing continued throughout the night at intervals of fifteen minutes to one hour. Toward dawn Confederate guns began to respond from the rear. With the morning Wilson was found to be gone. Beale's ordnance sergeant reported that the four squadrons had used thirty-one thousand rounds of ammunition. They had suffered no casualties.[24]

The next day some of the 9th Cavalry pushed beyond Rowanty Creek in the pursuit of Colonel Samuel P. Spear's Pennsylvania Regiment. Colonel Beale recounted that they came up near the front of the enemy column and were taking prisoners, but, as the dust settled, "the smallness of our party was discovered" and they were forced to withdraw. The colonel was separated from his command and reached the bridge (possibly over the Rowanty) after dark. Now alone, he said that he "led his jaded horse to a grassy bottom and laid down and slept."[25]

The prizes of the day had consisted of some Henry rifles, revolvers, and saddles. Now there were sufficient McClellan saddles and Colt revolvers to supply each man in the regiment. They camped along Hatcher's and Gravelly runs in Dinwiddie County (to the west of the Weldon Railroad), remained on picket duty and were, according to Colonel Beale, "comparatively inactive" until the middle of August, except for an excursion in late July to the north side of the James to fight at Malvern Hill.[26]

The McClellan saddle was a regulation U.S. army saddle, lightweight, easy on the horse, and comfortable for the rider. It was equipped with wooden stirrups covered by leather hoods. Other standard cavalry equipment consisted of an additional blanket other than the one used under the saddle, an oil cloth, a canteen, a revolver and cartridge box, a saber, and a rifle or carbine. The Southern cavalry was not always so fortunate as to have a saber or other than a single shot carbine. Should they capture a 7-shot carbine, they could not shoot it for lack of proper cartridges.[27]

To the east of Petersburg, General Burnside and the IX Corps occupied a deep railroad cut, 130 yards from the Confederate line. A mining engineer, Lieutenant Colonel Henry Pleasants, felt that, using the coal miners of the 48th Pennsylvania Volunteers, a mining shaft could be dug to a position under the Confederate fort. Both General Meade and Major Duane, chief engineer for the Army of the Potomac, were skeptical that it could be done. Pleasants had to fashion boxes for the dirt removal. He strengthened army cracker barrels with iron hoops from pork and beef barrels. An old bridge was torn down for lumber and two companies of the regiment were sent outside their lines to raid Confederate sawmills for additional lumber.[28]

The Confederates could hear mining sounds. They sank countershafts and tunnel listening galleries, but were unable to come upon the Federal miners. The resulting explosion on July 30, that came to be called the Battle of the Crater, was recounted by James Robert Reid, of the 34th Regiment, to his family and acquaintances around Beulahville.[29] When William Aylett heard about the explosion he wrote to Alice that he was appalled at "the slaughter of the poor negroes at Petersburg."[30]

Heth's division (and 22nd Battalion) were not with A. P. Hill and Beauregard below Petersburg at this time. They had been sent with Wilcox's division and the cavalry under Rooney Lee and Fitz Lee to the north side of the James.[31]

Both Confederate and Federal troops were transferred from the south side of the James to the north side and back. Lee's men from Petersburg would cross on a pontoon bridge from Drewry's Bluff to Chaffin's Bluff, inside the Richmond defenses, to go on to the White Oak Swamp area. Grant's men would move from Petersburg on the east side of the Appomattox River to cross to Bermuda Hundred and then over the James at Deep Bottom to the swamp area. The main road from Petersburg to Richmond passed through Drewry's Bluff. Halfway along there was a road that branched off to the left to the Howlett Line. A road ran from Petersburg by way of the Federal fortifications at the Appomattox River at Point of Rocks, with a connecting road to the bridge at Broadway Landing, that could take Grant to his double pontoon bridge over the James at Deep Bottom, into Henrico County and the area of the Long Bridge Road.[32] The New Market Road (Route 5) into Charles City County was only about 5 miles away.

General Ewell had taken charge of the Confederate forces on the north side of the James on July 27 when the II Corps under Hancock again moved into the area to threaten Richmond. Heth's division followed General R. H. Anderson back across to Chaffin's Bluff. Rooney Lee joined them on the 28th and other cavalry and infantry came up on the following day, causing Hancock to abandon this attempt.[33]

A powerful Confederate battery at Trent's Reach commanded the river there at the tip of the Dutch Gap Peninsula and the north end of the Howlett Line. Chief Engineer Michie said, "This barred all approach to Richmond on the part of United States war vessels." Butler asked him if a canal could be dug across Dutch Gap, where a 174-yard passage could eliminate 4¾ miles of river navigation. The canal was begun on August 10 but not completed until December 30, 1864.[34]

On August 10 General Lee's message from the signal station at Howlett house to General Ewell on the north side was intercepted by Butler's signal corps. It concerned the location of Tom Carter's artillery on Signal Hill (on the north side) at Cox's overseer's house and the possibility of all Confederate batteries, including the naval guns of Commodore John K. Mitchell and those at Howlett's, opening at the same time. Butler notified Grant that this might mean an attack on their troops and work force at Dutch Gap.[35]

The dredging troops (mostly black) were subjected to "continuous fire, first of heavy rifled guns and afterwards of mortars," resulting in the loss of mules, horses, carts, and men. Mortar-batteries fired vertically upon them from only 1,200 yards distance, causing frequent work stoppages while the troops sought cover in earthen dugouts.[36]

Colonel Carter had his tent 1½ miles to the rear, where his servants kept his cooking utensils and bedding, but he himself remained at the front. General Lee met Carter's servant, Martin, returning one morning amidst the clattering of the utensils he had used in cooking and serving breakfast. Also thrown over his saddle were the blankets to be aired during the day. Lee, upon his arrival at the line, teased Carter, saying that the troops must be moving if all the baggage was going to the rear. Upon the colonel's explanation that he slept on the line, Carter received Lee's commendation for remaining with his command.[37]

August 14-18 saw Lee's Rangers back in Charles City County. Colonel Beale wrote that on the hot morning of August 16 they were passing through a "bottom densely covered with undergrowth and huckleberry bushes." The brigade commander, General Chambliss, was killed and an ensuing hot fight caused them to temporarily fall back. They were now directed by Rooney Lee. An unadvised move led by Lieutenant Christian of Company H and Lieutenant Lawrence Washington of Company C created, Beale said, "a momentary. . . panic, [and] called forth bitter denunciation from our Major-General." He called the day "the most trying our regiment had ever experienced. Not one drop of water could be had; the heat was intense, and the wood was dense and tangled." They welcomed picket duty that night near "free, flowing water."[38]

South of Petersburg on the Weldon Railroad, Warren had his headquarters on the east side at Globe Tavern, just above Ream's Station and had instructions to destroy the railroad as far south as possible so as to cut off supplies. The cavalry had already damaged some of the tracks, but not beyond repair, when Warren with his V Corps and some cavalry under Colonel Samuel P. Spear set out the morning of August 18 to do a more complete job. It was hot and recent rains made the fields almost impassable for the artillery. The Confederates got word that they were on the way and confronted them with Heth's division and A. P. Hill's artillery.[39]

By the next day Meade had ordered out assistance by divisions of the II and IX Corps, further cavalry and 200 railroad men. The Confederates also received reinforcements, including Rooney Lee's men from north of the James, and they were concentrated on the Vaughan Road west of the railroad. Walker's brigade was one of the five under A. P. Hill's direction that attacked the enemy at 4 p.m., taking 2,700 prisoners. Hill's report to Beauregard at 10 p.m. shows that Walker's (with the 22nd Battalion) and another brigade were left occupying the ground.[40] Alfred B. Dabney of Lee's Rangers had sustained a gunshot wound across his back.

Yet the Federals remained in control of the railroad. A few days later they were back to tearing up the tracks. This time Hampton led his division, Rooney Lee's, two of Heth's brigades, and some other infantry against the Federals at Ream's Station, causing them to abandon destruction of the railroad. This time (August 25) Hill reported that he took 2,150 prisoners, 12 stands of colors, 3,100 stands of small arms, 32 horses and 10 caissons. The guns were 12-pounder bronze Napoleons and 3-inch rifled iron guns. Again Colonel Spear had led some of the cavalry and some of their fighting had been dismounted.[41]

The 9th Cavalry remained on picket duty at Ream's Station for a few more days. Richard Gwathmey of Company H had been killed. Philip Lipscomb of Company F had been wounded in his leg and it was amputated. On August 27, Lucian Jackson was wounded, but not seriously, and Walker Hawes sustained an injury in his groin. The regiment was back in its camp on Chappell's farm on Goose Creek in September. The following month Colonel Beale was given charge of the brigade.[42]

Carter was still at Chaffin's Bluff when Lee recrossed the James after the battles over the Weldon Railroad. At that time Lee joked with Carter's courier, Percy Hawes, "a youngster whose scant one hundred pounds covered the heart of a lion," over the prospect of making soup out of a fat little dog which was running around their camp.[43]

Pickett's men remained in the trenches on the Howlett Line throughout the summer. A record for August 29 shows the King William companies there. The fifty-piece Barton's Brigade Band (which included Charles Mosier of King William) was located near William Aylett's quarters. He wrote to Alice that they now had plenty of good music, even some of her favorites. The colonel was glad that Bob could be "of comfort to her" as he "knew he would be." Pat Fontaine had returned to camp in August and brought news that Alice, now the mother of three children looked younger and better.[44]

During a major portion of 1864 Colonel William R. Aylett was in charge not only of the 53rd Regiment but of the entire brigade as well. There was no further mention of either General Barton or Colonel Fry being in command. Upon General George H. Steuart being released from Federal prison, he "took Armistead's old Brigade, which Col. William R. Aylett had been commanding."[45]

The 30th Virginia Regiment, serving on the Howlett Line, experienced hardships of several kinds. In August they needed trousers, shoes, hats, and soap. When the inspector called back in January, he found the need twice as great. Their larder lacked sufficient vegetables and fruit. One Caroline man received peaches from home which he could have sold for $1.00 apiece. Due to their location on the river the men suffered from fevers and chills. The ubiquitous earthworks were hot and oppressive yet desertion was slight and "virtually non-existent" among the men of Company E (in which King William and Caroline were represented). Robert Peatross was sick and absent from the regiment from July 25 through September. He had served as the acting major in the early months of the year and his permanent promotion would take effect on November 5.[46]

Scouts from both the Confederate cavalry and infantry often

checked the Mangohick neighborhood. One day a lone figure on horseback, dressed in a woman's clothes and bonnet, appeared at the Jackson home. Jane Jackson invited the visitor in and was preparing to serve refreshments from her almost bare pantry when she noticed that her daughters were nudging each other and giggling. "Never before," she said later, "had she seen her girls behaving so outrageously!" But when the caller stretched a man's boot from beneath the flowing skirts, she recognized her son, Lucian, of Lee's Rangers. "Grabbing a broom," Mrs. Jackson said, "she chased him from the house."[47]

Union soldiers continued to drift through Mangohick, used the churches as overnight sanctuaries, and carved their initials on the benches. Bethel Church, on some unknown date, was broken into and the Bible stolen from the pulpit. Apparently a soldier shot out the lock on the door of Hebron Church. The ball passed through the door and lodged in the podium. Before leaving, this soldier or another inscribed in Hebron's Bible, "The Southern Confederacy died September 15, 1864, by a Yankee."[48]

CHAPTER 13

Cedar Creek, Chaffin's, and Hatcher's Run — 1864

Not since the early days of the war had the men from Mangohick been engaged on as diverse fronts as they were in the fall of 1864. From the rocky streams of the Shenandoah Valley to the fortified bluffs of the James and the swampy runs south of Petersburg they faced the determination of Grant and his Union forces to bring the war to an end.

The 9th Cavalry operated below Petersburg. The 53rd Regiment served on both the south and north banks of the James. The King William artillerymen generally remained on the north bank of the James with Tom Carter until he and they were called to Early's assistance in the Valley. The depleted ranks of the 22nd Battalion served on the fronts at Richmond and Petersburg.

A. P. Hill with most of the Third Corps was south of Petersburg. General Heth was at Deep Bottom on the north bank of the James. General R. H. Anderson went to Heth's assistance in July but a few weeks later he was given the command of the area of Culpeper and north of the Rappahannock. Anderson's troops, along with Fitz Lee's and Wickham's men, were to cooperate with Early along the Blue Ridge.[1] The 22nd Battalion's records show that John W. Davis was captured in July near Harper's Ferry and Reuben Gardner was captured near Harrisonburg on September 25.

In June, Early took the route from Cold Harbor to the Valley by way of Mechanicsville, the Meadow Bridges, Brook Turnpike (U.S. Route 1), the Plank Road (possibly Route 657) by Goodall's Tavern, the Old Mountain Road by St. Peter's Church (Route 33) through Trevilian's in Louisa and then went on to Charlottesville and Lynchburg.[2]

During August the Shenandoah Valley became a major theater of war. The course of the Shenandoah River is an anomaly to residents of Tidewater Virginia, where rivers flow to the east or southeast. It flows in a northeasterly direction toward Harper's Ferry before its waters join with the upper Potomac and find their way to the Chesapeake Bay. Hence travel down the Valley, meant moving in a northerly directly and up the Valley meant moving southward in the direction of Harrisonburg and central Virginia.

Grant put Sheridan in charge of the Army of the Shenandoah, consisting of the VI Corps, the XIX Corps, and General George Crook's Army of West Virginia. General Early was familiar with the area; Sheridan was not. Early kept his men on the move so it was not known until after the war that he was outnumbered three to one.[3]

General Armistead L. Long had gone with Early to the Valley to direct his artillery, but he became ill and had to relinquish his command to Lieutenant Colonel William Nelson. On September 2 Tom Carter was ordered to take over Early's artillery and he arrived in the Valley on September 9. For the next ten days there was occasional skirmishing along a line from Winchester to Martinsburg.[4]

There followed at least three major confrontations between Early and Sheridan in which King William Men were engaged: the Battle of Winchester, on September 19; the Battle of Fisher's Hill, on September 22 (up the Valley and on the north fork of the Shenandoah near Strasburg); and the Battle of Cedar Creek (between Strasburg and Winchester) on October 19. Among the opposing forces at Cedar Creek in the artillery under Colonel T. H. Carter was Captain W. P. Carter's Battery.[5]

Early had arrived in Lynchburg in time to prevent Hunter's attack. He pursued him to the mountains and then moved down the Valley to Staunton. General Early said that his purpose at this time "was to keep up a threatening attitude toward Maryland and Pennsylvania, and prevent the use of the Baltimore and Ohio Railroad and the Chesapeake and Ohio Canal, as well as to keep a large force as possible from Grant's army to defend the Federal capital." Early stayed for two months in the lower valley. Then on September 19 he moved a mile and a half out of Winchester and faced the enemy on Abraham's Creek and Red Bud Run,[6] with Colonel Carter as his new chief of artillery. This came to be known as the Third Battle of Winchester.

When a brigade under Confederate General John B. Gordon was pushed back into the woods, Carter had Braxton's battery open fire with canister (tin cases of cast-iron shot). Their firing continued until a brigade of Rodes's division could come to their assistance. That afternoon Crook's Army of West Virginia and the enemy cavalry moved around Early's left flank and forced him to withdraw back through Winchester. He had fought against Sheridan's 43,000 enlisted men and 2,225 officers. Early was supposed to have had some 13,000 men of all three arms — cavalry, infantry, and artillery. Later he wrote that many had already been lost in previous engagements and others were broken down, or left to guard supply trains. Under Colonel Carter's artillery command were 39 officers and 818 men.[7]

Fitz Lee was severely wounded and had to turn his command over to Wickham and later to Tom Rosser. Tom Carter, in the late afternoon, received a painful wound from a fragment of shell and had to turn the artillery command back temporarily to Lieutenant Colonel Nelson. Although Early's army suffered a reverse at this time, Carter reported that the "artillery was under perfect control to the last" and that the loss of the day was due to the "enemy's immense excess in cavalry." General Rodes, under whom Carter had fought starting with the Battle of Seven Pines, was been killed soon after midday.[8]

The next day Jed Hotchkiss, on his way down the Valley from New Market, at Hupp's Hill met the entourage bearing the body of the slain general. He wrote in his journal, "A severe loss, his men along the road lamented it deeply."[9] Certainly Tom Carter and others from King William shared this grief.

Early reformed his forces at Fisher's Hill, south of Winchester, where he was again attacked by Sheridan on September 22. At the Battle of Fisher's Hill the Confederate cavalry broke about sunset and some guns were lost. But, Early wrote, "The men and officers of the artillery behaved with great coolness, fighting to the very last, and I had to ride to some of the officers and order them to withdraw their guns before they would move. In some cases they had held out so long, and the roads leading from their positions into the pike were so rugged, that eleven guns fell into the hands of the enemy."[10]

Tom Carter was able to report for duty again on September 26. Early's forces were encamped at Brown's Gap in the Blue Ridge in the vicinity of Weyer's Cave (near Harrisonburg) to await reinforcements from beyond the mountains. Some of the batteries were engaged in the skirmishing at nearby Port Republic on the 26th and 27th. Then on the 28th Early began to move his army slowly back down the Valley toward Hupp's Hill and Strasburg.[11]

For the next several weeks there was continued skirmishing up and down the Valley. Rosser was in pursuit of the enemy forces who were burning houses, mills, barns, and stacks of wheat and hay, thereby destroying anything that would be of value to the Confederates. Early, having heard that Sheridan was planning to send some of his forces back to Grant, on October 12 moved his men back to Fisher's Hill. His topographical engineer, Jed Hotchkiss, and General Gordon surveyed the enemy position from the signal tower at the end of Three Top Mountain on October 17. After dark that night Hotchkiss brought Early a sketch of the terrain showing the enemy flanks on Cedar Creek as it flowed into the north fork of the Shenandoah, the roads to the enemy's rear, and their guards and pickets.[12]

A three-pronged attack by the divisions of Joseph B. Kershaw, Gordon, and Ramseur was planned for 5 a.m. the morning of October 19. Swords and canteens were left behind so the movement could proceed more quietly. Some infantry would be moving along the edge of the mountain and fording the Shenandoah. Others would cross over Cedar Creek, which gave the battle its name. The artillery would have to move along the

Valley Pike from Strasburg but was to remain behind until the attack commenced in order that the rumbling of their wheels on the macadamized road would not give away the element of surprise.[13]

General Early, travelling with those crossing the creek, said that by 3:30 a.m. they could see the enemy camps by moonlight. Upon the attack, Early immediately moved to Hupp's Hill and found the artillery moving up fast as planned. Colonel Carter, as the sun rose, had his batteries fire directly into the enemy's breastworks, forcing the men to flee while still blurry-eyed from sleep. General Long vividly described the attack as the enemy's slumber was broken by the sound of musketry. The drums and bugles called them to arms but the crack of rifles and sounds of battle were carried upon the breeze and no other sounds were heeded by the "flying multitude." Artillery, small arms, baggage, camp equipment, clothing, haversacks, and canteens were left behind. The temptation to plunder was too much for the hungry, ragged Confederate troops, who were weary from long marches without even the commonest comforts.[14]

The XIX Corps and Crook's men were in rout, but the VI Corps, on the right, had time to get under arms and take position. The morning became foggy and the area filled with the smoke from the artillery and small arms. When the fog lifted at 10 a.m., it could be seen that the VI Corps was in a strong position.[15]

Colonel Carter was ordered to concentrate 20 guns upon them. As Hotchkiss recounted, "The gallant and indomintable Col. Tom Carter soon had his own and some of the captured artillery playing on the Sixth corps and its batteries." Although the infantry, he went on to say, was only partially successful in their attack, due to the swampy character of the land along Meadow Run, yet "the Confederate artillery, formidable in the number and character of its guns and in the magnificent handling of these by its officers and men, soon forced the Sixth corps from its position, so that before noon the entire infantry command of the Federal army had been routed and driven nearly two miles beyond Middletown, and Early had halted in the pursuit." After this engagement an artilleryman of the VI Corps credited Early's batteries under Colonel Carter with being the best he had ever met.[16]

Early did not choose to pursue the enemy farther. He later stated that his men were much jaded, having been up all night. They had become scattered while passing over rough terrain and some were unfortunately engaged in plundering the enemy's camp. They had taken 1,300 prisoners and the general expected the Federals to continue their retreat. But by late afternoon the Union men found a gap in the Confederate line and counterattacked. General Gordon's men could give little resistance and soon Joseph B. Keshaw's and Stephen D. Ramseur's men, although seasoned veterans, began to panic. Ramseur was able to rally about 300 of his men and with the help of several pieces of artillery held the Federals off another hour until he, who had taken Rodes's command, was himself mortally wounded and the artillery ammunition ran out. Then Generals John Pegram and C. A. Evans were able to rally awhile to cover the withdrawal. However, a bridge on a very narrow road between Strasburg and Fisher's Hill gave way, blocking the retreat of the artillery, ordnance, medical wagons, and ambulances. Early's forces lost about 3,000 men that day and some of the enemy's guns which they had captured earlier in the day. Sheridan's army sustained a loss of 5,655 — killed, wounded, or taken prisoner.[17]

Corporal John M. Davis, of Carter's Battery, was killed at Belle Grove, where the Federal infantry was routed during the morning, and W. T. Douglas was taken prisoner at or near Strasburg. Colonel Carter reported that had they had 100 muskets when the enemy charged their train as they marched toward Hupp's Hill they could have saved it. Instead they lost all the enemy guns which they had captured that morning and twenty-three of their own. He also felt that had they had an additional battalion during the previous month they "could have held the Martinsburg Turnpike, the heights SW of Winchester, and prevented the fated progress of the (Federal) cavalry."[18]

After this engagement at Cedar Creek, Early withdrew his forces to New Market for a few weeks and then moved on to Staunton when inclement weather set in. Apparently Carter stayed with the general until sometime in early 1865. General Long, in his listing of the Army of Northern Virginia on November 30, 1864, shows Colonel Carter as chief of artillery for the Army Valley District. Under him were Nelson's, Braxton's, Cutshaw's and King's batteries, but no separate listing of the King William battery. By spring Early's forces had been reduced to one division of infantry (Gabriel C. Wharton's), six pieces of artillery, and a few cavalry, or about 1,800 men. He withdrew them to Waynesboro and then to Gordonsville where his staunch band threw themselves against Sheridan's flank and rear to no avail.[19]

———

Information on the events around Petersburg and Richmond during the fall of 1864 is not profuse. Official records are sparse and individual company and regiment records, as the war wound down, dwindled into nothingness.

In August Brigadier General James J. Archer, now released from a Federal prison where he had been held since his capture at Gettysburg, was assigned to the command of Archer's, Johnson's, and Walker's brigades. Walker was still recuperating from his amputation. Bushrod Johnson's Tennessee men were on provost duty around Richmond. Archer requested permission to replace them with Walker's men, who as Virginians would be closer to their homes. Colonel E. P. Tayloe was still leading the 22nd Battalion, in Walker's brigade.[20]

Benjamin A. Cocke of Company G, 22nd Battalion, had the previous year served as a clerk in the Richmond defenses. He was shown at Chaffin's farm in March 1865. However, it cannot be determined where the battalion was located during the fall of 1864 until it and Lee's Rangers were among those engaged below Petersburg.

At the end of September, the 53rd Regiment was brought from the Howlett Line in Chesterfield to be used at Chaffin's Bluff and Fort Harrison, in Henrico County. The fort was one and a quarter miles from the river, on Chaffin's farm, and was one of the strongest points of the Exterior Line as it stretched from the Chickahominy River to the James at Chaffin's Bluff.

The 53rd was completing its sixth month on the Howlett Line. On September 4, William Aylett tendered his resignation but no disposition was made of it. Aylett was not with his troops when they crossed the river and it is uncertain where he was. His brother wrote later to tell him that his regiment had been engaged in the unsuccessful attempt to retake Fort Harrison. Captain William E. Turner of Company D was leading the regiment. The word from Pat Fontaine was that the men were pleased that the colonel would not be pressing his resignation and that General Steuart was an "excellent fellow and regarded as a most excellent and gallant officer."[21]

Five defensive lines stood between Grant and the capital city. The engineers had built four military bridges spanning the river so troops would not have to pass through the city. General John Gregg, of Texas, commanded the New Market Line. All others on the north side reported to General Richard S. Ewell, called "Old Bald Head," a feeble one-legged man. Longstreet was still incapacitated.[22]

Anderson was recalled from the Valley to take over the divided command. He reached Chaffin's Bluff on September 28, but already Grant's forces were on the move against them. Beauregard remained in charge of some forces south of the river, but on September 20 he left Petersburg to inspect the defenses at Charleston and did not return.[23]

Lee did not expect Grant to attack so soon. He gave his artillery chief, General William N. Pendleton, leave to bury his son who had been killed at Fisher's Hill. From his headquarters at Dunn's Hill, just north of Petersburg, Lee directed his 53,000 men. Seventy percent of these were around Petersburg and others were in Chesterfield, principally along the Howlett Line and at the land and water batteries extending to Drewry's Bluff. He had 8,700 men on the north bank of the James, including the artillerists and second-class units around Richmond, and in the forward lines at Deep Bottom and Dutch Gap. There were eight vessels of the James River Squadron on the river, three of them ironclads.[24]

Grant's efforts at cutting the rail lines into Petersburg had been in process since mid-June. Now with Sheridan's success in the Valley, the Union commander was determined to push Lee out of Tidewater that fall. With Grant were the Army of the James, under Butler, and the Army of the Potomac, under Meade. Grant decided to begin his fall offensive by sending Butler and 25,000 men to the north side of the James. Meade would be held ready with 25,000 men to strike the supply lines around Petersburg. Another 50,000 men would be held at the mouth of the Appomattox River to keep the Confederates at Petersburg.[25]

On the night of September 28, two corps of the Union Army, the X Corps under General David B. Birney, and the XVIII under General Edward O. C. Ord, crossed to the north side of the James. Ord crossed on a pontoon bridge which had been hastily constructed in the early part of the evening at Aiken's Landing, two miles below Dutch Gap at the Varina Road. His men were drawn from the Bermuda Hundred front. General Birney came from Petersburg to cross the upper pontoon bridge at Deep Bottom and use the New Market and Darbytown roads. Kautz was to follow with his cavalry.[26]

As daylight broke both corps were pushing toward Fort Harrison. They were able to take the fort and drive Lee's men from both sides of it, but were unable to break the Confederate hold on the river due to the presence of gunboats. Nor could they reach the Confederate pontoon bridge or take Fort Gilmer, three quarters of a mile to the northeast. During the day Grant joined his men at Fort Harrison and General Ord was wounded.[27]

That morning those holding the Howlett Line could see clouds of cannon smoke over Chaffin's farm. Upon receiving word that General Ord had left Bermuda Hundred, Lee ordered Pickett to have troops readied to give assistance across the river. Pickett formed a provisional brigade, using one regiment from each of his brigades. The 53rd Regiment was one of those chosen. The brigade was put under Colonel Edgar B. Montague of the 32nd Regiment, (the co-leader of the 53rd with Colonel Tomlin in the early days of the war). They must have ridden the train north to cross the bridge just above Drewry's Bluff. Montague reported to General Ewell at 1 p.m. with the first troops to arrive from south of the James.[28]

Lee also crossed over and set up his headquarters on the Osborne Turnpike, which was defended by strong local forces. He urged Ewell to try to retake Fort Harrison. Other reinforcements did not reach there until late in the afternoon, that night or the next morning. No concerted action was launched against either flank of the enemy. Montague had to fight his own battle alone on the far south. The diary of the First Corps shows that Pickett's men on the afternoon of September 29 were pushing up toward Fort Harrison, but it does not show them in on the unsuccessful attempt the next day to retake the fort.[29]

Also during September 29, Kautz led his Federal cavalrymen, including Colonel Spear, to the northwest in a fruitless attempt to break the intermediate defenses and get into Richmond. By midnight they were on Mrs. Christian's farm, near Mechanicsville. In the cloudy darkness they "could find only entangling slashing — and each other." They fired into the night, causing the militia who manned the works to fire into the surrounding area. Kautz abandoned his thrust toward the city and turned his weary horsemen back through the night to rejoin the infantry. But Richmond had been alarmed and the tocsin sounded. General G. W. Custis Lee, the commander of the locals, had gone to the Deep South with President Davis, so General Seth M. Barton was given the task of organizing and equipping the convalescents called out from the hospitals and the prisoners from Castle Thunder to defend the capital.[30] Perhaps some of the convalescents were from King William County.

Grant and Meade, conferring at Deep Bottom, decided not to renew the offensive the next morning. Butler and the Army of the James, having spent the night entrenching and adapting the Confederate fortifications to their own use, went on the defensive at Fort Harrison.[31]

Confederate shelling, both from the gunboats and the batteries, into Fort Harrison that morning and early afternoon seemed to produce little effect. The afternoon was muggy, with no wind, and the thick acrid smoke seemed to hang over the field like a pall. By 3 p.m. the counterattack was considered a failure. Lee pulled his men back to their starting position on the Intermediate Line at Fort Johnson. Montague and his Provisional Brigade were moved to the fortifications between the New Market Road and the Osborne Turnpike. There, under Charles W. Field, they would assist Anderson and Barton, with his locals, in the defense of the northern sector, nearer Richmond, while Lee and Ewell continued to hold the Chaffin's sector. Rain began late in the afternoon and continued to fall into the next day.[32]

General Alfred Terry led four brigades of the X Corps that afternoon up the Darbytown Road and across the muddy cornfields in another attempt to penetrate the Intermediate Line. He was accompanied by Peter Michie, who was verifying a map which had been found August 16 on the body of General Chambliss. They attacked Fort Atkinson, but were repulsed. This is the closest the Federals would get to Richmond until the next April. Montague and his men were moved back to Chaffin's farm on October 2. No further mention is made of him or of Pickett's men during the skirmishes on the north side of the James during the next several weeks.[33] Colonel Aylett learned from his brother that two privates from his regiment had been killed and two wounded.[34]

In the meantime Meade had begun his offensive against the Confederate forces which held Petersburg. The Confederate entrenchments formed a semicircle around Petersburg from City Point to the Appomattox upstream. Two lines of trenches branched out to the southwest from the semicircle to Hatcher's Run. One was a primitive line of log works, barely covered with earth, along the Squirrel Level Road and the other was along the Boydton Plank Road. The Federals had trenches to the south of Petersburg to the Jerusalem Plank Road (Route 156 to Suffolk) and then westward across the Weldon Railroad and on to Hatcher's Run.[35]

Lee's forces continued to use the Weldon Railroad northward to Stony Creek Depot, eighteen miles below Petersburg. At that point they transferred their freight to wagons, which moved along the Flat Foot Road to Dinwiddie Court House and the Boydton Plank Road. Other caravans used roads across Gravelly Run and around Arthur's Swamp to meet the Boydton Plank Road near Hatcher's Run. Beyond the Plank Road the Southside Railroad brought supplies from the interior of the southland into the city.[36]

Hatcher's and Gravelly runs and Arthur's Swamp feed into Rowanty Creek. This creek and Stony Creek are tributaries of the Nottoway River as it finds its way into North Carolina and the Chowan River.

Hampton had his cavalry guarding the supply line along the roads from Stony Creek Depot to Petersburg. While some stood outpost duty along a picket line, others encamped farther back. Rooney Lee's division included a brigade of Virginians, including the 9th and 10th regiments, led by Colonel J. Lucius Davis since the death of Chambliss, and two brigades of North Carolinians.[37]

According to Richard Leftwich's obituary, Lee's Rangers, from encampments either to the south or southwest of Petersburg were involved:

> [at] Stoney Creek, Whitlock Swamp where Brigadier Chambers [Chambliss] was killed; in raid below Petersburg old church [Poplar Spring]; in expedition that captured lot of beef in Grant's rear, Reams Station; Plank Road where Warren made his raid; Hatchers Run, Dinwiddie C.H. . . .[38]

The raid for the beef took place in mid-September. From their camp on Cat Tail Creek (near Malone's Crossing on the Weldon Railroad), they went on a foray to Cabin Point on the James (below City Point). Their brigade held the roads while Rosser's drove out the 2,400 beeves from the cattle pound, 300 horses, and some wagons filled with supplies. Rosser gave the signal about daylight for them to charge the one or two squadrons guarding the road. Beale said, "Most of them were cozily sleeping in their tents, and quite unprepared for so early a visit. Some were made prisoners, and many, hastily rushing from their tents, and casting aside their blankets, with *white flags fluttering in their rear,* sought the protecting cover of the woods."[39]

During late September, the 9th Virginia encamped on Chappell's farm and Gresham's farm on Goose Creek, two miles northeast of Dinwiddie Court House. The Tarheels were just east of the county seat, on the Military Road near Stony Creek. Rooney Lee received orders to go across the James to assist Ewell against Butler. He took his cavalrymen along the Plank Road, only to be recalled before he reached Petersburg. The division was held on the Plank Road until late in the afternoon on September 29, when Hampton called the North Carolina cavalry to his assistance against Federal cavalry in the area.[40]

This was not just a cavalry raid but the left flank of Meade's thrust south of Petersburg while Butler was threatening at Chaffin's Bluff. Meade had directed General Warren of the V Corps and General John G. Parke of the IX Corps, with two divisions each, toward the Boydton Plank Road and the Southside Railroad. Their first objective was to take the junction of the Squirrel Level and Poplar Spring roads, at which point stood a redoubt at the end of the uncompleted Confederate entrenchments. On the morning of September 30, the cautious Warren spent several hours leading his men along the narrow woods-lined Poplar Spring Road and over a mill dam on Arthur's Swamp, just east of the Squirrel Level Road. Between 1 and 1:30 p.m., they broke Lee's defensive line across Peeble's farm and captured the lightly held Fort Archer. In mid-afternoon they pressed on.[41]

They were met by Heth's, General Cadmus M. Wilcox's, and Hampton's men, all under Hill's command. General Archer, now serving under Heth, was experiencing his first day of battle since his release from prison. He led his veteran troops, including the 22nd Battalion (with King William men) and the 55th Regiment, over the boggy ground and through what a major of the 55th described as an "almost impassable jungle of tangled briers, grape-vines, and alder bushes." Along the way some of them availed themselves of parts of blue uniforms from fallen Union soldiers. Late that afternoon they fired upon the Federals on the ridge until the enemy caissons brought up additional ammunition and Archer withdrew his men in the approaching darkness. They camped that night on the upper reaches of the Church Road (in the direction of the Plank Road). The rain that had drenched their fellows at Chaffin's earlier in the day now descended on them.[42]

From near Hatcher's Run, Rooney Lee personally led the 9th and 10th Cavalry in a dismounted charge to save an abandoned gun. Colonel Beale of the 9th Cavalry said that if they had been mounted they could have taken many more prisoners. They did take one colonel, many officers, and 500 privates, only to loose 50 prisoners the next day in a skirmish on the Squirrel Level and Vaughan roads (and Arthur's Swamp).[43]

By 3 a.m., October 1, Archer's men had been aroused to be assembled into Hill's fighting force of 4,750 men. But Warren's men had spent much of the rainy night throwing up a light line of entrenchments. By morning the rain was a drenching downpour. Heth's skirmishers ran into Warren's pickets by 7 a.m. The main line of the Confederates proceeded past their abandoned entrenchments along the Squirrel Level Road, now held by General Romeyn Ayres, of Warren's V Corps. Later in the morning, after the confusion of colliding with some Mississippi troops, the 22nd Battalion saw no need to proceed with the charge. Their officers "stood listlessly looking on" while Archer strove to "revitalize" the men. Their comrades in other units sustained casualties and left their dead lying on the field as they pressed toward the Federal lines at Fort Bratton. When the effort to roll up Warren's right and recapture Peebles' farm was abandoned, Heth returned his men to their old works near the W. W. Davis farm (in the direction of the main defenses of Petersburg).[44]

Colonel Beale said, "After a day or two passed in bivouac near Petersburg, we returned to Chappell's, on Goose Creek." He was made general of the brigade on October 17. About this time Hampton was making appeals for men to fill up the 10th and 13th under Beale, but the 9th was full with many waiting to join.[45] W. H. Clements had enlisted in early September only to be discharged in November for disability. Hansford Anderson had been taken prisoner October 11 on the Weldon Railroad.

Federal operations against the Southside Railroad and the Boydton Road crossing of Hatcher's Run continued. Grant instructed Meade to take the railroad on October 27. On the way Hancock, Warren, and Parke found slashed trees impeding them, the ford across the run obstructed by the felled trees, and Hill awaiting them. There were not enough ambulances to transport Federal wounded. Again the weather was against them as it rained heavily all night. The next day the Union troops were withdrawn to their former position. The 9th Cavalry had served dismounted on both sides of the Plank Road and "acted a conspicuous part," as they drove the enemy from several positions.[46]

That winter the 9th Cavalry continued the pursuit of Warren along the Weldon Railroad. Colonel Beale stated that they were under fire on several occasions "and suffered for want of rations and exposure to ice and sleet." Yet they spent much of the winter in comfortable quarters at Belfield Station (in Greenville County almost to the North Carolina line). The squadrons would take turns on picket duty thrity miles from camp. By February 5, 1865, they were back on Hatcher's Run and supported Gordon's infantry during the fighting that day.[47]

Provisions for those who held the defense lines around Richmond and Petersburg were becoming more scarce and expensive. William Aylett was at home in November. His letter of November 9 to Alice spoke of his sadness at leaving her. (Perhaps they lost their third child at this time.) The roads were in a bad condition as the colonel and George his servant, now barefooted, returned with the heavily loaded wagons. He promised to look for a house nearby so Alice could be with him, although the price of everything, including rent, was high. Cabbage in the area was selling for $5.00 a head and large turnips for $1.00 each. Aylett instructed Alice that her letters must be forwarded to Steuart's brigade.[48]

The 53rd Regiment inspection report for December 5, 1864, shows them near the "Clay House" on the Howlett Line. On October 19, Longstreet had returned to the command of the First Corps and was in charge of the forces on the north side of the James as well as at Bermuda Hundred, where Pickett's division was holding and continued to hold until relieved in early March 1865.[49]

The colonel spent a quiet Christmas, on the line and without Alice. He wrote to his wife that the men had received many boxes and they were always giving him something. One man had given him a gallon of apple brandy so he had toddy for Christmas, but there were no eggs for eggnog. He wrote that his ink had frozen and that he was sorry that her beef had proven to be poor.[50]

Even in General Lee's mess ingenious methods had been applied for some time. Lee kept a gift chicken which for over a year supplied an egg for the general's breakfast and thereby escaped the fate of the other biddies. She would lay her egg under Lee's bed. She made her roost on the baggage wagon and travelled with the army to Chancellorsville and Gettysburg. But in the winter of 1863-64, near Orange Court House, having become fat and lazy, she became a fine dinner for the general and some special guests.[51]

In November 1864, General Lee wrote to his wife, in Richmond, that "Col. [James L.] Corley [the chief quartermaster] has no socks." She must pack, weigh, and send hers and they will be distributed. He was living in "a very good abode about 1½ miles from Petersburg, south of the Appomattox....It is dreadfully cold. I wish I had a good wood to encamp in where I could pitch my tent. But there is none convenient. My door will not shut, so that I have a goodly number of cats & puppies around my hearth."[52]

That winter Heth stayed in Petersburg with his wife, and rode out to supervise the fortifications on Hatcher's Run. General Lee moved into Petersburg, on High Street. When he rode out to survey his lines and men, he determined that Walker's brigade was so depleted that it must be disbanded. There is no further mention of the 22nd Battalion in the listing of forces defending Richmond and Petersburg,[63] nor any indication as to which units the King William men were assigned.

According to Major Robert Stiles, who was in charge of the artillery at Chaffin's during the closing seven months of the war "...no intelligent man could fail to note the trend and progress of events." Atlanta had fallen and Sherman was marching to the sea and through the Carolinas, leaving little to the Confederacy "save its Capital and the narrow strips of country bordering on three railroads that fed it....One of our dreams was that Lee, having the inner line, might draw away from Grant, concentrate with [Joseph E.] Johnston, and crush Sherman, and then, turning, the two might crush Grant."[64]

CHAPTER 14
Elmira to Hilton Head — 1864-65

During the fall and winter of 1864-65, many King William men were far from their comrades in the Valley or in the defense of Richmond and Petersburg. They had been sent to prisoner of war camps stretched from Elmira, New York, to Hilton Head Island, South Carolina. The largest number would spend varying amounts of time at Point Lookout, Maryland, in the Chesapeake Bay, and Fort Delaware in the Delaware Bay. Smaller numbers were assigned to Hart's Island and David's Island in Long Island Sound. Most of the captured officers would be eventually on Johnson's Island, in Lake Erie, or Hilton Head Island, in the Atlantic Ocean off the coast of South Carolina and at the mouth of the Broad River. A few men would spend time at the Old Capitol Prison, in Washington, D.C., or at Elmira, an island prison on the Chemung River, fifty miles west of Binghamton, New York.[1]

Elmira, New York, was the hometown and burial place of Mark Twain. After the war, its state reformatory became a pioneer in modern penological methods. However, all accounts of the war years paint a grimmer picture. For the prisoners there, "Conditions were always bad, partly on account of insufficient shelter and partly because of a feud between the commandant and surgeon." The prison, opened in May 1864, was located on grounds lower than the level of the river and a "lagoon of stagnant water contributed to much sickness." There was a high fence around the prison area and the prisoners lived in tents until barracks could be built. Federal artillery stood guard over them. Faced with the prospect of either death by disease or shells, some men chose to tunnel their way to freedom.[2]

Patrick Sweet of Company D, 53rd Virginia, had been taken prisoner in May 1864 in King William. He was moved from Point Lookout to Elmira. Archie Turpin of the 5th Cavalry, who was taken prisoner in Mechanicsville in August 1864, was also held at Elmira. According to an unofficial record, J. W. Johnson of Carter's Battery died while imprisoned at Elmira and was buried in the National Cemetery in Woodlawn, New York.

The Old Capitol Prison in Washington had been built as a temporary capitol building after the British burned the original building during the War of 1812. It was used for suspected spies and Confederate prisoners.[3] Those who were pirsoners from King William did not stay there long. Joseph L. Lee of the 9th Cavalry, taken prisoner in Louisa in 1863, was exchanged sixteen days after his capture. John H. Beadles of the 22nd Battalion, taken at Falling Waters, was sent on to Point Lookout. The record of John Davis of the 22nd shows that he was sent to the Old Capitol Prison after his capture near Harper's Ferry, but there is no further account of what become of him.

Hart's Island is off the northern bank of Long Island Sound, opposite the Bronx. It has served as New York City's potter's field and as a United States Naval Hospital. David's Island is nearer New Rochelle and is also known as Fort Slocum.[4] The enlisted men from the 53rd Regiment who were taken captive in the closing days of the war were sent to Hart's Island, while their officers were sent to Johnson's Island.

Some wounded prisoners were sent to DeCamp Hospital on David's Island. Thomas R. Jones of Carter's Battery, wounded at Gettysburg, was released after his arm was amputated. John R. Lewis of the 53rd Regiment, also wounded in the arm at Gettysburg, was exchanged from this camp.

Point Lookout, Maryland, is a low, sandy spit of land located where the Potomac River empties into the Chesapeake Bay. It is marshy, indented with coves, and exposed to the heat of the summer and the freezing winds of winter. At the beginning of the war, there was a lighthouse there and a 400-acre resort containing a hotel and 100 cottages. Being in financial straits, the holders of the mortage offered it to the Federal government for a military hospital.[5]

After the battles at Gettysburg, Federal convalescents at Point Lookout were transferred to Baltimore and in the following month Confederate prisoners were sent to the Point. During October 1863, some of each shipment of prisoners were already suffering from smallpox or scurvy. The prisoners were kept in tents behind a high board fence. A medical inspection that November found the sick "in a filthy condition" with no stoves in their tents. The wells were shallow and diarrhea was prevalent. From twenty to thirty men were moved each day into the hospital, where the food was good. But for those who must remain in their tents the dispensary remained poor. A local county gazette described the prisoners as being in a pitiable condition — "all in rags." The poet, Sidney Lanier, was brought in as a prisoner in November 1863. He had a flute hidden up his sleeve and entertained his fellow prisoners with his piping. In June 1864, all officers well enough to be moved were transferred to Fort Delaware. Sidney Lanier was exchanged in March 1865, but the tuberculosis which he had contracted in prison led to his early death.[6]

There at Point Lookout in the fall of 1864 was John H. Beadles, who had been transferred from the Old Capitol Prison. His fellows from the

198

22nd Battalion who were also taken at Falling Waters, John H. Atkins and Ira Huckstep, had already died from disease. Reuben Gardner, from a capture in Harrisonburg, would soon be released. Rufus Waters, from his capture earlier in the year at Cold Harbor, remained in prison. Beadles would be exchanged in early 1865 and Robert and William Leftwich would be sent to Point Lookout in the closing days of the war.

Although relatively few cavalrymen were captured, five from King William County spent time at Point Lookout. Pulaski Sutton, who had joined the 9th Cavalry from "Towinque," near Mangohick, and was captured at Boonesboro, had already been exchanged. Robert Semple Ryland and William T. Robins, both also of the 9th, arrived there before the war was over, as did Douglas Rider of the 24th Cavalry, and John Turpin of the 5th Cavalry.

Fort Delaware was a fortification in the Delaware River opposite Delaware City. It was located on Pea Patch Island, a shoal on which local tradition claims a ship bearing a cargo of peas wrecked and the peas sprouted. The fort, built on thousands of piles, combined with batteries on the New Jersey shore to dominate the entrance to the Delaware River, which leads to Wilmington and Philadelphia. A dike around the island kept out the tides, which at times would have washed over the land.[7]

The first use of Fort Delaware for Confederate prisoners was to house 250 from Jackson's army in 1862. There were not sufficient accommodations within the fortress for all the captives so the commanding officer put the excess in the dungeons. Soon the Commissary General of Prisons ordered that barracks be built outside the walls. A request for additional guards was honored when the prison population had grown to 3,000 and 200 of them had escaped. During that winter most of the prisoners were exchanged, but plans were formulated to make the fort the largest prison camp in the country. Barracks were built all over the island. There was a large influx of captives after the battles at Gettysburg, bringing the total to 12,595 men. The number never fell below 6,000 until the last days of release after the war. Diseases were prevalent and water a major problem. A water-boat, sent up the creek to above the tidewater salt line, seldom reached that point. About 2,700 men, prisoners and guards, who died were buried on the New Jersey shore at Finn's Point.[8]

Unlike most other officers from King William, Andrew Leftwich, after his capture on the North Anna in May 1864, remained at Fort Delaware. Upon his arrival he joined members of Carter's Battery, who had been captured a few weeks prior in Spotsylvania, and members of the 53rd Regiment who had been captured at Gettysburg. Robert Beadles, captured at South Mountain in 1863, was already dead. James Madison would die of smallpox during Christmas week of 1864, and Gustavus Lipscomb would die a few weeks after Appomattox. These last two were buried on the New Jersey shore. William Ellett, Sergeant Beverly A. Littlepage, John Pemberton, William Penny, and Harvey Terry were exchanged in September 1864. Ellett and Pemberton were admitted to Chimborazo Hospital in Richmond, and soon furloughed to their homes in King William. Remaining at the fort were William Blake, Charles Madison, and John Tuck, all to be exchanged in February 1865. William Nicholson, T. N. Verlander, William Butler, and William Brown, like Andrew Leftwich, would be held until after the war.

Leftwich, in a letter to Sallie Tuck in November 1864, suggested that the next time she wrote to use larger paper and to write with the lines closer together. He also asked that she urge his father to write to him, for he had received no letter from him since he had been imprisoned. Andrew said that with Divine help he was striving to make himself content. Help did come in the assistance of an aunt of a fellow prisoner, Lieutenant E. P. C. Lewis. She wrote to him that month from Clifton Springs, New York, but did not sign the letter. She said that she had just returned from burying her husband in Wilkes-Barre, Pennsylvania, offered to send him some clothing, and enclosed $5.00.[9]

A January letter from Clifton Springs, this time addressed to "Lieutenant Andrew J. Leftwich, Prisoner of War, 31st Division, Officers barracks, Fort Delaware," headed "Dear friend and relative," and signed "M. L. Covett," told that she had received the permit for his clothes in his December letter. Since both he and Lieutenant Burrus had been sick, she hoped that the stewed fruit would help. She sent him (or them) a box containing: "a coat, pants, 2 pr. of cotton drawers, 2 woolen ones, 4 pr. woolen socks, 2 woolen shirts, 2 collars, 1 necktie, one pocket handkerchief, one hat, one pr. of shoes, 1 box of blackening, 1 piece of soap, 1 ct. of coffee, 1 ct. sugar, 2 papers tobacco, 2 doz. biscuits (some with a little cold meat inside), 2 cans of stewed fruit, 1 paper box containing 3 doz. small cakes, 1 loaf and half of cake, a few apples to fill in the space, paper of stationery and envelopes." She asked that he divide with Lieutenant Buruss and stated that she enclosed the permit in the box along with a letter to him and a letter to a General L. (?). Also she enclosed some buttons which had fallen out of the needle case which her daughter had sent.[10]

At that time there appears to have been only one King William man of the 53rd Virginia still being held at Fort Delaware. James H. Burch would be exchanged in February 1865. Lorimer Robinson had already been exchanged and Marius C. Campbell had died in September 1863, just before he was scheduled to be exchanged. There is mention in his record of being taken to Aiken's Landing on the James, so possibly his body was returned. John H. Seigle had died and been buried at Finn's Point. The officers of the regiment had been transferred to Johnson's Island.

Robert Campbell of the 53rd Regiment may have been returned to Fort Delaware before his brother, Marius, died. Robert and other King William men were among those officers who, in 1864, were used as pawns in the siege of Charleston, South Carolina. They were shifted from Fort Delaware to Morris Island in the Charleston harbor, to Fort Pulaski at the mouth of the Savannah River, then to Hilton Head Island in the Atlantic, and finally back to Fort Delaware.

Fort Pulaski fell to the Federals in 1862. The Union batteries had fired their rifled guns at the brick and mortar fortress from a considerable distance, causing a 100-foot breach in the wall. Morris Island and other islands in the Charleston harbor fell to the Federals in 1863. From the islands Union batteries, including the renowned "Swamp Angel," fired their bolts into the city. Confederate guns retaliated from Fort Sumter and Charleston.[11]

In the summer of 1864 General John H. Foster, Department of the South, had his headquarters at Hilton Head, South Carolina. The Confederates were holding fifty officers as prisoners in Charleston. It was reported that they were kept in a dangerous location in the city in range of the Federal mortars. Correspondence between General Foster and General Sam Jones, commanding the Confederate Department of South Carolina, Georgia, and Florida, failed to squelch the rumors. Foster required the removal of officers of comparable rank from Fort Delaware to Hilton Head for exchange.[12]

Among those sent to Hilton Head Island at that time and exchanged were General Edward Johnson (who had commanded Carter's Battery at Spotsylvania); General J. J. Archer (who would later command the 22nd Battalion); and General George H. Steuart (who would later command the 53rd Regiment). When General Grant heard that 500 to 600 more officers were being sent to Foster, he made it plain that he did not favor further exchange of prisoners.[13]

The story of the additional 600 officers who were sent to General Foster has been told by three of their number. Captain J. Ogden Murray, an officer of the 7th Virginia Cavalry, had been taken prisoner on the Valley Pike in November 1863. He called his account *The Immortal Six Hundred.* In their number he listed: Captain William P. Carter, Lieutenant W. E. Hart, and Lieutenant Festus King of Fry's or Page's Battery (actually Carter's Battery); Lieutenant Robert C. Campbell of the 53rd Regiment; and Lieutenant H. T. Coulter of the 53rd Regiment, said to be an assistant adjutant from King William Court House (although he is not listed on the monument at the courthouse). Lieutenant Peter B. Akers of Lynchburg, a member of the 11th Virginia Infantry who had been captured at Milford in May 1864, added his recollections to those of Murray. Captain J. J. Dunkle, a Franklin, West Virginia, man from the 25th Infantry who had been captured at Spotsylvania, wrote an account under the pen name of "Fritz Fuzzlebug."[14]

The 600 were called out from the officers' barracks at Fort Delaware on August 20, marched down to the wharf and packed like cattle in the hold of the steamship *Crescent City*. There the ventilation was poor, the light dim, and the odor of tar and grease prevailed. All were seasick as, thinking they would be exchanged, they were taken south by way of Fort Monroe. Their quarters were hot and reeked of human waste and vomit, but the captain refused to hose them out. After eighteen days they landed on Morris Island and were told that there would be no exchange. Murray said, "The day was hot, but we were once more in God's sunshine and out of the pest hole of the prison ship."[15]

The officers were kept on Morris Island in a three-acre pen surrounded by pine poles placed close together. Around the enclosure there was a twelve-foot-high parapet over which sentinels walked day and night and a ditch several feet wide. Inside there was a rope thirty feet from the wall. Prisoners were not allowed to touch the rope or appear to be going near it or they would be shot. Rows of tents which were made for two soldiers each held four prisoners. The atmosphere some mornings was pleasant, but the hot southern sun would soon make the sand almost unbearable to their bare feet. Then it would hold the heat until midnight. Other mornings were foggy and chilly.[16]

The Union batteries, Wagner and Gregg, were 250 to 400 yards from the prison enclosure. They continued to fire on the Confederate held forts — Fort Moultrie, 1,200 yards away on Sullivan's Island, and Fort Sumter, 700 yards away. Sometimes the retaliatory shells from Moultrie would fall short and land in their midst. The guns on Cumming's Point, 500 yards away, kept up their firing day and night into Charleston. At night the 300-pounder Federal rifled pieces would shake the island. Once a shell lost its projectile energy, it would fall rapidly, picking up velocity, then burst with the concussion of a thunderbolt. "Our ears were constantly greeted with the roar of artillery, the concussion of shells, the groans of the wounded, or the shrieks of the dying," one prisoner wrote. Some guards were wounded and some killed, but none of the prisoners were mortally wounded.[17]

Drinking water was obtained by digging holes in the sand. Their medicine was dispensed by a "red-headed cow doctor." It consisted of one opium pill or a dose of jamaica ginger, no matter what the complaint. They had to remain in their tents at night. Shells from Fort Sumter and other batteries fell in their midst. Murray remembered "Captain Will Page Carter" as "a loveable comrade, kind and generous, a dignified gentleman." Carter would say to those who could not rise from their bunks, "We can suffer, men, for principle; we cannot surrender without dishonor."[18]

In October, hopes arose again for exchange. The guns of Fort Sumter, Moultrie, Johnson, and those of Charleston ceased. The prisoners were marched down to the beach and loaded on two schooner hulks for thirty-six hours while the truce boats stood off Fort Sumter. The conference failed and the prisoners were marched back to the prison stockade in the afternoon. They did receive boxes of tobacco, sweet potatoes, and peanuts from the Confederate government. By December the sick, wounded, and influential had been exchanged and all the remaining loaded on gunboats for Fort Pulaski or Hilton Head.[19]

The service records for William Carter, Hart, King, and Campbell show that they were held on Hilton Head Island, but there is no notation that they had been previously held on Morris Island.

James F. Wilson of Company D, 53rd Regiment, was also at Hilton Head Island. He had been taken as a prisoner at Gettysburg, was held at Fort Delaware and had been in the smallpox hospital at Point Lookout. He was not shown as an officer on the company records nor listed by Murray or Dunkle as being among the "Six Hundred." Yet he died there on November 14, 1864, and was buried on the island.

On October 21, 1864 (some accounts say November), two hundred and twenty of the 600 were taken from Morris Island by the steamer *Cannonicus* to Hilton Head Island. They disembarked on a Sunday morning and encamped about a mile from the village in the same tents they had used on Morris Island. After a week they were moved into town to a large log house which had been built for and was still used as a prison for Federal deserters and criminals. Their rations for the first week had been good but in town they received only ten ounces of cornmeal and a half-pint of onion and cucumber pickle. To this was added in February 1865 four ounces of meat per diem and four ounces of potatoes.[20]

The prisoners were held at Hilton Head in a square enclosure that covered several acres. The general headquarters and barracks for the Union officers and men were on the beach and west side. A high plank wall separated these buildings from those on the north and east. In the northwest corner two 70-to-80-foot long buildings housed the Confederate prisoners. On the second story of one building was the hospital for the "yanks and rebs." There was a roll call three times a day, but otherwise the prisoners were allowed out of the buildings only twenty at a time. It was freezing cold and the chilly wind off the Atlantic blew through the cracks, but no fires were allowed inside. They had little clothing. Some had no shoes and few had blankets.[21]

Those few who had been able to buy frying pans cooked their cornmeal outside over a meager allotment of green pine or live oak. Others ate their meal raw. With the fall of McAllister (a fort below Savannah taken by Sherman's men on December 13), all but two companies of Union infantry and 30 cavalrymen were withdrawn from the island. The cavalry guarded the bridge to the mainland. While the opposite shore was held by Confederate pickets an escape was attempted, only to fail when the prisoners were betrayed by one of their own number.[22] They were there at the culmination of General William T. Sherman's "March to the Sea" at the end of 1864.

While Sherman and his 60,000 men rested outside of Savannah after their march across Georgia from Atlanta, Beauregard arrived in Charleston. For the evacuation of Savannah, Beauregard ordered the construction of a pontoon bridge, using the "plantation rice-flats" for pontoons. He arrived in Savannah on the night of December 16. Four nights later Hardee's 10,000 men, his artillery, and his trains made passage out of Georgia and across a series of bridges and causeways between islands and swamp lands to the South Carolina bank.[23]

The cold damp walls of the battered Fort Pulaski housed others of the six hundred. Lieutenant Hart's record shows that he spent some time at Fort Pulaski as well as Hilton Head. Lieutenant Coulter was exchanged in December from Fort Pulaski. B. W. Dabney of Company H, 53rd Regiment, although not an officer, had been sent from Point Lookout to a prison at Savannah (possibly Fort Pulaski). At the end of November 1864, he was sent to Camp Lee (Richmond) and exchanged.

Ogden Murray was among those held in Savannah harbor. He describes the guards as more humane than on Morris Island. But the daily ration was the same as on Hilton Head — 10 ounces of wormy cornmeal and a half-pint of onion and cucumber pickle. They slept on rough pine bunks in the fort casements, with no blankets or heat except for an occasional lump of coal in a camp kettle. Each division, consisting of twenty-eight men, had twelve sticks of pine wood a day and a stove which they could light at noon to do their cooking. Murray says that hunger drove the men to catching and eating dogs, cats, and rats. The colonel's wife had a pet cat which she begged them to spare. They honored her request although the temptation was especially great on Christmas Day. There were four inches of snow on the ground that day. They swapped memories of home and wondered if their comrades in camp had anything beyond their army rations.[24]

In early March 1865, the prisoners from Fort Pulaski (and it appears also from Hilton Head) were shipped northward on the large ocean steamer *Illinois*. This time they were allowed liberty of the ship and given good rations. They arrived off Norfolk on the morning the Confederates attacked Fort Stedman. None of the prisoners were allowed up on deck. After several days on the James, their steamer one night put back out to sea and landed them the next day at their former prison, Fort Delaware. They had been gone eight months. Soon they settled back into the life there of "law schools," "medical schools," and "divinity schools," and the roles of "prison gambler, barbers, tailors, laundrymen, workers in rubber, and a minstrel troop, which gave performances in the mess hall of the prison when the commandant gave the permission."[25]

At Fort Monroe in 1863, Rooney Lee had been well treated. General Lee wrote to his daughter Mildred that her brother's leg was nearly healed and, although it was stiff, he was walking around on it. He said that his son's "keepers are kind to him & give him all that is necessary." In November the commanding general wrote to his wife, "I see by the papers that Fitzhugh [Rooney] had been sent to Fort Lafayette. Any place would be better than Fort Monroe with [General Benjamin] Butler in command. It is probable he [Rooney] will be sent to Johnson's Island, where the rest of our officers are." The news had come to Rooney Lee, while he was still at Fort Monroe, that his wife, Charlotte, lay dying in Richmond. Rooney petitioned Butler that he be allowed a 48-hour leave to visit her. Although Custis Lee had formally offered himself as a hostage until his brother's return to prison, the petition was denied. Charlotte died the day after Christmas, 1863. By March 29, 1864, the young general had been exchanged and was back at Stuart's camp, near Orange Court House.[26]

Johnson's Island is two and one half miles from Sandusky, Ohio. The prison there was used exclusively for officers after the first year of the war. It consisted of seventeen acres enclosed by a fence. The crude barracks were two story. Conditions were generally good except when the cold winds blew off of Lake Erie. Some of the prisoners froze to death on New Year's Day, 1864.[27]

By the end of July 1864, Captain John Latane and Lieutenant Irving Sale, both of Company H, 53rd Regiment, had rounded out a year on Johnson's Island. Irving wrote to his mother that it was "a dull life, worse than anyone would imagine." They filled in their time making "fans of wood, Gutha Percha rings, crosses & chains with sets of shells from Lake Erie."[28]

In the cold misty dawn one morning on Johnson's Island, Captain Latane answered the roll call for a friend who had slipped away from camp during the night. With the close of the year Latane appointed a Captain John L. Hall to appear before Captain R. B. Moon, the adjutant quartermaster of the regiment, to collect the pay due him for the period July 1, 1863, to December 20, 1864.[29]

Lieutenant Archie B. Brown of Company D was captured at Dinwiddie Court House on April 1, 1865, and sent to this island prison. Colonel Aylett and Lieutenant James B. Hill, Company D, followed a few days later after their capture at Sayler's Creek.

Aylett wrote to both his wife and brother from Johnson's Island that he found there a host of friends and acquaintances and plenty of books to read. He had been brought to the prison by way of Petersburg and the Old Capitol Prison. The colonel kept in good health and spirits but regretted that he was not allowed to write more than one page at a time.[30]

Some of William Aylett's junior officers were no longer at Johnson's Island when he arrived. Captain Latane had been transferred to Point Lookout on March 21, 1865, and possibly also Lieutenant Sale. Irving Sale may have been exchanged by this time. He took his oath of allegiance in Richmond three weeks after the surrender at Appomattox.

The process for exchange of prisoners of war was worked out in 1862 between General D. H. Hill and Federal General John A. Dix. Colonel Robert Ould was the Confederate agent for exchanges and remained so until the end of the war, although exchanges ceased for periods of time starting in 1863. A quota system was calculated with a private as a unit, a non-commissioned officer as two units, on up to twenty to sixty units for a general. The "flag of truce boat," the paddle wheeled *New York* or some other bearing a white flag, would move up the James with Confederates from Fort Monroe to dock at Aiken's Landing or City Point.[31] The record of William Penny of Carter's Battery shows that, upon his release from Fort Delaware, he passed through Aiken's Landing on his way to Camp Lee in Richmond. An unofficial roster records Penny as dead from disease before the war was over.

A returning Virginia soldier observed other prisoners as they disembarked at Aiken's Landing. He wrote: "Those prisoners that trooped slowly over the gangplank, looking like the vanguard of the Resurrection, were from Fort Delaware. Scores seemed to be ill; many suffering from the scurvy, while all bore marks of severe treatment in their thin faces and wasted forms."[32]

General James J. Archer was among those taken prisoner at Gettysburg. He had been a classmate of Mary Chesnut's husband, General James Chesnut, Jr., at Princeton College, where he was called "Sally" for his feminine beauty. He was held at Fort Delaware and Fort Johnson before being exchanged in South Carolina. Mrs. Chesnut recorded in her diary in August 1864, that Archer visited in their home in Columbia, South Carolina (apparently after his release and before reporting to his assignment at Chaffin's Bluff). She said, "There is no trace of feminine beauty about this grim soldier now. He has a hard face, black-beard, shallow, with the saddest eyes. . . .He is abstracted, weary-looking in mind and body, deadened by long imprisonment." She said that his mother and sister had been permitted to visit him only once while he was in prison, at which time they had to stand thirty feet from him and were allowed no word or sign of recognition. Archer died soon after reaching Richmond. Mrs. Chestnut wrote: "He was only half alive here. . . .Poor, pretty Sally Archer; that is the end of you."[33]

The incarceration of experienced officers was felt back in the companies. Andrew Blake, second lieutenant of Company H, 53rd Regiment, was facing charges of misconduct before the enemy. He wrote a letter to General Cooper on November 26 to stress his relative youth and inexperience. He said that during the prolonged absence of both his captain and first lieutenant he had been responsible for the company command and for the increasing number of new men assigned to their ranks. The young lieutenant felt that he was unsuited to his duties and wished to resign his commission and become a member of the artillery. Colonel Aylett suggested Blake's resignation and wrote that the lieutenant's actions had not proved him to be incompetent or inefficient. Blake's resignation was approved by Generals Pickett, Steuart, and Longstreet and recommended to General Lee.[34]

Back in Hanover and King William that fall, a soldier from South Carolina searched for the body of his brother who had been mortally wounded during some of the cavalry fights in the spring. He had read in a New York paper that some of those who had been taken as prisoners had died and been buried on the way to the "White House." He found his friend, Middleton, buried in Hanover in the yard at "Summer Hill" and the grave marked by Mrs. Willoughby Newton. Dr. Brockenbrough of nearby "Westwood" accompanied the soldier across the Pamunkey to three graves by a roadside in King William. One of the graves was marked "Tingle." (Perhaps the Union soldiers had misunderstood the pronunciation of Pringle.) With continued digging they unearthed Pringle's remains in one of the other two graves. The men wrapped the body tenderly in a blanket, placed it in a coffin, and took it by wagon to "Summer Hill." Mrs. Newton, by the light of a lone lantern, read the Episcopal committal service. Young ladies and children covered the grave with fresh flowers.[35]

CHAPTER 15

Along the Appomattox — 1865

The early months of 1865 found the King William men participating in the last desperate efforts to save the Confederacy. The King William troops, who were scattered from the Valley to the James, would first be used in an attempt to prevent Sheridan from making contact with Grant in central Virginia. Failing that they then would be sent to the doomed trenches south of Petersburg and finally on the disastrous trek to Appomattox Court House.

Lee received word on February 4 that he had been confirmed by the Senate as General-in-Chief of the armies. Two days later he reported that action had been resumed against the enemy by Hill (Third Corps) and Gordon (Second Corps) along Hatcher's Run. He made no mention in his dispatches or letters of the peace conference at Hampton Roads on February 2 between Lincoln, Lincoln's secretary of state, William H. Seward, the vice-president of the Confederacy, Alexander H. Stephens, and Virginia Senator R. M. T. Hunter. The conference bore no fruit, nor did a letter written by Lee to Grant on March 2 requesting an interview with him concerning a military convention as a means to bring the war to an end. Grant declined an interview, saying that he had no authority to negotiate.[1]

R. L. T. Beale, now a general, wrote that the 9th Cavalry was on the right of the infantry at Hatcher's Run in February 1865. During the action on the 5th, "they suffered considerably" (although their service records show none from King William injured). It can not be determined if any of those remaining from the 22nd Battalion and still serving under General Hill were involved.[2]

Carter and his battalions were no longer in the Valley. Jed Hotchkiss wrote in his diary for February 1, as he sat in his tent that night drawing a map of the current position of their army, that Tom Carter stopped by. The colonel and two battalions would be leaving the next day for Richmond. The papers of Carter's courier, Page Powell, show that he was at Greenwood Station (near Charlottesville) on March 2. Doctor Freeman has concluded, "After the excessive losses of guns in the Valley, there seemed no good reason for retaining there, weaponless, so fine a combat officer as Col. Tom Carter."[3] But certainly, he was missed.

General Wesley Merritt of Sheridan's cavalry participated in the rout of Early at Waynesboro on March 2. He said of the general, "The veteran soldier was full of pluck and made a bold front for a fight, but his troops were overcome . . . and Early, with a few general officers, barely escaped capture by flight. All Early's supplies, all transportation, all the guns, ammunition and flags, and most of the officers and men of the army were captured and sent to the rear." Sheridan could now move through Central Virginia, wrecking the bridges and warping the rails of the Virginia Central Railroad. Another group under his command played like havoc with the James River and Kanawha Canal.[4]

An almost illegible letter from Colonel Aylett to his wife shows that the 53rd Virginia was to move out at 6 p.m. on March 9 from their position in Chesterfield County, near the Howlett Line. They would not be passing through Richmond. Some mention was made of Lynchburg.[5] It seems the 53rd Regiment may have been used to help block any approach by Sheridan from the southwest while others under General Pickett were to meet his cavalrymen should they move through Hanover County.

Sheridan used Grant's tactic of the year before and kept the Pamunkey between his cavalry and the Confederates. He reported that his activities along the railroad from Frederick's Hall to Beaver Dam and Hanover Junction drew Pickett's division, Bushrod Johnson's division, and Fitz Lee's cavalry below Ashland and to Hanover Court House. But, as Sheridan quipped, ". . . the enemy forgot his pontoon trains."[6]

General Ewell was aware of the need for pontoons but had been unable to obtain them in time. Through Ashland he had received word, apparently from a private scout calling himself "Thompson," that Sheridan had recrossed the North Anna River at "Oxford Ford" and the South Anna River at Wickham's ("Hickory Hill"). Thompson also wired that one of his scouts crossed the Pamunkey at Norman's (Norment's) Ford and fell in with the head of Sheridan's column. He said that the enemy cavalrymen were encamped near Mangohick Church and that their camp fires could be plainly seen from Hanover Court House.[7] Who was this "Thompson" who had ready access to the telegraph station at Hanover depot and had assistants both knowledgeable concerning local fords and adept at blending with passing Union horsemen?

On a previous occasion when Sheridan passed through Mangohick his men had entered the Thomas Jackson home searching for meat. They were thwarted by Albion Jackson's widow, named Martha but called Patty. When the soldiers suggested that the meat might be under the wood pile, she offered to help them move the wood. The search was abandoned although the meat was under the pile. Young Lucetta Jackson, Patty's sister-in-law, pled with them not to take her horse. They left without taking the horse, but returned for it later. This time the consequences of their presence in the neighborhood were more tragic.[8]

Thomas Price Jackson, Jr., had been assigned reconnaissance duty in the neighborhood due to the approaching enemy cavalry. He stopped off at his home to tell his family of his pending marriage to a local girl. Lucetta walked out with him as he left, and she had just turned back when twenty-four-year-old Tom was felled by a sniper's bullet. He was buried in the family cemetery beside the youngest brother, William Daniel, who had died of diphtheria before his fourteenth birthday. Brother Albion, who had died of pneumonia, was apparently buried elsewhere. Of the six Jackson brothers, only two survived the war: John, of Company E, 30th Regiment, and Lucian, who served with the 9th Cavalry.[9]

The family of James G. White, the friend of Sallie Tuck and her sisters, says that Sheridan and his men camped in the fields around his home, "Landsdowne," near Calno and Mangohick. White, 45 and discharged from Carter's Battery because of his age, must have fled to the woods for safety. His descendants still have the bowie knife which Mrs. White brandished to keep the cavalrymen from entering the house.[10]

Sheridan had at his command 13,000 enlisted men ready to fight. His record shows that they encamped at Mangohick on March 16, at the courthouse on March 17, and Indian Town (the Pamunkey Reservation) on March 18, and crossed on the next day over the repaired railroad bridge to the "White House." General Thomas Devin reported that his men followed at the rear of the train and passed through Ayletts on their way from Mangohick to the courthouse.[11]

———

Colonel Carter and his battalions (including the King William men now serving under Major Cutshaw) had joined the Confederates south of Petersburg. A map drawn by Nathaniel Michler shows a line of Federal forts stretching southward from the Appomattox, east of Petersburg, then westward across the Weldon Railroad to Hatcher's Run. The Confederate fortifications encircled the city and an uncompleted line reached out to Hatcher's Run.[12]

Lee's chief of artillery, Pendleton, made use of the colonel's expertise to, as he wrote, "refit the artillery battalion of the Second Corps." Pendleton put out special orders on March 20 which included instruction that "Nelson's, Braxton's and Cutshaw's battalions, Second Corps, will be re-equipped for the field under command of Col. Thomas H. Carter as soon as possible." The colonel must assemble the guns, bring in the horses and make arrangements for their continued forage. The chief of artillery considered these three commands as "veteran battalions" and he wished that they be "restored to full efficiency . . . on account of their tried superiority."[13] Yet there is no indication that they were used in the initial thrust for 1865 the following week. The chances are that they were not ready.

General John B. Gordon, in charge of the Second Corps, conceived a plan to cut Grant's left by the capture of Fort Stedman (in the northern segment of the line) and any forts behind the Federal line. He felt that this feat would cause the Union general to shorten his lines and pressure would be lessened on Lee's front. On March 24, Gordon requested that Pickett's division, that day under General "Maryland" Steuart, be sent to his assistance from north of the James. Gordon was warned that it would be unlikely that they could arrive in time to be of any assistance, nor did they arrive. Fort Stedman was taken in the early morning hours of March 25, but it was found to be untenable against strong enemy resurgence. By 8 a.m., General Lee ordered them to withdraw.[14]

General Sherman visited Grant at City Point on March 27. This general from the west now had his army at Goldsboro, North Carolina, 145 miles from Petersburg. He told Grant that he would be ready to move by April 10. His plan was, after threatening Raleigh, to turn toward the Roanoke River and Weldon, North Carolina, sixty miles from Petersburg. From Weldon he would head toward Burkeville, Virginia, to cut off Lee's possible retreat by rail to Danville. Grant feared that when Lee learned of Sherman's presence near the Roanoke River he might any night abandon his trenches at Petersburg and slip away. He took the initial move by instructing Sheridan to cross Hatcher's Run in the early hours of March 29 in an attempt to get to the west and rear of the Confederates.[15]

We can be certain that the 53rd Regiment and the 30th Regiment were by that time southwest of Petersburg. Both regiments would sustain injuries within the next three days at Dinwiddie Court House and Five Forks.

Pickett's division was made a mobile unit to work with Fitz Lee and Rooney Lee to keep Sheridan away from the Southside Railroad (now the Norfolk and Western) to Burkeville and Lynchburg at least until the roads dried out enough after the winter thaw and spring rains to allow Lee's poorly fed teams to move his wagon trains in the evacuation of Petersburg. Pickett's men were sent by train to Sutherland Station, then marched to the intersection called Five Forks (now Routes 613 and 627), several miles south of Route 460. There on March 30 and 31 they were met by Rooney Lee (with the 9th Cavalry), Fitz Lee, and Rosser. The troops passed through cold rain, crossed swollen streams, and moved along roads laced with mud holes. On the 31st they advanced toward the enemy at Dinwiddie Court House and remained in contact with Sheridan's men in attacks and repulses all day. It was reported that the men stayed in good spirits in spite of the inclement weather and the fact that they had little to eat.[16]

Major Robert Peatross of the 30th Regiment, under Generals Corse and Pickett, was wounded that day and two of his men were mortally injured. Lieutenant Archie B. Brown of Company D, 53rd Regiment, was taken prisoner. General Beale led his brigade through water up to their armpits to come to Pickett's assistance. The 9th Cavalry was engaged at both Dinwiddie Court House and Five Forks.[17] Fortunately there were no casualties among the King William cavalrymen during either confrontation or later on the way to Appomattox.

George Alfred Townsend, now back with the Union army as a correspondent after spending some time in England, wrote of the encounters at Dinwiddie Court House and Five Forks. He said that Sheridan, on his return from the Valley, had "scarcely time to change his horses' shoes before he was off, and after him much of our [Union] infantry also moved to the left." They passed their old breastworks on Hatcher's Run and pressed on southwestward to Dinwiddie Court House and engaged the Confederates along the Quaker Road. The next day they left the Boydton Plank Road and headed northward for a crossroads called Five Forks. There three of the five roads led to the Southside Railroad and the roads off of them unlocked all the country around. Along the principal road, the White Oak, Confederates had their log and earth breastworks and rifle pits. At the crossroads the land was high and dry. Nearby was a well-watered forest and the headwaters of Gravelly Run. A mile into the woods was a white-painted Methodist Church with green shutters.[18]

During the night General Pickett decided that it was more important to protect the approaches closer to the railroad (to the north) and the Confederate right flank (to the west) than to hold his position. At 2 a.m. his guns started back toward Five Forks and at 5 a.m. the infantry began the march back through the mud. Upon arriving at Five Forks the wagon trains were sent on to the north side of Hatcher's Run. Pickett received orders from Lee to hold Five Forks at all costs.[19] Twenty men from the King William members of the 53rd Regiment taken prisoner would be part of the cost sustained.

The line was formed at Five Forks with Rooney Lee, and possibly the 9th Cavalry, on the right to the west, adjoined by General Corse's brigade and the 30th Regiment. "Maryland" Steuart, with the 53rd Virginia, was positioned near the center. Fitz Lee's division, including the 4th and 5th Virginia Cavalry and directed by Colonel Thomas T. Munford, was on the extreme left to the east. That afternoon when the line was attacked by Sheridan and Warren (V Corps), General Pickett and Fitz Lee were across Hatcher's Run to the north, socializing with General Rosser over some shad he had caught. They were out of touch with their men when the Federals struck. Rooney Lee and Corse were able to hold on the right but the left was turned by Federal cavalry and infantry. Five thousand Confederates were taken captive. It turned out to be Lee's most costly day since the "Bloody Angle" the previous spring.[20]

Townsend, while seated by Sheridan's camp fire, wrote of the scene at the Methodist Church. He described the gallery for the servants and the varnished pulpit up front with a Bible bearing the inscription on the flyleaf, "Presented to the Gravelly Run Meeting House by the Ladies." He concluded with the statement, "That meeting house is a hospital tonight, running blood, and at Five Forks a victor's [Union] battle-flags are flying."[21]

The 53rd Regiment had been dealt another devastating blow. Among the prisoners taken from Company D were Sergeant Thomas Lipscomb; Corporal John Burch; and Privates James Chick, John Cooke, William Ellett, Warren Lipscomb, George Quarles, and Selim Slaughter. From Company H there were taken Eugene Clements, Americus Floyd, William Floyd, John Floyd, W. Garrett, Robert George, J. W. Hargrove, Henry Kelly, James Harvie Powell, J. P. Pumphrey, L. D. Trice, and George Tuck. Only Quarles appears to have been injured. He had his arm amputated, not at the meeting house, but at Fort Monroe. He was then put on the steamer *Hero of New Jersey* bound for a hospital in Baltimore. Later he was returned to Fort Monroe, where he died. All others, except Warren Lipscomb, were sent on to Hart's Island. Lipscomb was taken to Point Lookout.

With this last disaster there seemed to be more King William men in prison camps than in the ranks. Some had been exchanged and were possibly in Richmond hospitals or still on disability leave. A few prisoners from Carter's Battery had been exchanged and were now on active duty with Cutshaw's artillerymen. Those from the 22nd Battalion were serving in other undetermined units. About four dozen still rode with Lee's Rangers and a few men were with the 24th Cavalry and other units.

Robert Semple Ryland and Sergeant John Slaughter may have been either on detached service or leave while their fellows served around Petersburg. Ryland was taken prisoner on the Peninsula on March 16 and sent on to Point Lookout. Slaughter was taken prisoner on April 3 and released on April 20.

The only time we can be certain where any of the King William men were on the trek to Appomattox is when they appear on the lists of prisoners taken in Amelia County or at Sayler's Creek, near Farmville. Some members of the 22nd Battalion and Carter's Battery moved with General Gordon. The 53rd Regiment travelled with General Anderson.

On April 2 Lee sent word from Petersburg to General Breckinridge, now the secretary of war in Richmond, saying, "I see no prospect of doing more than holding our position here till night." He said that they had been cut off from the brigades on Hatcher's Run and that his lines at Fort Gregg had been broken. He would attempt to cross to the north side of the Appomattox that night, would cross back at Goode's or Beaver's (Bevil's) bridges, then concentrate his forces near the Danville Railroad. He advised that preparation be made for the evacuation of Richmond that night.[22]

Word may have already been received in Richmond that General A. P. Hill had been killed in the early morning hours. He had been shot as he and his courier tried to make their way along the Boydton Plank Road to General Heth's headquarters after the Confederate line had been broken.[23]

The defending forces in the trenches around Petersburg had already withdrawn to within the city, which was surrounded on three sides by Grant's men. Only the way to the north, across the Appomattox, lay open to the Confederates. If they could soon recross to the south side, they would be to the west of Grant's army. Longstreet was now leading both his First Corps and the Third, formerly under the direction of the now-fallen Hill. He and Lee moved their men and trains across the Appomattox on pontoons. Soon they were joined by Gordon and the Second Corps on the Old Hickory Road. High water made the first bridge, Bevil's, unusable. Before finding a crossing at Goode's Bridge, a few miles west of Skinquarter on present Route 360, they were joined by General Mahone and the forces from the Howlett Line. Upstream the defenders of Richmond under General Ewell and Custis Lee managed to cross the river by planking the railroad bridge at Mattoax.[24]

The concentration point was to be Amelia Court House, just a few miles to the west. Here General Lee had instructed that there should be food from Richmond to feed his men. As they began to arrive at the small village on April 4, they found that no rations had arrived from Richmond. The boxes that awaited them contained only ammunition for guns.[25]

Lee was using what is now Route 360 along the Southern Railroad. Grant was using present Route 460 along the Southside Railroad. The two roads and railroads crossed at Burkeville. Route 360 and the Southern Railroad then went on southwest to Danville, while Route 460 and the Southside Railroad wound their way westward along an old Indian footpath and later stagecoach route through Farmville and Appomattox to the mountains.[26]

Word from Farmville on the morning of April 4 was that Sheridan was already at Jetersville, just seven miles to the southwest of Amelia Court House. General Ord, commanding the Army of the James, was at Burkeville, only seventeen miles away. Already Grant was to the west of Lee. The Southern between Lee and Danville had been cut in two places.[27]

Pickett's men (including the 53rd Regiment) under Anderson's command did not arrive at Amelia Court House until the morning of April 5.

Earlier that morning Sheridan had directed the II Corps and the V Corps to move to Jetersville. Meredith's cavalry was also on the way.[28] Cary Kimbrough of the 53rd Regiment was captured at Jetersville on April 4.

On the march through Amelia County, from the courthouse on to the southwest, Longstreet and the First Corps led. Anderson followed with the Second Corps and then Ewell with the Third Corps. General Gordon, now in charge of the slowly moving wagon trains, was bringing up the rear. Lee had directed Gordon to take a turnoff above Jetersville and move the trains through Amelia Springs and Deatonville. Gordon continued westward at Deatonsville and then northwest along the Jamestown Road in order to converge with the others at Rice's Station on the Southside Railroad. Lee, Longstreet, Anderson, and Ewell took a southwestern fork at Deatonville that led them over several crossings of Sayler's Creek before reaching Rice's Station.[29]

The records of the 22nd Battalion show that the Leftwich brothers, Robert and William, and John Fox were captured at Amelia Court House on April 6. Benjamin Cocke, Andrew Leftwich's former mess mate, was captured at Amelia Springs on the same day. From this we may conclude that they were with Gordon and the wagons.

At 9:30 a.m. on April 6, Federals sighted two Confederate columns moving in a northwesterly directly. Humphreys waded his men across Flat Creek and commenced a running fight with Gordon's corps which continued over a distance of fourteen miles in the direction of High Bridge. General Gordon had to abandon many of his ammunition wagons due to the miry condition of the roads and the weakened state of his forage-starved horses.[30]

Perhaps it was at this time on their trek from Petersburg to Appomattox Court House that the wagon carrying Colonel Carter's papers got mired in the mud. The desk containing his reports was thrown out to lighten the load, but the frying pans and skillets were retained. The colonel could not fathom this selection, for, as he later wrote, they had received nothing to cook for several days and had subsisted on parched corn.[31]

Unfortunately communication was not maintained along the long Confederate line of march. Lee, travelling with Longstreet, had already reached Rice's Station, off Route 460 not far from Farmville, when Sheridan's cavalry and the VI Corps slipped through a gap behind them and blocked the movement of Anderson's and Ewell's men. In the ensuing battles, called Sayler's Creek, Ewell, Custis Lee, Corse, and three other generals, along with 800 men and officers, were taken as prisoners.[32] Among them were Colonel Aylett and Lieutenant James B. Hill of the 53rd Regiment. William Aylett was not injured.

General Lee rode up from Rice's and rallied some of the fleeing soldiers. Anderson's, Pickett's, and Bushrod Johnson's whereabouts were unknown. Those remaining of their commands, including the 30th Virginia and Wise's brigade, were placed under General Gordon and sent after nightfall to High Bridge. They were to cross the lower (wagon) bridge, burn both bridges behind them, and join Lee in Farmville.[33]

The majestic High Bridge spans 2,400 feet above the Appomattox River from a bluff in Prince Edward County to a bluff in Cumberland County. During the war it was a 60-to-125-foot-high wooden super-structure, built on twenty brick piers and used by the Southside Railroad. A Union detachment was sent to burn the bridge in order to trap the Confederates east of the river. However, the Confederates defeated the detachment on April 6, just prior to the battles at Sayler's Creek, thereby saving it and the lower wagon bridge for their own use. Mahone's division (formerly of Hill's corps), serving as the rear guard, had the responsibility for firing the bridges behind them. The orders were not promptly delivered and the green timbers of the wagon bridge were slow to burn.[34]

Longstreet's men continued from Rice's along a more southerly route into Farmville, there to cross to the northern bank of the Appomattox and to burn that bridge behind them. The night was cold; snow fell in Burkeville the next day. Those who trudged along the southerly route found the way crowded and the mud knee deep.[35]

The Federals took their prisoners from Sayler's Creek to Burkeville to encamp for two days at "Inverness," the home of a Mrs. Jeter. From there they moved them to City Point and then by boat to Point Lookout. Colonel Aylett and Lieutenant Hill were sent on to the prison on Johnson's Island.[36]

Upon their arrival in Farmville in the early morning light of April 7, the Confederate fighting men were given rations brought from Lynchburg. Earlier arrivals had been welcomed into the Farmville homes, fed, and put up for the night. Lee's breakfast that morning consisted of a cup of coffee in a home on Beech Street. Soon he rejoined his men as they crossed the Appomattox River into Cumberland County and burned the bridge. The men under Gordon's command were given their rations as they arrived on the north bank from High Bridge. Both they and Longtreet's men were expected to cook their food on that bank. The pursuit was hot on both sides of the river. For the late arrivals there was little or no time to receive rations or to light fires.[37]

General Wise may have brought a few men from King William with him on the northern route. Those who had served with Major Peatross in the 30th Regiment and Colonel Aylett in the 53rd moved with Longstreet on the southern way. The cavalry under Fitz and Rooney Lee, as usual, was on escort duty.

Fitz Lee commended the bearing of General Wise during the rigors of the retreat. In spite of Wise's age and life as a civil servant, Fitz said of the general, "His unconquerable spirit was filled with as much earnestness and zeal in April, 1865, as when he first took up arms four years ago." General Long described General Wise's appearance on the morning of April 7. In the absence of towels and a water basin, Wise had washed his face in a mud hole. The red clay still streaked his visage. With a blanket thrown over his shoulders, the old general resembled an Indian. General Lee greeted him, "Good morning, General Wise. I perceive that you, at any rate, have not given up the contest, as you are in your war paint this morning."[38] Anyone familiar with Cumberland County red clay will know that it has a certain adhesive quality.

General Humphrey's men found the bridges at High Bridge only partially consumed and they were able to use the lower deck. Hence, the Federals soon reached the north bank of the Appomattox River. This meant that Farmville, like Petersburg less than a week earlier, was surrounded on three sides. By early afternoon April 7, it was captured by the Union forces.[39]

The weary march continued. Many threw away their muskets, being too weary to carry them any farther. Others stayed close to the wagons, adding to the worries of the "half-maddened, half-stupefied teamsters." Horses and mules were left dead or dying in the mud. Upon reaching New Store, twenty miles from Farmville, the men were promised a rest until 1 a.m. April 8.[40]

They were now moving along the old stage road that led to Lynchburg. Already some of Lee's generals were recommending that he negotiate. In the afternoon the Federals tried in vain to pass a flag of truce. By 9 p.m. a flag of truce was passed and a letter from Grant was delivered to Lee. April 8 was a relatively quiet day on the march. Gordon's men were put in the advance and Longstreet's in the rear. General Pickett, Bushrod Johnson, and Dick Anderson, now having no men under their command, were authorized to return home.[41]

At Appomattox Court House the way again was found to be blocked, with no opening except to the north toward the James River. It was apparent that neither President Davis and his officials in Danville nor General Johnston and his forces in North Carolina could be reached. General Lee made one last desperate attempt to break through the enemy's lines, using General Gordon's men of the Second Corps, supported by the cavalry of Rooney Lee, Rosser, and Tom Munford. Of the aggregate of 298 men under Rooney's command, 174 were in Beale's brigade, led that day by Captain S. H. Burt.[42]

According to a history of the 9th Cavalry, "At Appomattox on the last morning, a tiny remnant of the 9th Cavalry was on the flank supporting the 14th Cavalry as the latter regiment made the charge which is one of several claimants to the honor of being the army's last. General Beale's son wrote that in that charge a color bearer of Company H, a young fellow from Rockbridge County, and another from the same county were killed. The later parole list shows only twenty-four men remaining with the regiment.[43]

Fitz Lee had expressed at a council meeting the evening before his desire to extract his cavalry should a surrender be "compelled the next day." Although, as he reported later, they were able to drive out the enemy cavalry quickly at sunrise, two corps of the enemy infantry soon arrived, causing them to retire to their own lines. Then he rode out with the portion of Rooney Lee's men closest to himself. He sent the men to their homes with the hopes that they and their private mounts could be reassembled and utilized later for the cause. But in a few days he realized "the impracticality of entertaining such hopes." He himself rode into Federal lines and accepted the terms offered to Lee's officers. The men, for the most part, were paroled at places convenient to their home localities.[44]

General Long described the action that morning by the infantry and artillery. General Gordon deployed only 2,000 of his men and thirty pieces of Long's artillery, parts of the commands of Colonels Carter, Poague, Marmaduke Johnson, and A. W. Stark. Although "the guns were served with the usual skill and gallantry," the infantry met with a much larger force. Gordon notified Lee that he would need heavier reinforcements to continue the advance. It was at this time that Lee sent a flag of truce to General Grant and an order to cease fire along his own lines. General Long passed the word along to his batteries and ordered the artillery to be parked east of the town of Appomattox.[45]

General Lee's letter to President Davis that morning said he had "7892 organized infantry with arms, with an average of seventy-five rounds of ammunition per man" and possibly no more than 2,100 effective cavalry. "If we could have forced our way one day longer, it would have been a great sacrifice of life, and at its end I do not see how a surrender could have been avoided."[46]

Upon reading Grant's terms for surrender, Lee reminded him that not only the officers and cavalrymen, but also some of the artillerymen, owned their horses. Grant replied that he would not rewrite the terms, but he would instruct his officers who took the paroles to allow all men who claimed their own horses and mules to take them home to work their farms. Sighting Lee, upon his return from the interview with Grant, his men raised their customary cheer for their beloved leader. But soon they broke off their cheers and raised their hats while tears streamed down

218

their faces.[47]

Four King William men were with Rooney Lee at the surrender: Edward Duncan, a coachmaker who had received a medical discharge but had re-enlisted; Pulaski Sutton of "Towinque," who had spent nine months in a Federal prison; the youngest Leftwich brother, Richard; and Sergeant William Mitchell, who had apparently been with the company without injury or capture since he signed with Captain Douglas at Ayletts in April 1862. About forty-two King William "Rangers" chose to ride off with Fitz Lee.

Colonel Carter is listed on the final records as a member of General Long's staff at the surrender. Lieutenant Lucian D. Robinson is listed as leading the Carter's Battery of Cutshaw's battalion. An additional eight others of the King William battery were at the surrender: Benjamin Beadles, a blacksmith who had spent nine months as a prisoner of war; A. E. Brooke, who had been in service little over a year; John Hay, a harness maker and battalion officer; William Heath; Beverly Littlepage, Harvey Terry, and John Tuck — three who had been exchanged from Fort Delaware; and William Tuck. All of these except Beadles and Brooke had signed on at Bond's Store, King William, in June 1861.[48]

The family of James Harvie Pollard of the 53rd Virginia affirms that he was at Appomattox. The records of Companies D and H, 53rd Regiment, show only one King William man, Charles Mosler, of Barton's Brigade Band, who received his parole at Appomattox. Others had been taken as prisoners earlier or for varying reasons were away from the ranks. None of the King William soldiers from the former 22nd Battalion presented himself for parole. Surrendering with the 30th Virginia were Almar Samuel and Lieutenant John W. Scott, both men of Caroline County who would marry and move to King William.[49]

Surrendering with Wise was James Robert Reid of Beulahville, who had joined the general and the 34th Infantry at Chaffin's Bluff in January 1863, and had come through the last twenty-seven months with only a nick through his ear sustained while on patrol duty. Reid kept his parole in his pocket the rest of his life. On the wall of his home in King William he hung the picture of his beloved general, Henry A. Wise.[50]

On that Palm Sunday morning, April 9, 1865, the marching and fighting that had taken them from one end of Virginia to the other, and even into North Carolina, Tennessee, Maryland, and Pennsylvania, was over for the men of King William. Now there remained the weary journey back to their homes in Mangohick and the surrounding countryside.

Certainly the families of upper King William must have seen the smoke that hung in the southwestern sky during the first week in April.

This time it was not from a burning bridge on the Pamunkey or from cannon fire along the Chickahominy, but from the burning capital of the Confederacy. Sam Anderson, of Mangohick, saw bits of partially burned paper float down from the upper atmosphere. Did he and his neighbors see the night sky again light up over Richmond as cannon fire from Camp Jackson signaled Lee's surrender at Appomattox? The next day the earth reverberated, at daybreak and noon, with the firing of a 100-gun salute.[51]

CHAPTER 16

Back Between the Mattaponi and Pamunkey — 1865-69

Six days after the surrender, a drenching rain was falling as General Lee and Rooney Lee rode across the pontoon bridge over the James and into Richmond. Lee's hat and clothes were soaked, as were those of the few officers who rode with him. Virginius Dabney, in his book, *Richmond, the Story of a City,* described Lee's meager entourage: "Behind them rumbled the rickety ambulance that served General Lee for his campaign kit. Behind that came two or three wagons, pulled by gaunt and jaded horses. The canvas top of one was missing, and a sagging, dripping old quilt was in its place." The former commanding general found his way to his residence on East Franklin Street. There a crowd was awaiting him. He grasped as many hands as he could, then made his way through the gate and up the steps. Bowing to the crowd, he entered the house and closed the door.[1]

In the weeks to come men from the Mangohick byways and other parts of King William would be returning to their families. A picture in *Harper's Weekly* depicted Confederate soldiers as they swore their allegiance to the United States in the Senate chamber of the capitol of the Confederacy. A picture in the Library of Congress shows former Confederate soldiers as they rested on the grounds of the Capitol Square in Richmond before continuing their journey home.[2]

James Harvie Pollard, age 39, of Company D, 53rd Regiment, reached his home at "The Glebe," the former Church of England rectory which stood off Route 610 near Enfield. He probably had already passed through Richmond, where he took his oath of allegiance to the United States on April 20. According to one of his descendants, "He arrived at home at night and was too ashamed of his appearance — long hair to his shoulders, dirty ragged clothes — to present himself to his family. Instead, he tapped on the window of one of the quarters to awaken an elderly servant and asked her to fix him a tub for a bath and to fetch him a razor and clean clothes from the house."[3]

Eighteen other King William men of the 53rd Regiment, having lost their leaders before Lee's arrival in Appomattox, did not present themselves for parole at the surrender. Instead they took their oaths in Richmond April 19 to May 20. Captain William Turner of Company D, Sergeant Thomas Redd, and Corporals Anderson Tuck and James Burch had either been wounded or in prison and exchanged. Sergeant Thomas Atkins and Private Charles Ancarrow, Robert Crow, Charles Crutchfield,

Thomas Powell, and William Turpin had been with the regiment without major injury since they signed with Colonel Tomlin in 1861. Lorimer Robinson and William Slaughter were apparently exchanged prisoners. John Davis had been a ship's carpenter and a hospital attendant. Eli Tucker had served as a teamster with the supply train. John Howell had been with his company since he signed on in Petersburg in 1863, whereas James Lipscomb, J. T. Rodgers, and William Wright had apparently only been with them a few months.

Sergeant William Powell, a four-year veteran of the 53rd, chose to take his oath at Burkeville between April 14 and 17. Sergeant William Cobb and Privates Alexander Davis, John Guthrow, James Hargrove, George Hargrove, and Robert Pollard took their oaths in Mechanicsville. The first three had signed with Colonel Tomlin in the early days of the hostilities. Pollard had been wounded in July 1863, possibly at Gettysburg, and Davis was on a three month disability leave.

The Hargrove brothers, John at age 26, and James at age 23, had joined the regiment at West Point on July 26, 1861. James had come through the war without major incident, but John was in Chimborazo Hospital in December 1863, and there is no further record of him. George Hargrove was a younger brother who had joined Company D in Kinston, North Carolina in January 1864. J. W. Hargrove, who was captured at Five Forks and held on Hart's Island, may also have been their brother. There is no record of when his name was entered on the roll of the regiment or whether he survived his imprisonment.

Five former members of the King William men in the 22nd Battalion took their oaths in Richmond, April 20-24. They were John Beadles, William Fox, Reuben Gardner, Sergeant Robert James, and William Pickles, all veterans of three or more years of service. Beadles and Gardner had been exchanged from prison. James had been wounded in 1862 and served on detached duty in Winchester.

Some members of Carter's Battery reported to Richmond, some to Mechanicsville, and others to Ashland. The majority had been on the roll since signing with Tom Carter in 1861. They were: Andrew Dunstan, Charles Madison, and John Pemberton, already released from prison; and Sergeant William Robins, Corporal Augustine Atkins, Corporal Thomas Jones, William Madison, Silas Tignor, and Stanley Trimmer, all of whom had suffered wounds. Sergeant Richard Robinson, Richard Allen, Corporal Roy Temple (who had been on detached service) and Giles Tignor had all served without major injury or imprisonment. J. M. Burruss, J. R. Douglas, and William Slaughter had been in service for a little over a year.

Cavalrymen of Lee's Rangers took their oaths at Farmville, or Black and White's Station (Blackstone), April 11 to 22, or at Richmond,

Mechanicsville, and Ashland, April 16 to May 30. Lieutenant Thomas Christian, Lieutenant James Pollard, Corporal Hansford Anderson, Charles Cocke, Richard Dunstan, Julien Edwards, James Gary, William Gary, William Gregory, Joseph Hay, John Hill, Joseph Lee, and Straughan Lukhard had joined the troop in the early days of 1861 when Rooney Lee was their captain. The term of service of James Campbell, Smith Davis, Presley Edwards, Edward Eubank, Josephus Figg, Oscar Gresham, Lucian Jackson, James Newman, James Robins, John Trant, and Logan Turner had begun either under Beverley Douglas or Thomas Haynes in 1862. Edward Davis had come with them in 1863. Augustin Broach, Alfred Dabney, M. R. Beadles, W. L. Garrett, Miles King, William B. Martin, Atwell Mooklar, Edward Pollard, and Thomas Satterwhite had been added to their number in 1864. No dates are shown in the records for William Eubank or J. C. Littlepage except for their oaths in 1865.

W. R. McGeorge, Philip Lipscomb, and Spencer Waring were members of Company F. McGeorge took the oath at Burkeville in mid-May. Lipscomb, in the Invalid Corps after his leg amputation following an engagement at Ream's Station, took the oath in Richmond on May 30. Waring, a former member of Carter's Battery who had been wounded at Seven Pines, also took his oath in Richmond.

Those in the Federal prisons in April 1865, feeling like "men without a country — soldiers without a flag," gave their assent to the oath of allegiance, or "swaller the yaller dorg" as they called it. By late June, all who had taken the oath were sent to their home states.[4] Virginius Dabney wrote of the men who passed through Richmond, "These haggard, weak and often ill men, clad in hardly more than rags, staggered into town after somehow making their slow and tortuous way back to the South."[5]

Seven King William men from Carter's Battery took their oaths in prison. Each had been on the company roll since June 1861. Sergeant William H. Robins was at Point Lookout. Captain William P. Carter, Lieutenant Festus King, Lieutenant William Hart, William Nicholson, L. B. Slaughter, and T. N. Verlander were at Fort Delaware. William Nicholson would be coming home to Mangohick without his brother. James Nicholson had been either killed or mortally wounded at Gettysburg, although his name was carried on the battery roll as a "prisoner in the hands of the enemy."

From Lee's Rangers, Sergeant Fleming Meredith, Sergeant John Lewis Slaughter, A. B. and Robert C. Hill, all having been taken as prisoners on April 3 and apparently still held in the Richmond area, took their oaths at the capital city on April 20. Lieutenant Robert Semple Ryland and Sergeant William T. Robins swore their allegiance at Point Lookout.

The men of the 22nd Battalion, Benjamin Cocke, John Fox, and the Leftwich brothers — Robert and William — took their oaths from Point Lookout June 10-14. Rufus Waters was sick with scurvy. He died in the Point Lookout hospital on June 4 and was buried in the prisoner-of-war graveyard. Andrew Leftwich swore allegiance at Fort Delware on June 16. We can only surmise the joy in the heart of James Leftwich of Mangohick as his sons arrived home, first probably Richard from Appomattox, then Robert and William from Maryland, and finally the eldest, Andrew, from Delaware.

At least seventeen King William men from the ranks of the 53rd Regiment came home from their imprisonment. Maeger Pollard, Corporal James Burch, and Sergeant John Slaughter were being held at either Point Lookout or Fort Delaware. Patrick Sweet would be coming form Elmira. Corporal John Burch, James Chick, Eugene Clements, B. W. Cluverius, William Ellett, and two Floyd brothers — Americus and William Columbus, John Floyd, W. Garrett, J. W. Hargrove, Henry Kelly, Sergeant Thomas and Warren Lipscomb, James Harvie Powell, J. P. Pumphrey, and George Tuck, had all been captured at Five Forks and must make their way home from Hart's Island. Selim Slaughter, brother of John, would not be returning from Hart's Island. He died there of pneumonia on May 20 and was buried on Long Island. Their brother William, who had been wounded at Gettysburg and held at Fort Delaware, was no longer in prison.

There were five King William officers of the 53rd Regiment in prison at the close of the war: Colonel Aylett, Captain John Latane, Lieutenant Archie Brown, and Lieutenant James B. Hill, at Johnson's Island; and Lieutenant Robert Campbell, at Fort Delaware. Latane, Brown, and Hill took their oaths June 12-18, although Latane said it was July 5 before he was released. Lieutenant Campbell had signed his oath on May 20.[6]

Colonel Aylett's family became increasingly concerned that he was still in prison. Etta Brockenbrough requested Mrs. A. D. Egerton, of Baltimore, a lady who apparently had ready contact with President Andrew Johnson, to use her influence to obtain his release. The colonel received a letter from Mrs. Egerton telling him that he must sign an application for amnesty and pardon, forward it through a persevering friend, and post a $2,000 bond.[7]

Major Robert Stiles the artillerist wrote: "When it was proposed to release the field officers at Johnson's Island, in the summer of 1865, I was one of those called upon by the prison authorities to aid in the preparation of the numerous requisite 'papers.' " Stiles found the commandant of the post, a Major Lee, to be a kind and courteous man who did not understand why he did not file his own papers. Stiles tried to explain that he wished to be given a parole upon his promise not to take up arms and given the option later either to take the oath or leave the country. His request was repeatedly denied until Mrs. Egerton arranged his release.[8]

On July 2 William Aylett wrote to his brother, Patrick, saying that he and other officers from Virginia had forwarded a letter to Governor Francis Pierpont (military governor of Virginia) asking for his "aid & intervention." They enclosed a letter to the President for the governor to endorse. William said that he had replied to his brother's "kind offer to supply me with funds" in a previous letter.[9] He took his oath on July 25 and probably not long after that started his journey home from Ohio.

As the year came to a close Aylett received word that his horse would not be coming back to him. Upon his capture at Sayler's Creek a friend, Henry A. Edmundson, had taken the colonel's servant, Tucker, and the horse to his farm in Halifax County. Edmundson wrote that it had been used by a Confederate scout and later by a local doctor before Sheridan's cavalry came through on April 29 and took the horse from the doctor's stable. Tucker, who continued to work on the Edmundson farm, sent his respects to the colonel and said that he did "what he thought was best to save your horse but he went up at last."[10]

The women were no longer meeting to sew uniforms for soldiers, but rather friendship quilts for newlyweds. One was fashioned in an applique pattern similar to a Hawaiian design. As was the custom in the 1870's, initials were used for the given names of both men and women. Among those names embroidered on the squares were A. T. Mooklar, J. C. Johnson, and W. A. Nicholson[11] — perhaps the groom's comrades in arms.

Andrew Leftwich and Sallie Tuck were married on May 1, 1866, at "Catalpa Grove," Sallie's home. Lucetta Jackson did not marry the "pretty boy," Almar Samuel, until December 8, 1868. The wedding was performed by a former chaplain, the Reverend Charles H. Boggs. The couple began their married life at "Montpelier," the Samuel family home near the Ni River in Caroline County. Julia Samuel Peatross, the wife of Major Peatross, gave them a hobnail bowl for a wedding present. Also about this time Letitia Nelson married Dr. D. B. Benson, the assistant surgeon of the 53rd Regiment.[12]

With hostilities at an end chaplains were free to return to their pulpits and worshippers to their churches without fear of marauding soldiers. Chaplain Boggs settled on his farm in King William. He continued to preach every Sunday and kept his home open to all ministers assigned to the King William Circuit until he was sent to Missouri in 1871 for four years. Boggs was of medium build and of compact size, with an intellectual forehead, a mouth that loved to smile, and dark blue eyes that would light up when he spoke. When a very old man and living out his retirement in Richmond, Lucetta and Almar Samuel's daughter, Alma, called on him to officiate at her marriage to Bennie Atkinson.[13]

The Reverend Patrick Henry Fontaine returned from his chaplaincy to marry his cousin, Annie Elizabeth Redd, in 1865. Having been ordained at the age of 17, he spent fifty-three years in the ministry before collapsing one day while conducting a worship service. He had become well known as a college professor of Latin, Greek, and mathematics. Fontaine was also an orator and a fluent writer.[14]

General Lee's son, Rob, was advised to take possession of the farm land in King William ("Romancoke," near West Point), which had been left to him by his grandfather Custis. His father was willing to assist him in the building of a house and purchase of machinery. Until this could be done the young Lee joined his brother Rooney and their cousin, John Lee, in 1865, in farming at the "White House," where they had built a "shanty." They used their own horses from their military days and some horses and servants which Rob had left at "Hickory Hill." The young farmers did not finish planting their corn until June 9, but, even with army servants and cavalry horses, Rob considered that crop the best he ever made.[15]

Dr. Douglas S. Freeman has pictured General Lee, in late May 1865, as he "rode out of Richmond, across the Chickahominy and on toward the Pamunkey." He passed Mechanicsville and the "gray earthworks that Early's men had thrown up precisely a year before." In King William, he "drew rein in the yard of Pampatike, home of his cousin, the gallant artillerist, Colonel Thomas H. Carter."[16]

General Lee arrived at "Pampatike" at the old-fashioned dinner hour of 3 o'clock. He was unannounced and unexpected, but the colonel at once recognized the horse and the rider. The ensuing days with the Carters were the happiest General Lee "had spent for many years." There were three children in the home. The youngest two, girls aged three and five, were the old gentleman's "special delight."[17]

While staying at "Pampatike," General Lee rode to "Chericoke," six miles downstream on the Pamunkey, to visit Corbin Braxton's widow. The younger Lees were invited over from the "White House" to a lavish meal. Rob and John, having been "for so many years in the habit of being hungry" did their best to lessen the quantity. General Lee was appalled at the extravagance and, while riding back to "Pampatike," commented to Colonel Carter that "we shall have to practice economy." Soon after this General Lee crossed the Newcastle ferry and made his way back to his residence in Richmond.[18]

After that Lee would visit his sons at the "White House," but Rob records that only once did their father stay with him at "Romancoke." Rob was a bachelor at the time and staying in the rather dilapidated overseer's house. The general was so dismayed at Rob's housekeeping that, upon arrival back in Richmond, he sent him a full set of plated forks and spoons. The family rejoiced at Rooney's remarriage in the fall of 1867.[19]

Eliza Douglas, wife of Major Beverley Douglas, died in 1866. Mrs. Douglas was only 44 years old and the family considered her "a deferred war casualty, victim of the hardships and malnutrition when already weakened by middle-age childbirth." She went out on a very cold day to carry delicacies to a sick friend and contracted pneumonia. Left behind were Bessie, age 18, Evelyn, age 12, and Mary Ellen, age 3.[20]

In 1868 Bessie and Mary Ellen Douglas were taken to visit relatives who were living in one of the row houses across the street from the Capitol Square in Richmond. By this time civilian officials had been reinstated in King William, but the state was still under the military governor and sentries walked the street just outside the iron fence around the square. Little Mary Ellen would wait until the uniformed guard reached the far end of the block before she would dart out to visit the children next door.[21] Aunt Mamie Pollard kept house at "Cownes" and helped to raise Mary Ellen. Teenage Evelyn was sent to the boarding school at Tappahannock which was started after the war by the Reverend John McGuire and his wife Judith. Bessie, a teacher, conducted a school for girls at "Cownes" for many years.[22]

James Powell of Mangohick had not served in the army but had been sent to the western part of the state to make wagons and equipment for the Confederacy. Upon his return home he took up his trade of coachmaker. His wife, Sarah, received the appointment of postmistress at Mangohick in February 1866. There was a cluster of shops at Mangohick where harness, wagons, and other farm equipment were either made or repaired. A black shoemaker, Gloster Anderson, lived nearby.[23]

Living at or near Mangohick were the Rider and Nicholson families. Daniel Rider, age 55, had served as the postmaster since 1844. He was also a saddle and harness maker. Benjamin J. J. Nicholson, age 49, was a wheelwright. His son, William, followed the trades of coachmaker and blacksmith and, in cooperation with members of the Powell family, operated the retail store at Mangohick. On rainy days when business was slack he would send a young apprentice to the second floor to paint caskets.[24]

CHAPTER 17

Home on Mangohick Byways — 1870

On April 27, 1870, Patrick Henry Aylett became the last "war casualty" from King William County, killed not by shot or shell but by falling debris, gallery or flooring in the Virginia State Capitol. It was during the closing days of Reconstruction in Virginia.

A dispute had arisen in Richmond concerning who was the duly constituted mayor of the city — one appointed by the last military governor of the district, or one chosen by the city council which had been appointed by the newly elected governor of the state. The Virginia Supreme Court of Appeals met on April 27 to render judgment. Spectators crowded into the visitors' gallery, causing the ceiling panels and girders to give away under the excessive weight. Moments before entering the building, Patrick Aylett had commented concerning the death of a friend, Hugh Pleasants, "We are all passing away."[1]

A survivor recounted that a falling mass of human beings "mingled with bricks, mortar, splinters, beams, iron bars, desks and chairs" plummeted in a cloud of plaster dust through the floor of the courtroom into the House of Delegates chamber on the first floor. Fortunately the legislature was not in session. The injured lawyer from King William was carried to the capitol grounds north of the building, where he soon expired. Sixty-two men had been killed, another 251 injured. In the ensuing days, among the meetings held to pay tribute to the deceased was one called by the Richmond *Press* to honor Pleasants and Aylett.[2]

A Virginia Constitutional Convention had been held in Richmond in the hall of the House of Delegates on December 3, 1867. It was presided over by the Federal judge, John Underwood, who had presided over the trial of President Davis earlier in the year and released him on $100,000 bail. Virginuis Dabney writes that "once it was divested of the disfranchising and test-oath features," the constitution "had a good deal to recommend it. First, it provided for a statewide system of public schools. ...It also established the secret ballot."[3]

The constitution specified that the counties be divided into townships with the governing board to be made up of a supervisor elected from each township. An amendment in 1874 substituted magisterial districts for townships. The newly elected Virginia General Assembly in 1869 ratified the 14th and 15th amendments to the United States Constitution which granted citizenship and voting rights to all male residents.[4]

Hansford Anderson, formerly of Lee's Rangers, obtained the job of assistant marshal for the 1870 United States Census. Listing by township, he began to canvas the county on June 13. He entered by family abode the names, ages, "color," occupations of both male and female, state or foreign country of birth and that of their parents, whether deaf and dumb, blind or insane, attended school during the year or could not read or write. He found only four in the township of Mangohick who had been born in a state other than Virginia and three others who were foreign born.[5]

The population of the Mangohick Township was around 3,340, only one third of whom were white. Others were listed as black or mulatto. Anderson did not show any as Indians except on the reservations in the lower part of the county. (Yet there were members of the Upper Mattaponi tribe living near Ayletts in an area called Adamstown and other families scattered throughout Mangohick.) The capricious listings in the 1850 through 1880 censuses regarding color or race, according to Dr. Helen Rountree, of Old Dominion University, cannot be relied upon.[6]

Farming was still the predominant occupation, including farmers and farm laborers of both sexes. There were in Mangohick Township five grist millers, six retail merchants, four coachmakers, five physicians, and two lawyers, as well as several carpenters, shoemakers, one saddle and harness maker, clerk in a store, blacksmith, and butcher. All of the eight teachers were women aged 18 to 42. There was one female trimmer and one seamstress. Fifty-three young people, both white and non-white, were attending school. Many others were working as farm laborers and domestic servants. Almost as many non-white women were shown as "keeping house" as white, 157 to 174. Four hundred fifty-seven males — white, black, and mulatto of age 21 or older — were counted as eligible to vote.[7]

The census of the Acquinton Township in the area of Ayletts, Enfield, and Manquin shows merchants (not all retail), clerks, blacksmiths, coachmakers, grist millers, sailors, preachers, a constable, and a stage driver. There was a seamstress and some of the teachers were male.[8]

By looking into the individual homes of Mangohick Township through the 1870 census and family recollections, we can see how, after the turmoil of war and change, life in the community continued. In the Jackson home, Thomas and Jane Jackson had only their bachelor son John, from the 30th Virginia Regiment, to farm the land. Living with them were Albion's widow, Patty, and their two small children, and a black boy who was employed as a farm laborer. After the death of the elder Jacksons, in 1879 and 1880, Lucetta and Almar Samuel and their five children moved down from upper Caroline. Within a few months Almar died of a brain tumor. Lucetta wore widow's weeds until her death at "Wyoming" fifty-six years later. John Jackson would spend his last years at the Old Soldier's Home in Richmond.[9]

Pulaski Sutton, age 44 in 1870 (a bachelor called "Mr. Hap Sutton" by his neighbors), was living alone at "Towinque," his mother having died in 1867. The farm was valued at $17,000 and his personal estate at $1,400. Nearby, possibly at "Bleak Hill," Andrew J. McDowell was farming $2,500 worth of land. James H. McDowell (probably his son) was running the grist mill. Twenty-seven year old Amanda kept house and there were children in the home, aged 15 years down to 6 months. Andrew McDowell was also the postmaster at Etna Mills.[10]

In 1870, James G. White was farming his mother's land at "Lands-downe." He lived there with his wife and three daughters, ages 16, 17, and 22. The two younger girls were attending school. Not far from the Whites lived Sam Anderson, a non-white farmer with $1,000 worth of land. Lizza Anderson, age 26, was keeping house. There were children aged 12 to six months. Twelve-year-old Lucy and ten-year-old John attended school that year.[11]

Andrew Leftwich, Sallie, and their daughters Gertrude, age 3, and Margaret, age 2, were living at "Catalpa Grove" with Sallie's brother, Charles, age 22, and sister, Lucy, age 23. Andrew, though shown as a farmer, also taught school. Later he would be the superintendent of the Poor Farm for the county and he would take his family to live at the farm in one of the cottages. Andrew's brothers Robert and Richard were living at "Walnut Grove" and assisting their father with the farming. Apparently their brother William was living elsewhere. By 1875 he was dead from the tuberculosis he contracted while in prison.[12]

On the Smoky Road (Route 609) lived Lucy Floyd Atkinson, age 50, and her three younger children, Irvin, 15, John, 13, and Cally, 10. Their father, Iverson L. Atkinson, had died before Cally was born and Lucy was shown as the farmer of the $2,000 estate. Her son by a former marriage, William C. Floyd, had returned from prison to his wife, Elizabeth, and their three children, ages 7, 8, and 10, but he would die before the year was out. Across the road from Lucy Atkinson, at "Tanyard," lived her brother, James H. Powell, who after his release from the county militia had made shoes for the Confederate army. Whenever Federals were known to be in the area, the Powell horses were kept hidden in a secluded place in the woods.[13]

Farther down the Smoky Road at "Claybank" lived Achilles Campbell, age 69, with his wife and four children. The eldest, James, age 24, of Lee's Rangers, had returned home with Dahlgren's saddle, bridal, and haversack. Not far away lived Robert Semple Ryland, also of Lee's Rangers, who ran his own grist mill, probably Dublin Mill, at the fork of the

Dorrell and Herring Creek.[14]

At "Glanvilla," off Route 600, John Latane had returned from prison to marry Ann Hallowell, sister of his brother's wife, Virginia. The two brothers owned the land together and farmed it. John and Ann had no children, but by 1872 Virginia and William had six. Miss Dora Ryland of "Roseville" was governess for the children in the late 1860's and early 1870's. The family attended St. David's Church, where John was a vestryman.[15]

Atwell T. Mooklar, 43, lived near the River Road (Route 600). He and his wife, the former Frances Ellen Fox, had a daughter Ellen, age 2, and a son Richard, age 1. They had lost an infant, Mary Susan, in 1867. Frances's sister, Mary A. (Nelson) Fox, 35, was keeping house. By the next year Frances Mooklar was dead at the age of 33. She was buried at "Retreat."[16]

At "Montville," Alice and William Aylett's family grew to seven children: Sarah, Pattie, Philip, Alice, William R., Bessie, and Patrick Henry. Mother Alice fell down the stairs to the basement in 1895. She received a concussion and died at the age of 56 years.[17]

The "Widow Nelson" and her daughters continued to live at "Wyoming." In 1870, Kate, age 29, was still single. Letitia and D. B. Benson had a year-old daughter. With them in the household were: J. S. Benson (perhaps the doctor's brother), 25, shown as the farmer; Harriet Lyons, 25, a black domestic; and William Benton, 12, a black farm laborer. Later the farm would be divided and Lettie and D. B. would build the house "Oglalla" for themselves and two daughters. Kate would marry John Pollard of "Mt. Zoar" late in life. They lived at "Wyoming" and had no children. Irvin Atkinson and his wife, the former Cornelia Nicholson, bought "Ogalla" in the 1880's and raised their four sons, Bennie, Willie, Bradley, and Douglas there. Cornelia's brother William came to live with them in his declining years.[18]

A young 19-or-20 year-old black man named Abram Underwood was living in Mangohick in 1870. Apparently he and 24-year-old Felitsen Underwood, who was keeping house for John P. Taylor[19] (perhaps at "Horn Quarter"), had chosen for their family name that of the Federal judge in Richmond. In a few years Abram Underwood would name his son for General Grant.

At or near Enfield in Aquinton Township was Ben Cocke (of the 22nd Battalion) apparently unmarried and living with his mother; Robert Campbell (of the 53rd Regiment), with his wife, the former Alice Hawes, still childless; and Captain Tom Haynes of the 9th Cavalry, with his wife Martha and 12-year-old son, Thomas. The Haynes family had lost their infants Martha and Lottie before the war and their nine-year-old Emma in 1864. In

1877 the captain, still paralyzed from his spinal injury, died and was buried at "The Grove."[20]

In 1870 two local post offices, along with Mangohick, were operated by women. Mary E. Powell was at Enfield and Millie Mahan was at the newly established office at Beulahville. Mary B. Leigh would take over at Ayletts in 1880 and Dora E. Furr would be appointed to the four-year-old office at Teck (later Duane on Route 604) in 1889. That same year Fannie B. Snead became the postmistress at Etna Mills. Lelia Gravatt would head the newly formed office at Calno in 1893. The new offices established 1870-1894 at Epworth (Routes 30 and 610), Manquin (Brandywine), Globe (Routes 610 and 608), and Venter (Routes 30 and 606) were operated by men.[21]

For a while the Teck Post Office was in the basement at "Retreat." The James Fox home had been bought in January 1865 by Dr. Joseph B. Moore. Two years later he and his wife Victoria sold "Retreat" to Rowland G. Tyler, of Detroit. Tyler married Mary Thomas, who lived just across the Mattaponi at "Vernon," in Caroline County. The old homestead, "Retreat," had a row of mulberry trees. One room in the house had wooden cabinets where silkworms had been kept in an early experiment in silk making. Family recollections in years to come would be of the strict Rowland Tyler, who was called "Wow-wow" by his great niece and great nephew, and who operated the Teck Post Office, 1891-1900. There was also a kindly great aunt "Sister Belle," Mary Thomas Tyler's sister, who entertained the visiting children "with singing 'Possum up the simmon tree,' and other delightful tunes on the rosewood square piano in the parlor."[22]

Masonic lodges had been organized. A Silentia Lodge no. 221 was chartered at Ayletts in 1866, but by 1876 it was extinct. King William Lodge no. 225 was chartered in 1868 with the mailing address of Hanover Court House. Its officers were H. A. Richards, Grand Master; James G. White, Senior Warden; and John W. Taylor, Junior Warden. The lodge members met each month on the Wednesday just before or during the full moon. By 1870 they were meeting at "Horn Quarter" and in 1871 at Sawville (Calno), King William County, where a frame two-story lodge hall was built on Route 30. In the 1880's the lodge's mailing address was given as "Mangohic (sic). Among its twenty-three members were the former Major Robert O. Peatross and James A. Powell (of Mangohick). The Powell family would keep James's apron and fez for several generations.[23]

According to a study made by Miss E. Louise Davis, a teacher in the King William schools, the public school system began in September 1870 with the appointment of R. L. Williams as superintendent. He was followed in 1872 by Dr. John Lewis, E. C. Hill in 1878, Colonel Johnson in 1882, and Dr. William Croxton in 1886. The schools were operated on the basis of three districts — Acquinton, Mangohick, and the town of West Point. There are few records for this period and very little is known. In 1872, $600 was levied for school expenses in Mangohick Township.[24]

For 1870 we can only deduce the location of the schools by the areas in which the teachers and pupils lived, for the majority had to walk to school or go on horseback. Those along Route 600, toward Ayletts, may have gone to Bessie Douglas, at "Cownes," or to Ellen Hill, who apparently lived at "Edge Hill." Those in the Beulahville area may have studied under Mary Waldane, who was living in the Munday home, under M. J. Fleet, who was living in the Latane home, or under I. S. Taylor, at "Wakefield." Those around Mangohick or Calno may have been instructed by M. A. Page, who lived with the Whites at "Landsdowne." A teacher, Margaret Rudd, apparently lived near Etna Mills. Near Enfield there were four teachers: Ben Cocke, Annie Timberlake, Henry C. Timberlake, and Cornelius Dabney.[25]

By 1885 there were ten schools in the district. Ayletts was in Acquinton District in 1887 when one acre of land was granted by W. D. Berkeley to the school board for a school there. The earliest land record for Mangohick District is the grant by A. T. Mooklar in 1892 of three acres for the Rider School (for white children). It was followed in 1894 by a grant by Sam Anderson of an acre and a half for the Rucker School (for black children). The former was probably located near Route 604 and Mangohick Church and the latter on Route 601, between Calno and "Bleak Hill."[26]

It is known that black children attended at least four other schools in upper King William in the latter part of the nineteenth century: Globe, Venter, Mangohick, and Hammtown. At the Globe School, Mrs. Mattie Dawson was the teacher and Henry Gwathmey was one of her pupils. At Venter, Charles and James Gwathmey were among the students. Lizzie Moore taught the Moore children and others at Mangohick. The building there now on Route 671 is a replacement of any earlier one which burned. The Hammtown School, on Routes 608 and 628 (near "Greenmount"), may have been taught by Annie Austin, the only non-white teacher shown by the 1870 Census in Mangohick Township.[27]

Perhaps Shoestring School for black children, at Ayletts on land given by William Berkeley, and Old Enfield and Enfield schools, on land given by Edgar Jackson in 1916, and T. A. Jackson in 1934, each had an earlier existence. Thomas A. Jackson was in school in the 1890's. He said that he was taught first in a church and then in a one-room school. The school term would run three or four months a year. Tommy Jackson lived to be over 100 and both encouraged and enabled many neighboring children to obtain an education. His daughter, Mrs. Jeanette Moore, taught at the Enfield School. The Rucker School later became known as the Rucker-Rosenwald School after it became the beneficiary of the Rosenwald philantrophy. John Rucker's daughter, Carrie, would teach there and his son, Stuart, would be a civic leader who encouraged his neighbors to exercise their right to vote.[28]

Colonel Tom Carter conducted a school for boys at "Pampatike." There was a school near Manquin called Leightown. Children in the McGeorge family and others attended a school at Tuck's Fork under Andrew Leftwich.[29]

In the 1880's at Etna Mills, Sidney Sweet went to school to Cora Hay, whose family kept a store at that crossroads. Miss Etta Snead taught in her home, "Fairview," which had been built at Etna Mills circa 1867. A Mr. Campbell taught in a school at Corinth Fork (Routes 614 and 604).[30]

The Jeter and Gravatt children, living at or near Calno in the 1890's, appear to have attended a school in that area. They studied *An Elementary English Grammar,* by Alonzo Reid (1880), which in two volumes could guide their study through high school or an academy.[31]

Soon after the turn of the century, Lewis B. Reese went to school to Miss Ida Moore, daughter of Dr. Joseph B. Moore of Ayletts. The school was located on Route 606, near Ventor and Turpin, in a locality called the "Big Swamp," and was attended by the children of the Billups and Reed families. Others attended the school in the Grange Hall, at Beulahville, and studied under Miss Lula Cook and Miss Pearlie Powell.[32]

Many of the churches had singing schools. In most churches there was no musical instrument, nor did the hymn books have musical notations. The hymns, marked by meter, were sung after someone had "raised the tune" and as the minister called out the verses line by line. Some congregations were fortunate to have a singing master in attendance who, with his pitch pipe or tuning fork, could instruct those wishing to learn to sing. Bethel Church, under the leadership of Alva H. Richardson and his wife, Kate, a music teacher, held several fairs to raise money for their first organ. Lewis R. Tunstall, a returned veteran of the 30th Virginia Infantry and a member of the singing class at Bethel, once remarked, "Listening to the 23rd Psalm set to music was the cheapest fun I ever bought."[33]

The music book used at Bethel may have been *Selections from the Psalms of David in Metric* (1870). The first book with musical notes which was used at Beulah was "an old yellow backed *Scepter* containing not only instruction for sight reading, but also hymns and beautiful anthems."[34]

Separate Baptist churches were organized by the black people of the area. Those who were members of Hebron Church withdrew in 1866 to form Mangohick Baptist. They met in the colonial church building, but it was 1924 before they could obtain a deed to the property from St. David's Parish through the county court. Their first pastor was the Reverend Thomas Chavis. Chavis served only a few months before his death and was succeeded by the Reverend John Collins. The Reverend William H. Stevens served from 1878 to 1885, the Reverend W. F. Byers for three years; then the Reverend E. C. Thompson served to 1893, at which time the Reverend W. H. Ford became pastor. A Sunday School was organized in 1878 with 38 members and J. E. Chick the superindent. Members of the Spurlock, Winston, Rucker, Anderson, Courtney, Moore, and Carter families and many others have been active at that church through the years.[35]

In 1865 the white members of the Beulah Women's Missionary Society helped some black members of the church organize and finance Providence Baptist Church, on Route 628 near Beulahville. Other black members of Beulah joined with twelve from Sharon Church to form an "organization" at the old Cattail Church. By 1871 they were known as the Mt. Sinai Negro Baptist Church.[36]

Rock Springs Baptist Church was organized in 1877 and built on Route 605 in the Enfield neighborhood. There Fannie Hill Latney and her husband, William called "Billy," would later attend with their twelve children and many grandchildren. On Sundays she could be seen on the front pew, holding her worn Bible.[37] Oak Grove Baptist Church on Route 615 was built in the twentieth century.

Saint Paul Baptist Church was organized in 1887 by members of the Providence Church for residents of the Globe community. The first pastor was the Reverend Horace Roane, who was assisted by Henry Taylor, Abraham Garlick, and Jack Gwathmey. Their families and others from the Baylor, Nelson, Temple, Pollard, Trent, Tunkett, and Jackson families made up the early congregation.[38]

The white congregations began to grow again and there was cooperation among the churches and denominations. The Reverend Richard A. Fox and the Reverend John Turnpin, of Beulah, preached a revival in September 1865 at Hebron, resulting in an increase in membership at that church. James G. White continued as Sunday School superintendent at Hebron. Andrew Leftwich returned to his job of Sunday School secretary. He had been elected to this position at the age of 18 and would serve in that capacity for fifty years. The Sunday Schools of upper King William held annual united celebrations, with Hebron, Beulah, Corinth, and the Chapel (later Epworth) participating.[39]

The Reverend John O. Turpin continued as pastor of Beulah Church until his death in 1884. Some of those years he was also serving as pastor

235

of Hebron. John W. Taylor was superintendent of the Beulah Sunday School in 1865, followed by George R. Trant, 1870, and Colonel J. C. Johnson, 1875-1888. Colonel Johnson remarked, "I would not have been what I am but for Beulah Church and her Sunday School."[40]

William B. Poynter was deacon at Sharon Baptist Church for forty years. The teachers around the turn of the century were Miss Florence Poynter, Miss Bettie Poynter Prince, Miss Maude Lipscombe, Mrs. E. S. Carter, and Mrs. Emma Farmer. Classes met in the sanctuary and in the corners of the balcony. The church was lighted by kerosene lamps and heated by wood stoves.[41]

When there was no assigned rector during the summer months at St. David's Church, students from the seminary filled the pulpit, making the church a "sort of training school for young ministers." The bishops of the diocese "expressed pride in the gallant little church." Besides the Aylett, Douglas, and Latane families, St. David's was attended by the Coates, Roanes, Blakes, Pollards, Leighs, Hills and Carters of King William.[42]

In 1875 Thomas Price Jackson wrote to his daughter, Lucetta Samuel, that the Sunday School at Bethel was improving since Miss Nannie Tunstall had become superintendent. The farmers were having a good growing season and producing better crops. He felt that the people of the land had experienced calamity after calamity because of their ingratitude to God. Bethel continued to be on the King William Circuit. Their Bible was found in one of the homes in the neighborhood and returned to the pulpit.[43]

Powell's Chapel was seven miles away from Enfield. Soon after the war the neighbors in that community began to gather on Sunday afternoons in the Leighton schoolhouse, on land owned by the Leigh family, and a Sunday School was started. On the second Sunday afternoon of each month the minister of the King William Charge would preach at both the chapel and the schoolhouse. A new church was organized in 1886. The Reverend Charles H. Green was pastor of the charge at that time. The founders were E. L. Pollard, Mr. and Mrs. E. R. Pollard, T. F. Cocke, Sr., Mr. and Mrs. E. V. Clements, and J. W. and W. T. Adrams. They called the new church McKendree, in honor of the first American-born Methodist bishop, William McKendree, who was born nearby.[44]

Members of the Abrams family had prior to this walked to Powell's Chapel and possibly passed the birthplace of the early bishop. Mary Abrams Smith, daughter of W. T. Abrams, has written that the small group met at "Chestnut Grove," the Pollard home on Route 605, to make plans to build a place of worship. In an arbor across the road, an altar, pulpit, and seats were constructed. Later two acres of land were purchased from nearby "Brookfield," home of Winston Dabney, and the lovely frame church was erected.[45]

J. C. Cocke was the Sunday School superintendent in 1880 at Powell's Chapel. Sometime between 1883 and 1887 the present building was constructed on one and an eighth acres of land dedicated by Miss Lucy Powell. It was renamed Epworth Methodist Episcopal Church. A Reverend Askew was pastor of the King William Charge at that time. Not until 1938 was the four-acre lot deeded to the church trustees, R. L. Mitchell, C. R. Reed, and Byrd L. Atkins.[46]

At Corinth Christian Church, Lucy T. Mooklar (second wife of A. T. Mooklar) was president of the Aid Society in 1879. A few years later the constituents decided to build a larger church. Bricks were made and fired in the field of William A. Sweet, and in 1888 a brick house of worship was dedicated. The Reverend Wallace Cave was pastor at that time time. On January 2, 1889, Laura Tuck and William Morrison were the first couple to be married in the new building.[47]

An unknown photographer visited Epworth Church, Sharon Church, Hebron Church, and homes in the area, including "Hill Top" farm and "Brookfield," circa 1890. The pictures, taken outside, show ladies in their big hats, floor-length skirts, and shirtwaists; men in their dark or gray suits, vests, and winged collars; girls in white dresses or pinafores; and boys in their Buster Brown suits. "Hill Top" farm at that time was the home of James Mordecai Abrams. There the photographer showed only the house. At "Brookfield," then the home of W. B. Wormeley, his wife, the former Delilah McKenzie, and three children, the family was ready to leave for church. The black man, Commodore, was waiting for them with the buggy. Father Wormeley was dressed in a Prince Albert coat, one of the boys had a rolled-brim hat, and sister Lucy was wearing a flat-brimmed sailor hat. According to a younger sister, the family attended "services at Corinth, McKendree, Epworth, Hebron, and even Rock Springs where they [as children] made enough noise outside that they were asked to come in and sit on the back seats."[48]

The towns of Ayletts and West Point took up their roles of river ports both for commerce and pleasure. The steamship *Isis,* starting on May 1, 1877, left West Point on Tuesdays as soon after the arrival of the steamer from Baltimore "as practicable." It was expected to arrive at Walkerton at 4 p.m., at Ayletts an hour later, and at Dunkirk by 6:20 p.m. The ship would start downstream on Wednesdays, leaving Dunkirk not earlier than 10 a.m. On Thursdays it would leave Walkerton not earlier tha 6 a.m. to make connection at West Point with the ship from Baltimore. The steamship *Roger* plied the Pamunkey on Fridays and Saturdays, making ports of call at "Canterbury" (near Lester Manor) and Doctor Wormeley's ("Manskin Lodge," near Hanovertown). Perishable commodities would be landed at the "White House" on Saturdays to be forwarded by freight to Richmond in the evening.[49]

Rob Lee tells of arranging for his father to visit their cousin in Gloucester County. He drove the general from "Romancoke" to West Point, where they boarded the Baltimore steamer, along with Rob's horse and trap. They landed at a wharf on the York, then drove the nine miles to "White Marsh," arriving at "supper time," or about 7:30 p.m. For their return they had to leave the house at 5 a.m. in order to catch the steamer back to West Point.[50]

Joseph Carter Fox operated a general store in Ayletts, beginning in 1881. He was 18 years old at the time and had been born during the war to Robert J. Fox, a county constable, and his wife, Ann Mahon Fox. An 1896 ledger shows that the store stocked the usual kitchen staples: sugar, flour, meal, molasses, nutmeg, ginger, alum, cloves, cinnamon, coffee, tea, bacon, ham, butter, rice, crackers, sardines, eggs, and salted cut herrings (by the barrel) and other fish. Fox sold for household use: brooms, cake soap, bed ticking and bedsteads, oil cloth, lamp shades, joints of stove pipe, cups and saucers, bluing, and stamps (5 for 10 cents).[51]

The ledgers for 1899 and 1900 show that Colonel Aylett bought black-eyed peas and potatoes (seed for the farm or garden); canned tomatoes; fresh oranges and lemons; carbolic acid and glycerine; yards of blue jean and checked dimity; a spool of silk thread and hooks and eyes; drawers and shoes; hame strings and a single tree (for hitching horses and mules); plow points; and window glass, mosquito netting, and fly paper.[52]

At the Ayletts store there were bolts of calico, cotton, flannel, domestic, lace, shirting, and collars. On the shelves there were also ready to wear articles: overalls, stockings, garters, corsets, and umbrellas. For the household medicine chests there was camphor, quinine, and bottles of chill tonic and liver regulator. The buyers would call for: corn, buckets, tar, nails, hoes, locks, paint, shells, rope, sulphur (for cut seed potatoes), Paris green (an insecticide for the garden), plugs of tobacco, and cigarettes. They would charge or pay their ferriage across the Mattaponi and receive credit for the delivery of chickens and sumac (used in tanning and dyeing).[53]

In the homes quinine was used, especially by those persons living along rivers and near swamps, for leg cramps, colds, chills, and fever. They applied mustard plasters for chest congestion, drank corn silk tea for the bladder, and used calamus root for indigestion.

In later years, when the Pamunkey Indians could not find their customary medicinal herbs, they would ask the pharmacist at Scott's Drug Store, on Main Street in Richmond, to order them. He would consult a book written in 1818, *The House Surgeon and Physician*, "designed to assist families, travellers & seafaring people in discerning, distinguishing, and curing diseases," and then send their requests on to New York. Some of the herbs requested were: quassia chips, for soothing the throat; sassafras bark, for indigestion and stomachache; aloe (gall of the earth), for a laxative; elm bark, to be chewed for a sore throat; ginger powder, for stomach distress; buck-u leaves, for a diuretic; croton oil and mustard, to cause blistering to reduce fever; strychnine powder, in small doses as a tonic and stimulant; snakeroot (sergentena root), as a tea for high blood pressure; and Indian tobacco (lobelia leaves), used in a tea for asthma or shortness of breath and also as a tincture for drenching horses.[54]

———

In order to see the "face" of King William during the postwar years we can turn to the portraits that hang on the colonial courthouse walls. There we find Judge John D. Foster, of Amelia and King and Queen, who was judge of the district that included King William during the reconstruction years. Also there are pictures of Judge James M. Jeffries of King and Queen who was judge of the circuit court, and Judge Owen Gwathmey of "The Meadow," who was judge of the county court.[55]

Major Douglas's portrait peers down from above the fireplace in the judge's chambers. Three who served in the state legislature, Colonel Aylett, Judge Roger Gregory, and Dr. John Lewis, look down from the wall in the courtroom or the jury room. Aylett was also commonwealth's attorney for the county and Gregory was also dean of the Department of Law at Richmond College. Thomas Dabney of the "Dorrell" was commonwealth's attorney. Octavius Winston and William D. Pollard, of "Octagon," were clerks of the court. Captain Thomas Haynes and Atwell Mooklar, of "Cloverdale" in Mangohick, were both treasurers. Mooklar was chairman of the board of supervisors. He and John W. Taylor, of "Ferry Farm" and "Wakefield," filled the office of sheriff. Dr. William Croxton was superintendent of schools. Portraits of Colonel Tom Carter, Captain William G. Pollard, and Patrick Henry Aylett, lawyer for the Confederacy, represent King William's role in the war.[56]

There are no portraits at the courthouse of Andrew Lefwich, Colonel J. C. Johnson, or Colonel Harrison Tomlin. Leftwich served for a number of years as commissioner of revenue. Johnson served as clerk of the county and superindent of schools. Colonel Tomlin remained a bachelor and made his home at "Queenfield," near the Hanovertown crossing.[57] In later years Tom Carter paid him a visit concerning a proposed change in the mail route to Ayletts. Carter wrote to William Aylett that the colonel, who had "never yet approved anything new," opposed it. The old gentleman liked to take walks about his farm. One day he collapsed and his body was found several days later by his neighbors.[58]

———

Beverley Douglas went as a delegate to the Democratic Convention in New York in 1868. In 1869, when Virginia was again allowed representation in the halls of Congress, he went to represent the First District, carrying his daughter, Bessie, along to be his hostess. The major was reelected to the 45th Congress without opposition. Unfortunately, just as Congress was recessing for the Christmas holidays in 1878, he died of pneumonia.[59]

Members of the House and Senate from Iowa, Illinois, Mississippi, and Missouri were appointed to escort the congressman's body home for burial. They came by train to Richmond and then by carriage and hearse to Ayletts. At the Pamunkey Ferry (Newcastle) the horses bolted and nearly went into the river. Friends met the cortege and accompanied it to St. David's Church. There Douglas's colleague from Illinois said, "He never thought of self, of his own interests or ambition, but moved forward fearlessly in the advocacy of what he believed right." Interment was in the Pollard family cemetery at "Mt. Zoar."[60]

Little Mary Ellen Douglas grew up to marry E. Spotswood Pollard in 1891. The ceremony, scheduled for mid-morning, was moved up so that the Reverend Sewell S. Hepburn, rector of St. David's, could participate in the unveiling of Lee's monument in Richmond. An ex-slave who had found his way to Canada and opened a store sent the "Cownes baby" a pair of white kid gloves for her wedding. The bride wore a cream-colored gown, with a boned bodice and a little bustle, and matching shoes.[61]

In 1896, when a Democratic Convention was to be held in Richmond for the election of someone to represent the Third Congressional District, a meeting was held at Mangohick to select a delegate. The following were elected to officiate at this local assembly: Thomas F. Cocke of Enfield, chairman; John R. Redd of Etna Mills, secretary; and John B. Gravatt of the former McDowell's Mill, assistant secretary. James D. Powell of Mangohick, and son of James, received fifty-one votes to be the delegate. Patrick H. Eubank of Etna Mills received five votes.[62]

A monument to the Confederate soldiers was unveiled in the brick-enclosed courtyard at King William on July 28, 1904. It had been, as Mary Burnley Gwathmey expressed in words of her father, "A war that should not have been, with intelligent Christian men on both sides, the differences should have been settled without one drop of blood being shed!"[63]

EPILOGUE

Along the Mangohick byways there still stand some of the old homes which witnessed the passing of men and their guns during the war years: "Horn Quarter," "Retreat," "Cownes," "Montville," and "Wyoming." Others have fallen into disrepair or been greatly altered. The churches — Bethel, Mangohick, Hebron, Corinth, St. David's, Cattail (Mt. Sinai) and Sharon — stand as quiet sentinels in the now-peaceful countryside.

At "Wyoming" a square piano once belonging to Julia Samuel Peatross, wife of Major Peatross, graces the parlor. A cupboard made by William Nicholson fills a corner niche. A hobnail bowl, the wedding gift to Lucetta Jackson and Almar Samuel, grandparents of my husband, rests on the dining room mantel. In an upstairs bedroom, Almar's picture with his two brothers, all in Confederate uniforms, hangs on the wall. Lucetta's tucked wedding petticoat lies in a trunk. Descendants of the "Widow Nelson" have been gone from "Wyoming" for nearly three-quarters of a century and the Atkinsons are now the owners of the old home.

Grant Underwood rests in the graveyard at Oak Grove Church and is fondly remembered. Leroy McAllister of Route 604 — a black man — has, since 1971, represented Mangohick Magisterial District on the county Board of Supervisors.

A concrete bridge spans the Pamunkey just downstream from where General Grant crossed the II and VI Corps. There is no public road to the former Hanovertown crossing. The morning and afternoon sun still casts long shadows across many open fields. Its lengthening rays weave their way between stands of oak, pine, maple, and hickory. At nighttime lights from an increasing number of houses and vehicles flicker along the still-narrow roads.

Dorothy Francis Atkinson
"Wyoming" 1990.

FOOTNOTES

Note: All references to individual service records and activities of individual companies are, unless otherwise indicated, from the National Archives Microfilm Publications (M324) "Compiled Service Records of Confederate Soldiers Who Served in Organizations from the State of Virginia" (National Archives & Records Service), or the "Virginia Confederate Rosters" (postwar), at the Virginia State Library, Archives Division.

CHAPTER 1

1. Joseph Martin, *A New and Comprehensive Gazetteer of Virginia* (Charlottesville, Va.: W. H. Brockenbrough, 1835), pp. 203-04.
2. Ibid.
3. Ibid.; James Mason Grove, *The Story of Todd's Bridge* (Williamsburg: 1983), pp. 1-18; Betsy Fleet, *Green Mount, A Virginia Plantation Family During the Civil War: Being the Journal of Benjamin Robert Fleet and Letters of His Family* (Lexington: University of Kentucky Press, c1962), p. 16n.
4. Willie T. Weathers, "Cownes: Records and Recollections," typescript (Tappahannock, Va.: 1983), p. 12. Malcolm H. Harris, *Old New Kent County, Some Account of the Planters and Places in New Kent County* (West Point, Va.: Malcolm Hart Harris, 1977), p. 843.
5. Charles Carter Page, "Page Workbook for King William County, Virginia, 1830." Ms. found at "Summer Hill," Hanover County, Va., owned by Mrs. W. B. Newton. Used by permission. Charles Carter Page was the son of Robert Page and Elizabeth Carter of Hanovertown and "Summer Hill." He married Sally Cary Nelson, daughter of Col. William Nelson of "Dorrell Plantation," King William County. They lived at "Difficult Hill," King William County.
6. United States Census Bureau, "King William County, Virginia, 1850."
7. Edward A. Smith, *The Early Post Offices of King William County, Virginia, 1825-1868* (King William County Historical Society, 1976), pp. 5-7.
8. Martin, p. 203.
9. Ibid.
10. Ibid., p. 204.
11. Fleet, p. 4n; Martin, p. 204; King William County Council, *King William County, Virginia* (1925), p. 34.
12. Martin, p. 204.
13. Alexander Slater, "Ledger, 1856," a handwritten ledger for an Ayletts store, King William County, Virginia. In the possession of his granddaughter, Emily Slater Stevens. Used by permission.
14. Fleet, p. 14n.
15. Notes from discussion with Virginia McGeorge Pearson, June, 1984.
16. Fleet, p. 8 (Feb. 14, 1860).
17. Ibid., pp. 16-17 (May 11, 1860).
18. Ibid., p. 15.
19. Martin, map — "Stage Roads through Virginia," engraved for the *Gazetteer of Virginia*, 1835.
20. County Council, p. 13.
21. Marshall Wingfield, *A History of Caroline County, Virginia* (Baltimore: Regional Publishing Co., 1969), p. 33.
22. Oliver W. Holmes, *Stagecoach East, Stagecoach Days in the Colonial Period to the Civil War* (Washington: Smithsonian Institution, 1983), pp. 43, 44.
23. Ibid., p. 46.
24. Ibid., pp. 47-48.
25. Angus James Johnston, II, *Virginia Railroads in the Civil War* (Chapel Hill: University of North Carolina Press, 1961).
26. Martin, pp. 204-05.
27. Alonzo Thomas Dill, *King William County Courthouse, a Memorial to Virginia Self-Government* (King William: King William County Board of Supervisors, 1984), pp. 9-28.
28. Martin, pp. 204-05.
29. John H. Gwathmey, *Twelve Counties Where the Western Migration Began* (Baltimore: Genealogical Publishing Co. Inc., 1981), pp. 82-83.
30. Harris, pp. 837 and 840.
31. Thomas T. H. Hill, "Record of the Officers of King William County, Virginia, Whose Photographs and Portraits Hang on the Walls of the Court House and a Few of the Officers Whose Portraits Are Not in the Court House" (1981), pp. 10-37, typescript. Used by permission.
32. Wyndham Blanton, *Medicine in Virginia* (Richmond: Garrett & Massie, 1933), pp. 363-64.
33. Ibid.; King William Real Estate, 1841; "Wyoming" plat, 1839, Thomas Dabney, surveyor; T. Dix Sutton, *The Suttons of Caroline* (Richmond: Richmond Press, 1941), p. 12.
34. Martin, p. 203; Maj. Gen. J. F. Gilmer, "Map of King William County, Virginia" (1865).
35. *Virginia Conference Annual, Methodist Episcopal Church, South, 1854.*
36. Bessie Peatross, "A History of Bethel Church, 1934," typescript.
37. County Council, p. 50; John Henry Foote *Sketches of Virginia* (Richmond: John Knox Press, 1966), p. 168 (licensed places used during the ministry of Samuel Davies); Jas. W. Peatross and Eliza Ann Davenport in "Peatross-Jackson Notes."
38. Garnett Ryland, *Baptists of Virginia, 1699-1926* (Richmond: Baptist Board of Missions and Education, 1955), p. 200; Mrs. William Elliott Fox, "Historical Sketch of Hebron Baptist Church, King William Co., Va. 1832-1932," typescript.
39. Ellen M. Cocke, "Centennial History of Corinth Christian Church, King William County, Virginia, 1832-1932."
40. Mary Burnley Gwathmey, "Beulah Baptist Church, King William County, Virginia . . . 1812-1962" (1962), pp. ix, 6 and 7.
41. Ibid., pp. 49-50; County Council, p. 56.
42. "Sharon Baptist Church" (King William, Va.,: 1975); Harris, p. 871.
43. "Sharon."

44. Ellen M. Cocke, *Some Fox Trails in Old Virginia* (Richmond: Dietz Press, 1939), p. 92; correspondence with Thos. T. H. Hill, 1986.

45. Wm. Meade, *Old Churches, Ministers and Families of Virginia* (Baltimore: Genealogical Publishing Co., 1978), I, 382; County Council, p. 58.

46. Fleet, p. 189; Olive Cosby Mason, "St. David's Church, Aylett" (1964), typescript.

47. Martin, p. 203; Harris, p. 815; E. Louise Davis, "Development of the Educational System of King William County" (King William High School, 1963).

48. Elizabeth Hawes Ryland, *King William from Old Newspapers and Files* (Richmond: Dietz Press, 1955), pp. 92-94.

49. Mary Mowbray Branch, "History of King William County Schools," in *Handbook for King Willam County Education Association* (1949), pp. 14-18; Fox, "Hebron;" conversation with Rose Frances Reid Ball, July, 1964.

50. Found among the papers of Alma Samuel Atkinson, 1977.

51. 1850 U.S. Census of King William County, Virginia; Lillian Latane Walters, "Recollections of Glan Villa," typescript.

52. 1850 Census.

53. Page, "Workbook."

54. Gilmer, "Map;" 1850 U.S. Census.

55. Walters; Mary Tyler Louthan, "Retreat," typescript.

56. Ibid.

57. King William County Deed Book 10, p. 265; Evelyn Acomb, ed., *The Revolutionary Journal of Baron Von Closen, 1780-83* (Chapel Hill: University of North Carolina Press, 1958), pp. 208-09; Harris, pp. 942-952.

58. Henrietta Nelson, "Petition to King William County, 1858," at the Virginia Historical Society. "Wyoming" plat, 1839; U.S. War Department, *Official Military Atlas of the Civil War* (Washington: U.S. Government Printing Office, 1891), plate xxi, no. 1.

59. Henrietta Nelson Papers in VHS.

60. Ibid.

61. County Council, p. 36; Atkinson recollections; Fleet, p. 43 (Dec. 22, 1860).

62. Harris, p. 952; Virginia Historic Landmarks Survey in the Virginia State Library.

63. Helen C. Rountree, "The Indians of Virginia: A Third Race in a Bi-racial State" (Norfolk: Old Dominion University, 1976), pp. 13 and 20, typescript.

64. Virginia Legislative Petitions, "King William County, 1843, B1207 & B1208." In Virginia State Library.

65. Ibid.

66. Commonwealth of Virginia, "Executive Letter Books, 1856-1860," pp. 47 and 49; Rountree, p. 13; Nell Marion Nugent, *Cavaliers and Pioneers* (Richmond: Virginia State Library, 1977), III, 290.

67. Harris, pp. 830 and 854.

68. John P. Little, *History of Richmond* (Richmond: Dietz, 1933), pp. 253-291.

69. Colvin, Steven A., *On Deep Water* (Verona, Va.: McClure, 1983), p. 17; Weathers, p. 16.

70. Fleet, p. 30 (Sept. 24, 1860), p. 67; Thomas H. Johnson, *Oxford Companion to American History* (N.Y.: Oxford University Press, 1966), pp. 72 and 108.

71. Fleet, p. 29 (Sept. 21, 1860).

72. Henry T. Shanks, *Secession Movement in Virginia* (Richmond, Va., Garrett & Massie, 1934), p. 62; John Beauchamp Jones, *A Rebel War Clerk's Diary* (N.Y.: Old Hickory Bookshop, 1935), I, 20.

73. Civil War letters to Misses Susan and Sallie Tuck of Mangohick. In the possession of Jean Leftwich Frawner. Used by permission.

CHAPTER 2

1. Tuck Letters: James G. White to the Misses Susan (C.) Tuck and Sallie (T.) Tuck, Sept. 5, 1861, from Allen's Grove. Letter to be delivered by Mr. Jno. Page. Stationery sold by J. W. Randolph, Richmond, 1861. Letters used by permission of Jean Leftwich Frawner.

2. Gwathmey, "Beulah," p. 21.

3. Tuck Letters: W. A. Williams to Miss Susan Tuck and sisters, July 3, 1861, from Camp Byron. (It also speaks of a Maryland colonel who was engaged in privateering and of ships that were tied up at Tappahannock.)

4. Colvin, pp. 16 and 66; Harris, p. 858.

5. Colvin, p. 67; Alonzo T. Dill, "West Point in 1861: a busy army camp," I and II, *Tidewater Review*, Feb. 4 and 11, 1987, p. 4, cols. 1 and 2.

6. Aylett Family Papers at the Virginia Historical Society.

7. Douglas Southall Freeman, *R. E. Lee: A Biography* (New York: Chas. Scribner's Sons, c1934), I, 382-389; G. W. Beale, *A Lieutenant in Lee's Army* (Boston: Gorham Press, 1918), p. 220.

8. Hill, pp. 18-21; correspondence with George D. Pollard on Pollard family; Willie T. Weathers, speech to King William County Historical Society on July 12, 1987.

9. R. L. T. Beale, *History of the Ninth Virginia Cavalry* (Richmond: B. F. Johnson, 1899).

10. Service Records; Fleming Meredith Papers, Virginia State Library.

11. Ibid.

12. Jack Coggins, *Arms and Equipment of the Civil War* (New York: Fairfax Press, 1962), pp. 63-67.

13. Colvin, p. 67; Harris, p. 799.

14. Robert K. Krick, *Lee's Colonels* (Dayton, Ohio: Morningside Bookshop, 1979), pp. 67 and 191.

15. Tuck Letters: Andrew J. Leftwich to his father (James Leftwich, 1807-1882), Mar. 20, 1864, from camp near Orange Court House.

16. Robert K. Krick, *30th Virginia Infantry*, Virginia Regimental History Series (Lynchburg, Va.: H. E. Howard, 1983), p. 5 and roster; Alma Samuel Atkinson (1881-1977) family recollections.

17. *Battles and Leaders of the Civil War*, Robert Underwood Johnson and Clarence Clough Buel, eds. (Secaucus, N.J.: Castle, 1983), II, 144-151 (Gen. Joseph B. Carr, USA). Hereafter cited as B. & L.

18. Ibid.
19. Aylett Papers: William Aylett to Alice, Sept. 4, 1861; Alice to William Aylett, Sept. 9, 1861.
20. Lee Family Papers in Virginia Historical Society: Thomas H. Carter to D. H. Hill, July 1, 1885.
21. 87th Regiment Militia: Letter with George T. Moren's service record.
22. Leftwich family recollections supplied by Jean Leftwich Frawner (1983) and Miriam L. Simmons (1986).
23. Stephen W. Sears, ed., *American Heritage Century Collection of Civil War Art* (New York: American Heritage Publishing Co., c1974), pp. 55, 229, and 239.
24. Aylett Papers: William Aylett to Alice, undated, from Camp Grafton.
25. James H. Brewer, *The Confederate Negro, Virginia's Craftsmen and Military Laborers, 1861-65* (Durham, N.C.: Duke University Press, 1969), pp. 7, 134, 136, and 166-67.
26. Aylett Papers: William Aylett to Alice, Feb. 26, 1862.
27. Fleet, p. 104 (Dr. Benjamin Fleet ["Pa"] to Fred, Feb. 8, 1862).
28. In possession of his great-niece, Mrs. James E. Walters.
29. Krick, *30th*, p. 7 and roster; Wingfield, *Caroline County*, pp. 239-241.
30. Tuck Letters: Andrew J. Leftwich to the Misses Susan and Sallie Tuck, Apr. 1, 1862.
31. Andrew J. Leftwich to Miss Sallie T. Tuck, Apr. 22, 1862.
32. Coggins, p. 33.
33. Fleet, p. 122 (Fred to Benny, Apr. 15, 1862) and pp. 24-25 (Benny's diary, May 6-13, 1862).
34. "Mangohick Baptist Church," re-typed 10-7-77 by C. J. Carter.

CHAPTER 3

1. Richard Wheeler, *Sword over Richmond: An Eyewitness History of McClellan's Peninsula Campaign* (New York: Harper & Row, c1986), p. 1.
2. B. & L., II, 121.
3. County Council, pp. 18-21; Alonzo Thomas Dill, *York River Yesterdays* (Norfolk: Donning Co., c1984), pp. 57-58.
4. B. & L., I, 692-709.
5. Thomas DeLeon, *Four Years in Rebel Capitals* (New York: Collier Books, 1962), p. 302.
6. *Official Records of the Union and Confederate Armies*, XI, pt. 3, 428-29 (Douglas). Hereafter cited as O. R. All references to Series 1.
7. B. & L., II, 266; Thomas J. Blumer, "The Pamunkey River: May - July 1862," *Tidewater Review - West Point, Va.*, p. 4, cols. 4-7.
8. B. & L., II, pp. 206 and 172.
9. Wheeler, pp. 166-67.
10. B. & L., II, 206 and 222.
11. Wheeler, p. 191.
12. Ibid., pp. 191-92.
13. George Alfred Townsend, *Rustics in Rebellion: A Yankee Reporter on the Road to Richmond, 1861-64* (Chapel Hill: Univ. of North Carolina Press, c1950), pp. 53-54.
14. Ibid.
15. Ibid.
16. Ibid.
17. Blumer, p. 4, cols. 4-7.
18. O.R., XI, pt. 3, 540-41 (Douglas).
19. B. & L., II, 319-322.
20. O.R., XI, pt. 1, 650 (Rush).
21. *Official Military Atlas of the Civil War*, pl. xxi, no. 1.
22. B. & L., II, 313, 320, 321, and 336.
23. Included in Judith W. McGuire, *Diary of a Southern Refugee during the War* (Richmond: J. W. Randolph & English, 1889), pp. 134-38.
24. Kenneth L. Stiles, *4th Virginia Cavalry*, Virginia Regimental History Series (Lynchburg: H. E. Howard, 1985), pp. 10-11.
25. O.R., XI, pt. 1, 997-98 (Kautz).
26. Ibid.
27. Ibid.
28. Colvin, p. 71.
29. Ibid., pp. 48-49, 72, and 79.
30. Fleet, pp. 126-28 (May 19-26, 1862).
31. Ibid., pp. 138-39 (June 16-24, 1862).
32. Ibid., pp. 147-151 (July 6-13, 1862).

CHAPTER 4

1. B. & L., II, 200-01 (Opposing Forces).
2. Ibid., pp. 221-24 (Smith, CSA).
3. Ibid., pp. 220, 227 (Smith), and 219 (Opposing Forces).
4. Ibid., pp. 225-230.
5. Douglas Southall Freeman, *Lee's Lieutenants, a Study in Command* (New York: C. Scribner's Sons, c1946), I, 240.
6. Ibid., pp. 240-41.
7. Ibid., p. 252.
8. Lee Papers: Hill to Carter, June 22, 1885.

9. Ibid., Carter to Hill, July 1, 1885.
10. Ibid.
11. Ibid.
12. O.R., XI, pt. 1, 975 (Rodes).
13. Service Records: Carter to Jas. A. Seddon, Jan. 5, Mar. 23, 1863, and Apr. 9, 1864; Carter to Samuel Cooper, Mar. 17, 1864; Douglas to Memminger, Aug. 28, 1863.
14. B. & L., II, 258-261 (Smith).
15. *R. E. Lee*, II, 69-74.
16. Aylett Papers.
17. Robert K. Krick, *9th Virginia Cavalry*, (Lynchburg, H. E. Howard, 1982), p. 6.
18. Marian Peterkin, "A History of Emmanuel Church, Brook Hill, Virginia," ed. Kathleen B. Francis (Glen Allen, Va.: 1986), p. 33, typescript at Virginia State Library.
19. *R. E. Lee*, II, 72-74.
20. O.R., XI, pt. 3, 567 (Douglas).
21. Krick, *9th*, p. 6; R. L. T. Beale, p. 17; Service Records.
22. B. & L., II, 271-75 (W. T. Robins, CSA) and note.
23. Interview with Mrs. W. B. Newton of "Summer Hill," Sept. 1988.
24. B. & L., II, 430; Fleet, p. 138.
25. B. & L., II, 347-350 (D. H. Hill).
26. Ibid.
27. Krick, *9th Va.*, p. 7; Henry Brainerd McClellan, *I Rode with Jeb Stuart: Life and Campaigns of Major-General J.E.B. Stuart* (Bloomington: Indiana University Press, c1958), p. 79; R.L.T. Beale, p. 29.
28. B. & L., II, 316-17 (Opposing Forces).
29. Ibid., pp. 350-361 (Hill); McClellan, p. 73.
30. B. & L., II, 350-361 (Hill).
31. Ibid., p. 397 (Longstreet); McClellan, p. 75.
32. *Confederate Soldier in the Civil War: The Campaigns, Battles, Sieges, Charges and Skirmishes* (New York: The Fairfax Press, 1977), p. 101. Hereafter cited as C. S. C. W.
33. B. & L., II, 334-39 (Gen. Fitz-John Porter).
34. Ibid., pp. 383-86 (Hill).
35. C. S. C. W., pp. 95-96; O.R., XI, p. 2, 652 (Rodes).
36. B. & L., II, 383-89 (Hill); McClellan, p. 79.
37. Ibid., pp. 389 and 401 (Longstreet).
38. Ibid., pp. 390-95 (Hill).
39. C. S. C. W., p. 100.
40. Fleet, pp. 135-138 (Fred to Pa: May 14, from New Kent; May 21, from near Richmond, and June 4, 1862, from Henrico. Fred to Ma, June 13, 1862, from Cox's farm).

CHAPTER 5

1. B. & L., II, 565 (D. H. Hill).
2. Ibid., p. 514 (Longstreet).
3. R. L. T. Beale, p. 29; McClellan, pp. 87-88.
4. Kenneth Stiles, *4th Virginia Cavalry*, pp. 15-16.
5. Blumer, p. 9, cols. 4-7.
6. G. Moxley Sorrel, *Recollections of a Confederate Staff Officer* (New York: Neale Publishing Co., 1905), p. 84.
7. Ibid., pp. 91-94.
8. Lee Papers at Virginia Historical Society.
9. B. & L., II, 454 (Gen. John Pope, USA).
10. Ibid., pp. 501-02 (Gen. W. B. Taliaferro, CSA).
11. Ibid., p. 496 (Opposing Forces at Cedar Mountain), pp. 262, 512, 515, 504, and 530 (Sketches).
12. Ibid., p. 530 (Redwood).
13. McClellan, pp. 86-88.
14. Ibid., pp. 89-92.
15. R. L. T. Beale, p. 30.
16. McClellan, p. 94.
17. B. & L., II, 530-33 (Redwood).
18. George S. Bernard, et al., *War Talks of Confederate Veterans* (Petersburg, Va.: Fenn and Owen, 1892), p. 9.
19. Ibid., pp. 10 and 12.
20. Ibid., p. 13.
21. Sorrel, pp. 96-97.
22. Bernard, pp. 15-17.
23. B. & L., II, 477 (Pope).
24. McClellan, pp. 103-09; R. L. T. Beale, p. 35.
25. R. L. T. Beale, pp. 35-39.
26. Ibid.
27. Ibid.; O.R., XIX, 208-09 (Pleasonton).
28. B. & L., II, 604-05 (Gen. John G. Walker, CSA).
29. Bernard, pp. 20-23.
30. B. & L., II, 621 (sketch) and 621n.
31. Ibid., pp. 604-09 (Walker).

32. Ibid., pp. 609-611 (Walker).
33. Aylett Papers.
34. B. & L., II, 560 (D. H. Hill).
35. McClellan, pp. 119-120.
36. Lee Papers: Carter to Hill, July 1, 1885.
37. McClellan, pp. 124-25.
38. Ibid., pp. 125-26.
39. Krick, 9th Va., p. 10.
40. B. & L., II, 558 (David L. Thompson, USA).
41. Ibid., p. 627 (Douglas).
42. Freeman, Lee's Lieutenants, II, 221.
43. Freeman, R. E. Lee, II, 390-91.
44. Service Records.
45. Lee's Lieutenants, II, 211-12.
46. Weathers, p. 17; Hill, "Record," p. 28.
47. B. & L., II, 636-37 (Douglas).
48. Wingfield, pp. 239-241.
49. Lee's Lieutenants, II, pp. 198-99, 221, and 275.
50. R. L. T. Beale, pp. 41-43.
51. Ibid., pp. 43-45.
52. Ibid.
53. Ibid., pp. 46-47.
54. McClellan, pp. 169, 177-179.
55. Aylett Papers.
56. Ibid.

CHAPTER 6

1. Tuck Letters: Dec. 7, 1862, from camp near Guinea Depot (Caroline County).
2. Krick, Lee's Colonels, pp. 410 and 342; B. & L., III, 146.
3. B. & L., III, 70-72 (Longstreet).
4. McClellan, p. 187.
5. Confederate Military History, Vol. III, Virginia, by Maj. Jed Hotchkiss (Secaucus, N.J.: Blue & Grey Press, n.d.), pp. 361-63. Hereafter referred to as Hotchkiss, Virginia.
6. Ibid.
7. Service Records; B. & L., III, 146-47 (Opposing Forces).
8. Sorrell, pp. 133-34.
9. B. & L., III, 70-71 (Longstreet).
10. Aylett Papers: Col. Aylett to Alice, Dec. 3 and 7, 1862.
11. B. & L., III, 120 (Gen. Darius N. Couch, USA).
12. Ibid., pp. 74-76 (Longstreet and map).
13. Lee's Lieutenants, II, 370-73.
14. R. L. T. Beale, pp. 56-57.
15. Ibid.
16. B. & L., III, 100-01 (Maj. W. Roy Mason, CSA) and 141 (J. H. Moore, CSA).
17. Jackson family recollections as told by Alma Samuel Atkinson, 1881-1977.
18. Sorrel, pp. 143-44.
19. McClellan, pp. 196-99.
20. Edward J. Stackpole, Chancellorsville: Lee's Greatest Battle (Harrisburg, Pa.: Stackpole, c1958), pp. 44-45 (map).
21. Tuck Letters: Jan. 2, 1863, from camp near Guinea; Jan. 25, from Camp Gregg.
22. B. & L., III, 118 and 119 (Couch).
23. Aylett Papers: Col. Aylett to Alice, Dec. 30, 1862 and Jan. 25, 1863, both from camp near Guinea.
24. Stackpole, pp. 64-65 and 93 (map).
25. Brewer, The Confederate Negro, p. 145.
26. Fleet, pp. 198 and 200 (Dr. Fleet to Fred, Jan. 20 and Feb. 3, 1863).
27. B. & L., III, 244 (Longstreet); Tuck Letters: Eli ?, Mar. 16, 1863, from a camp near Richmond.
28. Clifford Dowdey and Louis H. Manarin, eds., The Wartime Papers of R. E. Lee (Boston: Little, Brown, c1961), pp. 405 (Lee to Longstreet, Feb. 18, 1863), 417 (Lee to Longstreet, Mar. 27, 1863) and 418 (Lee to Seddon, Mar. 27, 1863).
29. Aylett Papers: Col. Aylett to Alice, Mar. 2 and 11, 1863, from a camp near Petersburg.
30. B. & L., III, 237 (Opposing Forces); Hotchkiss, Virginia, pp. 601-602.
31. Tuck Letters: Apr. 26, 1863. The Rev. George W. Trice, formerly from the Mangohick area, had served as pastor of near-by Mt. Horeb Baptist Church in Caroline County on Rt. 600 (Wingfield, p. 330).
32. Ibid., May 24, 1863, from Camp Jackson.
33. Ibid., Mar. 1, Apr. 5 and 26, 1863.
34. Fleet, p. 208 (Melville Walker to Benny Fleet, Mar. 3, 1863).
35. B. & L., III, 208 (The Rev. James Power Smith).
36. Coggins, p. 63; Lee's Lieutenants, II, 448-451.
37. Coggins, p. 73.
38. Stackpole, p. 26.
39. McClellan, pp. 219-224.
40. Ibid.; R. L. T. Beale, p. 61.

41. O.R., XXV, pt. 1, 804 (Lee); Krick, *9th*, p. 16.
42. Stackpole, p. 268.
43. Bernard, pp. 45-48.
44. Robert Stiles, *Four Years under Marse Robert* (New York: Neale, 1903), p. 168.
45. Ibid., p. 169.
46. Bernard, pp. 50-53; O.R., XXV, pt. 1, 796 (Lee).
47. Hotchkiss, *Virginia*, pp. 381-84.
48. O.R., XXV, pt. 1, 998-1000 (Carter).
49. Ibid.; Stackpole, pp. 238-245.
50. McClellan, pp. 245-48.
51. O.R., XXV, pt. 1, 999-1000 (Carter).
52. Bernard, pp. 56-57.
53. O.R., XXV, pt. 1, 804 (Lee) and 1000 (Carter).
54. Ibid., pp. 879-881 (Hardaway).
55. Ibid.
56. Ibid., pp. 881-82.
57. Stackpole, pp. 331-352.
58. Ibid.
59. Tuck Letters: May 9, 1863, from Hamilton's Crossing.
60. *Lee's Lieutenants*, III, 40-44.

CHAPTER 7

1. B. & L., III, 437-39 (Opposing Forces).
2. Ibid., pp. 152-53.
3. Fleet, pp. 225-29 (May 5 to May 12, 1863).
4. Alonzo Dill, "West Point in 1863 — a Union Outpost," *Tidewater Review-West Point*, Mar. 25, Apr. 1 and 8, 1987, sect. 1, pp. 4-5, cols. 1 and 2.
5. Ibid.
6. Dowdey, pp. 502-03 (Lee to Davis, June 7, 1863); Tuck Letters: to Sallie T. Tuck.
7. Aylett Papers: Wm. to Alice Aylett, June 23, 1863.
8. O.R., XXVII, pt. 3, 20 (Hooker).
9. Ibid., p. 20 (Dix); O.R., XXVII, pt. 2, 777-79 (Keyes and Lt. Col. C. Carroll Tevis, commanding infantry).
10. O.R., XXVII, pt. 2, 777ff; Hotchkiss, *Virginia*, pp. 690-91.
11. O.R., XXVII, pt. 2, 779 (Tevis).
12. Ibid.
13. O.R., XXVII, pt. 3, 861 (Wise).
14. Ibid.; O.R., XXVII, pt. 2, 783 (Wise).
15. O.R., XXVII, pt. 3, 861 (Elsey).
16. O.R., XXVII, pt. 2, 783 (Wise).
17. Ibid.
18. Ibid., p. 779 (Tevis).
19. Ibid., p. 784 (Wise).
20. McGuire, p. 222.
21. O.R., XXVII, pt. 2, 781-83 (Gillis).
22. Ibid.
23. O.R., XXVII, pt. 3, 862 (Pettigrew) and 876-77 (Wise).
24. Fleet, p. 224 and 239.
25. Fairfax Downey, *Clash of Cavalry* (New York: David McKay, c1959), pp. 77-8; Stackpole, p. 89.
26. Downey, p. 83.
27. Dowdey, p. 507 (June 9, 1863).
28. R. L. T. Beale, p. 67; Downey, p. 86.
29. Downey, pp. 99 and 100; McClellan, p. 266.
30. R. L. T. Beale, pp. 68-70.
31. McClellan, p. 295.
32. Captain Robert E. Lee. *Recollections and letters of General Robert E. Lee* (New York: Garden City, 1924), pp. 97-100; Stephen Tripp, "Fighting Them Over...Fitzhugh Lee's Capture," *Washington National Tribune*, June 4, 1896.
33. Ibid., p. 101
34. O.R., XXVII, pt. 2, 793-94 and 820 (Dix).
35. Ibid., p. 795-96 (Spear).
36. Ibid., p. 799 (Shingler).
37. Ibid., p. 798 (Godwin).
38. Ibid., p. 795-96 (Spear).
39. Fleet, p. 247 (June 26 and 27, 1863).
40. Colvin, p. 45.
41. O.R., XXVII, pt. 2, 794 (Dix) and 796 (Spear).
42. Emory M. Thomas, *The Confederate State of Richmond, a Biography of the Capital* (Austin, Texas: University of Texas, c1971), pp. 136-37.
43. O.R., XXVII, pt. 2, 821 (Dix) and 840 (D. T. Van Buren, Asst. Adj. Gen.).
44. Ibid., p. 852 (Spear).

45. O.R., XXVII, pt. 3, 953 (Col. E. D. Hall, CSA), 797 (Col. T. C. Singletary, CSA).
46. Ibid., p. 822 (Dix) and 838 (Getty).
47. Ibid., p. 842 (D. W. Wardrop, provisional brigade, USA). During an interview with the late W. Lynn Thomas (1983) of "Chestnut Grove," I learned that the cavalry often came that way; Harris, p. 855.
48. Gilmer map, "King William;" Elsie Edwards Garber and Sara Fox Wendenburg, "Map of King William County, Virginia," 1976; Ryland, pp. 78-79.
49. Thomas Dabney, surveyor, map of "Wyoming," 1839 and Atkinson family memorabilia.
50. U.S. Department of Interior, "Geological Survey: Virginia, Doswell Quadrangle," 1918.
51. "Map of the Vicinity of Richmond and Part of the Peninsula. From Surveys made by the order of Maj. Gen. J. F. Gilmer Chief Engineer, C.S.A."
52. O.R., XXVII, pt. 2, 841 (Foster) and 843-44 (Nixon).
53. Ibid., pp. 343 (Wardrop) and 838 (Getty).
54. Ibid., pp. 857-58 (Gen. John R. Cooke, CSA).
55. Ibid., p. 853 (Stratton).
56. Ibid., pp. 839 (Getty) and 844 (Nixon).
57. Gilmer, "King William;" interview with Edward Pollard (1984) concerning his ancestral home, "Cherry Hill."
58. Tuck Letters.
59. Fleet, pp. 248-49 (July 6-7, 1863).
60. O.R., XXVII, pt. 2, 839 (Getty) and 843 (Wardrop).
61. Ibid., pp. 820-24 (Getty).
62. Fleet, p. 251 (July 16, 1863, from 26th Regiment on Burton's farm.)
63. Tuck Letters: July 31, 1863, from Culpeper Court House.

CHAPTER 8

1. B. & L., III, 437-39 (Opposing Forces).
2. Ibid., pp. 267-270 (Gen. Henry J. Hunt, USA) and 251 (Col. John S. Mosby, CSA).
3. Ibid., pp. 262, 264, and 266 (maps 1-10).
4. McClellan, p. 296.
5. B. & L., III, 249-251 (Longstreet).
6. Aylett Papers: Wm. to Alice Aylett.
7. B. & L., III, 262, 264, and 266 (maps 1-10).
8. O.R., XXVII, pt. 2, 438 (Ewell); O.R., LI, pt. 2, 545-49 (Rodes).
9. Dowdey, pp. 524 (Lee to Ewell, June 22, 1863); O.R., LI, pt. 2, 545-49 (Rodes); O.R., XXVII, pt. 2, 455 (J. Thompson Brown, chief of artillery).
10. B. & L., III, 262, 264, and 266 (maps 1-10).
11. R. L. T. Beale, pp. 73-78.
12. Ibid., pp. 78-79.
13. Ibid., pp. 80-82.
14. Ibid., pp. 83-84.
15. B. & L., III, 262, 264, and 266 (maps 1-10).
16. Dowdey, p. 517 (Lee to A. P. Hill, June 16, 1863); B. & L., III, 249 (Longstreet).
17. O.R., XXVII, pt. 2, 637-39 (Heth).
18. B. & L., III, 438-39, 407 (Gen. Francis A. Walker, USA).
19. Hotchkiss, Virginia, pp. 400-02; Dowdey, pp. 534-35 (Lee to Ewell, June 28, 1863).
20. O.R., XXVII, pt. 2, 637-39 (Heth).
21. B. & L., III, 278 (picture).
22. O.R., XXVII, pt. 2, 602-03 (Carter).
23. Ibid.
24. R.L.T. Beale, pp. 85-86.
25. Lee's Lieutenants, III, 178, 299, and 308 (maps); B. & L., III, 439 (Opposing Forces).
26. Lee's Lieutenants, III, 130; B. & L., III, 342-45 (Longstreet); R. E. Lee, I, 362.
27. McClellan, pp. 343-47.
28. B. & L., III, 399-406 (Capt. Wm. S. Miller, with reference to McClellan).
29. R. E. Lee, III, 120-23.
30. Ibid.
31. Lee's Lieutenants, III, 179; O. R., XXVII, pt. 2, 603 (Carter).
32. Lee Papers: Carter to Hill, July 1, 1885.
33. Hotchkiss, Virginia, p. 418.
34. "King and Queen Letters from the Field, 1861-1865," The Bulletin of the King and Queen County Historical Society of Virginia, no. 11, July 1961, p. 3.
35. Ibid.
36. B. & L., III, 437-48 (Opposing Forces), 347 (Longstreet).
37. Aug. 11, 1863.
38. Dorothy Francis Atkinson, "Descendants of Iverson Lewis Atkinson and Lucy Ann Powell Floyd Atkinson" (King William: 1980), typescript.
39. Dowdey, pp. 539-40 (General Orders no. 74, July 4, 1863); B. & L., III, 420-23 (Imboden).
40. B. & L., III, 420-27 (Imboden) and pictures; Dowdey, p. 537 (Lee to Imboden, July 4, 1863).
41. B. & L., III, 422-27 (Imboden).
42. Ibid.

43. Service Records: Imboden to Col. Aylett, Nov. 11, 1863; Patrick Henry Aylett to President Davis, July 7, 1864; Pickett to Col. Aylett, Aug. 11, 1863; Interview with Dr. Bryan Mangum, current resident of "Montville," June 1964.
44. C. S. C. W., p. 169 (Longstreet).
45. Service Records; O.R., LI, pt. 2, 557-58 (Rodes).
46. Tuck Letters.
47. R.L.T. Beale, pp. 90-97; McClellan, pp. 356-364.
48. B. & L., III, 382 (map), 434-37 (Opposing Forces); B. & L., IV, 81-82 (Gen. Martin T. McMahon, USA).
49. B. & L., III, 429.
50. C. S. C. W., p. 169 (Longstreet).
51. O.R., LI, pt. 2, 558-59 (Rodes).
52. O.R., LI, pt. 2, 639-642 (Heth).
53. Tuck Letters: July 31, 1863, from Culpeper.
54. B. & L., III, 382 (map); O.R., XXVII, pt. 2, 603 (Carter).
55. O.R., LI, pt. 2, 558-59 (Rodes).
56. R. L. T. Beale, p. 97.
57. B. & L., III, 429-433 (Collins).
58. Ibid.
59. Aylett Papers: Alice to Wm. Aylett.

CHAPTER 9

1. Dowdey, p. 583 (Lee's report).
2. McClellan, pp. 368-370 (Stuart's report).
3. Ibid.; R. L. T. Beale, p. 98.
4. McClellan, pp. 372-74.
5. R. L. T. Beale, p. 100.
6. Dowdey, pp. 583-84 (Lee's report).
7. Aylett Papers.
8. Ibid., Alice to Wm. Aylett, July 15, 21, and 29, 1863.
9. Ibid., July 21 and Aug. 5, 1863.
10. Ibid.
11. Service Records: Pickett to Lee; Aylett to Gen. Cooper, June 30, 1864.
12. Dowdey, pp. 586-87 and 598 (Lee to Davis, Sept. 9, 1863).
13. Hotchkiss, Virginia, pp. 675-76.
14. Tuck Letters: July 31, 1863; Sept. (?), 1863.
15. Ibid., Aug. 30, Sept. 3, 13, and 25, 1863, all from at or near Orange Court House.
16. Armistead L. Long, Memoirs of Robert E. Lee (New York: J. M. Stoddart, 1886), p. 303.
17. Lee's Lieutenants, III, 239-246; R. E. Lee, III, 182-83.
18. McClellan, pp. 376-380 (Fitz Lee's letter).
19. Stiles, 4th Virginia, p. 37.
20. McClellan, p. 393; R. L. T. Beale, pp. 102-03.
21. R. L. T. Beale, pp. 102-03.
22. Tuck Letters: Oct. 20, 30, and Nov. 3, 1863.
23. Ibid.
24. Ibid., Dec. 29, 1863, Jan. 23, and Feb. 4, 1864.
25. Long, Memoirs, pp. 316-18; B. & L., IV, 88-91 (Gen. Martin T. McMahon, USA).
26. William Meade Dame, From the Rapidan to Richmond and the Spottsylvania Campaign (Baltimore: Green-Lucas, 1920), pp. 18-20.
27. Krick, 9th, p. 30.
28. R. L. T. Beale, pp. 105-06.
29. Krick, 9th, p. 30.
30. B. & L., IV, 5 (map); Fleet, p. 271 (Fred to Benny, Sept. 28, 1863) and pp. 290-92 (Benny's diary, Dec. 14-23, 1863); "Letters of Major John Robert Bagby," The Bulletin of the King & Queen County Historical Society of Virginia, Jan. 1962, pp. 1-8.
31. B. & L., III, 752 (Opposing Forces).
32. Krick, 30th, pp. 44, 59, and roster.
33. Joseph Park Thomas, untitled memoirs, Richmond, Apr. 16, 1919, pp. 11-12.
34. Aylett Papers: Alice to Wm. Aylett, Nov. 17, 1863; Wm. to Alice Aylett, Dec. 11, (1863).
35. B. & L., I, 647-652 (Gen. Rush C. Hawkins, USA); Webster's New Geographical Dictionary, p. 826.
36. Dowdey, p. 646 (Lee to Davis, Jan. 2, 1864).
37. Hotchkiss, Virginia, pp. 579-580.
38. Aylett Papers: Wm. to Alice Aylett, Feb. 17, 21, and 27, 1864.
39. Ibid., Dec. 11, 1863, and Feb. 21, 1864.
40. Ibid., Mar. 17, 1864.
41. Tucker's Records.
42. Tuck Letters: Mar. 12, 1864.
43. Ibid., pp. 32 and 44.
44. Long, Memoirs, pp. 318-19.
45. Ibid.
46. Ibid.
47. B. & L., IV, 96 (George E. Pond).

48. Fleet, pp. 308, 310, and 312.
49. From Jeannette Atkinson Sizer, 1988.
50. Fleet, p. 312n.
51. R. L. T. Beale, pp. 108, 110, and 179 (appendix).
52. Ibid.
53. Ibid.
54. G. W. Beale, pp. 138-39.
55. R. L. T. Beale, pp. 181-82 (appendix).
56. Ibid.
57. B. & L., IV, 95-96 (Pond); Weathers, p. 11.
58. R. L. T. Beale, pp. 111-12.
59. Fleet, pp. 312 and 316 (Fred to Pa, Mar. 9 and 21, 1864).
60. Ibid., p. 316 (Fred to Pa., Mar. 21, 1864).

CHAPTER 10

1. B. & L., IV, 98-101 (Grant).
2. Ibid.
3. O.R., XXXVI, pt. 1, 19 (Grant); Lee's Lieutenants, III, 388-89; R. E. Lee, III, 275.
4. Service Records: Carter's letter, Apr. 9, 1864.
5. O. R., XXXVI, pt. 1, 1038-1052 (Gen. Wm. N. Pendleton, CSA).
6. R. L. T. Beale, p. 116.
7. Tuck Letters: Mar. 12, 20, 27, and Apr. 4, 21, 1864.
8. Ibid., Mar. 27 and Apr. 4, 1864.
9. Ibid., Apr. 4 and 21, 1864.
10. Andrew A. Humphreys, The Virginia Campaigns of '64 (New York: Jack Brussel, n.d.), pp. 18-22.
11. Ibid., pp. 22-29.
12. O. R., XXXVI, pt. 1, 1084-87 (Long).
13. Humphreys, '64, pp. 29, 32, and 34.
14. Dowdey, p. 721 (Maj. Charles Marshall, aide-de-camp to Lee, to Ewell).
15. O. R., XXXVI, pt. 1, 1055 (Longstreet); B. & L., IV, 126-28 (Gen. E. McIver Law, CSA); Lee's Lieutenants, III, 365-66; R. E. Lee, III, 285-290.
16. R. L. T. Beale, p. 116.
17. Courtesy of Miriam Simmons.
18. O. R., XXXVI, pt. 1, 1084-87 (Long).
19. R. L. T. Beale, p. 117.
20. R. E. Lee, III, 309 (from Grant's memoirs).
21. B. & L., IV, 128 (Law).
22. Ibid.; Humphreys, '64, pp. 79-80; O. R., XXXVI, pt. 1, 1029 (Lee).
23. R. E. Lee, III, 312-15; Dowdey, p. 727 (Lee to Ewell, May 10, 1864).
24. R. L. T. Beale, pp. 118-19.
25. Lee's Lieutenants, III, 398-99; O. R., XXXVI, pt. 1, 1038-1053 (Pendleton) and 1084-87 (Long).
26. Pendleton's report and Long's report; R. E. Lee, III, 316.
27. Lee's Lieutenants, III, 401-02; Long's report.
28. Pendleton's report and Long's report.
29. B. & L., IV, 171-73 (G. Norton Galloway, USA); R. E. Lee, III, 325.
30. Pendleton's report and Long's report.
31. B. & L., IV, 195-200 (Beauregard).
32. Ibid., pp. 206-07 (Gen. Wm. F. Smith, USA) and 198 (map).
33. Ibid., I, 693-95 (Col. John Taylor Wood, CSA); R. E. Lee, III, 46-47.
34. R. E. Lee, III, 48-49; B. & L., II, 265-270 (Jas. Russell Soley, USN).
35. B. & L., IV, 207-08 (Smith) and 198 (map).
36. Ibid., pp. 146-47 (Grant); O. R., XXXVI, pt. 1, 20 (Grant).
37. Aylett Papers: Wm. to Alice Aylett, Apr. 13 and 17, 1864 and an undated scrap.
38. Ibid., Apr. 30 and May 9, 1864.
39. Ibid., May 9, 1864.
40. O.R., XXXVI, pt. 2, 213-17 (Barton), 229 (Lee) and succeeding pages.
41. Aylett Papers: May 11, 1864; O.R., XXXVI, pt. 2, 218.
42. Service Records: Aylett to Cooper, June 30, 1864; O.R., XL, pt. 2; Aylett Papers: May 15, 1864.
43. O.R., XXXVI, pt. 2, 219 (the officers' letter).
44. Service Records: Blake, Nov. 26 and 30, 1864.
45. McClellan, pp. 410-17; O.R., XXXVI, pt. 1, 792 (Sheridan); George L. Gillespie, USA, Map of Central Virginia (U.S. War Department, Engineers' Bureau, Oct. 1865).
46. B. & L., IV, 195-204 (Beauregard), 210-12 (Smith); Lee's Lieutenants, III, 478, 488, and 495.
47. Ibid.
48. Wingfield, pp. 239-241.
49. B. & L., IV, 480-86 (Gen. Imboden); Bryan L. Childress (of "Mari Hill"), "An Address to the King William County Historical Society, July 7, 1984."
50. Ibid.; William Couper, The V.M.I. New Market Cadets (Charlottesville, Va.: Michie, 1933), pp. 108-109.

51. O.R., XXXVI, pt. 1, 1038-1053 (Pendleton) and 1084-87 (Long).
52. Tuck Letters.
53. Krick, *30th*, p. 52.
54. R. L. T. Beale, p. 119.
55. Krick, *9th*, pp. 34-36.
56. O.R., XXXVI, pt. 1, 792-93 (Sheridan); Gillespie map.
57. Weathers, p. 18.

CHAPTER 11

1. O.R., XXXVI, pt. 1, pp. 276-79 (Gen. Rufus Ingalls, chief quartermaster, totals for Rapidan to Petersburg, 1864).
2. Humphreys, *'64*, pp. 119-120.
3. Dowdey, pp. 744-45 (Lee to Seddon, May 21, 1864).
4. Hotchkiss, *Virginia*, pp. 458-59.
5. R. L. T. Beale, pp. 121-23.
6. Humphreys, *'64*, pp. 127-132.
7. Ibid.
8. Ibid.
9. *R. E. Lee*, III, 395; O.R., XXXVI, pt. 2, 432, 467, and 826.
10. B. & L., IV, 244 (Venable).
11. Ibid., p. 124; Dowdey, pp. 732-33 (Lee to Breckinridge, May 17, 1864) and 747 (Lee to Davis, May 23, 1864).
12. O.R., XXXVI, pt. 1, 932 (Capt. Percy Daniels).
13. E. M. Sanchez-Saavedra, *A Description of the Country, Virginia's Cartographers and Their Maps, 1607-1881* (Richmond: Virginia State Library, 1975), pp. 89-102.
14. Ibid.; O.R., XXXVI, pt. 1, 291-303 (Michler).
15. O.R., XXXVI, pt. 1, 291-303.
16. Ibid.
17. B. & L., IV, 179 (Opposing Forces); O.R., XXXVI, pt. 1, 80ff.
18. Coggins, pp. 104-105.
19. O.R., XXXVI, pt. 1, 780-92 (Sheridan).
20. Ibid., p. 793 (Sheridan).
21. Nell Marion Nugent, ed., *Cavaliers and Pioneers* (Richmond: Virginia State Library, 1979), III - see paths 1702-1712; Martin, map.
22. O.R., XXXVI, pt. 1, 688 (Gen. Frank Wheaton) and 743 (Col. Otho H. Binkley).
23. Ibid., pp. 717-18 (Col. Reuben C. Benton), 531 (Capt. Geo. F. McKnight) and 756 (Col. Chas. H. Tompkins).
24. Ibid., p. 364 (Maj. W. G. Mitchell); O.R., XXXVI, pt. 2, 968 (Johnson to Fitz Lee).
25. Ibid., pt. 1, pp. 564 (Col. Wm. S. Tilton), 595 (Itinerary), and 551 (Itinerary).
26. Ibid., p. 80 (Dana).
27. Ibid., p. 304 (Spaulding).
28. Ibid., pp. 311-12 (Spaulding) and 295, 296, 300 (Michler).
29. Ibid., pp. 312 (Spaulding) and 804 (Gen. A. T. A. Torbert).
30. Ibid., pp. 300 (Michler) and 804 (Torbert).
31. Louis B. Wright, *The Prose Works of William Byrd of Westover* (Cambridge, Mass.: Harvard University Press, 1966), p. 375; Harris, pp. 913-14 and 952.
32. Harris, p. 952; "Campgrounds" information courtesy of Purcell Marshall, 1984.
33. O.R., XXXVI, pt. 1, 688 (Wheaton), 766 (Capt. Andrew Cowan), and 726 (Col. Wm. S. Truex).
34. Ibid., pp. 312-13 (Spaulding).
35. Ibid.; Benson John Lossing, *Mathew Brady, Illustrated History of the Civil War, 1861-65* (Washington: Fairfax Press, 1978), p. 311.
36. O.R., XXXVI, pt. 1, pp. 343 (Hancock), 364 (Maj. W. G. Mitchell) and other reports.
37. Ibid., p. 390 (Capt. Jas. Fleming).
38. Ibid., pp. 595 (Itinerary), 550 (Itinerary), 578 (Capt. Benj. F. Meservy), 564 (Col. Wm. S. Tilton), and 646 (Col. Chas. S. Wainwright).
39. Ibid., pp. 312-13 (Spaulding).
40. Ibid., pp. 991 (Itinerary), 989-990 (Gen. Edw. Ferrero), 931 (Daniels), and 242 (Surg. Thos. A. McParlin, army medical director).
41. Ibid.
42. Dowdey, pp. 752-53 (Lee to Seddon, May 27, 1864, and Lee to Davis, May 28, 1864).
43. Jedediah Hotchkiss, *Make Me a Map of the Valley, The Civil War Journal of Stonewall Jackson's Topographer* (Dallas: Southern Methodist University, 1973), p. 208. Hereafter referred to as Hotchkiss, *Journal*.
44. O.R., XXXVI, pt. 1, 1048 (Pendleton); *R. E. Lee*, III, 361-64.
45. Dame, *From the Rapidan to Richmond*, pp. 190-91.
46. O.R., XXXVI, pt. 1, 1058 (diary).
47. Ibid., p. 793 (Sheridan); R. W. Beale, p. 158; O.R., XXXVI, pt. 1, 811 (Gen. Wesley Merritt), 819 (Gen. Geo. A. Custer).
48. O.R., XXXVI, pt. 1, 242-43 (McParlin).
49. R. L. T. Beale, pp. 123-26.
50. Staunton, Va., newspaper, June 20, 1920.
51. O.R., XXXVI, pt. 1, 313 (Spaulding); O.R., LI, pt. 2, 969 (Johnson to Fitz Lee).
52. O.R., XXXVI, pt. 1, 313-14 (Spaulding).
53. Ibid.
54. Aylett Papers: Wm. to Alice Aylett, June 11, 1864.

251

CHAPTER 12

1. Humphreys, '64, p. 189.
2. *Lee's Lieutenants*, III, 513.
3. Humphreys, '64, pp. 169-170.
4. Ibid., pp. 162-63 and 171.
5. Ibid., pp. 162-63.
6. O.R. Atlas, plate xcii.
7. B. & L., IV, 214 (map).
8. O.R., XXXVI, pt. 1, 1048-1051 (Pendleton).
9. Ibid.
10. Humphreys, '64, pp. 188-89.
11. Dowdey, p. 782 (Lee to Davis, June 15, 1864).
12. O.R., LI, pt. 2, 1016 (Lt. J. R. Mitchell, CSA, com. detachment for local defense); R. L. T. Beale, p. 127.
13. O.R., XXXVI, pt. 1, 1051 (Pendleton); Dowdey, p. 742 (Lee to Beauregard, June 16, 1864).
14. Dowdey, pp. 740-42.
15. B. & L., IV, 540-44 (Beauregard); Fleet, pp. 326-27 (Fred to Dr. and Mrs. Fleet, May 22 and June 6, 1864).
16. Dowdey, pp. 785-94 (June 16-19, 1864); Humphreys, '64, p. 221.
17. Aylett Papers: Wm. Aylett to Alice, June 28 and 30, 1864.
18. Service Records: P. H. Aylett to Davis, July 7, 1864, and S. Cooper to P. H. Aylett, July 14, 1864).
19. O.R., XXXVI, pt. 1, 784 (Sheridan); Nugent, II, 42 and III, 108 and 147.
20. R. L. T. Beale, p. 129; O.R., XXXVI, pt. 1, 797-99 (Sheridan).
21. G. W. Beale, pp. 161-65; Stiles, *4th*, p. 55; Krick, *9th*, pp. 36-37.
22. Coggins, p. 51.
23. Ibid., p. 50.
24. R. L. T. Beale, pp. 132-34.
25. Ibid., pp., 134-36.
26. Ibid., p. 136.
27. Coggins, p. 154.
28. B. & L., IV, 545 (Maj. Wm. H. Powell, USA).
29. *R. E. Lee*, III, 464; conversation with Rose Frances Reid Ball, June 1964.
30. Aylett Papers: Wm. Aylett to Alice, July 20, 1864.
31. Humphreys, '64, p. 252.
32. *R. E. Lee*, III, 406; Richard J. Sommers, *Richmond Redeemed* (Garden City: Doubleday, 1981), p. 6.
33. *R. E. Lee*, III, 485-86; O.R., XL, pt. 1, 308ff (Hancock).
34. B. & L., IV, 575 (Gen. P. S. Michie, USA).
35. O.R., XLII, pt. 2, 106-07 (Butler, Grant et al.).
36. B. & L., IV, 575 (Michie).
37. Long, *Memoirs*, p. 386.
38. R. L. T. Beale, pp. 137-141.
39. B. & L., IV, 568-570 (Gen. Orlando B. Wilcox, USA).
40. O.R., XLII, pt. 1, 940 (Hill).
41. *R. E. Lee*, III, 490; O.R., XLII, pt. 1, 940-42 (Hill and J. G. Barnwell, USA); Krick, *9th*, p. 40.
42. Krick, *9th*, p. 41; R. L. T. Beale, p. 146.
43. *R. E. Lee*, III, 492.
44. Aylett Papers: Wm. Aylett to Alice, July 20, Aug. 6 and 18, 1864.
45. *Lee's Lieutenants*, III, 633; O.R., XLVI, pt. 2, 1268.
46. Krick, *30th*, pp. 55-61.
47. Alma Atkinson's recollections.
48. Jackson and White recollections of Bethel and Hebron.

CHAPTER 13

1. Dowdey, pp. 799, 826, 832, and 833 (Lee to Anderson, July 27 and Aug. 11, 1864; Lee to Hampton, Aug. 11, 1864; Lee to Early, Aug. 26, 1864).
2. Hotchkiss, *Journal*, pp. 211-12.
3. B. & L., IV, 501-05 (Wesley Merritt, USA); *Lee's Lieutenants*, III, 495.
4. O.R., XLII, pt. 1, 858-862 (Pendleton).
5. B. & L., IV, 432.
6. B. & L., IV, 492-93 and 522-24 (Early).
7. Ibid., p. 524; Coggins, p. 67.
8. O.R., XLII, pt. 1, 863 (Pendleton).
9. Hotchkiss, *Journal*, p. 230 (Sept. 20, 1864).
10. B. & L., IV, 524 (Early) and 509-511 (Merritt).
11. O.R., XLII, pt. 1, 864 (Pendleton).
12. B. & L., IV, 511-14 (Merritt), 525-26 (Early); Hotchkiss, *Journal*, p. 237 (Oct. 17, 1864).
13. B. & L., IV, 526 (Early).
14. Ibid., pp. 526-27 (Early); Long, pp. 364-65.

15. B. & L., IV, 527-28 (Early).
16. Hotchkiss, *Virginia*, pp. 507-08; Millard Kessler Bushong, *Old Jube, a biography of Jubal A. Early* (Boyce, Va.: Carr, c1955), p. 254.
17. B. & L., IV, 529 (Early) and note.
18. C. S. C. W., p. 279.
19. Long, pp. 355 and 671.
20. O.R., XLII, pt. 2, 1189, 1219, and 1284 (Archer).
21. Aylett Papers: P. H. Aylett to Wm. (no date).
22. Sommers, pp. 6 (map), 14, and 17.
23. Ibid., pp. 18 and 210.
24. Sommers, pp. 9-10.
25. Ibid., pp. 3-7.
26. Andrew A. Humphreys, *The Virginia Campaign of '65* (New York: Jack Brussels, n.d.), pp. 284-88.
27. Ibid.
28. Ibid., p. 288; Dowdey, p. 860 (Lee to Ewell, Sept. 29, 1864); Sommers, p. 69.
29. Sommers, pp. 94-95 and 427; O.R., XLII, pt. 1, 876.
30. Sommers, pp. 100-08.
31. Ibid., pp. 127-131.
32. Ibid., pp. 135, 136, 146, 150, and 166-69.
33. O.R., XLII, pt. 1, 876; Sommers, p. 158.
34. Aylett Papers: P. H. Aylett to Wm. (no date).
35. Sommers, pp. 178-79 and 236 (map); Bernard, map bet. pp. 128-29 (Michler-"Sketch of the Entrenched Lines in the Front of Petersburg").
36. Ibid.
37. Ibid., pp. 195-97 and 204.
38. Courtesy of Miriam Simmons, Richard Leftwich's granddaughter.
39. R. L. T. Beale, pp. 145-46.
40. Sommers, pp. 195-97 and 204.
41. Ibid., pp. 235-255.
42. Ibid., pp. 301-09; Humphreys, '65, pp. 291-92.
43. R. L. T. Beale, p. 146; Krick, *9th*, p. 41.
44. Sommers, pp. 309, 316, 328-336.
45. R. L. T. Beale, pp. 146-47.
46. Ibid.
47. Ibid.
48. Aylett Papers.
49. Humphreys, '65, pp. 304, 305, and 326.
50. Aylett Papers: Wm. Aylett to Alice (Dec. 27, 1864).
51. Long, *Memoirs*, pp. 241-42.
52. Dowdey, pp. 871-72 (Nov. 25, 1864).
53. *R. E. Lee*, III, 515, 516, and 530; O.R., XLII, pt. 3, 1235 (Special Order no. 284, Jno. Withers, Adj. Gen.); B. & L., IV, 593-94 (Opposing Forces).
54. Stiles, *Four Years*, p. 317.

CHAPTER 14

1. Service Records.
2. *Webster's New Geographical Dictionary* (Springfield, Mass.: G. & C. Merriam, c1972), p. 367; Francis Trevelyan Miller, ed., *Prisons and Hospitals, The Photographic History of the Civil War in Ten Volumes*, Vol. VII (New York: The Review of Reviews, 1912), pp. 77, 81, and 149.
3. Rod Gragg, *Civil War Quiz and Fact Book* (New York: Harper & Row, c1985), p. 5.
4. Webster's, pp. 489 and 317.
5. Edwin W. Beitzell, *Point Lookout Prison Camp for Confederates* (Abell, Md.: 1972), pp. 1-2.
6. Ibid., pp. 19-23.
7. Miller, p. 44; David Budlong Tyler, *Delaware - The Bay & River* (Cambridge, Md.: Cornell Maritime Press, 1955), pp. 95 and 111; Edward Noble Vallandigham, *Delaware and the Eastern Shore* (Philadelphia: J. B. Lippincott, 1922), p. 208.
8. Tyler, p. 98.
9. Tuck Letters: Nov. 12, 1864, from Fort Delaware, and Nov. 7, 1864, from Clifton Springs.
10. Ibid., Jan. 28, 1865, from M. L. Covett.
11. B. & L., II, 1-12 (Gen. Q. A. Gillmore, USA); B. & L., IV, 52-71 (Gillmore).
12. J. Ogden Murray, *The Immortal Six Hundred* (Winchester, Va.: Eddy Press, 1905), pp. 10-25; O.R., XXXV, pt. 2, pp. 161-175.
13. Murray, roster; O.R., XXXV, pt. 2, 254 (Grant).
14. J. J. Dunkle, *Prison Life During the Rebellion* (Singer's Glen, Va.: Joseph Funk's Sons, 1869), p. 27.
15. Murray, pp. 30-39 and 76-84.
16. Dunkle, p. 31.
17. Ibid., pp. 28 and 36.
18. Murray, pp. 42-52 and 71.
19. Ibid., pp. 57-61.
20. Ibid., pp. 91-95.
21. Dunkle, pp. 39-44.

22. Ibid.
23. B. & L., IV, 680 (Col. Alexander R. Chisolm, CSA).
24. Murray, pp. 84-86.
25. Ibid., p. 188.
26. Dowdey, pp. 598 (Gen. Lee to Mildred Lee), 625 (Gen. Lee to Mrs. Lee, Nov. 21, 1863), 685 (Gen. Lee to G. W. C. Lee, Mar. 29, 1864); Lee, p. 117.
27. Miller, p. 89.
28. (July 1864) — K. & Q. Bulletin no. 11, July 1961, p. 3, col. 2.
29. Lillian Walters; conversation with Betty Latane Walters, Oct. 1987.
30. Aylett Papers: Wm. Aylett to Alice, Apr. 20, 1865; Wm. Aylett to P. H. Aylett, July 2, 1865.
31. Miller, pp. 101, 107, and 109.
32. Ibid., p. 162 (quoting from Alexander Hunter, *Johnny Reb and Billy Yank*).
33. Mary Boykin Chesnut, *A Diary from Dixie*, Ben Ames Williams, ed. (Boston: Houghton Mifflin, 1961), pp. 428 (Aug. 6, 1864) and 477 (Feb. 10, 1865).
34. Service Records: Blake to Cooper, Nov. 26, 1864, and Aylett to Cooper, Nov. 30, 1864.
35. McGuire, pp. 305-07.

CHAPTER 15

1. Dowdey, pp. 898-99, 888-89 (Lee to Cooper, Feb. 4 and 6, 1865), 911 (Lee to Davis and Lee to Grant, Mar. 2, 1865); O.R. XLIV, pt. 2, 823-24.
2. R. L. T. Beale, p. 147; Service Records.
3. O.R. XLVI, pt. 1, 513 (Hotchkiss); *Lee's Lieutenants*, III, 632 and 632n).
4. B. & L., IV, 521 (Merritt).
5. Aylett Papers: Col. Aylett to Alice, Mar. 9, 1865.
6. O.R., XLVI, pt. 1, 477-78 (Sheridan).
7. O.R., XLVI, pt. 3, 1318 (Thompson and Ewell).
8. Alma Atkinson memorabilia.
9. Ibid.
10. White - Dabney memorabilia (Georgie A. Dabney, May 1988).
11. Humphreys, '65, p. 323; O. R., LXVI, pt. 1, 477-78 (Sheridan), 493 (Devin).
12. O.R. Atlas, plate lxxiv - Geo. Gillespie, "Map of Central Virginia Showing Maj. Gen. P. H. Sheridan's Campaigns."
13. O.R., XLVI, pt. 3, 1316-1329 (Pendleton, Lee, and Carter).
14. *Lee's Lieutenants*, III, 645-650.
15. Humphreys, '65, pp. 323-25.
16. *Lee's Lieutenants*, III, 657-660.
17. Ibid., p. 660; Humphreys, '65, pp. 334-35; R. L. T. Beale, p. 147.
18. Townsend, pp. xiii, 245-260.
19. *Lee's Lieutenants*, III, 660-61.
20. Ibid., pp. 668-671; B. & L., IV, 712-14 (map and Gen. Horace Porter, USA); O.R., XLVI, pt. 1, 1263-64 (Lee).
21. Townsend, pp. 246, 259-260.
22. O.R., XLVI, pt. 1, 1264.
23. *Lee's Lieutenants*, III, 678-79.
24. *Seven Fateful Days* (Farmville Herald, 1962), p. 12. Hereafter referred to as S. F. D.
25. Ibid., p. 12 and accompanying map; Dowdey, p. 900.
26. Nathaniel Mason Paulett, *Historic Roads of Virginia, 1607-1804* (Charlottesville, Va.: Virginia Highway & Transportation Council, 1977), p. 38.
27. S. F. D., pp. 12-13.
28. Humphreys, '65, pp. 374-75.
29. S. F. D., p. 13.
30. Humphreys, '65, pp. 379-381; S. F. D., p. 14.
31. Lee Papers: Thomas H. Carter to D. H. Hill, July 1, 1885.
32. S. F. D., p. 14; *Lee's Lieutenants*, III, 710.
33. *Lee's Lieutenants*, III, 712.
34. Jo D. Smith, *A History of High Bridge* (Richmond: 1987), pp. 5-7.
35. S. F. D., p. 14; Aylett Papers: Apr. 20, 1865.
36. *Lee's Lieutenants*, III, 713.
37. S. F. D., p. 15; *Lee's Lieutenants*, III, 715-16.
38. O.R., XLVI, pt. 1, 1304 (Lee); Long, p. 416.
39. S. F. D., p. 16.
40. *Lee's Lieutenants*, III, 718-19.
41. Ibid., pp. 719-721.
42. S. F. D., p. 18; *Lee's Lieutenants*, III, 726; Long, *Memoirs*, p. 421.
43. Krick, *9th*, pp. 43-44; R. L. T. Beale, p. 147.
44. O.R., XLVI, pt. 1, 1303-04 (Fitz Lee).
45. Long, pp. 420-21.
46. Ibid., p. 424.
47. *R. E. Lee*, IV, 139; Long, p. 424.
48. B. & L., IV, 752 (Opposing Forces); Service Records.
49. Pollard memorabilia (Virginia McGeorge Pearson, 1984); Service Records; Wingfield, pp. 239-241.
50. Reid memorabilia (Rose Frances Ball, 1984).

51. Community memorabilia through E. H. Pollard, 1964; Alfred Hoyt Bill, *The Beleagued City, Richmond, 1861-65* (New York, Alfred A. Knopf, 1946), pp. 284-85.

CHAPTER 16

1. Bill, p. 287; Virginius Dabney, *Richmond, the Story of a City* (Garden City, N.Y.: Doubleday, 1976), p. 197.
2. Bill, facing p. 271; Harry M. Ward, *Richmond, an Illustrated History* (Northbridge, California: Windsor Publications, 1985), pp. 134-35.
3. Virginia McGeorge Pearson, granddaughter of Pollard, Aug. 4, 1983.
4. Murray, p. 87.
5. Dabney, p. 201.
6. Service Records; Walters.
7. Aylett Papers: Egerton to Wm. Aylett, June 26, 1865, from Baltimore, Md.
8. Stiles, *Four Years*, pp. 352-54.
9. Aylett Papers.
10. Ibid., Edmundson to Wm. Aylett, Nov. 30, 1865, from Halifax Co., Va.
11. In Suzanne Fleet's possession, "Locust Grove," 1964.
12. Jean Leftwich Frawner, 1989; United States Census Bureau, "King William County, Virginia, 1870;" Atkinson memorabilia.
13. John James Lafferty, *Sketches and Portraits of the Virginia Conference* (Richmond, Va.: Virginia Christian Advocate, 1901), pp. 107 and 109.
14. Portrait and write-up at "Scotchtown," Hanover Co., Va.
15. Lee, pp. 160-61.
16. *R. E. Lee*, IV, 196-99.
17. Lee, p. 199.
18. Ibid.
19. Ibid., pp. 406 and 308.
20. Weathers, p. 18.
21. Ibid., p. 10.
22. Ibid., p. 21; 1870 Census.
23. Census.
24. Ibid.; Atkinson memorabilia.

CHAPTER 17

1. George L. Christian, *The Capitol Disaster* (Richmond, Va.: Richmond Press, 1915), p. 26; Dabney, p. 216.
2. Dabney, p. 217.
3. Ibid., p. 213.
4. Louis H. Manarin, *The History of Henrico County* (Charlottesville, Va.: University of Virginia Press, 1984), pp. 317-324.
5. 1870 Census.
6. Ibid.; Rountree, "The Indians of Virginia," p. 20.
7. 1870 Census.
8. Ibid.
9. Ibid.; Atkinson memorabilia.
10. 1870 Census; Smith, *Post Offices*, p. 12.
11. Ibid.
12. Ibid.; Frawner.
13. 1870 Census; Atkinson.
14. 1870 Census; Harris, p. 931; Erwin Scott Campbell, 1988.
15. 1870 Census; Walters.
16. 1870 Census; King William County Historical Society, *Old King William County Cemeteries* (King William County, Va.: 1968), p. 67.
17. 1870 Census; as told to Steven A. Colvin by Wm. A. Hoge, 1988.
18. 1870 Census; Atkinson memorabilia; Patty Barker, current owner of "Tanyard," 1989.
19. Ibid.
20. 1870 Census; *Old King William County Cemeteries*, p. 35.
21. Smith, *Post Offices*, pp. 5-17.
22. Mary Tyler Louthan, 1983.
23. Grand Masonic Lodge of Virginia Records, 1868-1880, courtesy of Jas. A. Brewer, Deputy Grand Secretary, June 21, 1984; Bartlett Powell, June 1984.
24. E. Louise Davis, "Development of the Educational System in King William County" (1962), pp. 3-5.
25. 1870 Census.
26. Davis, p. 4; Deed Book 6, p. 256; Deed Book 11, p. 4; Deed Book 12, p. 425.
27. Elizabeth Gwathmey McAllister, Feb. 1989.
28. Ibid.; Deed Book 32, p. 62; Deed Book 51, p. 167; "Two men who 'knew' black history . . . ," *Tidewater Review*, Feb. 27, 1985.
29. Hill, *Portraits*; Jean Leftwich Frawner, 1988.
30. Alberta Sweet Bowers, 1983; Etta Snead Ferguson, 1983; Atkinson memorabilia.
31. Marian Mitchell Moren, 1984.
32. Lewis B. Reese, 1984; Rose Frances Reid Ball, 1983.
33. Peatross, "Bethel History."

34. Moren; Gwathmey, "Beulah," p. 14.
35. "History of Mangohick Baptist Church," re-typed 10/7/77 by C. J. Carter, courtesy of Rosa Spurlock Brooks, 1989.
36. Gwathmey, "Beulah," p. 75; "Sharon."
37. "Fannie Hill Latney . . . ," Richmond *Times Dispatch*, Mar. 7, 1986, Section C, pp. 1 and 7.
38. "Centennial Celebration, 1887-1987, St. Paul Baptist Church, Aylett, Virginia," courtesy Elizabeth Gwathmey McAllister and Rosa Spurlock Brooks, 1989.
39. Fox, "Hebron."
40. Gwathmey, "Beulah," pp. 8, 11, and 49.
41. "Sharon."
42. Mason, "St. David's."
43. Peatross, "Bethel History;" T. P. Jackson to Lucetta Samuel, July 8, 1875.
44. Elizabeth McGeorge Townsend, "History of McKendree Methodist Church in King William" (1971), typescript.
45. Mary Thomas Abrams Smith, 1983.
46. "Epworth United Methodist Church 1883-1975," Dee Pendley, Pastor, courtesy of Virginia Woody Rice, 1989.
47. Alberta Sweet Bowers, "Corinth Christian Church" (1960), typescript.
48. Edna Abrams Richardson, 1983; Rosebud Wormeley Osbourne, as told to Teressa A. Pearson, Aug. 3, 1983.
49. Schedule in the possession of Mary Thomas Abrams Smith, June 1983.
50. Lee, pp. 407-410.
51. Ledgers, gift of Sara Fox Wendenburg to King William County Historical Society, 1988.
52. Ibid.
53. Ibid.
54. Dr. Philip B. May, Sept. 1984, using book published in Southhampton Co., Va., 1869.
55. Hill, "Portraits."
56. Ibid.
57. Colvin, p. 111.
58. Aylett Papers: Carter to Aylett, Feb. 7, 1882; Harris, p. 857.
59. Weathers, pp. 22-23.
60. Ibid.
61. Ibid., p. 26.
62. Democratic Committee of King William County, "Minutes — Caucus at Mangohick, August 31, 1896." In King William County Historical Society files.
63. County Council, p. 30; Gwathmey, "Beulah," pp. 20-21.

BIBLIOGRAPHY

Primary Published Sources

Acomb, Evelyn, ed. *The Revolutionary Journal of Baron Von Closen, 1780-83.* Chapel Hill: University of North Carolina, 1958.

The American Heritage Century Collection of Civil War Art. Ed. Stephen W. Sears. New York: American Heritage Publishing Co., 1974.

Battles and Leaders of the Civil War. 4 vols. Ed. Robert Underwood Johnson and Clarence Clough Buel. Secaucus, N.J.: Castle, 1983.

Beale, G. W. *A Lieutenant of Cavalry in Lee's Army.* Boston: Gorham Press, 1918.

Beale, R. L. T. *History of the Ninth Virginia Cavalry in the War Between the States.* Richmond, Va.: B. F. Johnson, 1899.

Bernard, George S., ed. *War Talks of Confederate Veterans.* Petersburg, Va.: Fenn and Owen, 1892.

Bland, H. C. "The Charge of the Partisan Rangers - a Reminiscence of the Civil War." *The Bulletin of the King & Queen County Historical Society of Virginia,* January 1987, pp. 4 and 5.

Chesnut, Mary Boykin. *A Diary from Dixie.* Ed. Ben Ames Williams. Boston: Houghton Mifflin, 1961.

Christian, George L. *The Capitol Disaster: A Chapter of Reconstruction in Virginia.* Richmond, Va.: Richmond Press, 1915.

Confederate Soldier in the Civil War: the Campaigns, Battles, Seiges, Charges and Skirmishes. New York: Fairfax Press, 1977.

Dame, William Meade. *From the Rapidan to Richmond and the Spottsylvania Campaign.* Baltimore: Green-Lucas, 1920.

DeLeon, Thomas Cooper. *Four Years in Rebel Capitals.* New York: Collier Books, 1962.

Dowdey, Clifford, ed. *The Wartime Papers of R. E. Lee.* Boston: Little, Brown and Co., 1961.

Dunkle, J. J. *Prison Life During the Rebellion.* Singer's Glen, Va.: Joseph Funk's Sons, 1869.

"Fannie Hill Latney . . ." Richmond *Times-Dispatch,* March 7, 1986, Section C, pp. 1 and 8, cols. 1-3.

Fleet, Betsy, ed. *Green Mount, A Virginia Plantation During the Civil War: Being a Journal of Benjamin Robert Fleet and Letters of His Family.* Lexington: University of Kentucky Press, 1962.

Hotchkiss, Jedediah. *Make Me a Map of the Valley: The Civil War Journal of Stonewall Jackson's Topographer.* Dallas: Southern Methodist University, 1973.

Humphreys, Andrew A. *The Virginia Campaign of '64: The Army of the Potomac and the Army of the James.* New York: Jack Brussel, n.d.

————. *The Virginia Campaign of '65: The Army of the Potomac and the Army of the James.* New York: Jack Brussel, n.d.

Jones, John Beauchamp. *A Rebel War Clerk's Diary.* 2 vols. New York: Old Hickory Bookshop, 1935.

"King and Queen Letters from the Field, 1861-1865." *The Bulletin of the King & Queen Historical Society of Virginia,* July 1961, pp. 1-4.

King William County Council. *King William County, Virginia.* 1925.

Lee, Captain Robert E. *Recollections and Letters of General Robert E. Lee.* New York: Garden City Publishing Company, 1924.

"Letters of Major John Robert Bagby." *The Bulletin of the King & Queen County Historical Society of Virginia,* January 1962, pp. 1-6.

Long, Armistead L. *Memoirs of Robert E. Lee.* Richmond: B. F. Johnson, 1886.

McClellan, Henry Brainerd. *I Rode with Jeb Stuart: The Life and Campaigns of Major General J. E. B. Stuart.* Bloomington: Indiana University Press, 1958.

McGuire, Judith W. *Diary of a Southern Refugee During the War.* Richmond: J. W. Randolph & English, 1889.

Martin, Joseph. *A New and Comprehensive Gazetteer of Virginia and the District of Columbia.* Charlottesville, Va.: W. H. Brockenbrough, 1835.

Murray, J. Ogden. *The Immortal Six Hundred, a Story of Cruelty to Confederate Prisoners of War.* Winchester, Va.: Eddy Press, 1905.

Nugent, Nell Martin. *Cavaliers and Pioneers.* Vol. 3, 1695-1732. Richmond, Va.: Virginia State Library, 1979.

Ryland, Elizabeth Hawes. *King William County from Old Newspapers & Files.* Richmond, Va.: Dietz Press, 1955.

Smith, Edward A. *The Early Post Offices of King William County, 1825-1968.* King William County Historical Society, 1976.

Sorrel, G. Moxley. *Recollections of a Confederate Staff Officer.* New York: Neale Publishing Company, 1905.

Stiles, Robert. *Four Years under Marse Robert.* New York: Neale Publishing Company, 1903.

Townsend, George Alfred. *Rustics in Rebellion: A Yankee Reporter on the Road to Richmond, 1861-65.* Chapel Hill: University of North Carolina Press, 1950.

"Two men who 'knew' black history . . . ." *Tidewater Review - West Point,* February 27, 1985, pp. 1 and 4, cols. 2-4.

Wright, Louis B., ed. *The Prose Works of William Byrd of Westover.* Cambridge, Mass.: Harvard University Press, 1966.

Official Documents and Maps

Bucholtz, Ludwig von. "Map of the State of Virginia." (Correction of the 9-sheet map surveyed by Herman Boye, 1825) 1859.

Commonwealth of Virginia. "Executive Letter Books, 1856-1860." Virginia State Library.

Commonwealth of Virginia. "Legislative Petitions - King William County, 1843." Virginia State Library.

Commonwealth of Virginia, Division of Historic Landmarks. "Virginia Historic Landmarks Survey of Horn Quarter." Virginia State Library, Picture Collection.

Dabney, Thomas, surveyor. "Wyoming" plat, December 4 and 5, 1839.

Gillespie, George L. "Central Virginia, showing Major General P. H. Sheridan's Campaigns . . . ." Washington: Engineer Bureau, War Department, October 1865.

Gilmer, Jeremy F. "Map of King William County, Virginia." Engineers' Office, Department of Northern Virginia, 1865.

King William County. Deed Books 6, 10, 11, 12, 32, and 62.

257

Michler, Nathaniel. "Richmond from Surveys under the Direction of Bvt. Gen. N. Michler, Maj. of Engineers & Bvt. Lieut. Col. P. S. Michie, Capt. of Engineers. By Command of Bvt. Maj. Gen. A. A. Humphreys, Brig. Gen. & Chief of Engineers." 1867.

United States Census Bureau. "King William County, Virginia, 1850."

_____. "King William County, Virginia, 1870."

United States Department of Interior. "Geological Survey, Virginia - Doswell Quadrangle." 1918.

_____. "Geological Survey, Virginia - Aylett, Beulahville, Hanover, King William, Manquin, Penola, Studley, & Tunstall Quadrangles," 1964-69. Courtesy of Sara Fox Wendenburg.

United States National Archives & Records Service. *Compiled Service Records of Confederate Soldiers Who Served Organizations from the State of Virginia.* (Microcopy 324).

United States War Department. *Official Military Atlas of the Civil War.* Washington: U.S. Government Printing Office, 1895.

Virginia Annual Conference, Methodist Episcopal Church, South. "Yearbook, 1854."

War of the Rebellion: A Compilation of the Official Records of the Union and Confederate Armies. 70 vols. in 127. Washington: U.S. Government Printing Office, 1880-1901.

Wendenburg, Sara Fox and Elsie Edwards Garber. "Map of King William County, Virginia." 1976.

Manuscripts

Atkinson, Dorothy Francis. "Descendants of Iverson Lewis Atkinson and Lucy Ann Powell Floyd Atkinson of King William County, Virginia." "Wyoming," King William County: 1980. Typescript in Virginia State Library.

Aylett Family Papers. Virginia Historical Society.

Bowers, Alberta Sweet. "Corinth Christian Church." 1960.

Cocke, Ellen M. "Centennial History of Corinth Christian Church, King William County, Virginia, 1832-1932." King William County Historical Society files.

Davis, E. Louise. "Developement of the Educational System of King William County." King William High School: 1962. Typescript. Courtesy of the King William County School Board Office.

Democratic Committee of King William County. "Minutes - Caucus at Mangohick, August 31, 1896." King William County Historical Society files.

"Epworth United Methodist Church, 1883-1975." Dee Pendley, pastor. Courtesy of Virginia Woody Rice.

Fox, Joseph Carter. "Ledgers, 1896, 1899, and 1900." Ayletts, King William County. Manuscripts in King William County Historical Society files.

Fox, Mrs. William Elliott. "Historical Sketch of Hebron Baptist Church in King William County, Virginia: Centennial Service, 1825-1925." Typescript in King William County Historical Society files.

Grand Masonic Lodge of Virginia. "Records, 1868-1880." Courtesy of James A. Brewer, Deputy Grand Secretary.

Gwathmey, Mary Burnley. "Beulah Baptist Church, King William County, Virginia: Highlights and Shadows, 1812-1962." (1962). King William County Historical Society files.

Hill, Thomas T. H. "Record of the Officers of King William County Whose Photographs and Portraits Hang on the Walls of the Court House at King William Virginia and a Few of the Officers Whose Portraits Are Not in the Court House." Courtesy of Rhoda Leslie MacCallum.

"History of Mangohick Baptist Church," re-typed 10-7-1977 by C. J. Carter. Courtesy of Rosa Spurlock Brooks.

"History of McKendree Methodist Church, King William County, Va." August 19, 1971. Typescript in King William County Historical Society files.

King William County Historical Society. "Old King William County Cemeteries." King William County, Va.: 1988.

Lee Family Papers. Virginia Historical Society.

Mason, Olive Cosby. "St. David's Church, Aylett: 1859-1964." Nov. 3, 1864. Typescript in King William County Historical Society files.

Meredith, Fleming. Papers. 9th Virginia Cavalry File: Box 24 of Department of Military Affairs; Virginia State Library.

Nelson, Henrietta. Papers. Petitions 1857 and 1858 and Letter to Wm. R. Aylett, 2-25-1859. Virginia Historical Society.

Page, Charles Carter. "Workbook - 1830 Tax Assessments for King William County". Manuscript found at "Summer Hill," Hanover County. Courtesy of Mrs. W. B. Newton.

Peatross, Bessie L. "A History of Bethel Church." 1934. Typescript in my possession.

Peterkin, Marian. "A History of Emmanuel Church, Brook Hill, Virginia." Ed. Kathleen B. Francis. Glen Allen, Va.: 1986. Typescript in the Virginia State Library.

Rountree, Helen C. "The Indians of Virginia: A Third Race in a Bi-racial State." Norfolk, Va.: Old Dominion University, 1976. Typescript in the Virginia State Library.

"Sharon Baptist Church - A bi-centennial booklet - John C. Penny, Pastor." King William, Va., August 1975. King William County Historical Society files.

"St. Paul Baptist Church: Centennial Celebration, 1887-1987." Courtesy of Elizabeth Gwathmey McAllister.

Slater, Alexander. "Ledger, 1856." A handwritten ledger for an Ayletts store, King William County, Virginia. Courtesy of Emily Slater Stevens.

Thomas, Joseph Park. Untitled memoirs of Co. E - 15th Virginia Regiment. Richmond, Va., 1919. Courtesy of James T. Francis.

Townsend, Elizabeth McGeorge. "History of McKendree Methodist Church." King William County, Virginia, Aug. 29, 1971. Typescript.

"Tuck Letters," written to the Misses Susan and Sallie Tuck 1861-64. Courtesy of Jean Leftwich Frawner.

Virginia State Library Archives Division. "Virginia Confederate Rosters." (Some of these have appeared in the Southern Historical Society Papers.)

Walters, Lillian Latane. "Recollections of Glan Villa," 1980. Typescript. Courtesy of the author.

Weathers, Willie T. "Cownes: Records and Recollections." Tappahannock, Va., 1983. Typescript. Courtesy of James Aldwin Hight, Jr.

Family Recollections and Memorabilia

Abrahams and Abrams - Mary Thomas Abrams Smith and Edna Abrams Richardson.

Atkinson - Alma Samuel Atkinson and Benjamin Overton Atkinson.

Aylett - Dr. Bryan Mangum, William A. Hoge, and Steven A. Colvin.
Bassett - Evelyn Martin.
Black Churches - Rosa Spurlock Brooks.
Black Schools - Elizabeth Gwathmey McAllister.
Campbell - Erwin Scott Campbell.
Douglas - Elizabeth Douglas Redd.
Fontaine - APVA at "Scotchtown," Ron and Alice Steele.
Fox - Sara Fox Wendenburg, Mary Tyler Louthan, and Sterling Louthan.
Hill - Thomas T. H. Hill.
Hutchinson, Snead, and Cocke - Etta Snead Ferguson.
Indian Medicine - Dr. Philip B. May.
Jackson and Samuel - Alma Samuel Atkinson and Boyd L. Samuel.
Jeter and Gravatt - Marian Mitchell Moren.
Johnson - Rose Frances Reid Ball.
Jones - Bryan Childress.
Latane - Lillian Latane Walters and Betty Latane Walters.
Leftwich - Jean Leftwich Frawner, Lavalia McGeorge Leftwich, and Miriam L. Simmons.
Long - Mrs. J. M. Long.
Mangohick Quilt - Suzanne Fleet.
Marshall - Purcell Marshall.
McGeorge and Pollard - Virginia McGeorge Pearson.
Newman - J. Thomas Newman.
Newton - Mrs. W. B. Newton.
Peatross - Jean Scott Thomas.
Pollard - Edward H. Pollard, George D. Pollard, W. Lynn Thomas, and Roberta Douglas Pollard.
Powell - W. Frazier Powell, Bartlett Powell, and Patty Barker.
Reese - Lewis B. Reese.
Reid and Sweet - Rose Frances Reid Ball, Alberta Sweet Bowers, and Julia Elizabeth Sweet Fogg.
Rider and Powell - Constance Christian.
Ryland - Anne P. Ryland.
Sizer - Jeannette Atkinson Sizer.
Slater and Burch - Emily Slater Stevens and Brantley H. Slater.
Timberlake - W. Earl Scott and Emma Previs Campbell.
Tomlin and Townsend - Mary H. Townsend.
Tyler, Thomas, and Louthan - Mary Tyler Louthan.
White and Dabney - Georgie Atkinson Dabney.
Wormeley - Rosebud Wormeley Osbourne and Teressa Atkinson Pearson.

Secondary Sources

Beitzell, Edwin W. *Point Lookout Prison Camp for Confederates.* Abell, Maryland: E. W. Beitzell, 1972.
Bill, Alfred Hoyt. *The Beleagued City, Richmond 1861-65.* New York: Alfred A. Knopf, 1946.
Blanton, Wyndham. *Medicine in Virginia in the Nineteenth Century.* Richmond, Va.: Garrett & Massie, 1933.
Blumer, Thomas J. "The Pamunkey River: May - June, 1862," *Tidewater Review - West Point, Va.,* December 31, 1986, pp. 7 and 9.
Branch, Mary Mowbray. "History of King William County Schools." *Handbook for King William County Education Association,* 1949, pp. 14-18.
Brewer, James H. *The Confederate Negro, Virginia's Craftsmen and Military Laborers, 1861-6.* Durham, N.C.: Duke University Press, 1964.
Bushong, Millard Kessler. *Old Jube, a Biography of General Jubal A. Early.* Boyce, Va.: Carr, 1955.
Cocke, Ellen M. *Some Fox Trails in Old Virginia.* Richmond, Va.: Dietz Press, 1939.
Coggins, Jack. *Arms and Equipment of the Civil War.* New York: Fairfax Press, 1962.
Colvin, Steven A. *On Deep Water.* Verona, Va.: McClure Printing Co., 1983.
Confederate Military History, vol. III - *Virginia,* by Jedediah Hotchkiss, Secaucus, New Jersey: Blue and Gray Press, n.d.
Couper, William. *The V.M.I. New Market Cadets.* Charlottesville, Va.: The Michie Co., 1933.
Dabney, Virginius. *Richmond, the Story of a City.* Garden City, N.Y.: Doubleday, 1976.
Dill, Alonzo Thomas. *King William County Courthouse, a Memorial to Virginia Self-government.* King William, Va.: King William County Board of Supervisors, 1984.
_____. "West Point in 1861 - a Busy Army Camp." *Tidewater Review - West Point,* February 4 and 11, 1987, p. 4, cols. 1 and 2.
_____. "West Point in 1863 - a Union Outpost," *Tidewater Review - West Point,* March 25, 1987, April 1 and 8, section 1, pp. 4-5, cols. 1 and 2.
_____. *York River Yesterdays.* Norfolk: Downing Co., 1984.
Downey, Fairfax. *Clash of Cavalry.* New York: David McKay Co., 1958.
Foote, John Henry. *Sketches of Virginia.* Richmond, Va.: John Knox Press, 1966.
Freeman, Douglas Southall. *Lee's Lieutenants, a Study in Command.* 3 vols. New York: C. Scribner's Sons, 1946.
_____. *R. E. Lee: A Biography.* 4 vols. New York: Chas. Scribner's Sons, 1934.
Gragg, Rod. *Civil War Quiz and Fact Book.* New York: Harper & Row, 1985.
Grove, James Mason. *The Story of Todd's Bridge - Dunkirk, an Account of the Rise and Decline of an Old Mattaponi River Settlement.* Williamsburg: 1983.
Gwathmey, John H. *Twelve Virginia Counties Where the Western Migration Began.* Baltimore: Genealogical Publishing Co., 1981.

Harris, Malcolm H. *Old New Kent County: Some Account of the Planters, Plantations, and Places in New Kent County.* 2 vols. West Point, Va.: Malcolm Hart Harris, 1977.

Holmes, Oliver W. *Stagecoach East: Stagecoach Days in the Colonial Period to the Civil War.* Washington: Smithsonian, 1983.

Johnson, Thomas H. *The Oxford Companion to American History.* New York: Oxford University Press, 1966.

Johnston, Angus James. *Virginia Railroads in the Civil War.* Chapel Hill, N.C.: University of North Carolina, 1961.

King William County Council. *King William, Virginia.* 1925.

Krick, Robert K. *Lee's Colonels.* Dayton, Ohio: Morningside Bookshop, 1979.

_____. *9th Virginia Cavalry.* Lynchburg: H. E. Howard, 1982.

_____. *30th Virginia Infantry.* Lynchburg: H. E. Howard, 1983.

Lafferty, John James. *Sketches and Portraits of the Virginia Conference.* Richmond, Va.: Virginia Christian Advocate, 1901.

Little, John P. *History of Richmond.* Richmond, Va.: Dietz Press, 1933.

Lossing, Benson John. *Mathew Brady, Illustrated History of the Civil War, 1861-65.* Washington: Fairfax Press, 1978.

Manarin, Louis H. *The History of Henrico County.* Charlottesville, Va.: University Press of Virginia, 1984.

Meade, William. *Old Churches, Ministers and Families of Virginia.* 2 vols. Baltimore: Genealogical Publishing Co., 1978.

Miller, Francis Trevelyan, ed., *The Photographic History of the Civil War.* 10 vols. New York: Review of Reviews Co., 1911.

Pawlett, Nathaniel Mason. *Historic Roads of Virginia: The Roads of Virginia, 1607-1840.* Charlottesville, Va.: Virginia Highway and Transportation Council, 1977.

Ryland, Garnett. *The Baptists of Virginia, 1699-1926.* Richmond, Va.: Baptist Board of Missions and Education, 1955.

Sanchez-Saavedra, E. M. *Description of the Country: Virginia's Cartographers and Their Maps.* Richmond, Va.: Virginia State Library, 1975.

Seven Fateful Days. Farmville Herald, 1962.

Shanks, Henry T. *Secession Movement in Virginia.* Richmond, Va.: Garrett and Massie, 1934.

Smith, Jo D. *A History of High Bridge.* Richmond, Va.: 1987.

Sommers, Richard J. *Richmond Redeemed: The Seige of Petersburg.* Garden City, N.Y.: Doubleday, 1981.

Stackpole, Edward J. *Chancellorsville: Lee's Greatest Battle.* Harrisburg, Pa.: Stackpole Co., 1958.

Stiles, Kenneth L. *4th Virginia Cavalry.* Lynchburg: H. E. Howard, 1985.

Sutton, T. Dix. *The Suttons of Caroline.* Richmond, Va.: Richmond Press, 1941.

Thomas, Emory M. *The Confederate State of Richmond, a Biography of the Capital.* Austin: University of Texas Press, 1971.

Tyler, David Birdlong. *Delaware - The Bay & River. A Pictorial History.* Cambridge, Md.: Cornell Maritime Press, 1955.

Vallindigham, Edward Noble. *Delaware and the Eastern Shore.* Philadelphia: J. B. Lippincott, 1922.

Ward, Harry M. *Richmond: An Illustrated History.* Northbridge, California: Windsor Publications, 1985.

Webster's New Geographical Dictionary. Springfield, Mass.: G. & C. Merriam, 1972.

Wheeler, Richard. *Sword over Richmond: An Eyewitness History of McClellan's Peninsula Campaign.* New York: Harper & Row, 1986.

Wingfield, Marshall. *A History of Caroline County, Virginia.* Baltimore: Regional Publishing Co., 1969.

Wise, Jennings Cooper. *The Long Arm of Lee.* Lynchburg: J. P. Bell, 1915.

ROSTERS OF KING WILLIAM MEN
Compiled from a study of photostatic copies of company records filed in the National Archives

The majority of the names listed may be found on the monument at King William Court House, although there are discrepancies in initials. The few others included, because of their family name and place of enlistment, may have been from King William County. Those for whom no record was found may have entered service during the latter days of the war.

The first date shows the time of registration (enlistment or conscription), followed by the place and enlisting officer. Bounty shows that they were eligible for additional payment on reenlistment. An r shows that the information appears only in an unofficial listing at the Virginia State Library.

Carter's Battery

ALLEN, JAMES W.: 6/1/61, Bond's Store; wounded 9/14/63 at Somerville Ford, left leg amputated; retired 7/26/64; application for artificial leg 7/30/64.

ALLEN, RICHARD H.: 6/1/61, Bond's Store; oath 4/20/65 in Richmond.

ATKINS, AUGUSTINE: Cpl., 8/1/61, Bond's Store; Capt. Carter; wounded 5/12/64 at Spotsylvania C.H., forearm fracture; oath 5/2/65 in Mechanicsville.

BEADLES, BENJAMIN H.: 6/1/61, Bond's Store; POW 7/5/63 at Waterloo Bridge, to Ft. Delaware & Pt. Lookout & exch. 5/3/64; paroled at Appomattox; blacksmith.

BEADLES, JAMES C.: 6/1/61, Bond's Store; KIA 7/3/63 at Gettysburg.

BEADLES, ROBERT S.: 6/1/61, Bond's Store, Capt. Carter; POW 7/5/63 at South Mountain, to Ft. Delaware & Pt. Lookout, d. 9/15/63; teamster.

BLAKE, WILLIAM B. (W.): 3/13/64, King William; POW 5/12/64 in Spotsylvania, to Fort Delaware & paroled 2/27/65 to City Pt.

BOSHER, THOMAS J.: Sgt., 6/1/61, Bond's Store, Capt. Carter; medical discharge 8/18/62.

BROOKE, A. E. (E. A.): 3/14/64, King William;r paroled at Appomattox.

BROWN, WILLIAM K.: 5/26/64, King William;r POW 5/12/64 at Spotsylvania, to Ft. Delaware & oath 6/19/65; 5'4", lt. hair, br. eyes & dk. complexion.

BURKE, JOHN WALLER: Sgt., 4/20/62, Yorktown, Capt. Carter; KIA 5/12/64 in Spotsylvania.r

BURRUSS, J. M. (W.): 2/1/64; oath 4/25/65 in Richmond.

BUTLER, WILLIAM H.: 6/1/61, Bond's Store, Capt. Carter; wounded 9/14/63 at Somerville Ford; POW 5/12/64 in Spotsylvania, to Ft. Delaware & oath 6/19/65; 5'9", br. hair, grey eyes & dk. complexion.

260

CARTER, THOMAS H.: Col., 6/1/61, Bond's Store; wounded 9/19/64 at Winchester;ʳ paroled at Appomattox.

CARTER, WILLIAM PLEASANTS (PAGE): Capt., 6/1/61, Bond's Store; wounded 5/31/62 at Seven Pines;ʳ inspector & mustering officer 11/62 to 10/63 & 3/64 to 4/64; POW 5/10/64 In Wilderness (5/12/64 In Spotsylvania), to Ft. Delaware & Hilton Head, oath 5/65; 5'8", br. hair, grey eyes & lt. complexion.

COBB, RICHARD N. (H.): 6/1/61, Bond's Store; absent 8/2/61; d. '62.ʳ

COCKE, EDWARD J.: Cpl., 6/1/61, Bond's Store; wounded 5/31/62 at Seven Pines & d. of wounds 6/23/62.

DABNEY, ALEXANDER T.: Lt., 6/1/61, Bond's Store, Capt. Carter; mortally wounded 9/17/62 at Sharpsburg.

DAVIS, BENJAMIN F.: 6/1/61, Bond's Store, Capt. Carter; mortally wounded 9/14/63 at Somerville Ford.

DAVIS, JOHN M.: Cpl., 6/1/61, Bond's Store, Capt. Carter; KIA 10/19/64 during Battle of Cedar Run.

DAVIS, WILLIAM A.: Sgt., 6/1/61, Bond's Store, Capt. Carter; on detached service 8/31/64.

DOUGLAS, J. R.: 3/6/64, Richmond; oath 4/27/61 in Richmond.

DOUGLAS, WILLIAM T.: 6/1/61, Bond's Store, Capt. Carter; POW 10/19/64 at Cedar Run, near Strasburg, d. 5/2/65 at Pt. Lookout & buried there; farmer.

DUNSTAN, ANDREW M.: 6/1/61, Bond's Store, Capt. Carter; POW 5/12/64 In Spotsylvania, to Ft. Delaware & Pt. Lookout, exch. 10/31/64; oath 5/2/65.

EDMUNDS, JAMES W. (P.): 6/4/61; pd. 3/8/62.

EDWARDS, JOHN DUVAL: Sgt., 6/1/61, Bond's Store, Capt. Carter; detached as ordnance sgt. 7/63 to 9/63, ordnance train cpl. 2nd Corps. AWW 1/64.

ELLETT, OBEDIAH R.: 7/15/61, Richmond, Capt. Carter; discharged 11/62; re-enlisted 1/1/64; wounded at Somerville Ford;ʳ POW 5/12/64 in Spotsylvania, to Ft. Delaware & exch. 2/27/65 to Richmond hospital.

ELLETT, WILLIAM M. (W): 6/1/61, Bond's Store, Capt. Carter; POW 5/12/64 in Spotsylvania, to Ft. Delaware & exch. 9/18/64 to Richmond hospital; furloughed to King William 9/30/64.

EUBANK, JAMES NELSON: Lt. or Sgt., 6/1/61, Bond's Store, Capt. Carter; wounded 9/14/63 at Somerville Ford; hospitalized 1/8/64, shoulder resection.

FONTAINE, PATRICK HENRY: Lt., also 53rd Regiment; 6/1/61, Bond's Store; returned to ministry 6/62.

FONTAINE, PHILIP AYLETT: Bond's Store, Capt. Carter; d. of fever 8/8/62 at home.

GRIFFITH, JOHN W.: 6/1/61, Bond's Store, Capt. Carter; KIA 5/12/64 at Spotsylvania C.H.

HARPER, ROBERT: 6/1/61, Bond's Store; medical discharge 5/30/62; d. '64 in Richmond hosp.ʳ

HART, WILLIAM E.: Lt., 6/1/61, Bond's Store; commanding co. & inspection off. 11/63 to 12/63; POW 5/10/64 In Wilderness (5/12/64 In Spotsylvania), to Ft. Delaware, Ft. Pulaski & Hilton Head, oath 6/16/65 at Ft. Delaware; 5'8", dk. hair, blue eyes & lt. complexion.

HAWES, WALKER A.: Lt., also 9th Va. Cav.; 6/1/61, Bond's Store; transf. to 9th Va. Cav. Co. H, 8/25/62.

HAY, JOHN: 6/1/61, Bond's Store, Capt. Carter; detached service 1/64, battalion ordnance officer; paroled at Appomattox; harness maker.

HEATH, WILLIAM A.: 6/1/62, Bond's Store, Capt. Carter; paroled at Appomattox.

HENDRICK (HENDRICKS), RICHARD: 6/1/61, Bond's Store, detailed as a teamster 1/64 to 6/64 & 10/64 to 2/65.

HENRY, JAMES H.: Sgt., 6/1/61, Bond's Store; detailed in Richmond 1/62.

HILLARD, ALEXANDER C.: 6/1/61, Bond's Store, Capt. Carter; d. at home of fever, '62.ʳ

HILLARD, JAMES: 6/1/61, Bond's Store, Capt. Carter; POW 7/5/63 at Waterloo Bridge & d. 12/18/63 at Pt. Lookout; artificier.

HILLARD, RICHARD: 6/1/61, Bond's Store, Capt. Carter; wounded at Seven Pines; discharged 8/10/62; re-enlisted 3/1/63; detached service 2/65; carpenter, 5'10", dk. hair, blue eyes, dk. complexion & age 38.

JOHNSON, J. W. (H.): d. in Elmira Prison & buried in Woodlawn Cemetery, N.Y.ʳ

JOHNSTON (JOHNSTONE), ROBERT B. (E.): 6/1/61, Bond's Store, Capt. Carter; (wounded at Seven Pines;) discharged, 6/1/64, overage; farmer from Ireland, 5'9", dk. hair, blue eyes, fair complexion & age 50.

JONES, THOMAS CATESBY: Cpl., 8/2/61, Bond's Store (Richmond), Capt. Carter; POW wounded 7/3/63 at Gettysburg, left arm amputated 7/20/63, to David's Is. & exch. 8/31/63; detailed to work at Tredegar '64; assigned to Invalid Corps 5/30/64; oath 4/18/65 in Richmond.

JONES, T. S.: 6/1/61, Bond's Store, Capt. Carter; KIA at Seven Pines.

JONES, WALKER: 1864, Richmond.ʳ

KELLY, MORDECAI A.: 6/1/61, Bond's Store, Capt. Carter; wounded 7/1/63 at Gettysburg, d. from wounds 7/19/63 in Winchester & buried there.

KING, FESTUS: Lt., 6/1/61, Bond's Store, Capt. Carter; shot through back 5/31/62 at Seven Pines; promoted for valor & skills on recommendation of Col. Carter 3/24/64; POW 5/10/64 in Wilderness (5/12/64 in Spotsylvania), to Ft. Delaware & Hilton Head, oath, 6/6/65 at Ft. Delaware; 5'10", lt. hair, blue eyes & lt. complexion.

KING, MILES C.: 6/1/61, Bond's Store; name cancelled, underage.

LANDRUM, RICHARD: 6/1/61, Bond's Store, Capt. Carter; d. of disease '62 in Richmond hosp.ʳ

LE MUNYOU, GEORGE: 7/10/61, Richmond, Capt. Carter; detailed as teamster; oath 3/25/65 at Fortress Monroe.

LIPSCOMB, BERNARD A.: also 53rd Regiment. 6/1/61, Bond's Store, Capt. Carter; hospitalized 12/61; discharged '62.

LIPSCOMB, EGBERT E.: 6/1/61, Bond's Store, Capt. Carter; detached as guard at Chimborazo Hosp. '63 & '64.

LIPSCOMB, GUSTAVUS A.: 9/1/63; POW 5/12/64 in Spotsylvania, to Ft. Delaware, d. 4/28/65 of pneumonia & buried on Jersey Shore.

LIPSCOMB, JAMES T.: 6/1/61, Bond's Store, Capt. Carter; oath 4/27/65 in Richmond.

LIPSCOMB, LANDON B.: 6/1/61, Bond's Store, Capt. Carter; discharged 8/16/62, overage; farmer, 5'10", blk. hair, blk. eyes, dk. complexion & age 36.

LIPSCOMB, R. H.: 6/1/61, Bond's Store, Capt. Carter; wounded 5/12/62 at Seven Pines; discharged '62.

LITTLEPAGE, BEVERLY A.: Sgt., 6/1/61, Bond's Store, Capt. Carter; POW 5/12/64 in Spotsylvania, to Ft. Delaware & exch. 9/18/64; paroled at Appomattox.

LITTLEPAGE, WILLIAM (B.): 6/1/61, Bond's Store; name cancelled 8/2/61.

LONGEST, JOHN C.: 8/11/62, Bond's Store, Lt. Hart; POW wounded 7/3/63 at Gettysburg & d. 7/31/63 from wounds.

MADISON, CHARLES J.: 6/1/61, Bond's Store, Capt. Carter; POW 5/12/64 in Spotsylvania, to Ft. Delaware & exch. 2/27/65; oath 4/24/65 in Richmond.

MADISON, JAMES R. (A.): 6/1/61, Bond's Store, Capt. Carter; POW 5/12/64 in Spotsylvania, to Fort Delaware, d. 12/27/64 of smallpox & buried on the Jersey shore.

MADISON, WILLIAM: 7/18/61, Richmond, Capt. Carter; wounded at Seven Pines;r oath 4/25/65 in Richmond.

MARTIN, JAMES: 6/1/61, Bond's Store, Capt. Carter; discharged 6/64, overage; farmer, 5'10", dk. hair, hazel eyes, fair complexion & age 45.

MITCHELL, ROBERT B. (W.): 7/17/61, Richmond, Capt. Carter; mortally wounded at Seven Pines.

MOORE, ANDREW J.: 7/1/61, Richmond, Capt. Carter; POW 5/12/64 in Spotsylvania, to Ft. Delaware, oath 6/30/65; 5'4", lt. hair, grey eyes & dk. complexion.

MOORE, JAMES D. (W.): 7/10/61, Richmond, Capt. Carter; d. 1/12/62 of typhoid in Culpeper.

NEALE, JUAN STANLEY: 6/1/61, Bond's Store, Capt. Carter; wounded at Seven Pines;r discharged 10/18/62, under 18.

NELSON, BENJAMIN CARY: 6/1/61, Bond's Store, Capt. Carter; shell wound in knee 7/3/63 at Gettysburg, detailed as ordnance sgt. '63, detailed in War Dept. '64; retired 11/30/64.

NEWMAN, WILLIAM B.: Sgt. & Lt., 6/1/61, Bond's Store; KIA 5/31/62 at Seven Pines.

NICHOLSON, JAMES DABNEY: 8/1/62, Richmond, Capt. Carter; KIA 5/12/64 in Spotsylvania.r

NICHOLSON, WILLIAM A.: 6/1/61, Bond's Store, Capt. Carter; POW woundedr 5/12/64 in Spotsylvania, to Ft. Delaware & oath; 5'9", lt. hair, blue eyes & dk. complexion.

PAGE, JOHN W.: 6/6/61, Bond's Store, Capt. Carter; d. 6/29/62 in Richmond hosp.; farmer.

PEMBERTON, JOHN W.: 6/1/61, Bond's Store, Capt. Carter; POW 5/12/64 in Spotsylvania, to Ft. Delaware & exch. 9/18/64 to Rich. hosp.; oath 4/25/65 in Richmond.

PEMBERTON, LEWIS H.: 6/1/61, Bond's Store, Capt. Carter; KIA at Sharpsburg.

PENNY, WILLIAM H.: 4/27/64, Gordonsville; POW 5/12/64 in Spotsylvania, to Ft. Delaware & exch. 9/30/64; d. of disease.

PRINCE, W. A.: 6/1/61, Bond's Store, Capt. Carter; POW 7/5/63 at South Mountain, to Ft. Delaware, d. of smallpox & buried at Finn's Pt. on Jersey shore.

REDFORD, RICHARD T. (B.): 6/1/61, Bond's Store, Capt. Carter; POW 7/5/63 at Waterloo Bridge, to Ft. Delaware, oath 6/14/65; 5'7", lt. hair, blue eyes & fair complexion.

RIDER, DOUGLAS (C.): also 24th Cavalry. 6/1/61, Bond's Store, Capt. Carter; discharged under 18, '62; farmer, 5'10", dk. hair, grey eyes, dk. complexion & age 17.

ROBINS, WILLIAM H.: Sgt., 6/1/61, Bond's Store, Capt. Carter; wounded at Seven Pines & Gettysburg;r oath 4/20/65 in Richmond.

ROBINSON, J. C.: 12/1/61, Davis Ford, Capt. Carter; leg broken '63; on detached service with Maj. Ruffin in Richmond 1/63.

ROBINSON, LUCIAN DABNEY: Lt., 6/1/61, Bond's Store, Capt. Carter; horse killed at Gettysburg 7/1/63, commanded co. 3/1/64 to 2/65; paroled at Appomattox.

ROBINSON, RICHARD C.: Sgt., 6/1/61, Bond's Store, Capt. Carter; artificer; oath 4/22/65 in Richmond.

RYLAND, ROBERT S.: Lt.; also 9th Va. Cavalry, 6/1/61, Bond's Store; trans. 9/18/62 to 9th Va. Cav. Co. H.

SALE, PHILLIP: 6/1/61, Bond's Store, Capt. Carter; wounded at Seven Pines; discharged 3/1/63.

SLAUGHTER, L. B.: 8/1/62, Bond's Store, Capt. Carter; POW 5/12/64 in Spotsylvania, to Ft. Delaware & oath 6/21/65; 5'10", dk. hair, blue eyes & dk. complexion.

SLAUGHTER, WILLIAM T.: 3/7/64, Richmond;r oath 4/27/65 in Richmond.

SMITH, JOHN: 7/10/61, Richmond, Capt. Carter; wounded at Fredericksburg;r discharged, overage; farmer, dk. hair, grey eyes, dk. complexion & age 46.

STILES, JOSHUA C.: 7/18/61, Richmond, Capt. Carter; detached to Ordnance Dept. Battalion 3/64 to 6/64; oath 3/25/65 at Fortress Monroe.

SWEET, T. C.: 5/14/62, Long Bridge, Capt. Carter.

TEBBS, GEORGE T.: Cpl., 6/1/61, Bond's Store, Capt. Carter; wounded at Seven Pines in both feet, one amputated; applied for position in Treasury Dept. with endorsement of Col. T. J. Evans & Maj. Douglas 9/7/63.

TEBBS, JOHN S. (C.): 6/1/61, King William; d. of disease in King William.r

TEBBS, ROBERT T.: 6/1/61, Bond's Store.

262

TEMPLE, ROY: Cpl., 6/1/61, Bond's Store; recommended for capt. of artillery '63; detached service 10/64 to 2/65; oath 4/20/65 in Richmond.

TERRY, HARVEY: 6/1/61, Bond's Store, Capt. Carter; POW 5/12/64 in Spotsylvania, to Ft. Delaware & exch. 9/30/64 to Camp Lee; paroled at Appomattox.

TIGNOR, GILES: 6/1/61, Bond's Store, Capt. Carter; oath 5/2/65 in Ashland, carpenter.

TIGNOR, SILAS DUNCAN: 6/1/61, Capt. Carter; oath 5/12/64 (Spotsylvania); oath 4/20/65 in Richmond.

TRIMMER (TRIMYER), STANLEY C.: 6/1/61, Bond's Store, Capt. Carter; wounded at Sharpsburg;r oath 4/20/65 in Richmond.

TUCK, JAMES (T.): 6/1/61, Bond's Store, Capt. Carter; wounded at White Oak Swamp 7/1/62, d. of fever 8/1/62; farmer, 5'5", blk. hair, blk. eyes, dk. complexion & age 22.

TUCK, JOHN (C. or H.): 6/1/61, Bond's Store, Capt. Carter; POW 7/5/63 at Gettysburg, to Ft. Delaware, exch. 2/18/65; paroled at Appomattox.

TUCK, WILLIAM C. (M.): 6/1/61, Bond's Store, Capt. Carter; paroled at Appomattox.

TURNER, CHARLES W.: 3/13/62, Goochland, Capt. Leake; transf. from Capt. Leake's Co. as 1st sgt. 10/8/62; detached service '64 & '65.

VERLANDER, E.: No record found.

VERLANDER, JOSEPH M.: 6/1/61, Bond's Store; d. 3/28/62 of typhold & pneumonia in Orange C.H. hosp.

VERLANDER, T. N.: 2/1/64; POW 5/12/64 in Spotsylvania, to Ft. Delaware, oath 6/2/65; 5', red hair, grey eyes & lt. complexion.

VIAR, HENRY W. (M.): 6/1/61, Bond's Store; discharged '62.

VIAR, WILLIAM H.: 6/1/61, King William.r

WARFIELD, (R.) WILLIAM: 6/1/61, Bond's Store, Capt. Carter; discharged.

WARING, SPENCER R.: Sgt., also 9th Va. Cavalry. 6/1/61, Bond's Store, Capt. Carter; wounded 5/31/62 at Seven Pines;r 4/1/64 transferred to 9th Va. Cav. Co. F.

WHITE, JAMES A.: also 9th Va. Cavalry. 6/1/61, Bond's Store; medical discharge 7/1/62 in Richmond; 6/9/63 enlisted in 9th Va. Cav. Co. H.

WHITE, JAMES G. (C.): Sgt., 7/23/61, Richmond, Capt. Carter; discharged 6/30/62, time expired; 5'7", dk. hair, blue eyes, fair complexion & nearly age 42.

WILTSHIRE, GEORGE H.: 6/1/61, Bond's Store.

WILTSHIRE, W. H.: 6/1/61, King William.r

WOODY, EZEKIEL L. (C.): 6/1/61, Bond's Store, Capt. Carter; wounded 5/31/62 at Seven Pines;5 discharged 6/1/64; sailor, dk. hair, blk. eyes, dk. complexion & age 45.

WOODY, JOHN (BEN) P.: 6/1/61, Bond's Store; wounded at Seven Pines 5/31/62;r POW 9/20/62 near Keedysville, Md.; d. 11/29/62 of typhold in Richmond hosp.

2nd Regiment Virginia Artillery - Company G
22nd Virginia Infantry Battalion - Company G

ADAMS, HAMILTON (C. W.): 2nd Artillery & Militia only, 1/31/62, Gloucester Point, Capt. Johnson, from Capt. Littlepage's Militia; sick 3/62 to 4/62 in King William.

ADAMS, LEROY C.: also Militia, 1/31/62, Gloucester Pt., Capt. Johnson, from Capt. Moore's Militia; sick '62-'63; discharged 10/4/63.

ATKINS, JOHN H.: 3/16/62, Richmond, Capt. Johnson; POW 7/14/63 at Falling Waters, d. 2/1/64 of disease & buried at Pt. Lookout, Md.

ATKINS, L. D. (see James D. in Militia): No record found.

BEADLES, JOHN H.: also Militia, 1/31/62, Gloucester Pt., Capt. Johnson, from Capt. Littlepage's Militia; POW 7/14/63 at Falling Waters, to Old Capitol Prison, Pt. Lookout & exch. 2/13/65; oath 4/20/65 in Richmond.

BLAKE, JOHN W.: also Militia, 1/31/62, Gloucester Pt., Capt. Johnson, from Capt. Moore's Militia; wounded gunshot in back near kidney & spine 6/26/62 at Mechanicsville & discharged 10/4/62; overseer, 5'10", br. hair, grey eyes, dk. complexion & age 35.

CLEMENTS, JAMES H.: 2nd Artillery & Militia only, 1/31/62, Gloucester Pt., Capt. Johnson, from Capt. Moore's Militia.

CLEMENTS, LEROY C. (Y.): 2nd Artillery & Militia only, 1/31/62, Gloucester Pt., Capt. Johnson, from Capt. Moore's Militia; d. 4/9/62 in Richmond.

COBB, JOHN M.: 2nd Artillery & Militia only, 1/31/62, Gloucester Pt., Capt. Johnson, from Capt. Littlepage's Militia; d. 3/18/62 in camp near Richmond.

COCKE, BENJAMIN A.: 3/15/62, Richmond, Capt. Johnson; detailed as clerk in Richmond defenses 3/62 to 10/63; POW 4/6/65 at Amelia Springs, to Pt. Lookout & oath 6/10/65; 5'9", dk. grey hair, br. eyes & lt. complexion.

DAVIS, JOHN W.: 3/17/62, Richmond, Capt. Johnson; detailed as wagoneer for battalion 5/23/62; POW 7/64 near Harper's Ferry & sent to D.C. prison 7/20/64.

FOX, JOHN B. (O.): 10/29/63, Culpeper C.H., Lt. Houle; POW nose broken 4/6/65 at Amelia C.H., to Pt. Lookout & oath 6/12/65; 6', dk. hair, grey eyes & dk. complexion.

FOX, WILLIAM H.: also Militia & Bounty, 1/31/62, Gloucester Pt., Capt. Johnson, from Capt. Moore's Militia; oath 4/24/65 in Richmond.

GARDNER, (J.) REUBEN: 7/20/61, Capt. Pollard, King Wm. C.H.; POW 7/14/63 at Falling Waters, to Baltimore Hosp. & exch. 9/26/63; POW 9/25/64 at Harrisonburg, to Pt. Lookout & exch. 10/29/64; oath 4/24/65 in Richmond.

GARDNER, JOHN C.: also Militia & Bounty, 1/31/62, Gloucester Pt., Capt. Johnson, from Capt. Moore's Militia; on roll 12/31/64.

GRAVATT, GEORGE W.: Sgt., also Militia, 1/31/62, Gloucester Pt., Capt. Johnson, from Capt. Moore's Militia; mortally wounded 8/28/62 at Manassas & d. 9/19/62 in Warrenton.

HAY, EDWARD: also Militia, 1/31/62, Gloucester Pt., Capt. Johnson, from Capt. Moore's Militia; overage 5/31/62.

HAY, FLEMING: also Militia, 1/31/62, Gloucester Pt., Capt. Johnson, from Capt. Moore's Militia; overage 5/31/62.

HUCKSTEP, IRA: 1/31/62, Gloucester Pt., Capt. Johnson; POW 7/14/63 at Falling Waters & d. 11/30/63 of disease at Pt. Lookout.

JAMES, ROBERT H.: Sgt., 1/31/62, Gloucester Pt., Capt. Johnson, from Capt. Moore's Militia; wounded 6/30/62 & sent home to King Wm.; on detached service 5/10/63 at Camp Jackson in Winchester; oath 4/24/65 in Richmond.

JOHNSON, JAMES CHRISTOPHER: Lt. Col. (also Militia?), 1/31/62, Gloucester Pt.; signed roll as commanding company 3/62 to 4/62; made lt. col. 11/5/62; medical discharge 11/5/62.

JOHNSON, JAMES E.: Lt., Bounty; 3/10/62, Richmond, Capt. Johnson; wounded 8/29/62; POW 7/14/63 at Falling Waters, to Johnson's Island & oath 6/11/65; 5'8", lt. hair, blue eyes, florid complexion & age 36.

JOHNSON, JOHN H.: Cpl., Bounty; 2/27/62, Richmond, Capt. Johnson; oath 4/24/65 in Richmond.

LEFTWICH, ANDREW J.: Lt., Militia & Bounty; 1/31/62, Gloucester Pt., Capt. Johnson, from Capt. Moore's Militia; detached to King Wm. to enroll conscripts 7/62 to 11/62; 7/63 to 8/63 signed roll as commanding company; POW 5/23/64 at North Anna, to Fort Delaware & oath 6/16/65; 5'8", lt. hair, blue eyes & ruddy complexion.

LEFTWICH, ROBERT WASHINGTON: Cpl., Militia & Bounty; 1/31/62, Gloucester Pt., Capt. Johnson; POW 4/6/65 at Amelia C.H., to Pt. Lookout & oath 6/14/65; 5'7", br. hair, hazel eyes & lt. complexion.

LEFTWICH, WILLIAM H.: Militia & Bounty; 1/31/62, Gloucester Pt., Capt. Johnson; POW 4/6/65 at Amelia C.H., to Pt. Lookout & oath 6/14/65; 5'6", br. hair, hazel eyes & fair complexion.

MARSHALL, JOHN W.: 2nd Artillery & Militia only; 1/31/62, Gloucester Pt., Capt. Johnson, from Captain Moore's Militia; 10 monthsr - over 35.

MOOKLAR, ATWELL T.: Lt., also 9th Cav. & Militia; 1/31/62, Gloucester Pt., Capt. Johnson; on roll 5/31/62.

MORAN, GEORGE: 3/17/62, Richmond, Capt. Johnson; 5/31/62 sick in Richmond.

PICKLES, WILLIAM D.: Militia & Bounty, 1/31/62, Gloucester Pt., Capt. Johnson, from Capt. Littlepage's Militia; oath 4/24/65 in Richmond.

PRINCE, ROBERT H.: Cpl., also Militia, 1/31/62, Gloucester Pt., Capt. Johnson, from Capt. Moore's Militia; KIA 8/28/62 at Manassas.

SLAUGHTER, JOHN C.: also Militia, 1/31/62, Gloucester Pt., Capt. Johnson, from Capt. Moore's Militia; wounded 7/1/63 at Gettysburg; wounded shoulder & lung 5/10/64 & d. 6/22/64 at Chimborazo Hosp.; farmer & age 30.

SLAUGHTER, JOSEPH: also Militia, 1/31/62, Gloucester Pt., Capt. Johnson, from Capt. Littlepage's Militia; wounded 7/1/63 at Gettysburg; on roll 9/30/64.

SLAUGHTER, WILLIAM B.: Cpl., also Militia, 1/31/62, Gloucester Pt., Capt. Johnson, from Capt. Littlepage's Militia; 3/15/62 detailed to work on gunboats at West Point; on roll 7/8/64.

SULLENS, GRANGER L.: also Militia, 1/31/62, Gloucester Pt., Capt. Johnson, from Capt. Littlepage's Militia; overage 5/31/62.

TUCK, GEORGE S.: also Militia, 1/31/62, Gloucester Pt., Capt. Johnson, from Capt. Moore's Militia; overage 5/31/62.

TUCK, RICHARD M.: also Militia, 1/31/62, Gloucester Point, Capt. Johnson; on roll 6/20/62.

WALKER, ANDREW (ALEXANDER) B.: also Militia & Bounty, 2/5/62, Gloucester Pt., Capt. Johnson; wounded 6/30/62 & d. 7/15/62 at St. Chas. Hosp. in Richmond.

WATERS, RUFUS W.: also Militia & Bounty, 1/31/62, Gloucester Pt., Capt. Johnson, from Capt. Littlepage's Militia; POW 9/16/62 at Hagerstown, paroled from N.Y. 11/10/62; POW 6/4/64 at Cold Harbor, d. 6/13/65 of scurvy at Pt. Lookout Hosp., Md. & buried in POW graveyard.

WOOLARD, GEORGE W.: also Militia, 1/31/62, Gloucester Pt., Capt. Johnson, from Capt. Moore's Militia; sick 7/62 to 8/62, discharged.

Other Companies of the 22nd Battalion

ALEXANDER, JOHN C.: Co. C & Militia, 3/16/62, Richmond, Capt. Johnson; overage.

MILLS, JAMES W.: Co. E, 5/23/62, Milford, R. S. Elan; d. 8/15/62 in Petersburg.

5th Virginia Battalion - Companies B & D
53rd Virginia Regiment Infantry - Companies D & H (as shown)

ABRAHAMS, JAMES H.: Cpl., Co. D, 5/13/61, West Point, Maj. Tomlin; wounded in arm 6/28/62 near Richmond, nurse in hospital '62; lt. in local defense '63.

ADAMS, C. W.: Co. H, no record found.

ADAMS, HAMILTON: Co. H, also 2nd Artillery & Militia. Oath 4/21/65.

264

ALLEN, WILLIAM T.: Co. H, 7/26/61, West Point, Maj. Tomlin; wounded in head 5/31/62 at Seven Pines, discharged 8/16/62; on Chester roll 12/64.

ANCARROW, CHARLES E.: Co. H, Bounty; 7/26/61, West Point, Maj. Tomlin; oath 4/20/65 in Richmond.

ATKINS, ABSALOM A.: Co. H, 7/26/61, West Point, Maj. Tomlin; wounded 8/26/62 at Fauquier Springs & d. ca9/25/62 at Jefferson, Culpeper County.

ATKINS, THOMAS L. (L. T.): Sgt., Co. H, Bounty, 7/26/61, West Point, Maj. Tomlin; oath 4/19/65 in Richmond.

AYLETT, WILLIAM ROANE: Col., Co. D, 5/13/61, West Point, Maj. Tomlin; wounded 7/3/63 at Gettysburg; wounded 5/16/64 at Bermuda Hundred; POW 4/6/65 at Sayler's Creek & to Old Capitol Prison & Johnson's Is., oath 7/25/65; 5'9", lt. hair, br. eyes, dk. complexion & age 32 (34).

BAYLOR, JOHN N.: Co. H, 7/26/61, West Point, Maj. Tomlin; discharged overage 8/16/62; 5'4"; sandy hair, hazel eyes, florid complexion & age 45.

BENSON, DOUGLAS BROWN, DR.: (lived in King Wm. after the war). Appointed asst. surgeon for regiment 1/1/63; on roll 11/64.

BLAKE, ANDREW C.: Lt., Co. H, 8/16/61, West Point, Maj. Tomlin; wounded slightly 6/18/62; detailed to King Wm. & King and Queen to enroll conscripts 8/62; wounded in arm & leg 5/16/64; resigned commission 11/26/64.

BLAKE, AUGUSTINE A. (J.): Co. H, 7/26/61, West Point, Maj. Tomlin; d. 2/8/62 in Camp of disease; shoemaker, 5'6", br. hair, hazel eyes & age 37.

BRAY, CHARLES: Co. D, 5/13/61, West Point, Maj. Tomlin; POW wounded 7/3/63 at Gettysburg (no further record).

BRAY, WILLIAM HARVEY: Lt., Cos. D, E & B, 4/21/62, Suffolk, Maj. Tomlin; appointed capt. Co. B 7/1/63 to take effect 7/27/63; KIA 7/3/63 at Gettysburg.

BROWN, ARCHIE BEALE: Lt., Co. D, 6/30/61, West Point, Maj. Tomlin; detailed as clerk of brigade 10/63; POW 4/1/65 at Dinwiddie C.H., to Johnson's Is. & oath 6/18/65; 5'10", lt. hair, blue eys, fair complexion & age 23.

BROWN, JOHN NEWTON: Lt., Co. D, 5/13/61, West Point, Maj. Tomlin; commanding company 1/62; wounded Seven Days, d. 7/12/62 in Richmond.

BROWN, T. HITE: Co. D, no record found.

BRUSHWOOD, GEORGE W.: Co. E, 5/13/61, West Point, Maj. Tomlin; detailed to build bridges at Fort Grafton 1/62; KIA 6/28/62 between Williamsburg Rd. & Richmond-York River R.R.

BURCH, E.: No record found.

BURCH, JAMES H.: Cpl., Co. D, 5/13/61, West Point, Maj. Tomlin; POW 7/3/63 at Gettysburg, to Fort Delaware & Pt. Lookout, exch. 2/18/65; oath 4/21/65 in Richmond.

BURCH, JOHN F.: Cpl., Co. D, 6/30/61, West Point, Maj. Tomlin; wounded 6/18/62, to Richmond hosp.; wounded 7/4/63; POW 4/1/65 at Five Forks, to Hart's Is., oath 6/21/65; 5'8", dk. hair, blue eyes & fair complexion.

BURRUSS (BURRESS), WILLIAM H.: Lt. Col., Co. H, 7/26/61, West Point, Maj. Tomlin; on guard at So. Quay 5/63; POW 7/3/63 at Gettysburg & d. 8/15/63 (8/9/63).

BUTLER, BENJAMIN: Co. H, 7/26/61, West Point, Maj. Tomlin; d. 6/25/62 in Richmond hosp.; farmer, 5'8", dk. hair, dk. eyes, ruddy complexion & age 21.

CAMPBELL, MARIUS G.: Sgt., Co. H, Bounty, 8/7/61, West Point, Maj. Tomlin; POW 7/3/63 at Gettysburg, to Fort Delaware & Pt. Lookout, d. 9/16/63 (2 days before exch.)

CAMPBELL, ROBERT C.: Lt., Co. D, Bounty, 5/15/61, West Point, Maj. Tomlin; POW 7/3/63 at Gettysburg, to Fort Delaware, Johnson's Is. & Hilton Head, oath 5/20/65 at Fort Delaware; 5'8", br. hair, grey eyes & dk. complexion.

CARNEAL, HENRY: Co. D, 6/30/61, West Point, Maj. Tomlin; KIA 7/4/63 at Gettysburg.

CATLETT, THOMAS B.: Co. D, 5/13/61, West Point, Maj. Tomlin; discharged 8/16/62 at Falling Creek, overage; farmer, 5'8", dk. hair, br. eyes & d. complexion.

CHICK, JAMES F.: Co. D, 5/13/61, West Point, Maj. Tomlin; POW 4/1/65 at Five Forks, to Hart's Is., oath 6/20/65; 5'9", dk. hair, br. eyes & dark complexion.

CLEMENTS, ELKANAH D.: Sgt., Co. D, 5/13/61, West Point, Maj. Tomlin; d. 6/15/63 of pneumonia in Richmond hosp.

CLEMENTS, EUGENE V.: Co. H, 2/14/64, Richmond, Col. Shields; POW 4/1/65 at Five Forks, to Hart's Is., oath 6/20/65; 6'6", lt. hair, blue eyes & lt. complexion.

CLUVERIUS, B. W.: Co. D. On roll 10/15/64; POW 4/1/65 at Five Forks, to Hart's Is., oath 6/6/65; 5'10", br. hair, grey eyes & lt. complexion.

COBB, WILLIAM T.: Sgt., Co. D, 5/13/61, West Point, Maj. Tomlin; detached to King Wm. for conscripts 8/62 & 9/62; oath 5/20/65 at Mechanicsville.

COOKE, JOHN H. (R.): Co. D. On undated roll for clothing; POW 4/1/65 at Five Forks, to Hart's Is. & oath 6/20/65; 5'9", dk. hair, dk. eyes & dk. complexion.

COSBY, WILLIAM H.: Co. H, 7/26/61, West Point, Maj. Tomlin; teamster.

COULTER, H. T.: Lt., Adjutant; POW at Spotsylvania, to Fort Pulaski, exch. 12/64.

CROW, PRESTON: Co. H, 7/26/61, West Point, Maj. Tomlin; POW 7/14/63 at Falling Waters, to Pt. Lookout, oath 1/21/64 in Baltimore; 6', br. hair, dk. eyes, dk. complexion & age 23.

CROW, ROBERT W.: Co. D, Bounty, 5/13/61, West Point, Maj. Tomlin; oath 4/27/65 in Richmond.

CROW, WILLIAM T.: Co. H, 7/26/61, West Point, Maj. Tomlin; in hosp. in Suffolk '62; teamster.

CRUTCHFIELD, CHARLES C.: Co. D, Bounty, 6/30/61, West Point, Maj. Tomlin; oath 4/21/65 in Richmond.

DABNEY, B. W. (J. W.): Co. H. Discharged 12/17/61 at Ship Pt. having supplied substitute - Wm. Lynch; POW 6/1/64 in King Wm., to Pt. Lookout & Savannah, Ga., exch. to Camp Lee 11/13/64.

DAVIS, ALEXANDER: Co. H, Bounty, 7/26/61, West Point, Maj. Tomlin; furloughed for 3 mos. for disability 2/65; oath 5/4/65 at Mechanicsville.

265

DAVIS, CHRISTOPHER R. (H.): Co. H, 7/26/61, West Point, Maj. Tomlin; discharged overage 9/5/62; bricklayer, 5'8", dk. hair, grey eyes, dk. complexion & age 38.

DAVIS, JOHN B.: Co. D, 7/10/61, West Point, Maj. Tomlin; ships carpenter & detailed at West Point hosp.; oath 4/24/65 in Richmond.

DAVIS, PARKS B. P.: Sgt., Co. D, Bounty, 6/30/61, West Point, Maj. Tomlin; 12/61 & 1/62 with Quartermaster at Yorktown; on roll through 6/64.

EASTWOOD, A. W.: Co. D, no record, see Militia.

EDMUNDS, JOHN: Co. D, 5/13/61, West Point, Maj. Tomlin; d. 4/3/62 of typhoid in Suffolk hosp.

EDMUNDS, WILLIAM J.: Co. D, Bounty, 5/13/61, West Point, Maj. Tomlin; in hosp. 10/10/62.

EDWARDS, KLEBER (R.): Lt., Co. H, 7/26/61, West Point, Maj. Tomlin; on roll 12/64.

EDWARDS, THOMAS: Sgt., Co. H, 7/26/61, West Point, Maj. Tomlin; 2/62 sent to King Wm. for negroes to work on fortifications; wounded in abdomen 5/64 & d. 5/11/64 in Richmond hosp.

ELLETT, WILLIAM H.: Co. D, 5/13/61, West Point, Maj. Tomlin; duty in Chimborazo hosp. 5/63; POW 4/1/65 at Five Forks, to Hart's Is., oath 6/21/65; 5'8", lt. hair, blue eyes & lt. complexion.

EUBANK, THOMAS: Co. H, 7/26/61, West Point, Maj. Tomlin; medical discharge 5/23/62.

FLEET, JOHN B.: Co. D, Bounty, 5/13/61, West Point, Maj. Tomlin; with Quartermaster at Yorktown 12/61; mortally wounded 6/28/62.

FLOYD, AMERICUS: Cpl., Co. H, Bounty, 7/26/61, West Point, Maj. Tomlin; wounded 7/3/63 at Gettysburg; POW 4/1/65 at Five Forks, to Hart's Is., oath 6/21/65; 6', dark hair, dk. eyes & florid complexion.

FLOYD, JOHN T.: Co. H, also Militia, 2/12/64, Richmond, Col. Shields; POW 4/1/65 at Five Forks, to Hart's Is., oath 6/6/65; 6'1", dk. hair, dk. eyes & dk. complexion.

FLOYD, WILLIAM COLUMBUS: Co. H, 12/4/63, Richmond, Col. Shield; POW 4/1/65 at Five Forks, to Hart's Is., oath 6/21/65; 5'8", dk. hair, grey eyes & fair complexion.

FONTAINE, PATRICK HENRY: Rev., also Carter's Battery. Chaplain of regiment; on roll 8/2/63 through 2/16/65.

FOX, J. B.: Co. H, no record found.

FOX, ROBERT JERRY: Co. H, 7/26/61, West Point, Maj. Tomlin; carpenter detailed to work on gunboats at Richmond '61; discharged overage after 4/63.

GARDNER, REUBEN: Co. H, 7/26/61, West Point, Maj. Tomlin; age over 45.

GARNETT, ARCHILLES G.: Co. D, 7/18/61, West Point, Maj. Tomlin; medical discharge 9/2/62 & referred to Gen. Winder; merchant, lt. hair, blue eyes, fair complexion & age 32.

GARRETT, W.: Co. H, also Militia, POW 4/1/65 at Five Forks, to Hart's Is. & oath 6/20/65; 5'10", dk. hair, dk. eyes & dk. complexion.

GARY, W. T.: Cpl., Co. H, Bounty, 7/26/61, West Point, Maj. Tomlin; detailed to work on fortifications at Nansemond Bridge 4/62; POW wounded 7/3/63 at Gettysburg & transferred from Baltimore hosp. to Richmond hosp. 5/16/64.

GEORGE, ROBERT W.: Co. H, 7/26/61, West Point, Maj. Tomlin; detailed to wkr on gunboats at West Point 2/62; POW 6/18/62 at Seven Pines, to Fort Delaware; POW 4/1/65 at Five Forks, to Hart's Is., oath 6/20/65; 5'8", lt. hair, blue eyes, lt. complexion & age 26.

GEORGE, WILLIAM H.: Sgt., Co. D, Bounty, 5/13/61, West Point, Maj. Tomlin; POW 7/3/63 at Gettysburg, wounded in leg & d. 7/13/63.

GREGORY, WILLIAM: Sgt., Co. ? also 9th Va. Cav., Co. H, Bounty, 5/13/61, West Point, Maj. Tomlin; transf. 9/15/62 to 9th Va. Cavalry, Co. H; oath 4/24/65 in Richmond.

GUTHROW, JOHN F.: Co. H, 7/26/61, West Point, Maj. Tomlin; detailed with forage wagons 10/63; oath 4/28/65 at Mechanicsville.

HARGROVE, GEORGE: Co. D, 1/1/64, Kinston, N.C.; oath 5/20/65 at Mechanicsville.

HARGROVE, J. W.: Co. H, POW 4/1/65 at Five Forks, to Hart's Is., 6', dk. hair, dk. eyes & dk. complexion.

HARGROVE, JAMES H.: Co. H, Bounty, 7/26/61, West Point, Maj. Tomlin; oath 5/20/65 at Mechanicsville.

HARGROVE, JOHN T.: Co. H, Bounty, 7/26/61, West Point, Maj. Tomlin; at Chimborazo Hosp. 12/3/63.

HAY, F.: Co. H, no record, see Militia.

HILL, ARCHIBALD GOVAN: Lt., Co. D, 7/26/61, West Point, Maj. Tomlin; in charge of working party at Fort Grafton 12/61; requested transf. to engineers 5/62; resigned at reorganization.

HILL, EDWARD CARMICHAEL: Lt., Co. D, Adjutant at Ft. Grafton 12/61; medical discharge 8/12/62.

HILL, JAMES B.: Lt., Co. D, Bounty, 6/30/61, West Point, Maj. Tomlin; signs roll as commanding co. 6/63, 8/63 & 10/63; hand fracture 5/10/64; POW 4/6/65 at Sayler's Creek, to Old Capitol Prison & Johnson's Is., oath 6/18/65; 5'10", dk. hair, grey eyes, florid complexion & age 24.

HILL, JOHN: Co. H, also 9th Va. Cav., 7/26/61, West Point, Maj. Tomlin; sent to King Wm. for negroes to work on fortifications 2/62; transf. 10/5/62 to 9th Va. Cav., Co. H.

HILL, ROBERT GARLICK (C.): Lt., Co. D, 5/13/61, West Point, Maj. Tomlin; released from duty 5/5/62.

HOUCHENS, THOMAS D. (H.): Co. H, 7/26/61, West Point, Maj. Tomlin; discharged overage 8/16/62; carpenter, 5'6", br. hair, dk. eyes, florid complexion & age 42.

HOWELL, JOHN HARVEY: Co. D, 3/1/63, Petersburg, Col. Aylett; oath 4/20/65 in Richmond.

HUCKSTEP, JULIAN B.: Co. D, Bounty, 5/13/61, West Point, Maj. Tomlin; carpenter; on roll 12/62.

JACKSON, ALBION: Sgt., Co. H, Bounty, 7/26/61, West Point, Maj. Tomlin; discharged 12/18/62 on furnishing substitute, Henry C. Kelly; d. of pneumonia during war.

JOHNSON, ROBERT S.: Co. H, 7/26/61, West Point, Maj. Tomlin; POW 9/19/62 at Sharpsburg, paroled 9/21/62 from a camp near Sharpsburg; oath 9/22/64 in Washington; volunteered in Winder Legion for defense of Richmond 8/3/64 & pardoned by Pres. Davis.

JOHNSON, W. T.: Cpl., Co. D, Bounty, 5/14/61, West Point, Maj. Tomlin; KIA 7/1/62 at Malvern Hill.

JONES, JAMES (E.): Co. E, 7/18/61, West Point, Maj. Tomlin; sick 4/62; overage.

JONES, WILLIAM W. (J.): Co. D, Bounty, 5/13/61, West Point, Maj. Tomlin; discharged overage 6/16/62.

KELLY, HENRY C.: Co. H, 12/18/62, Fredericksburg, Col. Grammer; on guard at So. Quay 4/63; POW 4/1/65 at Five Forks, to & Hart's Is., oath 6/14/65; 5'8", lt. hair, blue eyes & lt. complexion.

KIMBROUGH, CARY A.: Co. D, Bounty, 5/13/61, West Point, Maj. Tomlin; POW 4/4/65 at Jetersville, to Pt. Lookout & oath 6/10/65; 5'6'', br. hair, hazel eyes & dk. complexion.

LATANE, JOHN L.: Capt., Co. H, Bounty, 7/26/61, West Point, Maj. Tomlin; POW 7/3/63 at Gettysburg, to Fort Delaware & Johnson's Is., oath 6/12/65; 5'10", dk. hair, dk. eyes & lt. complexion.

LEWIS, JOHN R.: Sgt., Co. D, Bounty, 5/31/61, West Point, Maj. Tomlin; POW wounded in arm 7/3/63, to David's Is. & paroled to Chimborazo Hosp.; on roll 10/31/63; farmer.

LIPSCOMB, ARCHIE: Co. H, 7/26/61; d. in Suffolk Hosp.

LIPSCOMB, B. A.: Co. D, see also Carter's Battery. In Chimborazo hosp.; oath 4/25/65 in Richmond.

LIPSCOMB, FRAZIER H. (A.): Co. D, Bounty, 5/13/61, West Point, Maj. Tomlin; detailed to work on gunboats 2/62; 8/64 guard at Castle Thunder in Richmond.

LIPSCOMB, JAMES A. (H.): Co. H. Oath 4/28/65 in Richmond.

LIPSCOMB, THOMAS A.: Sgt., Co. D, Bounty, 5/13/61, West Point, Maj. Tomlin; wounded 7/3/63; POW 4/1/65 at Five Forks, to Hart's Is., & oath 6/20/65.

LIPSCOMB, WARREN (I.): Co. D, POW 4/1/65 at Five Forks, to Pt. Lookout & oath 6/14/65; 5'10", br. hair, blue eyes & lt. complexion.

LIPSCOMB, WILLIAM H.: Co. H, Bounty, 7/26/61, West Point, Maj. Tomlin; sick '62.

LITTLEPAGE, LEWIS LIVINGSTON: Co. D, 5/13/61, West Point, Maj. Tomlin; detailed to King William for negroes to work on fortifications 2/62; POW 7/3/63 at Gettysburg, to Fort Delaware & exch. 2/18/65.

MADISON, GEORGE H. (E.): Co. H, Bounty, 7/26/61, West Point, Maj. Tomlin; medical discharge 1/14/63.

MADISON, JAMES (W.): Co. H, 7/26/61, West Point, Maj. Tomlin; sick in Richmond '62.

MADISON, W. H.: Co. H, no record found.

MITCHELL, WILLIAM A.: Co. H, Bounty, 8/22/61, West Point, Maj. Tomlin; nurse in Richmond hosp. '62.

MITCHELL, WILLIAM F.: Co. D, 1864, 3 months.

MOON, RANSOM B.: Capt., Adjutant & quartermaster for regiment.

MOORE, J. B.: Co. D, issued clothes in the field 11/20/64.

MOORE, JAMES M.: Co. H, 7/26/61, West Point, Maj. Tomlin; medical discharge 7/24/62; 5'7", lt. hair, lt. eyes, sallow complexion & age 22.

MOSER, (MOSIER) CHARLES: Co. H, 7/26/61, West Point, Maj. Tomlin; assigned to Barton's Brigade Band 4/27/64; paroled at Appomattox.

NEALE, JAMES THOMAS: Cpl., Co. D, 5/13/61, West Point, Maj. Tomlin; wounded 9/17/62.

POINTER, WILLIAM B. (R.): Co. D, Bounty, 5/13/61, West Point, Maj. Tomlin; on roll 11/29/64.

POLLARD, BYRD G.: Co. D, 6/30/61, West Point, Maj. Tomlin; detached to Commissary Dept. in Yorktown 12/61; transf. to Richmond Howitzers 1/26/64.

POLLARD, D.: Co. H, no record found.

POLLARD, HENRY: Co. D, 5/13/61, West Point, Maj. Tomlin; slightly wounded 7/1/62 at Malvern Hill; did not re-enlist 8/16/62, overage; carpenter, 5'8", lt. hair, grey eyes, florid complexion & age 36.

POLLARD, JAMES HARVIE: Co. H, also Militia. At Appomattox, oath 4/21/65 in Richmond (age 39?).

POLLARD, MAEGER: Co. D, POW 3/22/65 in King Wm., to Pt. Lookout & oath 6/16/65; br. hair, blue eyes & dk. complexion.

POLLARD, OTWAY: Co. H, 7/26/61, West Point, Maj. Tomlin; discharged 1/14/63 by furnishing substitute, John Hay; conscript 2/19/64, Richmond, Col. Shield; oath 4/21/65 in Richmond.

POLLARD, ROBERT C.: Co. D, 4/21/62, Richmond, Col. Charters; wounded 7/4/63; oath 5/2/65 at Mechanicsville.

POLLARD, DR. WILLIAM GEORGE: Capt., Co. H, 7/26/61, West Point, Maj. Tomlin; inspection & mustering officer 7/62 & 8/62; requested be relieved of commission to return to medical practice 9/5/62, approved 10/23/62, mortally wounded 9/17/62 at Sharpsburg & d. at hosp. on David Smith's farm, age nearly 45.

POWELL, EDWARD T. (R.): Co. D, Bounty, 5/13/61, West Point, Maj. Tomlin; detailed to Commissary Dept. at West Point 1861, 1863, and 1864.

POWELL, JAMES HARVIE: Co. H, POW 4/1/65 at Five Forks, to Hart's Is., oath 6/21/65; 5'11", dk. hair, grey eyes & dk. complexion.

POWELL, THOMAS (C.): Co. D, Bounty, 6/30/61, West Point, Maj. Tomlin; oath 4/21/65 in Richmond.

POWELL, WILLIAMI H. (N.): Sgt., Co. D, Bounty, 5/13/61, West Point; Maj. Tomlin; oath between 4/14 & 17/65 at Burkeville Jct.

POWERS, JAMES W.: Co. D, 7/10/61, West Point, Maj. Tomlin; medical discharge 5/7/62; 5'10", dk. hair, dark eyes & dk. complexion.

PUMPHREY, J. P.: Co. H, 7/26/61, West Point, Maj. Tomlin; POW 4/1/65 at Five Forks, to Hart's Is., oath 6/21/65; 5'7", lt. hair, blue eyes & lt. complexion.

QUARLES, GEORGE H. (C.): Co. D, 5/15/61, West Point, Maj. Tomlin; POW wounded rt. arm 4/1/65 at Five Forks, arm amputated Fort Monroe hosp., transf. on USS Hosp. Steamer *Hero of Jersey* to Baltimore, oath 4/13/65 in Washington & d. 5/29/65 at Fort Monroe.

QUARLES, THOMAS D.: Co. H, 7/26/61, West Point, Maj. Tomlin; wounded 4/12/63 at Suffolk; wounded 6/19/64 near Bermuda Hundred, amputated rt. leg & d. 8/8/64 at Richmond hosp.; farmer & age 32.

REDD, THOMAS: Sgt., Co. D, 5/13/61, West Point, Maj. Tomlin; wounded slightly in face 5/31/62 at Seven Pines; oath 4/24/65 in Richmond.

RICE, THOMAS D.: Co. D, Bounty, 5/13/61, West Point, Maj. Tomlin; sick '62.

RICE, WILLIAM A.: Co. H, Bounty, 7/26/61, West Point, Maj. Tomlin; teamster; oath 3/25/65 at City Point; 5'10", bk. hair, dk. eyes, sallow complexion & age 28.

ROBINS, DANIEL (L.): Cos. E & B, 7/18/61, West Point, Maj. Tomlin; transf. to Co. B 5/1/62; wounded in the foot 7/1/62 at Malvern Hill; POW mortally wounded in back at Gettysburg 7/3/63 & d. at Gettysburg hosp. 7/29/63.

ROBINSON, ALBERT (B.): Co. D, Bounty, 5/13/61, West Point, Maj. Tomlin; detached as ship's carpenter at West Point 3/62 & 4/62; detailed with quartermaster 10/25/62; transf. to Co. G 8/12/64.

ROBINSON, EUGENE D.: Lt., Co. D, Bounty, 5/13/61, West Point, Maj. Tomlin; requested be capt. of engineers 6/3/63; POW 7/3/63 at Gettysburg, to Fort Delaware, Johnson's Is. & Pt. Lookout.

ROBINSON, LORIMER B.: Co. D, 5/13/61, West Point, Maj. Tomlin; POW wounded 7/3/63, to Fort Delaware & exch. from hosp. 7/31/64; oath 4/2/65 in Richmond.

ROBINSON, T.: Co. D, no record found.

RODGERS (RODGES), J. T.: Co. ? Oath 4/25/65 in Richmond.

SALE, JAMES IRVING: Lt., Co. H, Bounty, 7/26/61, West Point, Maj. Tomlin; detached to King Wm. & King and Queen to enroll conscripts 4/62; POW 7/3/63 at Gettysburg (same day appointed 1st lt.), to Fort Delaware, Johnson's Is. & Pt. Lookout, exch. 3/14/65; oath 4/28/65 in Richmond.

SEIGLE (SEICLE), JOHN HENRY: Co. D, Bounty, 5/13/61, West Point, Maj. Tomlin; POW 7/3/63 at Gettysburg, to Ft. Delaware & Pt. Lookout, d. 11/27/63 & buried at Finn's Pt., New Jersey.

SLAUGHTER, JOHN B.: Sgt., Co. D, 5/13/61, West Point, Maj. Tomlin; POW 4/6/65 at Amelia C.H., to Pt. Lookout & oath 6/19/65; 6', black hair, blue eyes & dk. complexion.

SLAUGHTER, SELIM: Co. D, 7/10/61, West Point, Maj. Tomlin; wounded 7/4/63; POW 4/1/65 at Five Forks, to Hart's Is., d. 4/20/65 of pneumonia & buried at Cypress Hills, Long Is.

SLAUGHTER, WILLIAM: Co. H, Bounty, 7/26/61, West Point, Maj. Tomlin; detached to adj. gen. office '62; provist guard at Hamilton's Crossing 4/63; clerk for Gen. Winder '63; POW wounded in hand 7/3/63 at Gettysburg, to Fort Delaware, exch. to Winder Hosp. 11/63; oath 4/22/65 at Richmond.

STEVENS, L. A.: Co. H, 4/4/65 at City Point; POW 4/6/65 near Farmville & oath 7/1/65 at Newport News; 5'6", dk. hair, dk. eyes & dk. complexion.

SULLENS, JAMES WILLIS: Co. D, 5/13/61, West Point, Maj. Tomlin; POW wounded 7/3/63.

SWEET, PATRICK H.: Co. D, 5/13/65, West Point, Maj. Tomlin; wounded 5/16/64; POW 5/30/64 in King Wm., to Pt. Lookout & Elmira, N.Y., oath 5/29/65; lt. hair, blue eyes & fair complexion.

SWEET, W. H.: Co. ? Oath 4/20/65.

TALIAFERRO, JOHN W.: Co. D, no record found.

TARRANT, JAMES H.: Lt., Co. D, 5/13/61, West Point, Maj. Tomlin; d. 9/10/62.

TAYLOR, ROBERT G.: Co. D, Bounty, 5/13/61, West Point, Maj. Tomlin; detached in P.O. in Yorktown 4/62; KIA 8/26/62 at Warrenton Springs.

THORNTON, STERLING S.: Sgt., Co. H, Bounty, 7/26/61, West Point, Maj. Tomlin; on roll through 7/12/64; in reserve forces under Capt. Clark, Rappahannock Dist.

TIMBERLAKE, HARRY C.: Sgt., Co. H, Bounty, 7/26/61, West Point, Maj. Tomlin; wounded rt. elbow 6/18/62 near Richmond-York River RR; medical discharge 9/26/63.

TOMLIN, HARRISON BALL: Col., 5/61 stationed at West Point; appointed col. 11/9/61; horse killed at Seven Pines; resigned 11/29/63 (age 48).

TRICE, L. D.: Co. H, POW 4/1/65 at Five Forks, to Hart's Is. & oath 6/20/65; 5'7", lt. hair, blue eyes & lt. complexion.

TUCK, ANDERSON: Cpl., Co. D, Bounty, 5/17/61, West Point, Maj. Tomlin; detached as ships' carpenter in West Point 4/62; wounded 7/3/63 at Gettysburg; assigned to Invalid Corps 10/27/64; oath 4/26/65 in Ashland.

TUCK, GEORGE P. (C.): Co. H, Bounty, 7/26/61, West Point, Maj. Tomlin; POW 7/3/63 at Gettysburg, to Pt. Lookout & Ft. Delaware, exch. 11/1/64; POW 4/1/65 at Five Forks, to Hart's Is. & oath 6/20/65; 5'5", lt. hair, blue eyes & lt. complexion.

TUCK, JAMES: Co. H, Bounty, 7/26/61, West Point, Maj. Tomlin; d. ca10/1/62 near Winchester; overseer, 5'8", dk. hair, dk. eyes, dk. complexion & age 19.

TUCK, JOHN F.: Co. D, Bounty, 5/13/61, West Point, Maj. Tomlin; d. 7/30/62 of disease.

TUCK, PATRICK H.: Co., D, Bounty, 5/13/61, West Point, Maj. Tomlin; POW 7/31/63 at Manassas Gap, to Pt. Lookout & exch. 5/3/64; medical discharge 9/12/64; farmer, 5'8", black hair, grey eyes, sallow complexion & age 28.

TUCK, RICHARD H.: Co. H, Bounty, 5/26/61, West Point, Maj. Tomlin; discharged 8/16/62 at Falling Creek, overage; farmer, 5'9", br. hair, hazel eyes, dk. complexion & age 45.

TUCK, WILLIAM H.: Co. H, 7/26/61, West Point, Maj. Tomlin; mortally wounded 6/1/62 or 6/2/62 & d. 6/29/62 at Richmond hosp.

TUCKER, ELI B.: Co. D, Bounty, 5/13/61, West Point, Maj. Tomlin; detached as teamster in supply train '62-'64; oath 4/25/64 in Richmond; 5'6", sandy hair, blue eyes, fair complexion & age 26.

TUCKER, THOMAS H.: Co. H, 7/26/61, West Point, Maj. Tomlin; detached to work on gunboats '61-'62; discharged 8/16/62, overage; carpenter, 5'5", dk. hair, dk. eyes, dk. complexion & age 38.

TURNER, LOGAN (C.): Co. D, 5/5/62, Zuni, Col. Tomlin; sick in King Wm. 7/62 & 8/62; transf. to Capt. Bagby's Co. Artillery Va. Volunteers, 12/10/62.

TURNER, WILLIAM J.: Capt., Co. D, Bounty, 5/13/61, West Point, Maj. Tomlin; wounded 9/2/62; wounded 7/3/63; oath 5/8/65 in Richmond.

TURPIN, WILLIAM H.: Co. D, Bounty, 5/13/61, West Point, Maj. Tomlin; oath 4/24/65 in Richmond.

WHITE, BENJAMIN F.: Co. H, 7/26/61, West Point, Maj. Tomlin, medical discharge 5/28/62, chronic rheumatism; farmer, 5'10", dk. hair, blue eyes, dk. complexion & age 39.

WHITE, LEE A.: Co. D, 1864, 6 months.r

WILSON, JAMES F. (W.): Co. D, Bounty, 5/13/61, West Point, Maj. Tomlin; POW 7/3/63 at Gettysburg, to Fort Delaware & Pt. Lookout (smallpox hosp.), d. 11/14/64 of erysipelas & buried at Hilton Head, S.C.

WRIGHT, WILLIAM H.: Co. H, 2/18/64, Richmond, Col. Shields; oath 4/25/65 in Richmond.

9th Virginia Cavalry - Company H

ANDERSON, HANSFORD: Cpl., 6/10/61, West Point, Maj. Tomlin; wounded in hip 6/9/63 at Brandy Station; POW 10/11/64 on Weldon R.R., to Pt. Lookout & exch. 2/10/65; oath 5/3/65 in Richmond.

BEADLES, M. R. (R. M.): 3/1/64, King Wm., Lt. Pollard; oath 4/16/65 at Black & Whites.

BOGGS, CHARLES H., REV.: Appointed chaplain of regiment 4/10/62; resigned 3/28/64.

BROACH, AUGUSTIN M.: 2/1/64, King Wm., Lt. Pollard; oath 4/20/65 in Richmond.

BURGESS, JAMES R.: 6/10/61, West Point, Maj. Tomlin; detailed as courier for Gen. Jackson 6/62; mortally wounded 6/9/63 at Brandy Station & d. 7/2/63.

BURKE, FELIX ROSCOE: Sgt., 6/10/61, West Point, Maj. Tomlin; detailed with prisoners 6/10/63; KIA 6/30/64 in King Wm.

BURRUSS, REUBEN H.: 5/2/61 in 3rd Ga., Co. D; transf. 2/12/62 to 9th Va. Cav. Co. H; on final roll 10/6/64.

CAMPBELL, JAMES W.: 9/7/64, New Market, Md., Lt. Pollard; on detached duty 1/25/65 in Danville hosp.; oath 4/25/65 in Ashland.

CARDWELL, JOHN L.: 2/15/64, King Wm., Lt. Christian, conscript assigned to Co. H.

CHRISTIAN, THOMAS JEFFERSON: Lt., 6/10/61, West Point, Maj. Tomlin; commanding co. 7/63, 8/63, 7/64 & 8/64; oath 4/26/65 in Richmond.

CLEMENTS, D. C. (E.): 3/28/64, King Wm., Lt. Pollard; KIA 10/1/64.

CLEMENTS, WILLIAM H.: 9/8/64; discharged 11/26/64 for disability; farmer, age 32.

COOKE, CHARLES H.: 6/15/61, Ashland, Capt. Lee; on detached service in Richmond hosp. 9/62 to 9/64 as wardmaster; oath 4/25/65 in Richmond.

CROXTON, WILLIAM VIRGINIUS: Lt. & Pvt., 6/21/61, Ashland, Lt. Douglas; dropped 4/29/62; served briefly as C.S. surgeon in Salisbury, N.C.; re-enlisted 2/1/64, King Wm., Lt. Pollard; on sick furlough final roll 10/6/64.

DABNEY, ALFRED B.: 4/12/64, King Wm., Lt. Christian; wounded by gunshot across back & neck 8/16/64; oath 4/15/65 in Virginia, retained horse.

DAVIS, EDWARD P.: 1/21/63, Camp Lee, Col. Shields; oath between 4/11 & 4/21/65 in Farmville.

DAVIS, SMITH: 9/22/62, Martinsburg, Capt. Haynes; oath 4/24/65 in Richmond.

DOUGLAS, BEVERLEY BROWNE: Capt., 6/10/61, West Point, Maj. Tomlin; absent attending Va. Legislature 11/61 to 2/62; at '62 reorganization became Maj. in 5th Va. Cav.; resigned 1/8/63.

DUNCAN, EDWARD A.: 6/15/61, Ashland, Capt. Lee; discharged ca12/61; re-enlisted 3/15/62, Capt. Douglas; medical discharge 2/1/63; re-enlisted 3/1/64; King Wm., Lt. Pollard; paroled at Appomattox; coachmaker, 5'3", lt. hair, grey eyes, lt. complexion & age 30.

DUNSTAN, RICHARD R.: 6/15/61, Ashland, Capt. Lee; extra duty as blacksmith 8/61 to 6/63; oath 4/21/65 in Richmond.

EDWARDS, JULIEN T.: 6/15/61, Ashland, Capt. Lee; detailed as courier to Gen. Jackson 6/62; carried mail from White House to Walkerton, 2/4/63 to 4/8/63; wounded gunshot rt. forearm 7/28/63; detached in Treas. Dept. & as nurse in Chimborazo hosp. 7/64 to 3/65; oath 4/25/65 in Richmond.

EDWARDS, PRESLEY COLEMAN: 9/22/62, Martinsburg, Capt. Haynes; oath 4/16/65 at Black & Whites.

EUBANK, EDWARD FENDALL: 9/7/62, New Market, Md., Lt. Pollard; detailed with prisoners 9/17/62; POW 6/30/64 in Sussex Co., to Pt. Lookout & exch. 3/16/65; oath 5/1/65 in Ashland; student.

EUBANK, WILLIAM SHELTON: Oath 4/28/65 in Ashland, farmer.

FIGG, JOSEPHUS: 3/15/62, Ayletts, Capt. Douglas; oath 4/24/65 in Richmond.

GARRETT, W. L.: 2/20/64, King Wm., Lt. Pollard; oath 4/25/65 in Richmond.

GARY, JAMES H.: 6/10/61, West Point, Maj. Tomlin; oath 4/24/65 in Richmond.

GARY, WILLIAM J., JR.: 6/21/61, Ashland, Lt. Douglas; oath 4/20/65 in Richmond.

GREGORY, JUNIUS C.: 6/17/61, Ashland, Capt. Lee; detailed as courier to Gen. Jackson 6/62; detached as hospital steward 7/62 until promoted in Medical Dept. 12/23/62.

GREGORY, ROGER: Lt. Col., 87th Va. Reg. Militia until mustered into CSA & subsequently in Lee's Rangers. (see Hill, *Record*, p. 2 and R. L. T. Beale, p. 172 - no record found.)

GREGORY, WILLIAM: 5/13/61, Maj. Tomlin into 53rd Va. Infantry; transf. to 9th Va. Cav. Co. H on 9/15/62; oath 4/24/65 in Richmond.

GRESHAM, OSCAR: 3/15/62, Ayletts, Capt. Douglas; oath between 4/11 & 4/21/65 in Farmville.

GWATHMEY, RICHARD BROOKE: 7/10/61, Ashland, Capt. Lee; horse killed 9/15/62 at Boonsboro, Md.; wounded 7/63 or 8/63; KIA 8/25/64.

HAWES, WALKER A.: 8/25/62, Waterloo Bridge, Capt. Haynes; wounded 6/9/63 at Brandy Station; detached as nurse at Charlottesville 11/63; wounded gunshot in groin 8/26/64; wounded gunshot in rt. hip 1/65.

HAY, JOSEPH: 6/10/61, West Point, Maj. Tomlin; detailed with wagons 6/62; oath between 4/11 & 4/21/65 in Farmville.

HAYNES, THOMAS WITT: Capt., 6/10/61, West Point, Maj. Tomlin; signed roll as commanding co. 4/62; wounded 6/21/62 at Upperville; signed roll as commanding co. 7/62 to 8/62 & 11/62; severely wounded gunshot through body 10/15/63 at Manassas; retired to Invalid Corps 3/13/65 - disabled for life.

HILL, A. B.: 3/1/64, King William, Lt. Pollard; POW 4/3/65 & oath 4/20/65 in Richmond.

HILL, JOHN: 7/26/61, West Point, Maj. Tomlin into 53rd Va. Inf.; transf. to 9th Va. Cav. Co. H 10/5/62; detailed with prisoners 6/63; oath 4/25/65 in Ashland.

HILL, ROBERT CHRISTOPHER: Also Militia, 9/22/62, Martinsburg, Capt. Haynes; POW 4/3/65 & oath 4/20/65 in Richmond.

JACKSON, LUCIAN: 6/4/62, Beaver Dam, Capt. Douglas; wounded 8/27/64; oath 4/25/65 in Ashland.

KING, MILES C.: 3/1/64, King Wm., Lt. Pollard; oath 4/28/65 in Richmond.

LACY, JOHN B. (F.): 6/10/61, West Point, Maj. Tomlin; mortally wounded 9/62 at Sugerloaf Mt., Md. & d. 9/19/62.

LEE, JOSEPH L.: 6/15/61, Ashland, Capt. Lee; POW 5/3/63 near Yanceyville, Louisa, in Old Capitol Prison, Wash. & exch. 5/19/63; oath 4/21/65 in Richmond.

LEE, WILLIAM HENRY FITZHUGH (ROONEY): Gen. (New Kent), Capt. of Co. H, June 1861; elected col. 4/29/62; made brigadier general 10/3/62; at Appomattox.

LEFTWICH, RICHARD T.: 3/1/64, King Wm., Lt. Pollard; paroled at Appomattox.

LITTLEPAGE, HARMON H.: 3/15/62, King Wm., Capt. Douglas; POW 11/14/62 at Bloomfield, Va. & exch. 11/18/62; KIA 6/30/63 at Hanover, Pa.

LITTLEPAGE, J. C.: Oath 4/27/65 in Richmond.

LUCKHARD (LUKHARD), CORNELIUS: Also Militia, 1/29/64, King Wm., Lt. Pollard; absent with leave on final roll 10/6/64.

LUCKHARD (LUKHARD), STRAUGHAN H.: 6/10/61, West Point, Maj. Tomlin; oath 4/26/65 in Richmond.

MARTIN, WILLIAM B.: 3/21/64, King Wm., Lt. Pollard; oath 4/27/65 in Richmond.

MEREDITH, FLEMING: Sgt., 6/22/61, Ashland, Lt. Douglas; POW 4/3/65 & oath 4/20/65 in Richmond.

MITCHELL, WILLIAM H.: Sgt., 3/15/62, Ayletts, Capt. Douglas; paroled at Appomattox.

MOOKLAR, ATWELL TEBBS: also Militia, 1/31/62, Gloucester Pt., Capt. Johnson; on roll 22nd Battalion 5/31/62; 2/16/64 enlisted in 9th Cavalry; King Wm., Lt. Pollard; 2/65 in hosp. with contused wound of the back; oath 5/1/65 in Richmond.

NEWMAN, JAMES I.: 4/30/62, King Wm., Capt. Douglas; oath 4/26/65 in Richmond.

NOEL, JAMES L.: 4/1/62, Ayletts, Capt. Douglas; discharged 5/5/62.

NOEL, JOHN P.: 6/30/63, King Wm., Capt. Haynes; mortally wounded 9/13/63 at Culpeper & d. 10/14/63.

PEMBERTON, JOHN: Cpl., 6/10/61, West Point, Maj. Tomlin; horse killed at Brandy Station 10/11/63; mortally wounded gunshot rt. arm 5/12/64 & d. 5/19/64 in Richmond.

PEMBERTON, R. C.: 2/15/64, King Wm., Lt. Pollard; absent on leave last roll 10/6/64.

POLLARD, EDWARD SPOTSWOOD: also Militia, discharged 3/17/62; re-enlisted 1/22/64, Richmond, Maj. Peyton; oath 4/25/65 in Ashland.

POLLARD, JAMES: Lt. (New Kent), 6/10/61, West Point, Maj. Tomlin; signed roll as commanding co. 1/62, 2/62, 9/63, 10/63, 11/63 & 12/63; wounded 6/23/64 at Nance's Shiop & foot amputated 7/4/64; oath 5/3/65.

ROBINS, JAMES ARMISTEAD: 9/22/62, Martinsburg, Capt. Haynes; detailed to procure horses from Orange C.H., 11/1 to 11/16/63; oath 4/25/65.

ROBINS, WILLIAM TODD: Sgt., 6/10/61, West Point, Maj. Tomlin; detailed as courier to Gen. Jackson 6/62; wounded gunshot in left thigh ca5/16/64; POW 4/3/65 in Amelia Co., to Pt. Lookout & oath 6/17/65; 5'6'', lt. br. hair, grey eyes & lt. complexion.

ROBINSON, LUPER M.: 10/15/63, Culpeper, Lt. Christian; on final roll 10/6/64.

RYLAND, ROBERT SEMPLE: 6/1/61, Bond's Store, into Carter's Battery; transf. 9/18/62 to 9th Va. Cav. Co. H, near Strader's Mill; detailed with prisoners 5&6/63; detailed as nurse for Capt. Haynes 9/63 through 3/64; POW 3/16/65 on Peninsula in Hamilton, Va., to Pt. Lookout & oath 6/17/65; 6', br. hair, hazel eyes & lt. complexion.

SATTERWHITE, THOMAS PALMER: 3/12/64, King Wm. Lt. Pollard; oath 4/20/65 in Richmond.

SELDEN, BRAXTON: Sgt., & Pvt., 6/10/61, West Point, Maj. Tomlin; horse killed at Mingo Flats, W.Va., 8/61; detailed as a courier to Gen. Whiting; POW mortally wounded by shell in left leg at Funkstown, Md., d. 8/3/63 & buried in Mt. Olivet Hosp. Cemetery, Frederick, Md.

SHELLY, RICHARD HOLLIDAY: 3/15/62, Ayletts, Capt. Douglas; medical discharge 11/5/62; sailor, 5'10", dk. hair, grey eyes, dk. complexion, & age 27.

SLAUGHTER, JOHN LEWIS: Sgt., 6/10/61, West Point, Maj. Tomlin; detailed as courier to Gen. Jackson 5&6/62; detached 9/63; POW 4/3/65 & oath 4/20/65 in Richmond.

STRAUGHAN, DAVID: 7/12/61; Ashland, Capt. Lee; discharged 9/12/62, overage; farmer 5'11", dk. hair, grey eyes, lt. complexion & age 35.

SUTTON, PULASKI: also Militia, 1/17/63, Lloyd's, Capt. Haynes; POW 7/10/63 in Boonsboro, Md., to Pt. Lookout & exch. 3/17/64; paroled at Appomattox.

TAYLOR, JOHN P.: in Chimborazo Hosp. 12/64 to 2/65.

TRANT, JOHN HILL: 9/1/62, Fairfax Station, Lt. Pollard; detached in Richmond Passport Office under Gen. Winder 3/64 to 4/64; oath 5/2/65 at Mechanicsville.

TUCK, LEWIS M.: 6/10/61, West Point, Maj. Tomlin; thought POW 7/62 to 2/63, no record.

TURNER, BEVERLEY BRADSHAW: 5/21/61 in Hanover Artillery, Richmond, Col. Baldwin; transf. to 9th Va. Cav. Co. H on 9/14/61, camp near Big Spring in Mingo Flats, Capt. Douglas; wounded 9/62 at Centreville; transf. to Ordnance Dept. 4/63.

TURNER, LOGAN: 3/15/62, King Wm., Capt. Aylett; oath 4/20/65 in Richmond.

WHITE, JAMES A.: 6/1/61, Bond's Store, in Carter's Battery; medical discharge 7/1/62; enlisted 6/9/63 in 9th Va. Cav. Co. H, Camp Lee, Maj. Peyton; detached service in Passport Office & Provost Marshal Office in Richmond due to old break of arm 6/63.

In Other Companies of the 9th Cavalry

CAMPBELL, MANASSEH: Co. B, 3/2/62, Bowling Green, Lt. Baker; horse killed at Middleburg, 6/19/63; on roll through 8/64.

EUBANK, PHILIP COWLES: Co. F, 6/10/61, Tappahannock, Capt. Cauthorn; in Richmond hosp. 8/24/64; farmer.

LIPSCOMB, PHILIP EMMETT: Co. F, served in 5th Cav., Co. E in '61; enlisted 3/23/62 in 9th Va. Cav. at Urbanna, R.S. Cauthorn; wounded 6/9/62 at Brandy Sta.; wounded 10/63 near Manassas; wounded at Reams Sta. & leg amputated 8/25/64; retired to Invalid Corps 11/4/64; oath 5/30/65 in Richmond.

McGEORGE, W. R.: Co. F, 2/1/64, Center Cross, Wm. O. Oliver; oath between 5/14 & 5/17/65 at Burkeville.

WARING, SPENCER ROANE: Co. F, 6/1/61, Bond's Store, Capt. Carter, in Carter's Battery; wounded 5/31/62 at Seven Pines; transf. 4/1/64 to 9th Va. Cav., Lebanon, Wm. A. Oliver; oath 4/25/65 in Richmond.

Other Regiments

ATKINS, T. S.: see Thos. L. in 53rd Co. H.

BEADLES, J. A.: see Jas. H. in 87th Militia.

BEADLES, R. B.: No record found.

BLAKE, LLEWELYN: Sgt., 5th Inf., Co. E, 3/15/62, Gloucester Pt., M.P. Todd; POW 5/6/64 at Yellow Tavern, to Pt. Lookout, exch. 9/18/64; oath 4/18/65 in Richmond.

BRAXTON, TOMLIN, DR.: Asst. surgeon; POW '61 at Lewisburg, to Camp Chase, Ohio, paroled 6/62.

BRAXTON, WILLIAM ARMISTEAD: Mosby's Command, Surgeon; d. of wounds 11/16/64.

BURCH, EDWARD: Sgt., 15th Inf., Co. I, 5/29/61, Williamsburg, Maj. Peyton; detailed in commissary dept. 9/24/61; paroled at Appomattox.

BUTLER, DAVID: 24th Cav., Co. K, 8/1/62, So. Quay, Capt. Norfleet; detached as scout 5/64-9/64; POW 4/9/65 in Petersburg.

CLEMENTS, M.: No record found.

CLEMENTS, T. W.: No record found.

COOKE, R. H.: No record found. (A James Cooke was a prisoner at Fort Delaware.)

CROW, ALONZO: 24th Cav., Co. E, 3/7/63, King & Queen C.H., Capt. Hord; on roll 1/27/65, carpenter.

CROW, R. H.: see Robt. W. in 53rd Co. D.

DABNEY, J. W.: no record found.

EUBANK, JAMES H.: 4th Heavy Artillery & 4th Inf. Co. K, 5/9/62, Hanover C.H., Col. P. R. Page; wounded & in Jackson Hosp. in Richmond 4/1/65, POW 4/3/65, oath 5/3/65.

FOX, R.: No record found.

GREGORY, DAVID: 9th Inf., Co. H, 6/11/61, Fletcher's Chapel, R. A. Neblett.

GRESHAM, JOHN H.: 4th Heavy Artillery & 34th Inf., Co. K, 5/30/61, West Point, Maj. Tomlin; from King & Queen Artillery of Va. Volunteers - 4th Regt. Capt. Bagby's Co.; wounded 5/31/62 at Seven Pines; detailed to Signal Corps 4/29/63 by Gen. Elzey.

GRESHAM, RICHARD H.: 4th Heavy Artillery & 34th Inf., Co. K, 1/10/63, Chaffin's Bluff, Col. T. J. Page; from 4th Regt. Va. Heavy Artillery; wounded 7/8/64 in left shoulder.

GWATHMEY, J. H.: No record found.

HOOPER, JAMES H.: 24th Cav., Co. F, 3/20/63, King & Queen C.H., Capt. Allen; KIA 6/15/64 at Riddle's Shop.

HOOPER, JOHN T.: 24th Cav., Co. E, 4/23/63, Exol, Capt. Blake; oath 5/1/65 in Richmond.

HORTON, T. B.: Capt., 11th Infantry, POW 5/64 at Spotsylvania, to Fort Delaware & Morris Island.

JACKSON, EDWIN: 30th Inf., Co. E, 7/7/61, Marlboro Pt., Maj. Peatross; KIA 9/17/62 at Sharpsburg.

JACKSON, JOHN: 30th Inf., Co. E, 6/24/61, Marlboro Pt., Maj. Peatross; discharged 11/61; conscript 8/18/63 in Orange County; oath 5/3/65 in Ashland.

JACKSON, THOMAS PRICE: Sgt., 30th Inf., Co. E, 5/13/61, Fredericksburg, Maj. Peatross; wounded slightly in leg at Drewry's Bluff; killed while home on furlough 3/16/65 by Sheridan's raiding party.

JOHNSON, J. P.: No record found.

JONES, HENRY JENNER: VMI Cadet Corps, Co. D, KIA 5/15/64 at New Market; age 17.

LIPSCOMB, J. H.: see Jas. A. in 53rd.

LIPSCOMB, W. I.: No record found.

LACY, W. D.: No record found.

LITTLEPAGE, J. L.: see Junius in 87th Militia.

LITTLEPAGE, Sutherland G.: Navy, 1861, in QM Dept. for four years.r

MADISON, E.: No record found.

MADISON, J. T.: see James in Carter's Battery.

McGEORGE, JOHN L.: Pamunkey Artillery.

MITCHELL, W. F.: see Wm. A. in 53rd.

MORAN, A.: No record found.

NELSON, C.: see T. C. in 4th Cav., Co. G

NELSON, THOMAS CARY: 4th Cav., Co. G, 4/30/62, Ashland, W. B. N.; mortally wounded 6/24/64 in thorax at Samaria Church & d. 6/25/64 on the way to Richmond hosp.

OWENS, J.: No record found.

PEAY, JAMES K.: 24th Cav., Co. E, 3/7/63, King & Queen C.H., Capt. Hord; paroled at Appomattox.

POLLARD, C. T.: No record found.

POLLARD, G. O.: No record found.

POLLARD, G. W.: see W. G. in 53rd, Co. H.

POWELL, G. T.: see Thos. in 53rd, Co. D.

PULLER, ANDREW B.: No record found.

REID, JAMES ROBERT: 4th Heavy Artillery & 34th Inf., Co. K, 1/16/63, Chaffin's Bluff, Col. Page; wounded in rt. ear on picket duty 8/10/64; paroled at Appomattox.

RIDER, DOUGLAS: 24th Cav., Co. C, 10/15/63, Camp Elzey, Capt. Littleton; POW 4/8/65 at High Bridge, to Pt. Lookout & oath 6/17/65; 6'1", br. hair, grey eyes & lt. complexion, horse killed on New Market Heights 12/12/64.

ROANE, JAMES A.: 8/8/63, Hanover Jct., Capt. Littleton; oath 5/2/65 at Mechanicsville.

ROBINS, L. S.: No record found.

RODGERS, HEROD: 24th Cav., Co. E, 3/7/63, King & Queen C.H., Capt. Hord; oath at Appomattox.

SHELLEY, B.: No record found.

SHELLEY, JAMES ROWE: 4th Battalion, 1861 in Local Defense.r

SHELLEY, WILLIAM: Lt., Navy, 6/10/61; gunner 7/10/63; on CSS Torpedo '63 & '64.r

SILVEY, R.: 12th Inf., Co. E.

SIZER, M. S.: No record found.

STRAUGHAN, S. P.: No record found.

SWEET, W. H.: see W. A. in 87th Militia.

TERRY, CHARLES: 24th Cav., Co. E, 3/7/63, King & Queen C.H., Capt. Hord; on roll 8/64.

TERRY, W.: No record found.

TERRY, W. O.: No record found.

TERRY, G. R.: No record found.

TRIMMER, C.: see Stanley C. in Carter's Battery.

TUCK, M. C.: No record found.

TURPIN, ARCHIE B.: 5th Cav., Co. E, 7/12/61, Gloucester Pt., M. P. Todd; POW 5/28/64 at Mechanicsville, to Elmira, N.Y., oath 5/13/65; 5'11", dk. hair, hazel eyes & fair complexion.

TURPIN, JOHN O.: 5th Cav., Co. E, 1/1/63, Guinea Station, E. C. Fox; horse killed at Springfield 9/24/64; POW 4/4/65 in Dinwiddie, to Pt. Lookout, oath & 6/20/65; 5'5", lt. br. hair, blue eyes & fair complexion.

TURNPIN, R. B.: No record found.

VIAR, H.: see Henry W. in Carter's Battery.

VIAR, WILLIAM (P.): 24th Cav., Co. E, 3/7/63, King & Queen C.H., Capt. Hord; d. in Chimborazo hosp. 11/6/64 of typhoid.

WHITLOCK, LOGAN W.: 24th Cav., Co. E, 3/7/63, King & Queen C.H., Capt. Hord; POW 3/18/65, to Pt. Lookout & oath 6/22/65; 5'8", br. hair, hazel eyes & lt. complexion.

WILLEROY, WILLIAM: Cpl., Pamunkey Artillery, 4/22/63, Chaffin's Bluff, Col. Maury; paroled at Appomattox.

87th Regiment Virginia Militia

ADAMS, HAMILITON: Co. D, Capt. Green, 12/16/61, King Wm. C.H.; transf. to Capt. Johnson.

ADAMS, LEROY C.: Co. C, Capt. Moore, 12/16/61, King Wm. C.H.

ALEXANDER, JOHN C.: Co. C, Capt. Moore, 12/16/61, King Wm., C.H.; detailed as nurse 1/9/62.

ALLEN, TEMPLE R.: Co. C, Capt. Moore, 12/16/61, King Wm. C.H.; sick with typhoid & d. 1/12/62.

ANCARROW, THOMAS: Co. D, Capt. Green, 12/16/61, King Wm. C.H.; transf. to Capt. Johnson 2/5/62.

ATKINS, ALVERY L.: Co. C, Capt. Moore, 12/16/61, King Wm. C.H.; discharged 1/16/62.

ATKINS, JAMES D.: Co. C, Capt. Moore, 12/16/61, King Wm. C.H.; discharged 2/5/62.

BAYLASS, SILAS P.: Co. C, Capt. Moore, 12/16/61, King Wm. C.H.: discharged 2/4/62; plasterer, 5'7", lt. hair, blue eyes, fair complexion & age 34.

BEADLES, JOHN H.: Co. D, Capt. Green, 12/16/61, King Wm. C.H.; transf. to Capt. Johnson 2/5/62.

BLAKE, JOHN W.: Co. C, Capt. Moore, 12/16/61, King Wm. C.H.; on guard at Gloucester Pt.; discharged 2/5/62.

BRAXTON, WILLIAM B.: Co. D, Capt. Green, 12/16/61, King Wm. C.H.; detailed as courier & orderly by Col. Gresham & Maj. Saunders.

BROACH, AUGUSTIN M.: Co. D, Capt. Green, 12/16/61, King Wm. C.H.; exempt by substitute 1/18/62.

BROWN, JOSEPH: King Wm. C.H.; detailed on govt. work at West Point 1/20/62.

BURGESS, CHARLES: Co. C, Capt. Moore, 12/16/61, King Wm. C.H.

BURTON, MARION H.: Co. C, Capt. Moore, 12/16/61, King Wm. C.H.

BUTLER, JOHN: Co. C, Capt. Moore, 12/16/61, King Wm. C.H.; discharged 2/5/62.

CARDWELL, JOHN L.: Sgt., Co. C, Capt. Moore, 12/16/61, King Wm. C.H.; discharged 2/5/62.

CLEMENTS, JAMES H.: Co. C, Capt. Moore, 12/16/61, King Wm. C.H.; discharged 2/5/62.

CLEMENTS, LEROY Y.: Co. C, Capt. Moore, 12/16/61, King Wm. C.H.; on guard at West Point 1/31/62; discharged 2/5/62.

CLEMENTS, WILLIAM H.: Co. C, Capt. Moore, 12/16/61; King Wm. C.H.; medical discharge 1/2/62 at Gloucester Pt.

COBB, JOHN M.: Co. D, Capt. Green, 12/16/61, King Wm. C.H.; transf. to Capt. Johnson 2/5/62.

COCKE, JOHN: Sgt., Co. C, Capt. Moore, 12/16/61, King Wm. C.H.

DANSEY, THOMAS: Co. D, Capt. Green, 12/16/61, King Wm. C.H.; detailed to govt. work at West Point 1/20/62.

DAVIS, CORNELIUS: Co. D, Capt. Green, 12/16/61, King Wm. C.H.; transf. to Capt. Johnson 2/5/62.

DAVIS, JAMES: Co. D, Capt. Green, 12/16/61, King Wm. C.H.; detailed on govt. work at West Point 2/20/62.

DAVIS, JAMES M.: Sgt., Co. C, Capt. Moore, 12/16/61, King Wm. C.H.

DAVIS, JOHN: Co. D, Capt. Green, 12/16/61, King Wm. C.H.; transf. to Capt. Johnson 2/5/62.

DAVIS, SMITH: Co. D, Capt. Green, 12/16/61, King Wm. C.H.

DAVIS, THOMAS L.: Co. D, Capt. Green, 12/17/61, West Point; detailed to Adj. & QM at West Point.

DAVIS, TRAVIS: Co. D, Capt. Green, 12/17/61, West Point; detailed to Adj. & QM at West Point.

DEW, WILLIAM: Co. D, Capt. Green, 12/16/61, King Wm. C.H.; Capt. 9th Regt. & Adjt., Gloucester Pt.

DIKE, HENRY M.: Co. D, Capt. Green, 12/16/61, King Wm.

DILLARD, THOMAS F.: Co. D, Capt. Green, 12/16/61, King Wm. C.H.; exempt 2/1/62.

DOUGLAS, GEORGE F. (T.): Co. D, Capt. Green, 12/16/61, King Wm. C.H.; transf. to Capt. Johnson 2/5/62.

DOWNER, WILLIAM T.: Sgt., Co. C, Capt. Moore, 12/16/61, King Wm. C.H.; discharged 1/12/62 at Gloucester Pt.

DUNN, JOHN: Co. D, Capt. Littlepage, 1/28/62, Gloucester Pt.; detailed on govt. work at West Point 1/20/62.

EASTWOOD, WILLIAM: Co. D, Capt. Green, 12/22/61, West Point; detailed to Adj. & QM at West Point.

EDWARDS, CAPT.: ?

ELLETT, WILLIAM: Co. D, Capt. Littlepage, 2/1/62, Gloucester P.

EUBANK, EDWARD F.: Cpl., Co. C, Capt. Moore, 12/16/61, King Wm. C.H.

EUBANK, RICHARD, JR.: Co. ?. Furnished substitute & discharged 2/8/62.

FERGUSON, ANDREW: Co. C, Capt. Moore, 12/16/61, King Wm. C.H.; discharged 2/5/62; bricklayer, dk. hair, grey eyes & fair complexion & age 35; volunteer to 55th Regt., Co. F.

FLOYD, JOHN T.: Co. C, Capt. Moore, 12/16/61, King Wm. C.H.

FOX, JAMES O.: Co. C, Capt. Moore, 12/16/61, King Wm. C.H.: discharged 2/5/62.

FOX, WILLIAM H.: Co. C, Capt. Moore, 12/16/61, King Wm. C.H.; on guard at Gloucester Pt. 1/31/62; discharged 2/5/62.

GARDNER, JOHN C.: Co. C, Capt. Moore, 12/16/61, King Wm. C.H.; detailed as nurse 1/19/62; discharged 2/5/62.

GARNETT, ROBERT B.: Co. C, Capt. Moore, 12/16/61, King Wm. C.H.; medical discharge 12/26/61.

GARNETT, THOMAS: Co. C, Capt. Moore, 12/16/61, King Wm. C.H.

GARNETT, WILLIAM: Co. C, Capt. Moore, 12/16/61, King Wm. C.H.; discharged 2/5/62.

GARNETT, WILLIAM A.: Co. C, Capt. Moore, 12/16/61, King Wm. C.H.; on guard at Gloucester Pt. 1/31/62; discharged 2/5/62.

GLASS, HENRY: Co. D, Capt. Green, 12/22/61, West Point; detailed to Adj. & QM at West Point.

GRAVATT, GEORGE W.: Cpl., Co. C, Capt. Moore, 12/16/61, King Wm. C.H.; discharged 2/5/62.

GREEN, J. BEVERLY: Capt., Co. D, no record.

GREGORY, ROGER: Lt. Col., 87th Regiment Va. Militia. 12/14/61, Richmond.

HARDGROVE, WILLIAM: Co. D, Capt. Littlepage, 1/30/62, Gloucester Pt.; transf. to Capt. Johnson 2/5/62.

HARPER, DOWNING: Co. D, Capt. Littlepage, 1/2/62, Gloucester Pt.; transf. to Capt. Johnson 2/5/62.

HAWES, RICHARD: Co. D, Capt. Green, 12/16/61, King Wm. C.H.; detailed 12/26/61 to King Wm. to hire slaves for service in CSA; exempt 1/4/62.

HAY, EDWARD: Co. C, Capt. Moore, 12/16/61, King Wm. C.H.; discharged 2/5/62.

HAY, FLEMING: Co. C, Capt. Moore, 12/16/61, King Wm. C.H.; discharged 2/5/62.

HAYNES, ALEXANDER F.: Sgt., Co. D, Capt. Green, 12/16/61, King Wm. C.H.; transf. to Capt. Johnson 2/5/62.

HILL, ROBERT C.: Co. D, Capt. Green, 12/16/61, King Wm. C.H.; exempt by substitute 1/19/62.

HOGANS, WALKER: Co. D, Capt. Green, 12/16/61, King Wm. C.H.; exempt by substitute 1/10/62.

HOUCHINGS, JOHN C.: Co. D, Capt. Green, 12/16/61, King Wm. C.H.

HUCKSTEP, IRA: Co. C, Capt. Moore, 12/16/61, King Wm. C.H.; discharged 2/5/62.

JETER, WILLIAM: Co. D, Capt. Green, 12/16/61, King Wm. C.H.; exempt 1/5/62.

JOHNSON, AMMON: Sgt., Co. D, Capt. Green, 12/16/61, King Wm. C.H.; detailed to King Wm. for delinquents 12/22/61.

JOHNSON, JAMES E.: Co. C, Capt. Moore, 12/16/61, King Wm. C.H.

JOHNSON, WILLIAM C.: Lt., Co. D, Capt. Green, 12/16/61, King Wm. C.H.

JONES, JOHN T.: Co. D, Capt. Green, 12/16/61, King Wm. C.H.; transf. as surgeon 1/26/62.

KING, JAMES C.: Cpl., Co. D, Capt. Green, 12/16/61, King Wm. C.H.; exempt by substitute 1/18/62.

LACY, JOHN P.: Co. D, Capt. Green, 12/16/61, King Wm. C.H.; discharged 1/8/62.

LATANE, WILLIAM C.: Sgt., Co. C, Capt. Moore, 12/16/61, King Wm. C.H.; exempt by substitute 1/24/62.

LEFTWICH, ANDREW J.: Cpl., Co. C, Capt. Moore, 12/16/61, King Wm. C.H.

LEFTWICH, ROBERT W.: Co. C, Capt. Moore, 12/16/61, King Wm. C.H.; discharged 2/5/62.

LEFTWICH, WILLIAM H.: Co. C, Capt. Moore, 12/16/61, King Wm. C.H.; discharged 2/5/62.

LEIGH, JOHN R.: Co. C, Capt. Moore, 12/16/61, King Wm. C.H.; medical discharge 2/1/62; farmer, 5'10", lt. hair, blue eyes, fair complexion and age 45.

LIPSCOMB, CORNELIUS: Co. D, Capt. Green, 12/16/61, King Wm. C.H.; exempt to rept. to pres. of Richmond & York R.R.

LIPSCOMB, HUDSON B.: Co. D, Capt. Green, 12/16/61, King Wm. C.H.; exempt to rept. to pres. of Richmond & York R.R.

LIPSCOMB, JUNIUS: Co. D, Capt. Green, 12/16/61, King Wm. C.H.; detailed to govt. work at West Point 1/20/62.

LIPSCOMB, STERLING B.: Co. D, Capt. Green, 12/16/61, King Wm. C.H.; detailed to King Wm. for delinquents 12/22/61.

LIPSCOMB, WILLIAM J.: Sgt., Co. D, Capt. Green, 12/16/61, King Wm. C.H.; detailed to King Wm. for delinquents 12/22/61.

LITTLEPAGE, HARMON H.: Capt., Co. D, Capt. Green, 12/16/61, King Wm. C.H.; present at Gloucester Pt. 12/61 & 1/62.

LITTLEPAGE, JUNIUS A.: Co. D, Capt. Green, 12/16/61, King Wm. C.H.; exempt as surgeon 1/1/62.

LONG, ANDREW J.: Co. D, Capt. Green, 12/16/61, King Wm. C.H.; exempt 1/5/62.

LUKARD, CORNELIUS: Co. D, Capt. Green, 12/16/61, King Wm. C.H.; exempt by substitute 1/25/62.

LUKARD, HARDIN A.: Co. D, Capt. Green, 12/16/61; King Wm. C.H.; exempt 2/8/62; farmer, 5'10", lt. hair, blue eyes, lt. complexion & age 32.

LUKARD, WILLIAM: Co. D, Capt. Littlepage, 1/19/62, Gloucester Pt.

MAHON, SILAS: Co. C, Capt. Moore, 12/16/61, King Wm. C.H.

MARSHALL, JOHN W.: Co. C, Capt. Moore, 12/16/61, King Wm. C.H.; discharged 2/5/62.

MARTIN, FRANCIS: Co. D, Capt. Green, 12/16/61, King Wm. C.H.; detailed to King Wm. for delinquents 12/22/61; exempt over-age 1/1/62.

McGEORGE, JAMES R.: Co. D, Capt. Green, 12/16/61, King Wm. C.H.

McGEORGE, WILLIAM J.: Co. D, Capt. Green, 12/16/61, King Wm. C.H.

MOOKLAR, ATWOOD T.: Lt., Co. D, Capt. Green, 12/16/61, King Wm. C.H.; transf. to Capt. Johnson 2/5/62.

MOORE, JOSEPH BROADMAN: Capt., Co. C, Capt. Moore, 12/16/61, King Wm. C.H.; present at Gloucester Pt. 12/61 & 1/62; inspection & mustering officer 1/31/62.

MOREN, GEORGE T.: Co. C, Capt. Moore, 12/16/61, King Wm. C.H.

MORRISON, JOHN W.: Co. C, Capt. Moore, 12/16/61, King Wm. C.H.; discharged 2/1/62.

MUNDAY, GEORGE: Co. C, Capt. Moore, 12/16/61, King Wm. C.H.; detailed to work on harness at Yorktown 1/21/62; discharged 2/5/62.

NEALE, ROBERT K.: Sgt., Co. D, Capt. Green, 12/16/61, King Wm. C.H.

NORMENT, DANIEL W.: Sgt., Co. C, Capt. Moore, 12/16/61, King Wm. C.H.

PALMER, THOMAS H.: Co. D, Capt. Green, 12/22/61, Gloucester Pt.; medical discharge 2/5/62.

PERKINS, A. H.: Co. ?, Discharged 1/31/62.

PICKELS, WILLIAM D.: Co. D, Capt. Green, 12/16/61, King Wm. C.H.; transf. to Capt. Johnson 2/5/62.

PILCHER, SAMUEL D.: Cpl., Co. D, Capt. Green, 12/16/61, King Wm. C.H.; sent to King Wm. for delinquents 12/22/61; detailed as QM Sgt. 1/19/62.

POLLARD, EDWARD S.: Co. D, Capt. Green, 12/22/61, Gloucester Pt.; detailed as courier for Col. Gregory; exempt 1/4/62.

POLLARD, JAMES H.: Co. C, Capt. Moore, 12/16/61, King Wm. C.H.; exempt by substitute 1/20/62.

POLLARD, LEWIS: Co. C, Capt. Moore, 1/2/62, Gloucester Pt.; exempt by substitute 1/20/62.

POWELL, JAMES A.: Lt., Co. C, Capt. Moore, 12/16/61, King Wm. C.H.; signs as commanding co. 1/62; discharged 1/8/62.

POWELL, JAMES H.: Co. D, Capt. Green, 12/22/61, Gloucester Pt.; exempt as tanner 1/8/62.

POWELL, WILSON C.: Lt., Co. C, Capt. Moore, 12/16/61, King Wm. C.H.; asst. QM for battalion 1/19/62 near Gloucester Pt.

PRINCE, ROBERT H.: Co. C, Capt. Moore, 12/16/61, King Wm. C.H.; discharged 2/5/62.

PURCELL, JOHN H.: Co. D, Capt. Green, 12/16/61, King Wm. C.H.

READ, JAMES H.: Co. D, Capt. Green, 12/16/61, King Wm. C.H.; exempt 1/27/62.

SHENAULT, BROOKEN: Co. D, Capt. Littlepage, 1/2/62, Gloucester Pt.

SLAUGHTER, JOHN C.: Co. C, Capt. Moore, 1/2/62, Gloucester Pt.; discharged 2/5/62.

SLAUGHTER, JOSEPH: Co. D, Capt. Green, 12/16/61, King Wm. C.H.; transf. to Capt. Johnson 2/5/62.

SLAUGHTER, WILLIAM B.: Co. D, Capt. Green, 12/16/61, King Wm. C.H.; transf. to Capt. Johnson 2/5/62.

SMITH, WILLIAM A.: Co. D, Capt. Littlepage, 12/27/62, Gloucester Pt.

STEVENS, LEWIS A.: Cpl., Capt. Moore, 12/16/61, King Wm. C.H.; discharged 1/24/62.

SULLENS, GRANGER: Co. D, Capt. Littlepage, 1/28/62, Gloucester Pt.; transf. to Capt. Johnson 2/5/62.

SUTTON, PULASKI: Co. C, Capt. Moore, 12/16/62, King Wm. C.H.; discharged 1/24/62 at Gloucester Pt. overseer, 5'9", lt. hair, lt. eyes, lt. complexion & age 36.

SWEET, WILLIAM A.: Co. D, 12/27/61, Gloucester Pt.; medical discharge 1/4/62.

TAYLOR, EDMOND: Co. C, Capt. Moore, 12/16/61, King Wm. C.H.; discharged 2/5/62.

TOMPSON, GEORGE W.: Co. D, Capt. Littlepage, 12/22/61, Gloucester Pt.; exempt overage 2/13/62.

TRICE, JAMES A.: Co. ? Exempt by substitute 1/13/62.

TUCK, GEORGE S.: Co. C, Capt. Moore, 12/16/61, King Wm. C.H.; discharged 2/5/62.

TUCK, RICHARD M.: Cpl., Co. C, Capt. Moore, 12/16/61, King Wm. C.H.; detailed 12/61 to King Wm. for delinquents; discharged 2/5/62.

TWISDALE, JOHN E.: Co. C, Capt. Moore, 12/16/61, King Wm. C.H.; exempt by substitute 1/23/62.

TYLER, WASHINGTON: Co. D, Capt. Green, 12/16/61, King Wm. C.H.; transf. to Capt. Johnson 2/5/62.

WAGNER, CONWARD: Co. D, Capt. Littlepage, 12/22/61, Gloucester Pt.; transf. to Capt. Johnson 2/5/62.

WALKER, A. B.: Co. D, Capt. Littlepage, 1/2/62, Gloucester Pt.; transf. to Capt. Johnson 2/5/62.

WESTMORE, WARREN: Co. D, Capt. Littlepage, 1/2/62, Gloucester Pt.

WATERS, RUFUS W.: Co. D, Capt. Green, 12/16/61, King Wm. C.H.; transf. to Capt. Johnson 2/5/62.

WINSTON, OCTAVIUS M.: Co. C, Capt. Moore, 12/16/61, King Wm. C.H.; detailed to King Wm. for delinquents 12/22/61; detailed as chief clerk to QM & asst. commissary 1/19/62.

WOOLARD, GEORGE W.: Co. C, Capt. Moore, 12/16/61, King Wm. C.H.; discharged 2/5/62.

WYATT, BENJAMIN P.: Co. C, Capt. Moore, 12/16/61, King Wm. C.H.

INDEX

277

278

279